Norwegians on the Prairie

Norwegians on the Prairie

Ethnicity and the Development of the Country Town

ODD S. LOVOLL

Published in cooperation with the
Norwegian-American Historical Association

MINNESOTA HISTORICAL SOCIETY PRESS

www.mhspress.org
The Minnesota Historical Society Press is a member of the Association of American University Presses.

Manufactured in the United States of America

10 9 8 7 6 5 4 3 2 1

⊚ The paper used in this publication meets the minimum requirements of the American National Standard for Information Sciences—Permanence for Printed Library Materials, ANSI Z39.48–1984.

ISBN-13: 978-0-87351-603-7 (paper)
ISBN-10: 0-87351-603-6 (paper)

Library of Congress Cataloging-in-Publication Data

Lovoll, Odd Sverre.
    Norwegians on the prairie : ethnicity and the development of the country town / Odd S. Lovoll ; foreword by Todd Nichol.
        p.   cm.
    Co-published with the Norwegian-American Historical Association.
    Includes bibliographical references and index.
    ISBN-13: 978-0-87351-571-9 (cloth : alk. paper)
    ISBN-10: 0-87351-571-4 (cloth : alk. paper)
    1. Norwegian Americans—Minnesota—History. 2. Norwegian Americans—Minnesota—Ethnic identity. 3. Norwegian Americans—Minnesota—Social conditions. 4. Minnesota—History. 5. Minnesota—Ethnic relations. 6. Immigrants—Minnesota—History. 7. Frontier and pioneer life—Minnesota. 8. Benson (Minn.)—History. 9. Starbuck (Minn.)—History. 10. Madison (Minn.)—History. I. Norwegian-American Historical Association. II. Title.
    F615.S2L68 2006
    977.6'0043982—dc22
                                                                    2006006787

For Peter Magnar and Jon Elias Lovoll

Contents

Maps and Chart

Tables

Foreword

In 1988 Odd S. Lovoll completed and the Norwegian-American His-
torical Association published a groundbreaking study of Norwegian-
Americans in the context of metropolitan life, *A Century of Urban Life:
The Norwegians in Chicago before 1930*. In the present volume Professor
Lovoll has again pioneered a new field of inquiry. *Norwegians on the
Prairie: Ethnicity and the Development of the Country Town* is the first
full-length treatment of Norwegian Americans in the small towns to
which so many of them were drawn.

Representing the traditions of both the Norwegian-American Historical Association and the Minnesota Historical Society, Odd Lovoll here
presents scholarship of the highest order in an eminently readable way.
His book is an invitation to get acquainted with Benson, Minnesota, and
a multitude of towns like it. The conventions, customs, and characters
of small-town Norwegian America await the reader in every chapter.

The association is grateful to Odd Lovoll for yet another contribution to Norwegian American history. It is a privilege as well to thank
the Minnesota Historical Society Press for the opportunity to join in
copublishing this study.

I thank Greg Britton and Shannon Pennefeather of the Minnesota
Historical Society Press for their partnership in the work of editing and
publishing this book. In approving publication of this book, President
John R. Tunheim and the members of the Norwegian-American Historical Association's board of directors have again shown strong support of
the association's publication program. I thank them.

Todd W. Nichol
Editor

Preface

In undertaking a study of three small towns in west-central Minnesota—Benson in Swift County, Starbuck in Pope County, and Madison in Lac qui Parle County—I hoped to gain insight specifically into the small-town and rural experience of Norwegian immigrants and their descendants and more broadly into the ethnic dimension in shaping the social, cultural, religious, and political environment of country towns. By the criteria set in the federal census, Norwegians were statistically the most rural of all major nineteenth-century immigrant groups: to a high degree they lived in towns of 2,500 or fewer citizens or in agricultural settlements. In the early twentieth century, their children did not conform to the prevailing exodus to the cities but instead engaged in farming in proportions that surpassed by a wide margin that of any other immigrant population. The expansive midwestern setting allowed them to exercise ethnic separateness while taking part in the life of the larger community. More than any other factor, it was family stability and high rates of in-group marriage through several generations that sustained ethnic communities. Norwegian Americans became enterprising participants in the creation of the small midwestern town, as townspeople and as farmers in the town's environs; their old-world cultural heritage became a vital resource in adjusting to the demands and opportunities of frontier society and in fashioning the marketplaces that served their commercial and social needs.

Benson in Swift County was selected as a case study because of its early founding in 1870 as a railroad town, its location in a typical prairie agricultural setting, and the demographic composition of the area, heavy with Norwegian settlement in town and in the surrounding townships. While an approximate reconstruction of the town's social and historical development employing ethnicization theory seemed desirable at the outset, the more serious concern of the study became to view the histories of the people of Benson and of those who farmed on the prairie landscape surrounding town as a context and framework in which to explore how ethnicity expressed itself in this special environment and how various ethnic groups interacted and shaped a shared local identity and a place to call home while continuing to celebrate their differing immigrant roots.

In order to determine how representative Benson was as a "Norwegian" country town, the research expanded to include Starbuck in Pope County and Madison in Lac qui Parle County. These two towns, though founded a decade or so later than Benson, made possible an insightful comparative approach. The Norwegian American population did not display a monolithic front but differed in old-country regional loyalties and, although heavily Lutheran, engaged in hostile controversy on divergent doctrinal positions. An uncompromising pietism transcended religious strife and made the Norwegian Lutheran church in America—molded, like American Protestantism, in a rural and small-town environment—in its formative decades, and even much later, advocate adherence to a strict moral code and turn its force against such perceived evils as demon rum. Even in political loyalties, although Norwegians on the western prairie engaged heavily in reform and third-party politics, they associated with different camps. Like other ethnic groups—especially in urban places—they disbursed into a variety of social classes and roles but, even so, a strong tendency to remain in blue-collar occupations persisted, not only among the immigrants but also in the American-born generations.

The narrative is set against the broad background of the expanding frontier, the emergence of the state of Minnesota, and Norwegian immigration in the Upper Midwest. The patterns of migration and their convergence in western Minnesota can thereby be clarified and the perimeters of ethnic life in the state established. The presettlement population of Native Americans is included as well—their presence on the western frontier, their total absence in Turner's romanticized thesis of the West, and the abiding insensitivity toward them. In contrast, a strong Norwegian presence was evidenced in the acceptance of celebratory events such as May 17, the homeland's national holiday, as a community festival. The story is brought up to the present time and the loss of family farms, a changing economic reality that had an adverse impact on rural ethnic communities. As the United States from the late 1960s rediscovered its culturally pluralistic society, ethnic festivals have been revived and given new content by what can be termed a "chamber of commerce ethnicity" in order to attract attention to the town. These and other ethnic activities and traditions speak to persistent Norwegian ethnocentric emotions that can be traced to pioneer days.

Engaging in the extensive fieldwork this study required, I incurred a large debt of gratitude to many individuals and institutions. I can list only a few names here; many more will be identified elsewhere in the text or in the endnotes. A great benefit of doing fieldwork is gaining a new circle of friends and developing a strong identity with the community in question. I had earlier established contact with the Benson community when doing research for *The Promise Fulfilled* in 1995–96. My main field assistant was Clara Swingseth, who tirelessly guided my inquiry; Mildred Torgerson, director of the Swift County Historical Museum—whose help I had received in 1971 while researching Norwegian American regionalism for my doctoral thesis—shared her great knowledge of the area with me. Marlys Gallagher, current director of the museum, and her assistant, Lowell Moen, offered invaluable and enthusiastic help for the present work and consistently made me feel at home.

On June 28, 2001, my wife, Else Lovoll, and I were guests of Bjørgvin Lodge of the Sons of Norway at a picnic in Ambush Park in Benson. The cordial reception and assurances of assistance convinced me of the feasibility of a project that could succeed only through local involvement. A dinner invitation to Garfield and Charlotte Haugen's Lillehaugen Inn bespoke small-town hospitality. Sandy Thompson, director of the Benson area chamber of commerce, gave encouragement and assistance in the initial stage of systematic research, which began in February 2002. A broadly distributed questionnaire garnered valuable information and announced the project to the community; the local radio station KSCR broadcast interviews about the study; the *Swift County Monitor-News*, published by Reed Anfinson, reported on it; and the earlier publisher, Ronald Anfinson, and his wife, Patricia Ann Roth Anfinson, provided me with special historical issues and a copy of her *County Cookbook* with historical notes.

Throughout the two years of research and writing, Paul Kittelson, mayor of Benson; John Thompson, county commissioner and president of Bjørgvin Lodge; Janet K. Lundebrek, president of the First Security Bank; and Ginter Rice, longtime resident of Swift County, gave generously of their time and knowledge and advanced the project considerably. I should also like to mention Robert Mikkelson, Orie Mills, Verna Gomer, and Ernest Anderson as valuable contacts. A special word of gratitude goes to Diane Schuerman, manager of the Country Inn & Suites, for her hospitality and generous permission to conduct interviews and arrange meetings in the hotel's dining room. I was well received by the clergy and staff when visiting churches of various denominations, Protestant and Catholic; Joan Moline, financial secretary at Our Redeemer's Lutheran Church, was most generous in her assistance. Officials at the Swift County Courthouse were consistently cordial and furnished valuable data about the county.

Gary G. Erickson of Willmar more than anyone else engaged himself in the research with dedication and stamina. I am truly grateful for his willingness to do interviews, to respond to specific research requests, and to design maps with diligence and competence. Historian Jon Willand, an expert on Madison and Lac qui Parle County, demonstrated an unusual degree of generosity of spirit and mind by sharing with me his considerable store of knowledge. Lorraine Connor, curator, and her assistant, Celesta Haugen, at the Lac qui Parle Historical Society enthusiastically embraced the research; Ann Maguire, local historian, shared precious insights; Ethel Shelstad, feature writer at the *Western Guard*, provided copies of her newspaper articles about the area; Meredith Sherman Ulstad furnished literature on the county's history. In Pope County, Merlin Peterson, curator at the Pope County Historical Society; Hannah Sanders, local historian; Leland Pederson and Arnold (Arne) Pederson, both active in community affairs, all contributed substantially to the research endeavor.

My earlier research associate and later doctoral student Terje Mikael Joranger contributed material on his study of Valdres settlements in Pope County. I enjoyed my discussions with Scott Anfinson and Rodney Rice about their childhood and youth in Benson; with Richard Lundebrek, MD, who returned to Benson to practice medicine; and with the brothers Dan Lageson and Scott Lageson, who moved to Benson to operate DS Lageson's Restaurant. Such individual advents to a place called home are promising signs of revival and growth in a small western country town. I wish also to thank the staff at the Minnesota Historical Society for their patience and assistance, and especially Deborah Miller, who during research at the society was at every turn helpful.

Colleagues at my academic home, the Department of History at St. Olaf College, by their friendship and support made the challenging task easier. The department's academic administrative assistant, Nancy Hollinger, was attentive and considerate beyond the call of duty. Nothing would have been possible without a generous grant from the Ella and Kaare Nygaard Foundation administered by St. Olaf College. The financial support enabled me for short periods to have the expert assistance of two salaried coworkers, both graduate students at the University of Minnesota, David LaVigne and Aaron Hanson, who accompanied me on research excursions and conducted archival and library research. Todd Nichol of the Norwegian-American Historical Association offered strong encouragement and gave informed advice. I thank them all most sincerely. I also wish to thank editor Shannon Pennefeather at the Minnesota Historical Society Press for a cordial and productive working relationship in preparing the manuscript for publication. I am grateful to the three outside reviewers—professors Joseph Amato, Jon Gjerde, and Ann M. Legreid—for their careful reading of the manuscript and for their helpful suggestions, which greatly improved the published version of the study.

My wife and my family, as in past publications, made the endeavor worthwhile; their love and their support were constant sources of inspiration and perseverance. I dedicate the book to my two youngest grandchildren, Peter Magnar, born May 16, 2002, and Jon Elias, born September 6, 2004. They make the future seem all the more bright.

Norwegians on the Prairie

One

The Western Expansion

THE FIELD OF INQUIRY

Settlement on the American frontier illuminates immigration's centrality in the history of American society. By 1800, as settlers streamed into the region, the northern frontier had crossed into Illinois, which gained statehood in 1818; then decade by decade it moved west, to Wisconsin and Iowa, to eastern Minnesota, then on to the western part of the state and from there into the northern Great Plains, to the Dakotas, and beyond. In 1860 Minnesota and Iowa formed part of the westernmost tier of states; in most sections the frontier line was then close to the ninety-fifth meridian. Ray Billington sees the frontier as a process, "the repeated rebirth of civilization along the western edge of settlement during the three centuries required to occupy the continent."

The western advance was both rural and urban; small towns and villages gradually dotted the agricultural landscape even in pioneer days. As Billington explains, "An urban frontier was truly a part of advancing settlement. . . . Towns sprang up as if by magic." Along the navigable inland waterways trading posts and farm villages evolved into commercial centers to serve the surrounding farming communities; some were founded by speculators, or by merchants, or by politicians, mainly driven by the twin motives of power and profit. As the railroad lines pushed westward, town sites were platted at regular intervals, generally on public lands granted the railroad companies by the government. Many railroad towns became thriving frontier business ventures. In western Minnesota, the towns that are the subject of the present study—Benson in Swift County, Starbuck in Pope County, and Madison in Lac qui Parle County—all owe their existence to the railroad.[1]

The western expansion represented a convergence of numerous migratory patterns, from settled areas farther east or from beyond the Atlantic Ocean. Norwegians participated fully in the settlement of western lands. The early—and from the mid-1860s massive—emigration of footloose and land-hungry Norwegian peasants explains their prominence on the western northern frontier. There, as pioneer in Norwegian emigration history Ingrid Semmingsen maintains, they wished to re-establish the conservative way of life they were accustomed to in rural Norway, but with a greatly improved social and economic status.[2]

Not all became farmers. Many found a livelihood in the villages and country towns that came into being on the western frontier. In fact, Norwegian immigrants and their descendants appear to have possessed a special bond with the small town and country life. Indeed, towns must be viewed as an intrinsic part of the western frontier, not as a separate development. The federal census defines villages and towns below 2,500 residents as rural; only incorporated places of 2,500 or more are "urban" according to the plan adopted by the U.S. Bureau of the Census. Harvey Walker argued in 1927 that "such a distinction may be justified in the eastern states, where there are many large cities, but in states which are largely agricultural . . . the community of 2,500 or less affords a large part of the urban life in the state." Oliver Knight agrees; in "Toward an Understanding of the Western Town" he disregards population figures in defining urban places: "It is the substance of an urban place—the function that it performs regardless of size—that will open our vision to the reality of the town and frontier." Despite small sizes, the village of Benson and other towns under consideration were, as Thomas White Harvey shows in his study of towns in the Red River Valley, urban in their social, cultural, and commercial design and function. Benson, for instance, did not in terms of population qualify as an urban place until the mid-1930s; however, it had since 1908 enjoyed status as a city. By the criteria set in the federal census, Norwegians were statistically the most rural of all major nineteenth-century immigrant groups. Farming became their major livelihood: in 1900, 49.5 percent of all Norwegian-born "heads of household" were, according to the federal census, engaged in agriculture—as owners or renters of farms or as laborers. As many as 54.3 percent of the immigrants' children—the second generation—were farmers. No other nationality even came close.[3]

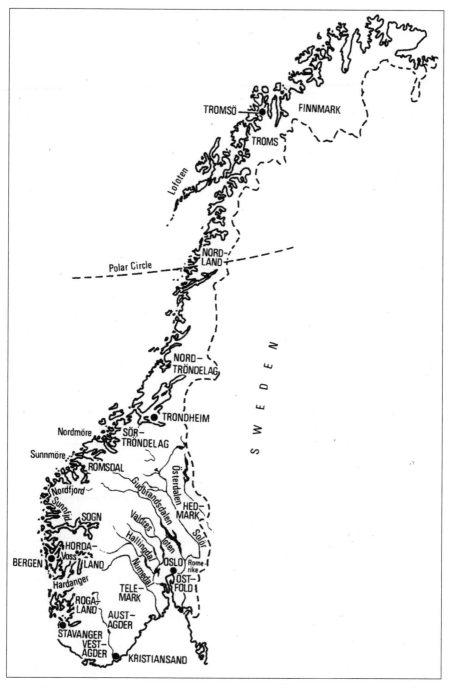

Map of Norway. This map does not indicate administrative boundaries but shows the principal valleys, districts, and towns from which the emigrants came.

Time of emigration, pattern of settlement, and regional origin in Norway as well as the function of family networks in the immigration drama may do much to explain the situation. It is significant that traditions of going to the United States were well established in the regions of Norway that would be most affected by emigration long before a transformation of the rural economy occurred there. The districts most heavily involved in the overseas movement were those least able to respond to change, lacking resources to modernize agricultural production. A strong anti-urban bias among Norwegian immigrants, an opinion transferred from these districts of the old country, may be detected in their preference for life outside large urban areas. They came from the inner fjord districts in west Norway and the mountain valleys of east Norway. These early immigrants greatly influenced the shape of the Norwegian American community, imbuing it with their values and traditions.

In 1910, following a new wave of Norwegian immigrants who were more likely to choose an urban occupation, still only 42.2 percent of first- and second-generation Norwegians were urbanized, that is, living in towns with 2,500 or more residents. In 1910 first- and second-generation Norwegians numbered 1,011,125; of these, 403,858 were of the immigrant generation. About 80 percent of the Norwegian stock, the immigrants and their American-born children, resided in the upper middle west. As recently as 1940 more than half of all midwestern Norwegians lived on farms or in small villages and towns.[4]

The progeny of Norwegian immigrants, as Table 1 documents, did not in the early twentieth century follow the trek to the cities in numbers comparable to other nationalities; instead they inhabited small towns or resided in surrounding farming communities in exceptional numbers. "The emigrants came to stay on the land," T. A. Hoverstad wrote in 1915 about Norwegian farmers in the United States, and "their children remain on their lands after them." Few would argue that a strong rural attachment among Norwegian immigrants did not exist; indeed, it became an idiosyncratic trait. They were dedicated to farming as a way of life.[5]

In America their basic rural orientation reinforced strong nationalistic and ethnocentric emotions. Recognizing the primarily cultural and historical basis of ethnicity, it is fair to advance the proposition that ethnic cohesiveness—though marred by religious and regional differences—has to a remarkable degree characterized Norwegians in America throughout

TABLE 1

Urban and Rural Distribution in Percentage of the Overall, Norwegian, Swedish, and German Populations in the United States and Minnesota by Generation, 1900, 1920, and 1960[a]

| | | 1900 | | 1920 | | 1960 | |
		Rural	Urban[b]	Rural	Urban	Rural	Urban
National	Total Population	61	39	49	51	na	na
	Norwegian						
	Immigrant	63	37	54	46	na	na
	Second Generation[c]	74	26	64	36	na	na
	Swedish						
	Immigrant	46	54	36	64	na	na
	Second Generation	54	46	43	57	na	na
	German						
	Immigrant	38	62	33	67	na	na
	Second Generation	43	57	38	62	na	na
Minnesota	Total Population	66	34	56	44	38	62
	Norwegian						
	Immigrant	72	28	61	39	37	63
	Second Generation	82	18	66	34	47	53
	Swedish						
	Immigrant	62	38	49	51	31	69
	Second Generation	70	30	56	44	33	67
	German						
	Immigrant	69	31	60	40	42	58
	Second Generation	74	26	65	35	47	53

Source: Ruggles, Sobek, et al. *Integrated Public Use Microdata Series: Version 2.0.* Minneapolis: Historical Census Projects, University of Minnesota, 1997.

a. Complete national data not available for 1960
b. "Urban" defined as incorporated places with 2,500 or more residents
c. Second generation determined by at least one parent born in country of origin

their history. They clearly qualify as an ethnic group, as Milton Gordon has it, "based on a social-psychological sense of peoplehood stemming from history." An investigation of the Norwegian experience in America may thus disclose unique social and cultural patterns of adjustment. In an earlier study, the author of this book states, "no fully satisfactory explanation for extraordinary ethnic fervor among Norwegian Americans may ever be found." As an explanatory factor, however, one may naturally point to Norway's underdog position among Nordic nations and as a consequence its defensive sense of national inferiority. The dramatic events toward the end of the Napoleonic Wars in 1814 saw the rebirth of the Kingdom of Norway after a four-hundred-year union with Denmark; the most lasting symbol of newfound independence was the constitution adopted at Eidsvoll on May 17 of that year. In the fall of 1814, however, the great powers in Europe forced Norway into a personal union with Sweden—the creation of a Swedish-Norwegian monarchy under a common king, referred to as the Twin Kingdoms of Sweden and Norway, each with its own national governance. The union lasted until 1905. A growing Norwegian nationalism and self-assertion was directed against the dominance of Sweden in this uneven marriage; especially during the last quarter of the century, rural areas witnessed a rapid growth of active nationalist sentiments. British historian T. K. Derry has pointed out how development of the arts—with such names as the violinist Ole Bull, the dramatist Henrik Ibsen, and the composer Edvard Grieg—after 1830 contributed to an independent Norwegian identity and full self-confidence.

Norway's small population, to a large extent residing in widely spread and isolated rural communities, encouraged an extreme localism and a sense of kinship with others from the same area. Furthermore, a feeling of place relating to the spectacular landscape and the indelible mental images it created bestowed a perception of primordial identity and a sense of permanency in ethnic relations. The small community and its striking features became Norway for most of those who participated in the overseas exodus. They left, it has been claimed, with strong nationalistic aspirations and a love for the homeland in their hearts. Norwegian immigrants, in the manner of other nationalities, transferred national peculiarities and circumstances, localism, religious loyalties, and ethnic biases to American soil, facilitating cultural retention and transfer of the spoken language as well as historical memories and a full measure of ethnic icons to American-born generations. Norwegian immigrants transplanted traditions in food and customs, values in social conventions and in religious life and beliefs, and, to be sure, prejudices against other nationalities and faiths.[6]

The journey to America begins.

Norwegian immigrants' cultural baggage, combining with that of other nationalities, obviously had an impact on developments in the new land. The Norwegian American social critic Thorstein Veblen wrote in 1923, "The country town is one of the great American institutions; perhaps the greatest, in the sense that it has had and continues to have a greater part than any other in shaping public sentiment and giving character to American culture." What happens, then, if the national origin and characteristics of the residents are taken into consideration? The main field of inquiry—a case study, if you will—relates mainly to the Norwegian population in west-central Minnesota. Ethnic diversity and interaction nevertheless became a part of the balance sheet as a new society took shape on the western prairie. How did the Norwegian American experience in the special environment of the country town differ from that of the big city or the farm? How did Norwegians enter into economic life? What was their place in the social structure? In what manner did they step into the political arena? How did their Lutheran faith survive and change? Who were the religious and secular leaders? How did their relative strength influence their own adjustment as well as have an impact on the larger society? How did generational succession and shifting so-cietal attitudes affect the expression of Norwegian ethnicity? These are some of the major issues the present study seeks to interpret within the framework of multiculturalism.[7]

An in-depth case study, employing a varied methodology and adopt-ing a strong humanistic approach, will be made of the city of Benson and of Swift County. These locations remain the major research site throughout the study. Benson, founded as a railroad town in 1870, is viewed, first, in the context of the agricultural communities it served and was sustained by and, second, in the broader context of state his-tory. Comparisons are made to the cities of Starbuck and Madison, founded a decade or more after Benson, in order to determine how rep-resentative a "Norwegian" town Benson is in empirical terms limited to characteristics such as occupational and social structures, political participation, and religious life and institutions. Following a presenta-tion of Benson's early history, a full discussion and comparison will be made in chapter four.

The intent is to view the histories of the people of the country town and those who farmed the surrounding prairie landscape as a context and framework in which to explore how ethnicity expressed itself in this special environment and how the various ethnic groups interacted and coalesced into a shared place-specific identity while celebrating in-dividual immigrant roots. In historiographical terms, the intention is not to provide a history of the region as such but rather to use its his-tory as a backdrop against which to portray select aspects of historical change and generational succession in order to elucidate the nature of a Norwegian American presence.

The period covered runs from the mid-nineteenth century to the present. It may be said that the day the immigrant stood on the deck of the vessel that would take him to America and waved good-bye to the homeland, he had begun a process of change and accommodation to a new society. It had actually begun even earlier, to cite Marcus Lee Hansen, "when he first dreamed of the far-off land." After his arrival he faced a process of ethnicization from immigrant to some kind of ethnic American. A new chapter, again as Hansen has it, "in the history of the Norwegian stock" was marked by the appearance of American-born chil-dren who, Hansen insists, were in reality neither Norwegian nor American. They were in ethnic terms Norwegian American like their parents even though how they related to and defined that identity might diverge considerably from the ethnic tenets of the immigrant generation. As sociologists define the term, ethnicity involves, to cite Mary Waters, "the *belief* on the part of people that they are descended from a common ancestor and that they are part of a larger grouping." Werner Sollors holds that in the socialization of an ethnic group across generations, aspects of its values, norms, and identifying patterns of behavior are increasingly altered, a process he describes as "the invention of ethnicity." One may, then, claim to have arrived at today's situation, where for individuals of European descent structural ethnicity and ethnic boundaries no longer prevail. Ethnic identity has become a matter of subjective choice— creating a postethnic America—and a voluntary affiliation with a specific ethnicity, or with none. A common view is that ethnicity is primordial, a personal inherited characteristic, and that ethnic groups are stable entities; the idea, then, that membership in an ethnic group need not be inherited but instead voluntary is naturally a direct challenge to this widely held view. While accepting the subjective and perceptual notions of the nature of ethnicity, it is nevertheless evident, as this study endeavors to show, that as a cultural group Norwegian Americans for several generations engaged in a dynamic strategy of adaptation and accommodation. In the final analysis, it was their place and acceptance in American society and history that remained the primary motivation when defining their ethnic identity—frequently placing it within the assimilative design of American history—and establishing acceptable group credentials.[8]

Following the lead of Jon Gjerde's prizewinning monograph *The Minds of the West,* this study considers migratory and cultural patterns in the special environment of the middle west and the process of redefining bonds of family, church, and community. The migration overseas represented a separation and a subsequent reunification in America; there on the immense land settlements could be created of kin, neighbors, and fellow parishioners from the homeland. As this study shows, family stability and high rates of inmarriage through several generations sustained ethnic communities. The Lutheran church represented the most visible connecting links between the Norwegian and Norwegian American cultures. It was a focal point and a conservative force in country towns and rural settlements. Just as with American Protestantism in general, it was the country town and the rural environment that formed the Norwegian Lutheran church in America. The numerous religious schisms in Norwegian communities in the late nineteenth century, caused by a pervasive religious controversy over Lutheran doctrine and church polity, contained an element of cultural conflict as well based on regional backgrounds in the homeland. An aggressive pastorate exercised great power through the Lutheran church and secured its position as a central institution. While engaging in religious warfare, the church nurtured a sense of community by adhering to a common set of values and traditions.[9]

The expansive midwestern setting allowed for a high degree of ethnic separateness and thus retention as well as reinvention of transplanted national cultures; nevertheless, the immigrants and their descendants took an active role in the life of the larger community. They were enterprising participants in the creation of the small midwestern town as a national American institution and had a decisive voice in shaping it.

If, as Richard Lingeman maintains, the history of America is the history of its small towns, then viewing the small town through the prism of ethnicity will further clarify its constituent parts and their relative influence on the town's social and cultural growth. Lingeman also claims that "for better or worse, small town values, convictions, and attitudes have shaped the psyche of this nation." Considering the ethnic component in this process will help us understand how it came to be so, even when, as in this study, we limit ourselves to an examination of the rise of the small town in the middle west—in reality western Minnesota—from the second half of the nineteenth century. All three towns and the counties in which they are located have had substantial, though by no means exclusive, Norwegian populations throughout their history, making them ideal subjects for this study.[10]

Early Minnesota

On their way west Norwegians joined old-stock Americans and newly arrived immigrants of other nationalities, the great majority northern Europeans. Most Norwegians, as well as other immigrants, had first settled on farmsteads farther east, and many arrived in west-central Minnesota with American-born children. All responded to the adventure and promises of the American frontier, moving west in ever increasing numbers.

The story of this central drama in American history, a celebrated tale filled with romance and legend, is well known. Less appreciated is the displacement of indigenous populations induced by this westward movement. Nelson Klose defines the frontier as "that advancing line of civilization where it comes into contact with the Indians and the wilderness." It was, he states further, the attraction of land and its resources, in other words an agricultural frontier, that kept the line moving westward.[11]

Some consideration of the native residents in the presettlement period is consequently in order. The Dakota (Sioux) tribe occupied lands in the southern half of what became the state of Minnesota. They were known as the people of the *Oceti Sakowin* or Seven Council Fires, the seven tribes of the Sioux confederacy. In the 1830s and 1840s four well-defined eastern bands of the Dakota inhabited lands in present Minnesota. The largest, the Mdewakanton, lived in the southeast along the Mississippi River to where it meets the Minnesota River and some distance up along that waterway. The Wahpekute, the smallest tribe, hunted in southern Minnesota between the Des Moines and Cannon rivers. The Wahpeton and Sisseton bands of the Dakota nation resided farther up the Minnesota River and were the Natives displaced by white settlement in west-central Minnesota. Some bands of these tribes lived near Lac qui Parle, Big Stone Lake, and Lake Traverse. They built their villages on the prairie landscape and pursued a mixed economy. They hunted buffalo, deer, duck, and geese, caught muskrats and turtles, fished in the lakes, rivers, and small streams, gathered wild turnip, and did simple farming. As observed by the pioneer missionary Samuel Pond in 1834, "All the ground planted by them was dug up by the women with hoes"; they cultivated a little corn "and such vegetable food as grew spontaneously." In spite of the large tract on which the Dakota had to draw for their supplies, they not infrequently, as Pond explains, "suffered from want of food . . . whenever game is scarce and the cold severe."[12]

The Ojibwe (Chippewa) nation controlled the forested northern part of the state. "As late as the 17th century," however, as Mitchell Rubinstein and Alan Woolworth explain, "the Dakota were established at and around Mille Lacs Lake." In a belt of hardwood forest, where most lived, there was a wealth of vegetation that "supported a large population of animals and birds and a wide variety of plants." Both nations lived a subsistence lifestyle but otherwise had distinct cultures and languages and systems for leadership, for hunting and war parties, for religious leadership, and for passing on knowledge. Both had flourishing cultures long before their first contact with Europeans. The Ojibwe were in fact relative late-comers, arriving in northern Minnesota from the eastern Great Lakes in the late 1600s and 1700s. They acquired guns through their participation in the fur trade with the French and became formidable intruders and enemies of the Dakota, who were ousted from their ancient hunting grounds. In a half century of warfare the Ojibwe advanced south beyond their territory around Lake Superior as far as the Mille Lacs area.

The Dakota lived under the influence of British fur traders who competed with the French; the British operated from Mackinac and Prairie du Chien. The Dakota became the prairie dwellers the white men knew, attracted to the plains by the introduction of horse culture and the availability of bison. The British replaced the French traders after American independence in 1783. Not until the War of 1812 did the United States enforce with troops and a military fort its legal rights in the Minnesota country. In 1819 Fort Snelling was established above the junction of the Minnesota and Mississippi rivers as a sentinel in America's frontier defense program as well as to promote westward movement.[13]

With the founding of Fort Snelling, Indian missions and civilian Indian agents entered Dakota and Ojibwe territory. Twenty-five-year-old Lawrence Taliaferro in 1819 was appointed Indian agent at St. Peter. According to William Watts Folwell, he became for twenty years "the most important and influential civil official on the upper Mississippi." He played an important role at the so-called "grand conference" between the Dakota and Ojibwe nations at Prairie du Chien in August 1825, where negotiations resulted in a dividing line between their respective territories. The agreed-upon boundary stretched in a general southwest direction from the junction of Goose River, a North Dakota streamlet, with the Red River of the North to a point on the St. Croix about eight miles below Osceola, Wisconsin. The two nations, as they had in the past, engaged in warfare but also experienced peaceful coexistence and interaction.

Because Native Americans were intensely religious and devoted to their beliefs, missionaries faced considerable challenge in attempting to convert them to Christianity. Besides, as Folwell reminds us, the Christians the Natives met set a poor example in "their greed and licentiousness." Several Protestant mission societies offered sponsorship of missions to evangelize the Ojibwe and Dakota, but some individuals made their way to the Natives without it. The brothers Samuel W. and Gideon H. Pond, young laymen from Connecticut, came independently, "without commission or license from any religious body," writes Folwell. In the spring of 1834, then twenty-six and twenty-four years old, they appeared at Fort Snelling determined to work among the Dakota. Theodore Blegen views the two brothers as "major figures in the history of Minnesota missions." With keen observation, they studied the Dakota language and wrote about the customs and lifeways of the Natives with whom they associated for nearly twenty years.[14]

THE TERRITORY OF MINNESOTA

Minnesota achieved territorial status the summer of 1849. The total number of people within the area that became the state of Minnesota was fewer than 4,000; included in that number were Metís, or mixed blood, but not Native Americans. The commercial river port of St. Paul, the largest city in the territory, had at the most some 900 residents, and the two lumbering towns of Stillwater and St. Anthony had 609 and 248 respectively. There was only a bare beginning of rural settlement with some farming on the prairie lands by Lake St. Croix in what would become Washington County. The whole subsistence of the white population was transported up the Mississippi River by steamboat. A regular line between St. Paul and points downriver was put in service in 1847. Earlier, steamboats had sailed when they had a full load of cargo; the first one reached the post at Fort Snelling as early as 1823. It was a small beginning, but, as Blegen states, "the hope of multitudes to come motivated the drive for territorial status."[15]

It was Henry H. Sibley, fur trader, hunter, adventurer, and later Minnesota governor, who, as a delegate to Congress from the rump of Wisconsin Territory, on March 3, 1849, secured passage of the bill creating the Territory of Minnesota. On April 2, 1849, President Zachary Taylor, earlier commandant of Fort Snelling, commissioned as territorial governor Alexander Ramsey of Pennsylvania. Given the present study's focus on ethnicity, it may do well to quote Blegen's assessment that "Early and late in Minnesota history, Yankee influence has been important." Sibley was born in Detroit of New England stock, and Ramsey was a native Pennsylvanian of Scotch and German background. The "onrushing of thousands," as Blegen writes, in the 1850s recruited settlers from many nationalities, but the old-stock American population constituted a majority. "The Yankee element lent special character and color to Minnesota institutions and folkways of the decade," Blegen concludes. A strong Yankee presence persisted in Benson and in other regional market towns as they came into being. Members of this group formed a prominent and influential social and professional elite.[16]

Minnesota Territory was almost entirely within Native American lands; there was no room for its swelling population save a triangle between the St. Croix and Mississippi rivers ceded by the Dakota and Ojibwe in 1837. "The great [Dakota] cession in Minnesota Territory is the outstanding negotiation with the Indians of the border," writes historian Frederic L. Paxson. In 1851 Governor Ramsey conducted treaty councils with the Dakota. In his negotiations he was responding to the predominant and absorbing interest of the territory's white settlers to acquire lands occupied by the Dakota west of the Mississippi River, what newspapers referred to as the "Suland." On July 23, 1851, the treaty at Traverse des Sioux was approved by thirty-five leaders of the upper Dakota; a nearly similar one was signed with the lower Dakota at Mendota on August 5. White settlers gained close to 24 million acres of land, some 19 million in Minnesota.

The Dakota reserved a slice of land ten miles wide on each side of the Minnesota River from Lake Traverse to the Yellow Medicine River and reluctantly began moving to their designated areas in early 1853. The area was legally opened for settlement in the summer of 1853, but because it was not yet surveyed it was not to be offered for sale until 1855. While pre-emption laws allowed occupation of surveyed lands only, pioneers did not refrain from trespassing into the region west of the Mississippi; they became squatters there, occupying land they had not purchased. By the close of that year the "Suland" was nearly empty of Native Americans, forced out by this rapid influx of settlement. In August 1854 Congress granted to Minnesota squatters the pre-emption rights for settlers on unsurveyed lands, as it had in other states, and as those squatters had assumed it would.

In a series of land cessions beginning in 1837 the Ojibwe also lost their lands to white settlers. They were as a matter of government policy consolidated on large reservations, but pressure to release reservation lands for white settlement led to changes. The Dawes Allotment Act of 1887, intended to provide individual lots of land to enrolled members of any reservation, freed unlotted lands for sale to the general public. The treatment of Native Americans in public land policy was tragically unfair to say the least. Their hereditary lands were taken from them as the agricultural frontier swept over them.[17]

Minnesota Statehood

The federal census of 1860 evidences prodigious population growth during the preceding decade. By 1860 there were 172,032 residents in Minnesota; of these about 66 percent were American born. Of the native born, 27 percent came from New York and the middle states, 22 percent from the middle west and west, and 17 percent from New England. Minnesota's population was not yet as cosmopolitan in national origin as it later would become through immigration. Even so, in excess of 29 percent of the total population was foreign born, the Norwegians being the third-largest group after the Germans and the Irish.[18]

Minnesota had by then achieved statehood, a complicated and involved process. The fundamental document moving the territory toward statehood was the enabling act passed by Congress on February 26, 1857, which delineated the geographical limits of the state and set in motion the process that would, if Congress gave final approval, lead to statehood. Contingent on if and when Minnesota became a state, and in keeping with precedent, grants of public lands were made, including allocation of two sections (16 and 36) in each township for schools, seventy-two sections for a state university, and grants for various other purposes beneficial to the incipient state.[19]

The admission of Minnesota as the thirty-second state was delayed by the bitter Kansas-Nebraska conflict on the question of slavery. Minnesota adopted its constitution in October 1857 and submitted it to President James Buchanan on January 6, 1858. He sent it to the Senate on

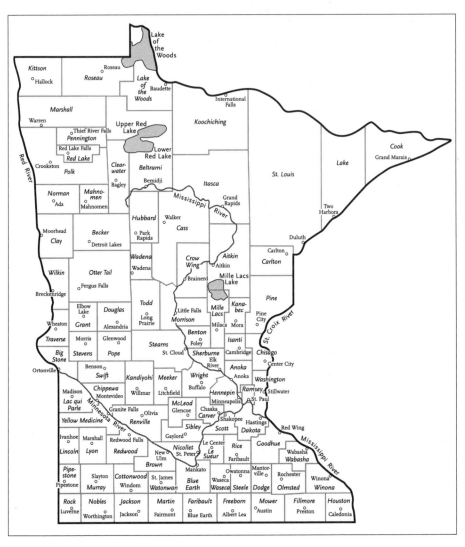

Map of Minnesota Showing Counties and County Seats

January 11, but various political controversies, mainly between southern and northern senators, delayed approval until April 7. The House concurred with the Senate on May 11, 1858, and President Buchanan then signed the bill into law. Governor Henry Sibley, elected by Minnesota voters the previous year under the territorial election machinery, was sworn in along with other officers. Following adoption of a state constitution, a legislative body had also been elected in 1857. On May 14, 1858, the *Saint Paul Daily Minnesotian* declared, "We are a State of the Union."[20]

Before the final congressional vote to admit Minnesota was taken, a provision permitting unnaturalized aliens to vote became an issue of debate in both the Senate and the House, as did the provision opening suffrage to "civilized" Native Americans. Granting voting rights to immigrants would later have a significant impact on state politics; the foreign born could vote four months after applying for citizenship. The whole subject was thoroughly debated in the Senate before its approval was granted; the bill was then sent on to the House. As Folwell explains, many a speaker denied or ignored the well-understood distinction between the rights of citizenship and the privilege of voting.

Opposition to foreigners and to Catholics, which had been growing since the rise of foreign immigration in the early part of the century, led to formation of a secret political organization in 1849, the Order of the Star-Spangled Banner, better known as the Know-Nothing Party. The steady tide of Irish and German immigrants to the industrial North was viewed as a threat to political solidarity and caused apprehension among dissident politicians. The passage of the Kansas-Nebraska Act in 1854, establishing "popular sovereignty" on the question of slavery in the new states, convinced many unionists that the party's program of native white Protestantism would hold the nation together, and the Know-Nothings gained political ground in their antiforeign and anti-Catholic movement. One reason for opposing suffrage for foreigners before they were naturalized citizens related to the basic controversy of the Kansas-Nebraska question and was held by many senators and representatives but unavowed by most. Representative Thomas L. Anderson of Missouri disclosed this fear vigorously during the House debate, predicting what would happen if the Minnesota bill with this particular provision was passed: "I warn gentlemen from the South of the consequences. . . . The whole of the Territories of this Union are rapidly filling up with foreigners. The great body of them are opposed to slavery. Mark my word: if you do it, another slave State will never be formed out of the Territories of this Union. They are the enemies of the South and her institutions."

In the end, of course, it was concern with the West that widened the sectional tensions that led to civil war.[21]

THE CIVIL AND DAKOTA WARS

Minnesota was only three years into statehood when the Confederates opened fire on Fort Sumter on April 12, 1861, forcing its surrender and thereby starting the American Civil War. The war placed heavy demands on the infant state's manpower and resources. Minnesota contributed more than 24,000 men from all ranks of life—the majority volunteers—for service in the Union armies. These men also took part in suppressing Native Americans during the Dakota War. They came from varied backgrounds: American born, Irish, German, Norwegian, Swedish, and other nationalities. Of the small Norwegian population—11,893—estimates suggest that at least 800 volunteered for service; some historians have set the number much higher, including a recent study that found 1,200 volunteers, plus another 200 farmers in and around New Ulm who were mustered to meet the Dakota. Young Norwegian men in Minnesota were also recruited to serve in the famed Fifteenth Wisconsin Regiment, a Norwegian military unit. During the course of the hostilities, eleven regiments of infantry as well as special artillery, cavalry, and sharpshooter units were raised in Minnesota. "Minnesota troops," Blegen states, "played a valiant part in the far-flung battles and campaigns of the Civil War."

The enormous conflict was a watershed experience for Norwegians in America. This heroic, dramatic, and idealized period in their history marked a decisive phase in their adjustment to life in the New World. A strong feeling existed that they had earned a legitimate place in America. Norwegian blood had been spilled in defense of the nation, and famed heroes of their ethnicity gained public recognition. Soldiers returning from battlefields at the end of the war, many of them having enrolled in the armed forces shortly after landing in America, headed west in large numbers to become pioneers on the American agricultural frontier or to settle in nascent marketplaces. Many made their homes in the village of Benson and in other western trading centers or claimed land in emerging western townships and counties.

In Minnesota there were many signs of transition. In the legislature, elected at the end of the territorial period in 1857, the Democrats obtained majorities in both houses. Their gubernatorial candidate Sibley was elected by popular vote and the Democratic legislature successfully placed its candidates in state offices. The Republican Party, pledging to keep slavery out of the territories, became a sectional party in the North and in Minnesota caused a political shift from Democratic to Republican control. The Civil War also moved Norwegian Americans, guided by immigrant journals, into the fold of the Republican Party. The northern faction of the Know-Nothings joined the Republicans against the Democrats; the Republicans avoided their antiforeign and anti-Catholic thought in order to attract the immigrant vote. Beginning in 1859 and lasting almost to the end of the century the Republican Party held predominant, nearly monopolistic power in the state's political affairs.[22]

It was in the midst of the Civil War that the Dakota, from their reservations along the upper Minnesota River and under the leadership of Little Crow, finally vented their frustrations by taking up arms against their white oppressors. A second treaty in 1858 had further reduced the Dakota reserve; the entire treaty system and the government's Indian policies were greatly flawed. Native Americans and their way of life were being engulfed by the westward movement of land-hungry settlers and by the advance of railroads, farming, and industry.

Congressional passage on May 20, 1862, of the much-advocated Homestead Act, which granted 160 acres of public land to anyone who lived on it for five years, expressed the urgency of making free land available, moved the agricultural frontier westward, and created farm prosperity. Because of Republican concerns about the immigrant vote—the foreign born made up about 30 percent of Minnesota's population—the party adopted a friendly attitude on the homestead question. It was rewarded with the coveted support of immigrants.[23]

The Episcopal bishop Henry B. Whipple, a defender of Native Americans, had warned of the evils and dire consequences of the government's dishonest treatment of the Dakota and other nations in a letter to President Abraham Lincoln written more than five months before the conflict erupted. Whipple, who had moved to Faribault in Rice County in 1859, became a familiar figure through his missionary labors in different settlements and among the Ojibwe and the Dakota.[24]

The U.S.–Dakota War was triggered by an August 17, 1862, incident in Acton Township, western Meeker County, on the edge of the Big Woods when a hunting party of four Dakota from the Lower Sioux Agency killed five settlers on Howard Baker's farm. The settlers, all with roots in New England, were buried in a single grave in the Ness Norwegian Lutheran Church southwest of Litchfield; a memorial was dedicated in 1878. The fact that these Yankees were buried by a Norwegian immigrant church was likely a reflection of convenience; it was simply the nearest cemetery. The attack was not planned, but it led to a series of bloody battles that continued through that fall. Labeling the conflict "Minnesota's Other Civil War," Kenneth Carley estimates that "at least 450—and perhaps as many as 800—white settlers and soldiers were killed, and considerable property was destroyed in southern Minnesota." The concluding event in 1862 was the hanging of thirty-eight Dakota in Mankato on December 26. This dramatic reprisal did not, however, end the settlers' fear of attacks. Although small numbers of Dakota, including scouts and their families, were allowed to stay, virtually all the Dakota, including many who had remained friendly with the whites, were banished from the state. Their numbers in Minnesota had by 1866 been reduced from close to 7,000 to only 374.[25]

During the days of fighting, isolated homesteads were assaulted by bands of Dakota, who spread out to strike remote areas on the fringes of settlement. On August 20 warriors attacked the Norway Lake settlement located north of the city of Willmar in Kandiyohi County. Founded in 1858 on the rolling prairie surrounding the lake, the settlement had about one hundred Norwegian residents in 1860; some Swedish settlers lived a few miles farther west by West Lake, later known as Monson Lake, in Arctander Township. Coming by way of Quebec from Sweden, the small group of settlers—the two brothers Anders P. and Daniel P. Broberg with their families—arrived at their selected claims by Lake Monson on July 15, 1861. They were the first to suffer the wrath of the Dakota; fourteen or more white settlers in the Swedish community were killed. The two Broberg families encountered the Dakota on their return from religious services at the neighboring home of Andreas L. Lundborg. The scene of the attack, in which nearly all the Brobergs were killed, is preserved in Monson Lake State Park.[26]

There were many acts of individual courage and astonishing survivor stories among the white settlers. The story of Guri Endresen Rosseland from Vikør in Hardanger, Norway, is especially well known. In 1857 she had settled with her husband, Lars, and their children by Lake Solomon, south of Norway Lake. On August 21, the day after the attack at Lake Monson and Norway Lake, the Dakota struck the Rosseland farm, killing Lars, the oldest son, and his wife, wounding another son, and carrying off two of the daughters as captives. Guri hid with her youngest daughter in a cellar some distance from the house. They fled but returned the next day, finding her wounded son alive. In a farm wagon pulled by oxen she transported them along with two injured neighbors through regions controlled by the Dakota to safety in Forest City, about thirty miles farther east. There she found her two abducted daughters, who had managed to escape their captors.[27]

In an 1866 letter to her mother in Norway, Guri recalls the atrocities of the conflict and gives an account of her experience during the Dakota War. Piously she reminds her mother that "God permitted it to happen thus, and I had to accept my heavy fate and thank Him for having spared my life and those of some of my dear children." News of the attacks on pioneer settlers spread quickly in Norway and was used to argue against emigration. The attacks had confirmed western settlers' worst fears. One letter sent from St. Peter, Minnesota, in September 1862 and reproduced in newspapers in Norway gave this account: "That which I suspected and wrote about in my last letter has come about. The Indians have begun attacking the farmers. They have already killed a great many people,

and many are mutilated in the cruelest manner. Tomahawks and knives have already claimed many victims." Much of the material on the conflict that appeared in Norway's newspapers was gleaned from the Norwegian-language weekly *Emigranten* (The Emigrant), which had begun publication in January 1852, printed in a simple log cabin

Guri Endresen Rosseland wrote of her ordeal during the U.S.–Dakota War of 1862.

in Newark, in Wisconsin's Rock Prairie area. The descriptions presented a frightening scenario that might have discouraged people from setting out for the promise of America. There was a short-term decline in emigration as a result, but it did not last long: mass emigration from Norway commenced after the end of the Civil War.[28]

Guri's positive report about her surviving family members might suggest some of the circumstances that caused emigration not only to rebound but to assume epic proportions. "I must also let you know," she writes, "that my daughter Gjærtru has land, which they received from the government under a law that has passed, called in our language 'the Homestead law,' and for a quarter-section of land they have to pay $16, and after they have lived there five years they receive a deed and complete possession of the property and can sell it if they want to or keep it if they want to. She lives about twenty-four American miles from here and is doing well." Thus the promises of an agricultural West were widely promulgated.[29]

"A Glorious New Scandinavia"

In 1850 Fredrika Bremer, forty-nine years old and a much-celebrated Swedish author and feminist, made a strenuous journey to the Midwest. Having traveled from Chicago, visiting Swedish and Norwegian settlements along her route, and up the Mississippi River from Galena, Illinois, she was welcomed in St. Paul by territorial governor Alexander Ramsey and his wife, Anna. Bremer became their guest in the governor's mansion.

Her countrymen who arrived later in such great numbers were hardly accorded the same warm welcome, yet they proved themselves to be god-fearing and hardworking settlers of the territory and later state. Indeed, they became the object of much propaganda and other inducements to attract them to the region. Bremer had a prophetic vision of the significant role they would play, declaring "What a glorious new Scandinavia might not Minnesota become!" and claiming "The climate, the situation, the character of the scenery agrees with our people better than that of any other of the American States, and none of them appear to me to have a greater or more beautiful future before them than Minnesota."[30]

In 1850 there were not many Scandinavians in Minnesota Territory; the federal census lists four Swedish-born persons. The first log cabin built by Swedes in Minnesota was apparently constructed at Hay Lake in Washington County by three young Swedes who arrived from Illinois after having emigrated from the province of Västergötland in Sweden in the spring of 1850. One of them, Carl Fernström, made an exploratory tour to the north and came back "so enthusiastic about the lakes and forests of Minnesota, which had reminded him of Sweden, that in October that same year he returned with his two friends, Oscar Roos and August Sandahl, all three in their early twenties, and together they made themselves at home on a forty-acre tract on Hay Lake." The territory's landscape, with its thousand lakes and densely wooded areas, might indeed be reminiscent of certain regions of the Scandinavian homelands.[31]

In his 1938 study of Norwegian settlement, Carlton C. Qualey found by examining census schedules that there were nine Norwegians in Minnesota Territory in 1850. Two were soldiers stationed at Fort Snelling; another was a seventeen-year-old servant girl "somewhere in Wabasha County." Hjalmar Rued Holand identifies the first Norwegian woman to settle in Minnesota as Ingeborg Levorsdatter Langeberg, who arrived in St. Paul in 1850 and for one year served as a maid in the residence of Governor Ramsey. The other six listed in the 1850 census were the first Norwegians to take up residence in Minnesota; they settled at Long Prairie in the later Todd County. A reservation had been established there in 1848 for the Ho-Chunk (Winnebago) tribe of Wisconsin. These six—Ole Tollefson, his wife and two children, Søren Olson Sørum, and Isabelle Nelson, the last two being married in 1850—had been employed at Fort Atkinson, Iowa, and in 1848 had accompanied the Ho-Chunk north. As Holand has it, "in 1848 the government was tired of trying to civilize the Indians and decided to move the entire tribe 300 miles to Minnesota." The four continued to work for the government in the new location for two years before "returning to white people's society."

Another early settler was Nils Nilsen, born in Modum, in the County of Buskerud, Norway, in 1830, who arrived in St. Paul in 1849, having first worked that same year in the lead mines in Galena, Illinois, and on a farm near Decorah, Iowa. Holand credits him with being Minnesota's first Norwegian settler. After being variously employed in St. Paul and Stillwater until 1882, "he purchased a large farm in the vicinity of New

York Mills" in Otter Tail County. His experience typifies that of many pioneers in Bremer's prophetic "glorious new Scandinavia."[32]

NORWEGIAN IMMIGRATION AND EARLY SETTLEMENT

Only two or so decades passed after the U.S. arrival of pioneer immigrants from Norway in 1825 before Norwegians found their way to Minnesota—more evidence that they had come to a nation on the move. The first group of Norwegians to respond to the appeal of American freedom and opportunity were the much-celebrated Sloopers. Their July 4, 1825, departure from the city of Stavanger on the southwest coast of Norway onboard the small sloop *Restauration* provided a colorful opening to a major historical development. The many circumstances and motives that in the nineteenth century and into the twentieth made Norway one of the major countries of emigration cannot be covered in the present study. In short, Norway experienced wrenching economic changes and significant population growth, from fewer than 900,000 residents in 1801 to more than 1.7 million in 1865. A high birth rate and a steadily falling death rate gave Norway one of the highest percentages of such growth in Europe. These sixty-some years saw nearly a doubling of the number of people who sought subsistence in an economy that did not modernize quickly enough to keep pace with the demands placed on it.

Population growth was not itself a cause of emigration, but it lay behind the gradual structural changes and transformation that Norwegian society went through in the nineteenth century, influenced both by economic liberalism and democratic reform based on the May 17, 1814, constitution. Emigration reflected the spirit of change that characterized the age. It became a dramatic national experience that during a century of emigration, 1825 to 1925, moved nearly 800,000 Norwegians overseas. During the nineteenth century nearly all those emigrants came to the United States, which had a practically limitless need for new citizens to settle the country's wide-open spaces and to develop its enormous resources.[33]

The Sloopers arrived in the port city of New York on October 9, 1825, after a voyage of fourteen weeks; they numbered fifty-three, crew and passengers and a baby born in transit. They were Quakers, Quaker

On July 4, 1825, the small sloop Restauration *left Norway with the first boat-load of Norwegian emigrants.*

sympathizers, and Haugeans, followers of the lay religious leader Hans Nielsen Hauge—all subjected to persecution by the religiously monopolistic Lutheran State Church. The religious motive for immigration appears not to be replicated in the later exodus; indeed, from the mid-1840s religious liberties were enacted in Norway. The free exercise of faith gradually changed and even, it has been claimed, Americanized Norwegian religious life. Hauge himself—in spite of persecution and imprisonment for his lay activity—and his many followers did not leave the Lutheran State Church but worked for a renewal of Norwegian Christian life within its framework. Their activities made obvious the peasantry's growing class consciousness and an objection to the power held by the official classes.[34]

The liberal philosophy that imbued the Constitution of 1814 gave the individual freedom of movement and made emigration a matter of personal choice. It was a voluntary migration. The Sloopers first settled in Kendall Township on the shores of Lake Ontario in western New York State. In the mid-1830s most of them responded to news of better opportunities in the West and moved to the fertile Fox River Valley south-west of Chicago, founding a colony there. Not until the frontier for Norwegian settlement had moved west to Illinois and there were colonies ready to receive newcomers did Norwegians begin arriving in large numbers. "America letters," relating the advantages of the New World, convinced flocks of Norwegian peasants to seek a future across the Atlantic. Annual group emigration resumed, in the early years mainly from the central highland valleys and the western coastal districts but before the Civil War ended it had taken hold throughout the kingdom. Although there were localized differences in intensity, emigration occurred from all nineteen of Norway's counties. In this founding phase contacts were established between earlier immigrants and their kin and friends back home in all parts of the country. Later immigrants' destinations might thus be settlements of people from their own community in Norway who spoke a familiar local vernacular and preserved the traditions of home. With this comforting circumstance, the overseas migration fueled itself. By the end of the Civil War nearly 78,000 Norwegians had come to America.[35]

Norwegians participated from the mid-1830s in a westward movement that by 1900 reached from the southern tip of Lake Michigan to eastern Montana, matching the general march of the American population. Within this vast region they established agrarian settlements with distinct regional composition: people from specific Norwegian communities settled together and became neighbors again in America. The immigrants re-created the rural Norwegian community to an astounding degree. There was, to be sure, a certain intermingling of people from different districts within each community, especially as settlement moved westward, but a tendency to associate with "their own folk," as expressed by the immigrants themselves, persisted. Norwegian localism became a strong force in the formation of settlements. As the author has stated in an earlier publication, "Bonds of kinship to the pioneer colonies strengthened this regional tendency as the older immigrant farming communities gave up their youth to new settlements farther west," and "familial connections also guided immigrants to specific destinations in America." The heaviest concentration of Norwegian farming communities developed in the northern part of the so-called Homestead Act triangle between the Missouri and Mississippi rivers.[36]

Norwegian immigrants did not confine themselves entirely to farming and rurality. An urban colony emerged in the prairie seaport of Chicago in 1836 when a few newcomers remained in the fledgling city rather than moving on to the Fox River Valley, choosing instead to enter an urban economy. By 1860 the colony was well established; it would have a significant cultural and political influence on the entire Norwegian American community. Chicago had by then—in a nearly miraculous transformation—moved from being a village of five log cabins in 1832 to a bustling city of close to 110,000 inhabitants, more than half of whom were either immigrants or the children of immigrants. The Norwegian colony had 1,573 members, 62 percent of them residing near Milwaukee Avenue on the sparsely settled west side of the north branch of the Chicago River. As Norwegians left the Milwaukee Avenue district to continue their trek northwestward, they were replaced by successive neighborhoods of Poles, Russian and Polish Jews, and Italians. By the turn of the twentieth century, the neighborhoods around Humboldt Park had become "the great Norwegian center." The district described as "Little Norway" by the 1920s extended north to the Logan Square community and east to the Wicker Park district. They numbered about 56,000, counting only the immigrants and their children; 63 percent of them lived in the Norwegian districts on the northwest side of Chicago.

The Norwegian colony was but one of a large number of easily identifiable ethnic enclaves in Chicago's landscape; in the urban environment the many immigrant groups created their separate social worlds. It was a home for Norwegian immigrants that differed from life in the country town; there a small population and closeness to country living encouraged community activity and mutual cultural influence with citizens of other national backgrounds. There no one could live entirely in an ethnic world. The comprehensive ethnic colonies formed in America's great cities, on the other hand, enabled immigrants to live in two worlds and experience a public as well as a private sphere. Residential clustering and institutional growth within the colony widened the perimeters of the latter. The urban colony in some striking ways functioned as a city within a city. There were social associations, fraternal and athletic clubs, dramatic and musical groups, and ethnic business enterprise and professional services. The Norwegian Lutheran Church—its accustomed role the formation of rural communities—entered into the city as a missionary and never gained the strength it enjoyed in rural and small-town settings. It transferred its prejudices and fears to the new environment and viewed the city as a direct threat both to Lutheranism and to Norwegian heritage. It instilled in its urban parishioners, and by extension the entire Norwegian Lutheran community, a strong rejection of the city's evils, thereby reinforcing an ingrained distrust of urban life. The churches and their subsidiary charitable and social services were visible evidence of adaptation to greater needs in the harsh urban environment. There they competed more directly with temporal interests than in the country town or in Norwegian American farming communities; indeed, within the urban colony a manifest division existed between church members and those active in secular endeavors, between church people and lodge people.[37]

The urban colony and the country town were communities different from the church-centered rural settlements of Norwegian Americans. In these segregated communities, the immigrants could work, play, and worship with other Norwegians, not infrequently from the same part of Norway, and in relative isolation from outside intrusion. Norwegian agrarian settlement spread into Wisconsin in the 1840s. Wisconsin Territory was organized in 1836 and gained statehood in 1848. The Norwegian pioneers were two brothers, Ole and Ansten Nattestad, who had emigrated from Numedal, Norway, in 1837, coming first to the ill-fated Beaver Creek settlement in Illinois, where most of the residents died from malaria. Among those who perished was Ole Rynning, author of a famous immigrant guide, *Sandfærdig beretning om Amerika* (True Account of America), published in 1838. Rynning's account circulated widely in Norway, and together with the mass of America letters it greatly influenced later emigration. The summer of 1838, while Ansten was in Norway, Ole left Illinois for Wisconsin. He founded the settlement known as Jefferson Prairie in Rock County, which grew rapidly when Ansten returned the following spring with a large group of people. Some of the newcomers went farther west and established a community on Rock Prairie: the Luther Valley settlement, as it has been called, after the congregation formed there in 1844.[38]

As newcomers poured into Wisconsin, both territory and state, it remained the center of Norwegian settlement and activity until the Civil War. A number of notable settlements were founded; these play an important part in the annals of Norwegian American history. Several more communities were established in the south and east of the state; especially noteworthy were the prosperous settlements by Lake Koshkonong in eastern Dane and western Jefferson counties. The village of Stoughton in Dane County became a Norwegian enclave, as explained by Svein Nilsson in *Billed-Magazin* (Picture Magazine) in 1870: "What especially attracted my attention to Stoughton is the strongly Norwegian character of the town. A newcomer from Norway who arrives here will be surprised indeed to find in the heart of the country, more than a thousand miles from his landing place, a town where language and way of life so unmistakably remind him of his native land." In terms suggested by Ray Billington, one may trace "an urban frontier"—even if one considers only the commercial centers with a dominant Norwegian presence—beginning most notably in Wisconsin, from there moving into northern and central Iowa and southeastern Minnesota, and onward to the west-central part of the state and the regions considered in the present study. Benson, Starbuck, and Madison, along with several other urban places, belong in this westward trajectory.[39]

The early settlements both acted as receiving stations for newcomers and served as mother colonies for new farming communities, each which in turn might become a new point of departure. The Muskego settlement, founded south of Milwaukee in 1839, gained a unique position: the Muskego church, started the winter of 1843–44 and dedicated in March 1845, has been recognized as the first Norwegian Lutheran Church in America; the first Norwegian-language newspaper, *Nordlyset* (Northern Lights), was published there in 1847. As stated in *The Promise of America,* "The lines of development are clear—the church and the press were to be the two most important institutions established and supported by Norwegian immigrants."[40]

Nineteenth-century Norwegian immigration was regularly a rural-to-rural movement. In some ways it might be characterized as a conservative migration, a desire to continue an accustomed way of life, to preserve traditional values associated with a rural existence. Around 1850 Norwegian settlers came to an area in north-central Wisconsin they named "Indielandet," located in Portage and Waupaca counties. They had already found their way to the western part of the state toward the end of the 1840s; the coulee country along the Mississippi River, from Crawford County to Barron County, was almost a solid strip

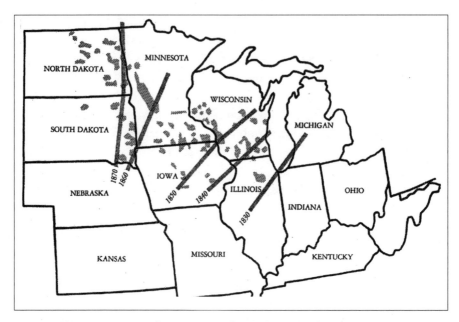

Map Showing Westward Movement of Norwegian Settlement

of Norwegian settlements. By the 1870s the major areas of Norwegian settlement had been established; they have in the main persisted until the present time.[41]

In the late 1840s Norwegian settlers joined with thousands of old-stock Americans in the westward push into Iowa, following closely on the heels of Native Americans and traders. Hjalmar Holand dates the beginning of Norwegian settlement in the state to 1846, when Ole Halvorson Valle—who came from Numedal, Norway, to Rock Prairie in 1841—started to farm southeast of St. Olaf in Clayton County. "It is with this year," writes Holand, "Clayton County's and Iowa's Norwegian history begins." Iowa gained statehood in 1846, and in the following years Norwegian immigrants coming directly from Norway, making their way from New Orleans by boat, or joining in the movement from older communities in Illinois and Wisconsin formed new settlements in the state. According to the census, in 1850 there were only 330 of them, a number that increased to 8,048 in the following decade. Washington Prairie in northeastern Iowa's Winneshiek County became a Norwegian center; the little town of Decorah gained special fame as the center of

Norwegian Lutheran church and educational activities and newspaper publishing. Norwegian settlers also moved to central Iowa, especially to Story County and particularly Story City. Like Decorah, it may be viewed as a Norwegian town in the founding of urban places during the movement west. Pastor C. A. Clausen, an early Lutheran religious leader, was in 1853 instrumental in founding the village of St. Ansgar, which became the nucleus for an extensive Norwegian settlement in Mitchell and adjoining counties.[42]

The party that came to Mitchell County moved from Rock Prairie, Wisconsin. In describing this vast movement, it is important to bear in mind the process of settlement: a stage migration westward. Holand's description is both colorful and enlightening:

> The main requirements of the early settlers were wood, water and tillable land, and when no more land possessing these essential qualities could be found in the Fox River region, they looked for it in the nearest areas where it still could be had. Most of Illinois was treeless; therefore the first settlers took the road to Wisconsin. From there their path went northwestward, from one forest grove to the next, through northeastern Iowa to Minnesota.... Several settlements in Minnesota were settled directly from Fox River, but most were founded by men from Rock Prairie, Fox River's first offspring, which, with the possible exception of Koshkonong, is the mother of more Norwegian settlements than any other district.[43]

The large Goodhue County, Minnesota, was opened to settlement in spring 1852; settlers began arriving in 1854, but the first Norwegian to take up residence there was, according to Holand, Matthias Petersen Ringdahl from Fåberg, Norway, who in 1851 came to Red Wing, later moving onto a farm near the present town of Zumbrota. The future river town of Red Wing in 1851 consisted of three or four houses, but already the settlers could "buy their food and sell their products" there, much closer than the alternative marketplace, Decorah.[44]

The early 1850s introduced the first period of settlement in Minnesota, which lasted until 1865, and the pioneering of the state's southern counties; the number of Norwegians in Minnesota rose from 6,769 in 1857 to 11,893 in 1860 to 49,569 in 1870. The earliest settlement area was south of Goodhue County: beginning in 1851 parties of Norwegian settlers moved to western Houston and eastern Fillmore counties. From this core, settlement expanded west along the Iowa border. In southern Houston County the Norwegian Spring Grove settlement, founded in 1852, became a center in one of America's most densely settled Norwegian colonies. Minnesota's boom—hawked by newspapers and land speculators—is reflected in the dramatic increases in the Norwegian American population.[45]

In his essay on Spring Grove, Carlton Qualey maintains that it "was one of the important distribution points for Norwegian settlement in the American Northwest, and [that] there are hundreds of Norwegian Americans in western Minnesota and the Dakotas whose ancestors stopped for a time in Spring Grove Township before going on farther westward." It was a common route for settlers in Pope, Swift, and Lac qui Parle counties and in the several urban places populated by Norwegian immigrants.[46]

The prairies to the west awaited white settlers. But, as Holand describes, "Straight through Minnesota, from St. Cloud to Mankato, there was in olden days a large forest known as the Big Woods. . . . It was about 100 miles long and from 10 to 40 miles wide, and was for many years like a barrier to settlement farther west." The Park Region lay beyond the Big Woods to the northwest, a country of lakes, meadowland, and prairie. The Norway Lake settlement in northwestern Kandiyohi County—founded in 1858 by migrants from Rock Prairie, Wisconsin—was the only large Norwegian community formed there before the Dakota War. Most of these early settlers left during the hostilities, but others began coming after a two-year hiatus.[47]

Settlers were reluctant to move out on the prairie beyond the Big Woods before railroad lines were built for easy transportation. They instead engaged in a long and costly process of turning the heavily forested areas into farms. Immigrants feared the open prairie, its fierce winds and wildfires, its lack of timber for fuel or building except along the waterways. It took time to overcome the threat of open landscape, for Norwegians as well as for other pioneers, but, as Folwell explains, "the lure of free or cheap land soon gave opportunity for learning the attractions and advantages of the prairie."[48]

Concluding Remarks

The emergence of small towns in western Minnesota belongs mainly to the post–Civil War years. Many, if not all, were a result of railroad extension into the Park Region. The present study views this white settlement in a broad historical context; the frontier's rapid advance thus provides the setting for an analysis of the founding and early life of railroad towns and other agricultural centers that came into being. Ethnicity, with heavy focus on the Norwegian American experience, serves as a main interpretive tool within the analytical framework of cultural pluralism.

Even tracing the nature of the small town, as Lingeman does, from the colonial period to the present represents a fruitful approach. Benson, Madison, Starbuck, and other small commercial centers share with the New England towns, "imbued with Puritan Congregationalist ideals," the circumstance that they came into being on a frontier wilderness, though two centuries apart. Town development repeated itself in shifting geographic environments as America expanded westward. On the other hand, Billington reminds us that, indeed, "To the casual observer these pioneer villages varied little from the towns in the East, but actually they differed markedly in the sophistication of their economic activity, institutions, and attitudes." And Lingeman shows us the variety that existed as he follows the historical path of "town jobbing" in the Old Northwest, in Ohio and Indiana, "along rivers and streams; on trails, traces, and later roads, around crossroads taverns; near military posts; at fords and passes, or near the gristmills that ground the first settlers' corn."[49]

There were, as Lingeman's chapter headings suggest, the mining camps and cow towns of the Great West, the homesteads and prairie junctions of the Great Plains, and the town, city, and factory of a later day: even though they had a particular economic base, they exhibited in their social and cultural life many similarities throughout their existence. Lingeman attributes to the frontier town "a leveling force as well as an escape hatch," claiming "the people who went west arrived theoretically as equals, with equal opportunities for all." By the 1890s the small town had reached its apotheosis, Lingeman states, and was providing a comfortable middle-class lifestyle and a secure existence for the people who set the tone. Lewis Atherton in his treatise *Main Street on the Middle Border* shows how in nineteenth-century midwestern society a horse culture prevailed, gearing settlers "to the strength and limitations of horsedrawn transportation." But, Lingeman reminds us, "the threats or contradictions to that life were still segregated off some place—across the tracks, in Polish town . . . where the new immigrants lived." A further threat to the complacency of the small town was the rural exodus, depriving it of its economic base and robbing it of its young as they looked to growing urban centers and distant factories for opportunities.[50]

The immigrant presence was obvious in many midwestern villages and towns from their beginnings and is much in evidence in the towns under consideration; indeed, immigrants might well found, name, and boom small towns and villages on their own. Authors of fiction have depicted the immigrant adjustment and influence. In Sinclair Lewis's cutting portrait of the small midwestern town Gopher Prairie (Sauk Centre, Minnesota, serves as its prototype) in the 1920 novel *Main Street,* Carol Kennicott, the central figure, finds novelty in the drab and sterile town environment only when she visits the Norwegian fair in the Lutheran Church: "There, in the *bondestue,* the replica of a Norse farm kitchen, pale women in scarlet jackets embroidered with gold thread and colored beads, in black skirts with a line of blue, green-striped aprons, and ridged caps very pretty to set off a fresh face, had served *römmegröd og lefse.*" It was the "mild foreignness" that she reveled in. But Carol laments that these foreign women were also "being Americanized into uniformity, and in less than a generation losing in grayness whatever pleasant new customs they might have added to the life of the town." Rapid assimilation was the creed of the day; few would join Carol Kennicott in decrying its unfortunate consequences—the loss of cultural diversity.[51]

The small western towns, as well as the farming communities and urban colonies, constituted an environment where a transfer and reinvention of ethnic cultures could occur and persist. The country town on the western prairie was a much more complex place than Lewis's fictional account suggests. More than a Yankee bastion, it was also immigrant laden, as was its agricultural hinterland. Taking into account the American frontier's westward advance through presettlement, territorial, and statehood periods offers a context in which to consider the fate of Native Americans, the patterns of westward migration—with full participation by Norwegian immigrants—and the historical and cultural forces that came into play in the founding and growth of the state of Minnesota.

Two

The Village of Benson

BECOMING A CENTRAL PLACE

The village of Benson—the county seat from its founding in 1870—served as a central place for Swift County. Townspeople, villagers, and farmers throughout the county had business to conduct in the courthouse. In commerce and farm trade Benson interacted most directly with the farm population in its hinterland, though it might compete with other local trading centers and, as a major stop on the railroad line in west-central Minnesota, extend its reach to the Minneapolis mills where much of the county's wheat was transported or engage in financial transactions with other distant urban centers. Locally, of course, the prevailing horse culture of the nineteenth century greatly limited commercial and cultural intercourse to communities within a distance easily traversed by horse-drawn conveyances.

Improved transportation offered by the railroad explains both Benson's early beginnings and the prosperity it enjoyed as a trading center; Starbuck and Madison would share a similar history when railroad tracks crossed into those parts of Minnesota more than a decade later. These events occurred during the period of mass emigration from Norway—and from Europe more generally—and the accompanying increase in Norwegian settlement in Minnesota. As the Minnesota River Valley and other parts of the West were opened to white settlement, the pace of westward movement quickened. Norwegians concentrated in well-defined regions of the state and were among the earliest settlers to arrive in Swift, Pope, and Lac qui Parle counties, where they constituted a large portion of the rural pioneers whose arrival predated the dawn of the three villages.

A dominant Norwegian presence characterized all three urban places and their hinterlands and evinced similar developments, though Starbuck and Madison did not share in the excitement of the pioneering decade of the 1870s and its formative influence on the country town. Benson's early history and relations with the farming communities in its close upland is the main focus of the present chapter; the two other central places and their constituencies will be considered in greater detail later.

The population of Swift County was not only Norwegian, though this ethnicity was the most represented, but included people of varied European backgrounds. A survey of the townships reveals that, like the Norwegians, other groups lived in more or less segregated communities. Regional identity and loyalty based on Old Country localism influenced patterns of Norwegian settlement in west-central Minnesota, even in the country town, but they were much more visible in farming communities, where immigrants created a local Norwegian cultural world in language and in mundane as well as festive traditions, mightily played on by Lutheran religiosity.

THE MINNESOTA VALLEY

The summer of 1850 saw the beginning of steamboat navigation on the Minnesota River; before then, writes Edward D. Neill, "no large vessel had ever disturbed the waters of this stream." On July 18 the *Anthony Wayne*, which the year before had reached the Falls of St. Anthony on the Mississippi River, made it almost to Mankato on the Minnesota. The following year the most important event was the treaty with the Dakota "by which," Neill continues, "the west side of the Mississippi and the valley of the Minnesota river were opened to the enterprise of the hardy emigrant."[1]

Steamboating on the Minnesota occurred regularly between 1852 and 1871, increasing as settlement created demands for the transportation of freight and passengers. The Minnesota river trade ran mainly between the wharfs in St. Paul and Mankato, to the mouth of the Blue Earth River, but for a part of the season—April, May, June, and July—boats occasionally ventured as far as Fort Ripley and the Redwood and Yellow Medicine Indian agencies. All merchandise to Chippewa County, of which Swift

County was a part until 1870, traveled along the Minnesota River by wagons, usually drawn by oxen; until 1870 most of the settlers' necessities were brought from New Ulm or beyond. Before the founding of Benson, Norwegian business pioneers, men like N. P. Strom and Thomas Knudson, procured the wares they sold in their shanty stores in this cumbersome manner. The coming of the railroad radically altered the mode of transportation. The Minnesota Valley Railroad Company, organized in 1864, completed its line between St. Paul and Mankato in 1868. It was, in the manner of several other railroad companies, a land-grant railroad, approved by the state legislature under the 1857 Land Grant Act of Congress.[2]

The first railroad line in Minnesota, only ten miles in length, was opened in 1862 between St. Paul and St. Anthony; railroad construction then proceeded slowly, but by the end of 1865 there were 210 miles of track in the state. This first line heralded the network that would eventually link the state's farming communities, villages, and towns. The company responsible for the first ten miles of track optimistically bore the name "St. Paul and Pacific Railroad." This road, whose bonds were purchased by James J. Hill and partners in 1878, laid the foundation of the famed Great Northern Railway, which prospered under Hill's dominant leadership.[3]

The St. Paul and Pacific Railroad, as it struck westward and northwestward, reached Willmar in Kandiyohi County in 1869 and Benson in Swift County in the fall of 1870. As Thomas White Harvey reminds us in his thesis, in which he describes how the railroads pushed into western Minnesota's prairie counties, "The wholesale founding of railroad towns that took place from the late 1860s to around 1920 formed the Western urban network." By locating town sites at intervals of about eight miles, the St. Paul and Pacific Railroad determined that four trading centers should be founded in Swift County: Kerkhoven, De Graff, Benson, and Randall, or Clontarf, as it was renamed by the original Irish settlers who moved the town site to a new location. Of these four, only Kerkhoven and Benson prospered during the first six years.[4]

Railroads engaged in land marketing and became the chief promoters of town sites. Prominent Swedish immigrant Colonel Hans Mattson, of Civil War fame and a pioneer farmer, served from 1868 as land agent for the St. Paul and Pacific Railroad. Land and immigration were two major factors in the peopling of the state. The St. Paul and Pacific Railroad adopted a special Scandinavian immigration policy and was until the spring of 1871 the leading colonization railroad, seeking to create a chain of Scandinavian settlements along its main line. The predominance of Norwegian and other Scandinavian settlers in western Minnesota was thus a result of deliberate policy enacted by the railroad company and also by the state government. Mattson's reason for accepting the appointment as land agent was, he explained to his Scandinavian audience, "in order to see to it that—as far as possible—this country which I described in the Scandinavian papers a year ago would fall into the hands of Scandinavians." Mattson refers to his successful work as secretary for the Minnesota Board of Immigration, established in 1867, to populate with Scandinavians the even-numbered sections, the government land, along the main line. In 1868 his assignment was to fill the odd-numbered sections, the railroad's own land, along the line.[5]

The Minnesota Board of Immigration sent out advertising pamphlets in Dano-Norwegian, Swedish, German, and Welsh; pamphlets and newspaper articles carried propaganda advertising the advantages Minnesota offered. Sören Listoe, assistant editor of the Norwegian-language *Nordisk Folkeblad* (Nordic People's Newspaper) in Minneapolis produced and distributed in large numbers both articles and pamphlets emphasizing the suitability of the climate for Scandinavians; the natural scenery; the economic geography, noting agricultural products, industries, cities, and railroads; how to get along during the first years as a farmer; the location of the largest Scandinavian settlements; and the best places to establish new ones. Listoe furthermore claimed for Norwegians a special political knack that would work to their advantage in Minnesota; a case in point was the political career of Lars K. Aaker of Goodhue County, who was appointed to the federal land office in Alexandria, Douglas County, destined to become a region of heavy Scandinavian settlement.[6]

In late 1869 the Minnesota Board of Immigration was replaced by a new board to advance the settlement of the state, founded on petition from a German emigration society and the Scandinavian Emigration Society for the State of Minnesota, formed earlier that year with Aaker as its president. As a consequence state immigration promotion operated to a large extent under the auspices of various immigrant groups, a circumstance that reflected those groups' self-interest but also the commercial necessity for American capital to allow immigrant groups to operate among their own, where it had no direct access. State immigration promotion declined in the 1870s as the land-grant railroads became more powerful and took over most of the land and town site marketing.[7]

MIGRATION AND SETTLEMENT

Expansion of railroad lines into the West coincided with the arrival of legions of Norwegian peasants seeking security through land ownership. Mass emigration from Norway to the United States occurred in the period between 1865 and 1915, when in the course of fifty years almost 677,000 Norwegians took part in the overseas crossing. Norway's population increased despite this heavy loss of citizens, passing the 2 million mark around 1890; by 1910, toward the end of the era of mass emigration, Norway's population stood at 2,391,782. Norwegians crossed the Atlantic in three massive waves, the first one, beginning after the Civil War, lasted until 1873. The second and greatest period of migration was in the 1880s, when eleven out of every thousand Norwegians were leaving the homeland annually. Movement to the New World reached a climax in 1882, when more than 28,000 people left Norway. The first decade of the 1900s witnessed the final great exodus.

In absolute numbers there were throughout these fifty years more immigrants from the Norwegian countryside than from the cities, although after 1871 Norway's small urban centers had in percentages of their populations—figured in number of emigrants per thousand—a greater loss of citizens to emigration than did rural Norway. Those possessing urban skills or business acumen might in America more easily head for the city and the small town. The fact remains, however, that until 1930 the majority of Norwegians arriving in America came from rural regions; between 1871 and 1930 only about 31 percent of all emigrants left an urban residence, and many who came from urban areas hailed from an agricultural district, emigrating only after having sojourned in a town. And there was a clear age variable over time. The pioneer emigration had displayed a family character, with father, mother, and children emigrating or with father and son emigrating first to prepare for the others' arrival; in the half century of mass migration after the American

Civil War, family emigration gave way to individual emigration of young single people, a youth migration with a marked predominance of men, especially from the countryside.[8]

Minnesota's total population had by 1870 jumped to 439,706. Of these, 279,009 were native born, many with immigrant parents, others coming from the North Atlantic or north-central states; 160,697 were foreign born. Of those, 46,606 were from British countries, including 21,303 Irish; Scandinavian immigrants numbered 59,390; and Germans, 48,457. Folwell describes the situation as "An American commonwealth truly, with an infusion to the amount of thirty-seven per cent of the most virile, industrious, ambitious, and moral of foreigners, who had come from far-off countries to a free land to make homes and raise families."[9]

The Norwegian stock, immigrants and their children, accounted for 49,569; of these, 33,697 were immigrants and 12,381 were born in Minnesota, 2,591 in Wisconsin, 530 in Iowa, 242 in Illinois, and 128 elsewhere. The shifting birthplaces—and it was still a mostly youthful population, only one generation removed from the first immigrants—suggest engagement in the westward movement. Norwegian immigrants and their American-born children constituted a little more than 11 percent of the state's inhabitants. This substantial Norwegian population in 1870 concentrated in southeastern and southern Minnesota; the regions north of the Minnesota River had been left largely untouched. For some of the reasons mentioned earlier, this circumstance soon would change.

In the second period of settlement, which Carlton Qualey dates from 1866 to the middle seventies, the state's other large area of Norwegian concentration was created, chiefly in the western and northwestern counties. "Norwegians by the thousands," Qualey writes, "poured into the Park Region and into the Red River Valley. . . . From southeastern Kandiyohi County there extended in a northwesterly direction an almost unbroken series of Norwegian settlements covering a territory bounded on the west by prairies and on the northeast by forests." Norwegians formed a larger percentage of the total population there than in the more densely occupied southeastern districts. They consequently could wield greater social and political influence in that part of the state, a circumstance frequently neglected by area historians. Many of the new settlers were Civil War veterans: encouraged by a special homestead bonus for soldiers that required only one year's residence, they moved into the Park Region in large numbers. "So many earlier soldiers were among the first settlers in the Park Region," Hjalmar Rued Holand writes, "that a list of them looks like a roll call of the [Norwegian] Fifteenth Wisconsin Regiment."[10]

NAMING BENSON

Norwegian pioneer settlers who streamed into the Park Region and the Red River Valley in some cases played a role in naming agricultural towns and townships on the farming frontier. These names had a variety of origins and were not always given after long reflection. For many town sites that were rapidly founded, their names at times seem like an afterthought. Madison of course is one of a number of cities and villages named for the fourth president of the United States. The source of Starbuck's name appears to be more speculative, though a likely explanation is that the village was named after an officer of the Northern Pacific, Sidney Starbuck, who in 1882 held an important position on the railroad's branch lines. Indeed, the railroad had a decisive voice in naming trading centers along its line. Many samples of cursory naming practice may be cited. In Fillmore County, for example, twenty-four villages were platted before the state was admitted to the Union in 1858. The towns of Chatfield, Elliota, and Carimona were laid out in 1854; the next year a second Carimona village and a Fillmore village followed. Fillmore County, created in 1853, honors president Millard Fillmore, as does the village of the same name; Chatfield was named after Judge Andrew Gould Chatfield, who presided there at the first court held in the county; Carimona was named for a Ho-Chunk chief; and Elliota honored its first settler, Julius W. Elliott, who arrived in 1853 from Illinois. But in the county is also the railway village of Peterson, after the Norwegian immigrant Peter Peterson Haslerud, who in 1867 donated land to the railroad, and even the town of Norway, settled in 1854 and named in honor of the native country of most of the settlers.[11]

Place names thus honor locations and people of lesser and greater prominence and even individuals with very little social recognition at all. The origin of the place name Benson, a common enough name, is in some dispute. Edward Neill, in an early work published in 1882, gives the following explanation:

> Ben H. Benson was born in 1846 in Norway and in 1861 came to America. He worked in various places and in 1869 went to Benson, Swift county, Minnesota; was employed as a clerk three years, then kept a boarding house in Appleton; in 1875 took a claim in this town; was in mercantile business at Benson eighteen months also at Canby then returned to his farm. The town of Benson was named for him.

Following this information, Neill informs readers that Benson married Matilda Larson on November 22, 1872, and that the couple had four children, three boys and one girl, but Neill does not explain why he was so honored or where he came from in Norway. Benson was of course a pioneer settler, and there are many examples of early arrivals being honored through townships and trading centers named after them. No amount of speculation will convincingly resolve the issue, but Neill's early statement has in any case been given credence in later publications.[12]

Warren Upham's 1920 compilation of Minnesota geographic names simply restates Neill's explanation but adds, "Others have regarded this name as chosen in honor of Jared Benson of Anoka, who at that time and during many years was a prominent citizen and civic leader." Jared Benson was born in Mendon, Massachusetts, in 1821 and in 1856 came to Minnesota, where he engaged in farming and cattle raising. He was a member of the Minnesota House of Representatives in 1861–62, 1864, 1879, and 1889. His candidacy for the honor of giving name to Benson is naturally strong. When Jared Benson spoke at the 1885 county fair in Benson, the *Benson Times* reported his visit, stating "The address of Hon. Jared Benson, of Anoka, for whom our town was named, was a prominent feature of the occasion, and was listened to with marked attention." The disagreement in regard to whose name the town bears might reflect existing tensions between the self-conscious Yankee element and immigrant self-assertion, in this case Norwegian, a background claimed by nearly 37 percent of all Bensonites in 1880. American-born Edward Thomas, of Luxembourg descent—then the proprietor of the Republican *Benson Times*—and citizens with Yankee credentials would surely have harbored biases in favor of a prominent Republican New Englander, although that does not in itself disprove their assertion. Current consensus and logic nevertheless seem to bolster the claim on behalf of Ben Benson.[13]

FRONTIER BENSON

Norwegian settlers, people like Ben and Matilda Benson and their children, arrived in west-central Minnesota years before the coming of the railroad. "The advance guard of the army of civilization that first penetrated the solitude of Swift county, was a small body of Norwegians, who in 1866, settled at Camp Lake," writes Edward Neill. Ole Corneliusen is generally given credit for being the first to establish himself in the vicinity of the later village of Benson; in 1866 he claimed land in Six Mile Grove Township after having walked all the way from Olmsted County in southeastern Minnesota. Walking great distances was not as unusual as it may seem to a modern-day reader; travel on foot was a striking feature of pioneer life. Later, most likely the same year, Lars Christenson (Kjørnes) arrived in wagons pulled by oxen; he made a claim and built a house in the same township as Corneliusen, two miles from Benson. He was born in 1839 in Stedje Parish in Sogndal, Norway, and married Anna Johannesdatter Stedje before they both emigrated in 1864; the young couple spent two years in northern Iowa and southern Minnesota before moving to the Benson area. In 1868 Christenson was appointed postmaster; in winter he carried the mail from New London in Kandiyohi County on snowshoes, or so the story goes. The example of Swift County requires a revision—or at least a reconsideration—of the belief that Norwegians were rarely the first to settle on the frontier but generally followed Yankees. In Swift County and elsewhere in western Minnesota they in several instances were the farming pioneers in a foreboding prairie landscape.[14]

The village of Benson, on the other hand, clearly came into being as a result of Yankee capitalist interests; even so, immigrant participation in its early life is obvious: immigrants gave leadership and created commercial activity. Indeed, its history may be seen as a cultural microcosm of frontier transformation. Norwegian villagers played a central role, benefiting from the Norwegian agricultural communities that sprang up in Benson's environs.

Benson was surveyed and laid out by Charles A. F. Morris in the spring of 1870 for the First Division of the St. Paul and Pacific Railroad Company on a portion of its land grant. The village began simply as a series of stakes set into the unyielding prairie sod. It was located, to be precise, on the southwest quarter of Section 5, Township 121 north, Range 39 west in Torning Township, then included in Benson Township. Morris, who surveyed several railroad towns, used a standard symmetric plan; Benson is thus viewed as having a typical layout. Tom Schmiedeler described the plat as follows: "It shows half blocks subdivided into 20 residential lots, all of which are oriented to the tracks. Benson's business district evolved facing the tracks along Atlantic and Pacific Avenues, the names of which, as well as the general design of the town, were replicated in Morris and Willmar."[15]

Following the platting of Benson, the railroad could offer lots for sale to potential residents. Settlers had, however, arrived in advance of the railroad. When the town site was being surveyed, N. P. Strom attempted to convince the railroad company to locate the village a short distance from the plat, at his claim on the banks of the Chippewa River, a tributary to the Minnesota River. Strom's claim was called Chippewa Landing, Benson's earliest name. The company found Strom's asking price too high and declined. Strom, or Strøm—obviously a Norwegian name—filed on a homestead in the later Torning Township on September 25, 1868. He is typical of the many young men who saw business opportunity as the terminus of the railroad moved westward. The Lathrop brothers, A. W. and W. V., of Yankee background born in New Jersey, are additional examples. They erected a sod hut mercantile store on Strom's claim early in 1870. Thomas Knudson also built a sod hut there. They all later moved their businesses to the railroad plat, where Knudson, appealing to his compatriots, opened a Norwegian saloon. The *Benson Times* for February 23, 1876, lists one Knud Knudson as the proprietor of Norsk Saloon and Billiard Hall, perhaps the same establishment. Thomas Knudson had by then opened a mercantile business; he became a prominent member of the Norwegian business community and was active in Benson's early civic life. Born in Hallingdal, Norway, in 1850, he came to the United States at age fifteen, settling first in Iowa and five years later moving to Benson.

Frontier conditions reigned. At about the time Knudson opened his

*The pioneer settler
Ole Corneliusen and
wife Randi in 1916*

saloon, Louis Meldahl and R. Sunde opened a store in a sod shanty, described by Neill: "It consisted of a few posts driven into the ground, against which was banked sod; the roof being of straw. . . . In this primitive edifice were sold very many goods." Their names do not appear in the 1875 state census for Swift County, but R. Sunde is listed in 1870 as postmaster of the brand-new Benson post office; in 1874 he was succeeded by another Norwegian, Ole Wenaus. Another future Norwegian merchant and civic leader of prominence was Theodore Hansen, whose early claim to fame was having purchased the first railroad ticket to Benson; he was born in Nittedal, northeast of Oslo, in 1846, and came to the United States at the age of twenty-two after having attended a military academy (*underoffiserskole*) in Halden, then Fredrikshald. Hansen came first to Michigan and then in 1870 to Benson, where he established a general merchandise store. Demonstrating movement away from the crude frontier life, Hansen early on erected a frame building for his business, the first one on Main Street and a direct contrast to the other two businesses in their "sod and makeshift shacks."[16]

In his detailed history of 1882, Neill lists businesses, hotels, law firms, churches—all indicating the village's steady growth. Participation by Norwegian immigrants, especially in various small businesses, is by no means hegemonic but nevertheless prevalent in the pioneering years. The Norwegian-born journalist Paul Hjelm-Hansen, who as a special agent for the State of Minnesota in 1869 "through the Norwegian-American press blazed the way for the Scandinavian settlers to the Red River Valley," regarded businessmen as the true bearers of civilization into the prairie wilderness. On his journey to "the Red River Country" in 1869, traveling by Mississippi steamer to Minneapolis from his home in La Crosse, Wisconsin, he stopped at the river town of Red Wing. There on the dock he met "two of our young, able, and brave countrymen with their young and gracious wives" on their way "out into the West to make their way as businessmen on the wild prairie." Hjelm-Hansen extolled them as having a special place "among the honest and enlightened young Norwegians who in this country advance civilization."[17]

The village of Benson had by the mid-1870s a population of 300 and could boast four general stores, three hotels, two drugstores, two machinery houses, one bank, and two saloons. The 1875 state census covering Benson Township, which included the later Torning Township and beyond as well as the village of Benson, listed 688 names, nativity, and nativity of parents. These people sustained the growing number of businesses. As many as 296 were born in Norway, 168 male and 128 female, suggesting, though men outnumbered women, the many family units recorded in the census. American-born Norwegians numbered 128 for a combined 61 percent Norwegian stock. Other immigrant populations were small: 62 first- and second-generation Swedes, 48 Canadians, 6 Swiss, 5 Irish, 3 Brits, 3 Scots, and 1 Dane. There was no German settler among them. The Yankee group numbered 57; many were bankers, lawyers, and other professionals in the small frontier community.[18]

Memories of the presettlement period were close at hand; the pioneer period was in its infancy in the 1870s. Ambush Park on the banks of the Chippewa River is today a reminder of an incident related by Samuel W. Pond, a missionary to the Dakota. Early in April 1838, Samuel's brother Gideon, in order to study Dakota language and life, joined a hunting party residing on Lac qui Parle and traveled to the Chippewa Valley. As the hunters divided, they left a party consisting of mostly women and children in a camp at the fork of the Chippewa near where Benson

*Theodore and Mary
(Vangen) Hansen and
oldest son Harold, late
1870s. Hansen built
the first wooden store
building in Benson.*

would eventually be located. The camp was visited unexpectedly by the Ojibwe leader Hole-in-the-Day with nine followers. They professed peace and were given hospitality. During the night, the Ojibwe arose on an agreed signal, seized their guns, and killed all but three of the Dakota. A woman escaped with a wounded boy and found the advance Dakota party. Pond joined one of the hunters in burying the mutilated bodies. A bloody revenge followed promptly in August. Hostility between the two nations persisted until white settlers forced the Ojibwe and the Dakota off their lands less than thirty years later.[19]

THE VILLAGE OF BENSON IN ITS RURAL SETTING

The "Indian Era" might clearly have ended in 1865, as Stanley Anonsen asserts. Rare visits to Benson by the Ojibwe were—as in 1882, when "a party of thirteen Chippewa [Ojibwe] Indians gave our people an exhibition of Indian dancing"—inequitably dismissed by the *Benson Times* as lacking "the trimmings and superfluities of civilization." Economic growth became the main preoccupation for townspeople and farmers alike. In this regard, Benson's strong Norwegian business community represented a natural response to the large and heavily concentrated Norwegian farming districts in its close upland. "Farmers on foot, or with horses and oxen, had to shop within a radius of six to twelve miles in order to return home to care for livestock before nightfall," writes Lewis Atherton. The village, incorporated February 14, 1877, consequently had as its natural marketing area mainly the surrounding townships, including heavily Norwegian Six Mile Grove, Camp Lake, and Swenoda. Residents of townships farther east, Kerkhoven, Hayes, and Pillsbury, would also conduct business there, but they frequently turned to more convenient trading centers, located inside as well as outside Swift County.[20]

In spring 1870, businessmen, several of them Norwegian, including a general merchant, a hardware dealer, and a hotel and grain dealer, moved to the hamlet of Kerkhoven. The thinly settled area did not give much promise of growth, and by 1875 there were hardly more than fifty residents according to Stanley Anonsen's estimate. Besides Benson and Kerkhoven, two more trading centers emerged at this time, at the county's two waterpower sites—Appleton and Swift Falls. While Lewis Atherton claims that "every town expected to become the county seat," the village of Appleton was the only strong contender with Benson, and no direct challenge was launched. Many of the settlers who arrived in the 1870s were of New England stock and veterans of the Civil War; the Yankee element remained strong. The Lathrop brothers, A. W. and W. V., played an important role here, as they had in Benson, platting the village of Appleton—named for a Wisconsin town—at a site by the Pomme de Terre River. In 1872 they erected the first flour mill on its banks; only in 1879 did a railroad line reach the mill town, providing adequate communication and making Appleton prosper. The closest railroad was until then Benson; twice weekly a stagecoach carried mail and passengers between the two towns.[21]

The hamlet of Swift Falls received its name from the waterfall located on the east branch of the Chippewa River in Camp Lake Township. It was founded on land purchased from the railroad by J. M. Danelz. He and his mother, Ulricka Danelz, emigrated from Sålla, southwest of Stockholm, Sweden, in 1869, when J. M. was thirty years old, and arrived in Benson the following year. He staked a claim in Camp Lake Township, acquired ownership of the waterfall site, and shipped timber from St. Paul to construct a mill. His financial partner was Theodore

Hansen of Benson, who by then was in a position to invest the considerable amount of $6,000 in the enterprise. The first flour was produced on June 9, 1873. Norwegian farmers and others from miles around hauled their grist to this mill; the demands placed on it sometimes required farmers to wait two or three days for their flour.[22]

The village of Benson enjoyed superior advantages in the competition with other trading centers. Not only was it the county seat; for a year or so it was the terminus of the St. Paul and Pacific Railroad, a circumstance that greatly stimulated business. Benson served as a market for the territory one hundred miles to the west, north, and south. Wheat was hauled for further transportation from the neighboring counties; household goods and farm equipment were purchased for the return trip. In fall 1876 the federal land office was moved west from Litchfield to Benson. The *Benson Times* announced the move as "truly good news for Benson and the upper country." Later, following its opening, the newspaper reported that the "Land Office is daily thronged with anxious land hunters," concluding that this "argues well for the value of land in the county." As Neill writes, "A veritable 'boom' struck the place in 1876." The prosperity created speculation in town lots and sections of land, and the hotels overflowed with immigrants. "So eager were the newcomers," Neill continues, "that many claims were made before the snow went off the ground." The following year the town's infrastructure was developed through street improvements, the laying of gravel, and completion of a drainage system, "so that the village, at all times[,] is dry."[23]

Benson had rapidly evolved into a central place, different from the surrounding agricultural neighborhoods. Norwegian farmers came to town from their church-centered enclaves to sell the products of their land, to do business with compatriots who had entered American economic pursuits in town, or to seek the services of Yankee bankers and professionals. The Norwegian "townies" adjusted to American life in a trajectory that differed from that of Norwegian country folk; the latter cultivated a more segregated ethnic existence. Even so, the town-dwellers and farmers intermingled extensively. Norwegians in town set the tone for secular ethnic cultural expression, ethnic festivals, and commercial activity; their country cousins found comfort in a heavily Norwegian urban place while simultaneously contributing their own cultural flavor.

Considering the role of villages like Benson and the surrounding smaller towns and hamlets—even when emphasizing an ethnic predominance—Lewis Atherton might find justification for his claim that the country town provided leadership in the Midwest's development: the "history of the Middle Border has been largely the history of towns" and the boom-or-bust philosophy of competing trading centers.[24]

Thorstein Veblen, on the other hand, in a 1923 article viewed the country town in negative terms for its exploitation of its farmer neighbors: "the townsmen are engaged in a vigilant rivalry, being competitors in the traffic carried on with the farm-population." Competition, Veblen insists, "does not hinder collusion between the competitors with a view to maintain and augment their collective hold on the trade with their farm-population." It was this unfriendly depiction of the country town and its business psychology to which Atherton later objected. He did not see a collective exploitation intended both to control the farm trade and to inflate the real estate value in the town, as Veblen did; he criticized Veblen's proposition that real estate represented the one community interest that bound the townsmen together as they hoped to realize on speculation in inflated values. Veblen stated further that "the business of the town arranges itself under such regulations and usages that it foots up to a competition, not between the business-concerns, but between town and country, between traders and customers." The profits in any one town as a result were, according to Veblen, excessively large for the work done, deriving from the fact that the number of concerns doing business exceeds what is necessary to "carry on the traffic."[25]

Veblen's article fell into a common disparaging view of life in small rural communities and country towns, a strong literary and economic criticism often expressed in the 1920s. Atherton in his objections pointed to factors that refuted negative opinions of business dealings, such as the detail that even during horse culture days no one town had monopoly of the farm trade. He also points to retail advertising in country town newspapers by stores in larger cities a distance away; the *Benson Times,* as an example, carried a St. Paul business directory and solicited advertising from competing trade centers in Swift County. In Veblen's propositions, Atherton states, he "failed to distinguish between motivations and the extent to which these were realized."[26]

The economic boom Benson experienced beginning in 1876 might seem on Veblen's terms like an excessive establishment of services. And it may be illustrative of the West's role in shaping American attitudes toward material goods, as Ray Allen Billington has written: "The creation of wealth by the continuing exploitation of successive layers of natural resources, and the steady flow of that wealth eastward, helped engender a state of mind in which material progress became the sole measure of many people." There were by the end of 1876 in the small village of Benson, home to only some 300 people, five general stores, two drugstores, a hardware store, a blacksmith shop, a law office, and three saloons—the latter despite the fact that Benson had voted to be dry, though this opinion was changed at a town meeting before year's end. There were additionally two machinery houses, three hotels, and a branch farm machinery business. Clearly these enterprises were directed as much or more toward the farm population as toward townspeople.

Joseph A. Amato, in his article "Business First and Always," states "early Midwestern towns . . . housed two types of businesses: retail and artisanal." He identifies as the most important early artisans the blacksmiths, the cobblers, the harness makers, and the wagon makers. Norwegian immigrant artisans mastered these skills: pioneer settler Ole Corneliusen was, for example, a wagon maker by trade. Norwegian farmers in the vicinity of Benson might work part-time as blacksmiths or in other artisanal activity in town; some after a time gave up the farm for life in the village. Martin Syverson, born in 1873 in Rolling Forks, Pope County, Minnesota, to Norwegian immigrant parents, typifies an occupational career. At twenty-one he married Ingeborg Monson and began farming at Swift Falls. Six of nine children were born there, the last three in Benson, where the family moved. In Benson Martin became a blacksmith, a skill likely transferred from his farm operation. In the final issue of 1876, the *Benson Times* declared as it listed the town's recent improvements, "We do not know of a town in western Minnesota that has made so great an increase proportional to its size, as Benson within a year." There was, however, nothing in this economic expansion that suggested support for Veblen's assumption of evil intent toward and exploitation of the farm population. Instead, though a social distance obviously existed between the agricultural population and the townspeople, a synergistic relationship is visible between town and country, an interdependence in their economic activity.[27]

Local newspapers boomed the sale and transportation of farm products. In fall 1875 Frank M. Thornton, register of deeds and the first railroad station agent—and in time prominent in business—built an elevator in town, later much expanded; in 1877 a second elevator was erected, which became the Farmers' Elevator. Minnesota's principal crop from the beginning of cultivation was spring wheat, which was well adapted to the soil and climate; in 1875 more than 30 million bushels, at twenty-three bushels to the acre, were produced. In all western pioneer communities, wheat was the principal cereal; it was an immediate cash crop. Norwegian immigrant farmers produced large wheat crops on their holdings in the surrounding townships; deliveries to Benson for further shipment were highlights of the busy harvest season and an opportunity to enjoy the sociality and modest distractions the village offered. Farmers coming to town with their grain-filled wagons were a regular feature of the village landscape. The *Benson Times* boasted in its issue of April 10, 1876, "Benson may well feel proud of the name she is gaining as a wheat market. All of last week the elevators were full, almost running over." There was also a spirit of rivalry: the newspaper reported in its initial issue, February 16, 1876, on the authority of the Minneapolis Millers Association that "Benson had shipped more wheat than Willmar."[28]

Even during the boom, disaster struck. On July 9, 1876, swarms of Rocky Mountain locusts invaded the county and within a few days practically destroyed the grain fields. Many immigrant farmers who had arrived that spring lost the first crop they had planted. Tragic accounts of farmers forced to abandon their lands had a chilling effect on the attraction western Minnesota had enjoyed as an agricultural region, and immigration slowed. The locust invasion into large areas of the state had begun in 1873 and lasted for four years; at first the incursion was by swarms of locusts; they stayed long enough to deposit their eggs so that the next assault was by their offspring. Bearing a resemblance to the common grasshopper, the strange insect was called grasshopper or simply 'hopper. In supporting state aid for farmers, the *Benson Times* in 1876 explained, "The people in some of the counties afflicted with the grasshopper pests, are many of them in suffering condition, and in many cases not for one year only but for three and even four years." Even though Swift County, according to the newspaper, was not as badly affected as many others in the southern and western part of the state, farming families endured great privations on the Minnesota frontier. Funds to assist the destitute farmers were made available by a legislative act the following spring.[29]

In an extensive effort to destroy the pest, ingenious methods were devised, including invention of the "hopperdozer," plowing infested fields, crushing the larvae with rollers, firing piles of straw near hatching grounds, and even catching and destroying the young before their wings developed. Some ministers and lay people voiced their opposition to this endeavor on religious grounds. Their disapproval reflected both a strict religious Puritanism that characterized many Norwegian settlements and the powerful influence of the Norwegian Lutheran clergy under frontier conditions. The *Benson Times* reported in its June 9, 1877, issue that "Mr. Davidson, a very intelligent Norwegian farmer, was in town this week and we were much surprised and pained to hear him advocate the foolish and stupid religious doctrine, that it is wicked to kill the grasshopper, as God had sent them to punish us for our sins." His minister had convinced him that "the Almighty will not allow the 'hoppers to eat up a man's crop if he is not wicked" and that only sinful men's crops were being destroyed. The newspaper commented editorially:

> we feel like doing what we heard a prominent Scandinavian businessman say he would do, a few days ago in speaking of a certain preacher who had told his congregation that it was wicked to kill the 'hopper, he said, "he is my preacher but I'll give him hell when I see him." . . . And that is how we feel, we should like to make such fellows "smell brimstone" if nothing more.

The following month, on July 10, 1877, as Anonsen expresses it, "the swarms of the pest disappeared as miraculously as they had come in the previous year." Agricultural prosperity and migration to the affected regions resumed.[30]

EARLY SWIFT COUNTY

Benson functioned as a major locality for all of Swift County, and in its cultural identity and commercial success the village was greatly influenced by the history of the region and the cultural heritage of those who made it their home. Thus a summary of the county's historical and social circumstances is pertinent. The county was named in honor of Henry Adoniram Swift, governor of Minnesota in 1863, and established on February 18, 1870, formed from part of the territory belonging to Chippewa County. By legislative act the county seat was established at Benson. That year the combined population of Chippewa and Swift counties was only 1,467 white inhabitants; by far the largest number resided in what remained as Chippewa County. Its county seat was at the village of Chippewa City, opposite the present site of Montevideo, which, although not without controversy and political maneuverings, became the permanent county seat in 1870, at the same legislative session that established Swift County. Chippewa County had been organized only two years earlier, in 1868; until then it constituted a part of the vast area belonging to Renville County, the entire territory north, on the eastern bank of the Minnesota River. The several legislative acts that divided this territory illustrate the orderly procession of the westward movement in the spirit of the Northwest Ordinance of 1787.[31]

Edward Neill described the surface of Swift County as an "undulating prairie, interspersed with timber along the borders of streams." He judged the soil to be good, to be well watered, and to possess excellent drainage. The Chippewa River flows through the central portion of the county, the Pomme de Terre River through its western part. The Minnesota River crosses the southwest corner.[32]

A special edition of the *Swift County Monitor* for June 24, 1927, describes the frontier trails and river travels for those moving to Swift County. This source helped Stanley Anonsen explain the travails of early settlement. Pioneers traveled up the Minnesota River to Traverse des Sioux or to New Ulm. If the water was high they could go beyond New Ulm and then follow the river trail with oxen. In smaller boats settlers could reach the mouth of the Chippewa or the Pomme de Terre and then continue up these streams to their claims. Another possibility was to use a land route to Hutchinson and then travel through Meeker and Kandiyohi counties to the lake settlements and on to the western prairies. A third option was to journey up the Mississippi as far as Sauk Centre or St. Cloud and then head southwesterly, through the village of Paynesville, and on to the Camp Lake settlements in northeastern Swift County.[33]

A few early settlers might venture out on the treeless prairie in anticipation of the railroad's arrival, but most preferred settlement by rivers and lakes, where wooded sites gave timber for buildings and fuel for warmth during the cold winters. A dugout might serve as the first dwelling; the settler generally found a hillside and dug a cellar with the front opening on a level with the lower part of the ground. On the flat prairie a dugout might be a simple hole in the ground with a roof; logs, poles, brush, and grass were needed for the front and roof of the primitive, temporary dwelling. Fish and game were important resources, as food and as income, which was another reason to locate near water. In pioneer days, to quote Anonsen: "Swift county represented but a patchwork of settlements—in the northeast, in the north central, in the northwest, and a thin line along the banks of the Chippewa and the Pomme de Terre rivers." A settler arriving in Benson in spring 1870 relates that traveling by wagon from Willmar—then the railroad terminus, the tracks being completed to Benson only that fall—the party felt disappointed by the scenery, which "consisted of flat prairie dotted with sloughs and inhabited by millions of mosquitoes." They saw "only one person enroute, who crawled out of his dugout to look at us as we drove by."[34]

Iver Knudson came to Kerkhoven Township in 1867 with two other Norwegian pioneers, Nels Ole Broten (Nils O. Braaten) and Andrew Monson. Knudson filed a claim in Hayes Township, then a part of Kerkhoven, as did Monson; Lake Monson, which is crossed by the line between the two townships, is named for him. Knudson gained prominence as one of the first three county commissioners; the other two were A. W. Lathrop and C. E. Foster, both of Yankee background. Their first meeting was held January 3, 1871, in Lathrop's store in Benson. In the Swift County Commissioner Records, Knudson's name is given as Iver Knudtsen. No further details have been uncovered, but his appointment to this high office bears witness not only to his competence but also to the political strength of the Norwegian settlers. Two other Norwegians demonstrated ethnic influence by entering the early civic arena in 1871; the commissioners made Halvor Helgeson coroner, later county treasurer, and Oley Thorson became the new county's first judge of probate, having earlier served as a county commissioner in Chippewa County. It is told that in winter he would ski from his home in Camp Lake Township to the county seat at Chippewa City, a feat that required

Berit Hagebak outside her sod hut in Lac qui Parle County about 1870.
Pioneer settlers stopped here to drink coffee and let their horses rest.

him to leave before daybreak and brought him to his destination at sunset. By keeping the Chippewa River woods on his right he would never lose his way.

Thorson's obituary in 1902 relates that he came to Swift County in 1866 "with the first settlers" and "was among the hardy pioneers who broke the first soil in Camp Lake township." Thorson was a Civil War hero, which enhanced his status among his compatriots as well as in the general community, assuring his success in public affairs. As suggested earlier, the Civil War boosted both Norwegians' self-confidence and greater acceptance by their American neighbors. Veterans were held in especially high esteem. Thorson was one of many who after the end of hostilities responded to opportunities on the western frontier. He came to Wisconsin from Valdres, Norway, in 1857 at age sixteen and enlisted in 1861, first in a Missouri infantry unit and later in a Wisconsin cavalry unit, where he served until the end of the war.[35]

THE TOWNSHIPS

Norwegians were the dominant, nearly exclusive population in a number of townships. By the early 1900s Norwegian farmers owned considerable acreage in Swift County, but their holdings varied greatly from one township to another, from nearly 90 percent of the total acreage in Kerkhoven Township to zero percent in Fairfield. It is therefore helpful to outline the ethnic composition of the county's townships. Several were organized at the initial commissioners meeting on January 3, 1871. Twenty-one townships were eventually established in Swift County, each surveyed six miles square and consisting of thirty-six square-mile sections. Only Appleton, which has its southwest corner cut off by the Minnesota River, does not fit this model, making it the smallest township in the county. All townships were established in the course of the following eight years or so; the last one was Torning, where Benson was platted; it was organized by the county commissioners at a meeting on March 18, 1879. By 1880 the county's population had risen from approximately 600 to 7,473.[36]

Benson held its first township meeting in April 1871. In 1880, 90 percent of all residents were foreign born or of foreign-born parentage. Norwegians were the largest group, with 32 percent of the population. Other townships surrounding the village of Benson were more Norwegian. In Camp Lake Township the Norwegian population, first and second generation, accounted for 75 percent of all residents. In Hayes Township the percentage rose to 45, although Norwegians there were surpassed by Swedes, who made up 48 percent of all residents. Hegbert Township was 64 percent Norwegian and Kerkhoven 71 percent. In Six Mile Grove Township Norwegians numbered 71 percent as well, and in Swenoda, 56 percent. In Torning Township, excluding the village of Benson, 60 percent of residents were Norwegian. In West Bank Township, the last of the "Norwegian" townships, they numbered 67 percent. These townships provided a majority of the coveted potential customers who would sustain Benson's commercial life; their Norwegian roots became a major factor.[37]

Even though the Norwegian "stock," in the language of the census, in 1880 accounted for 29 percent of all residents in Swift County and was the largest ethnic group, Norwegians shared the county with other

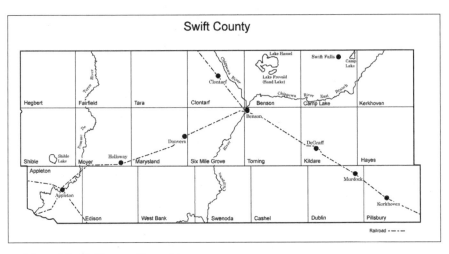

Map of Swift County Townships

nationalities and Benson met competition as other trading centers developed. The self-segregation of nationalities—as people of a similar past reunited in the rural middle west—is readily apparent, as Jon Gjerde points out; this tendency made cultural transfer possible. Gjerde explains, "Family, friends, and countrymen crossed hundreds, even thousands of miles to return in a sense to webs of affiliation based on kinship and nationality in the rural settlements of the West. . . . This pattern of movement had enormous significance not only for the individuals who migrated but also for the cultural development of the region."[38]

The other major nationalities in Swift County in 1880 were Irish, 22 percent of the county's population; Swedes, 11 percent; Germans, nearly 11 percent—but ethnic Poles from the German Empire are included in these statistics; and Canadians, 7 percent, most of French origin. An imposing 83.3 percent of the county population of 7,473 were in 1880 either immigrants or the children of immigrants, evidence of immigration's central role in westward expansion. The level of clustering and settlement isolation is suggested by the fact that Clontarf Township had only one Norwegian resident; Dublin Township, eight; Kildare Township, three; and Fairfield, Marysland, and Tara townships, zero. These townships were basically Irish, with the exception of Fairfield, which was 59 percent German.

Self-segregation of Norwegian-speaking settlements explains why one

TABLE 2

Countries of Origin for Immigrants and Second-Generation Americans in Swift County, 1880[a]

| | Number of Individuals and Percentage of County Population | | | | | |
| | Immigrants | | Second Generation | | Total | |
	N	%	N	%	N	%
Canada	309	4.1	230	3.1	539	7.2
Denmark	16	0.2	23	0.3	39	0.5
German Empire[b]	386	5.2	412	5.5	798	10.7
Great Britain	68	0.9	136	1.8	204	2.7
Ireland	574	7.7	1,091	14.6	1,665	22.3
Norway	1,185	15.9	962	12.9	2,147	28.8
Sweden	477	6.4	338	4.5	815	10.9
Other foreign country	66	0.9	124	1.7	190	2.6
Non-duplicated totals	3,081	41.3	3,316	44.4	6,397	85.7

Source: U.S. Census, 1880

Note: Swift County total population was 7,473 in 1880. Percentages in the table are for the total population.

a. Second generation determined by at least one parent born in country of origin

b. A portion of the German population was from German Poland. Census enumerators did not consistently distinguish.

today meets individuals in their mid-seventies and on occasion even younger who master nineteenth-century rural vernaculars, men like Ernest Anderson, born in 1932, and Leonard Mitteness, born in 1921, who both speak the dialect of the district of Nordfjord on the west coast of Norway, brought over by grandparents. Both men grew up in the Nordfjord settlement by Swift Falls in Camp Lake Township, Mitteness on the so-called Nordfjord Prairie, on the north side of the Chippewa's east branch. An old-country linguistic heritage is evidenced as well by the many who speak English with a settlement accent or a "Norwegian brogue," as it is described in local parlance. Old-timers still remember what they call "lines" or boundaries between ethnic groups that should not be crossed: a country road or a stream might serve as a marker.[39]

An effort organized by the Catholic Colonization Bureau of St. Paul brought Irish settlers to Swift County. The project's main promoter was

Bishop John Ireland; his motive was to move as many fellow Catholics from the crowded and unhealthy conditions in large eastern cities to the opportunities offered in the wide-open spaces of the West. Ireland proposed plans for Catholic colonies in 1875; copying earlier colonization plans, he entered into contracts to purchase railroad land. By July 1877 the Catholic Colonization Bureau had acquired more than 4,000 acres and began settling families of indigent colonists on eighty-acre tracts; it was, as the *Swift County Advocate* wrote, an expression of "John Ireland's Jeffersonian ideal of placing nearly every citizen on a farm of his own." In Swift County, Catholic settlers took land around Clontarf in Clontarf Township and around De Graff in Kildare Township; these were the two main Catholic colonization projects; Graceville in Big Stone County was another major one. In Minnesota's western triangle a number of other colonies were established, each with a resident Catholic priest and often parochial schools. Most historians of Catholic colonization treat it largely as an episode in the western history of the United States; the small colonies did not ameliorate the problem of social injustice created by industrialization, and they made only a modest contribution to settlement in Minnesota.[40]

The Swift County lands, embracing four townships, were, however, quickly taken up by Catholic settlers: by 1880 Cashel Township was 62 percent Irish; Kildare Township, 71; Clontarf Township, 73; and Tara Township was the most Irish, 78 percent. Marysland Township was 52 percent Irish, and Dublin Township, 33 percent. Within Swift County's Catholic colony, comprising by the end of the 1870s 117,000 acres of railroad land and probably as much state land, Bishop Ireland's agents platted the two towns of De Graff and Clontarf, fourteen miles apart. De Graff began as little more than a railroad station, and Clontarf—originally Randall, renamed after the Irish town near Dublin—was built entirely by the colonists.[41]

James Shannon insists it would be a serious mistake to assume that even in the beginning the Catholic colonies were exclusively Irish settlements, although he admits that when the first settlement opened in Swift County in 1876 most of the settlers who came to it were Irish-born or their children. Irish Catholics were joined by French Canadians; Canada is listed in the 1880 census as "British America" and those of French background are not identified. Many Canadian Catholics settled among the Irish Catholics, but others did so as well: to cite Shannon, "Many French, Belgian, German, and English—and a few Polish—Catholics answered Bishop Ireland's invitation to Minnesota."[42]

It is important to bear in mind that several French Canadian Catholic families had settled in Swift County before John Ireland established his colonies there. Their relationship with the Irish might even be colored by a sense that the latter enjoyed a lower social status than the former. The earliest settlers in Clontarf, later dominated by Irish settlers, were actually French Canadians settling on the French Plains, which extended into Benson Township to the east, a major area of French Canadian settlement. The memorial pamphlet distributed at the St. Francis Xavier School dedication in Benson in 1953 relates the story of Firmin Bedard, who settled in Benson Township in 1871 and became the trustee and leader of the French settlement established just north of the village of Benson, encouraged by Bishop Ireland's announced plans to build Catholic churches in Swift County. A later French settler was Arsidas Benoit, who sold his 132-acre farm in the parish of St. Jude in Quebec, Canada, and moved to Minnesota in 1876, purchasing a 240-acre farm some five miles from the village of Benson. In 1880 Canadians constituted the second-largest ethnic group in Benson Township, 29 percent of all residents; almost no Irish had settled there. Canadian representation fell to 18 percent in Dublin Township, 12 percent in Kildare Township, and only 10 percent in Clontarf Township. French Catholics "who came to Swift County found what they sought—good land near a parish church," Shannon claims.[43]

German settlement, usually Protestant and particularly Lutheran, concentrated in the western townships, with Fairfield, at 59 percent, claiming the largest population. Moyer Township to the south was 38 percent German; Shible Township to the west was 23 percent German; and there were also scatterings of Germans in Clontarf, Dublin, Six Mile Grove, and West Bank townships, the latter two being heavily Norwegian. Considering the dominance of German-speaking people in Minnesota as a whole—between 1860 and 1905 they constituted the state's largest foreign-born group—and, according to Hildegard Binder Johnson, "the persistence of the original German core region in the Minnesota Valley

TABLE 3

Foreign-Born Population in Swift County, 1880–1950

Number of Persons Born in

Year	Canada	Denmark	Germany[a]	Great Britain	Ireland	Norway	Sweden	Total Population	Percentage Foreign Born
1880	309[b]	16	362	68	573	1,187	477	7,473	40
1890	222	38	652	84	348	1,822	784	10,161	39
1900	188	50	780	68	304	1,739	840	13,503	29
1910	109	51	581	55	202	1,316	626	12,949	23
1920	106	78	398	47	114	1,043	540	15,093	15
1930	74	70	315	24	41	776	374	14,735	11
1940	50	40	204	20	17	483	250	15,469	7
1950	45	34	135	17	5	258	154	15,837	4

Source: Inter-University Consortium for Political and Social Research. *Study 00003: Historical Demographic, Economic, and Social Data: U.S., 1790–1970.* Ann Arbor, MI: ICPSR.

a. A portion of the German population was from German Poland. Census enumerators did not consistently distinguish.
b. Canadian born referred to as "British American" in 1880

and the concentration of Catholic Germans in Stearns County," their relatively low representation in Swift County in 1880, if perhaps explained by emerging patterns of settlement, is nevertheless notable.[44]

Edison Township, which until 1889 carried the name New Posen, lists the majority—52 percent—of its residents as being from the German Empire. They were, however, mainly of Polish or Russian background, from regions within the empire's boundaries. In 1887 the settlers formed St. Joseph's Catholic Church, located in Section 23. The name *New Posen* may derive from Poznan, which with other peasant villages in Upper Silesia, then within Prussia, "were the homes of the first Polish migrants to Minnesota as they were of most American Poles until the 1880s," as Frank Renkiewicz writes.[45]

If we take into account only the immigrant generation, Swedish-born Minnesotans in 1905 replaced Germans as the state's largest foreign-born group. In Swift County, counting both the immigrants and their American-born children, Swedes numbered 815 in 1880; of these as many as 58.5 percent were foreign born. In comparison the Norwegian population numbered 2,147, of which only 46.1 percent were immigrants. The difference—that is, the proportionately larger Norwegian second generation—may reflect the fact that the nineteenth-century Swedish exodus began two or more decades later than the Norwegian one. The third Scandinavian nationality, the Danes, were only 39 strong in Swift County that year, of which 16, or 41 percent, were immigrants. Swenoda Township—south of Six Mile Grove—represents Scandinavian commonality in its name, which combines the three nationalities, Swedes, Norwegians, and Danes. It was, however, largely Norwegian: the first- and second-generation Norwegians made up 58 percent of all township residents; the Swedes, 13 percent; and the Danes, only 4 percent. There were also some Danish residents in the village of Benson and in Pillsbury Township. Pillsbury, with its commercial center Kerkhoven, was 59 percent Swedish and thus in percentage the county's main Swedish township; other substantial concentrations of Swedes were found in typical Norwegian townships such as Benson, Camp Lake, Hayes, Kerkhoven, and Torning, again indicating a sense of Scandinavian unity.[46]

No township consisted of a single ethnic group: in delineating ethnic self-segregation it is easy to lose sight of the interaction, negative and positive, that occurred among the various populations, in business dealings and political life, in cultural clashes and social affairs. There were, to be sure, language barriers and religious differences, which encouraged prejudice and distance, but as a new community developed in the prairie wilderness the major thrust would be one of movement toward a common effort. It is, however, in any study of the region's history significant to bear in mind the dynamics embedded in the differing pasts of the people who made their homes in Swift County. Their greatest common trait was that the entire county was nearly 100 percent white—most residents being of northern European extraction—and would remain so for most of its history.[47]

THE NORWEGIAN *BYGD*

Nationality may be said to represent an imposed identification that neglects the import and intimacy of local identities. Immigrant localism affected all ethnic groups in America: well known is the spirit of *campanilisimo,* the fellowship of friends and neighbors, among Italian Americans and their commitment to family and a narrow regional social network, also the *landsmanschaften,* local lodges, organized by Jews from particular eastern European towns.

In the spirit of local loyalties, Norwegian settlements may be defined not only by nationality but just as much by the rural Norwegian community from which the settlers had emigrated. The empirical evidence in Swift and neighboring counties demonstrates that the *bygd* phase of Norwegian settlement had a greater strength in the later history of settlement than the author as well as other historians have assumed. A *bygd* is a Norwegian country community, neighborhood, or district. In Swift County specific *bygd* groups were predominant in a number of townships, giving them character and reinforcing a traditional agrarian outlook. In considering regional identities, it is important to bear in mind that very few, if in reality any, Norwegian settlements consisted exclusively of one *bygd* population. There were certainly local prejudices and lack of familiarity with other dialects; indeed, the first introduction to unfamiliar peasant vernaculars might only have occurred after arriving in America. People from a different district or valley might be the real foreigners. Nevertheless, most settlements had sprinklings of people from several parts of Norway, in pioneer times in Illinois and Wisconsin as well as in western Minnesota, although they might occupy different areas of the colony. In general, one regional cultural identity dominated the entire settlement numerically—not infrequently representing a specific parish within a larger district in the homeland—and gave name to the settlement. And it is possible to locate those that were regionally pure, such as apparently the Nordfjord settlement in Camp Lake Township.[48]

Even though regionalism was common to all immigrants, loyalty to the local district seems to have had particular significance for Norwegians. The extreme isolation of rural communities in Norway, caused by the country's topographical conditions, may go some distance in explaining the deep consciousness of local origin harbored by its immigrants. Arthur C. Paulson may not be far from the truth in his claim that "customs, jealousies, and ideals which had been implanted in the lives of the inhabitants of a *bygd* by several hundred years of isolation within a narrow mountain valley were retained with almost religious fervor

Halvor and Bergitte ("Betsy") Rodahl outside their home in Swenoda Township

in America." Regional tensions existed and might even be reinforced by direct contact; among immigrants they resulted in a competition concerning which *bygd* group had contributed most to the building of America; a certain pecking order seems to have developed.

Someone writing about the Sogning—a person from Sogn—insisted that "because of the beauty of the natural environment he grew up in before coming to America, the Sogning typifies that which is best in the Nordic population." The writer further concludes that the "Sogning women as well as Sogning men love freedom and accept equality, and they are therefore well suited for democracy and the American state of affairs, institutions as a whole. So that they will live long over here to the honor of their country and their people." These claims were a part of an evolving identity within an assimilative context. A case study may be made of this Norwegian *campanilisimo,* to use the expressive Italian term for local loyalties, by looking at Norwegian patterns of settlement in Swift County. Norwegian localism, as will be seen later, also exerted powerful influence in the settlement patterns of Pope and Lac qui Parle counties and in the local *bygd* identities of those who made their homes in Starbuck and Madison. With the possible exception of blood relation, localism expressed the most poignant impulse in the "web of affiliation" that formed a strong bond among Norwegian settlers. Specific rural identities may be determined by looking at Norwegian farm names adopted as surnames alongside a patronymic, the dominant rural custom—hence, the many Hansons, Pedersons, Olsons, Andersons, and the like among the immigrants.[49]

The Norwegian community in Benson Township is heavily identified with Gudbrandsdalen, Norway's central valley; there were also pioneers from Trøndelag. The earliest settlers, arriving from Wisconsin in 1867 on a land-seeking journey, homesteaded by Lake Hassel and Lake Moore; like other early settlers who preceded the railroad they preferred wooded areas by water. These pioneers were Ole Andreas (Andrew) Pederson and John Olson, both from the Være farm in Strinda, now a part of the municipality of Trondheim, and Johannes Torgerson from Gudbrandsdalen. Their names do not, of course, reveal regional background.

The Norwegian settlement bordered on the French Plains or Frenchmen's Prairie, as it was also called, to the east. Pederson took land on the south shore of Lake Moore, land still in the family, showing stability over several generations. The Torgerson farm was located west of Lake Frovold, now Sand Lake; he first lived, in the manner of many pioneer settlers, in a dugout. Organization of a congregation consisting mainly of Gudbrandsdøls, the Lake Hazel Lutheran Church, in 1871 fortified the local cultural identity. Linguistic differences were the most obvious cultural products. Verna Gomer related a story of local cultural dominance: her husband's Swedish grandfather, Andrew Gomer, born in Östergötland, married Ragnhild Ulmoe from Vågå in Gudbrandsdalen; they settled among the Gudbrandsdøls by Lake Hassel, and he had to learn their dialect in order to be accepted. The *Swift County Monitor-News* on July 6, 1967, deplored the congregation's disbanding, reminding its readers that it had begun with "immigrant homesteads, oxen and prairie and [was] ending with second and third generation Americans, modern transportation and the average farm at least double the size of those early days."[50]

Nordfjordings were most numerous by Swift Falls, about twelve miles northeast of the village of Benson in Camp Lake Township. J. D. Korstad has written about this settlement:

It is located in the hilly terrain on both sides of the Chippewa River, although mostly on the north side. The land lay open when the first Nordfjordings came here. The first one of these was Ole Davidson Skarsten from Olden, who came to this area from Wisconsin to seek land the summer of 1869. He found the land around the waterfall at Swift Falls attractive and decided to settle there. He returned to the settlement by Rio, Wisconsin, and from there he, his brother Elias, and Rasmus Simonson Raudi went west in their prairie schooner, with their equipment and their cattle to Swift Falls the fall of 1870. They became the founders of this settlement.

Simply by looking at family names on grave markers in the St. Pauli Norwegian Lutheran church cemetery, one can identify the locations in Nordfjord where many of the settlers had their roots, including such singularly isolated and small farmsteads as Mitteness in the inner part of the fjord and Svor in the outer. Korstad makes another revealing observation about the St. Pauli congregation, organized in 1877, describing it as

> one of the few—perhaps the only one in Amerika—which consists exclusively of people of Nordfjord descent. . . . It is said to be in ethnic terms "pure" . . . [which] explains, one would assume, why the young people there can speak their dialect clearly, fluently, and authentically and why the special Norwegian-American words and expressions, which as a matter of course are mixed into their speech, appear to have become solidly embedded in their language.[51]

Several of the pioneer settlers in Kerkhoven Township who arrived from Goodhue County or neighboring Rice County in 1867 were from Hallingdal, in Norway's central highland. Among their number was Nels O. Broten, and the first township election, in 1872, was held in his home. Pillsbury and Hayes townships were then part of Kerkhoven Township; they separated as individual townships in 1876 and 1877, respectively. Thosten O. Quamme (Kvamme) and Ole Sondrol, both from Valdres, and Henrik H. Sagadalen from Hallingdal had arrived the year before

St. Pauli Church south of Swift Falls, built in 1898. The congregation was organized in 1877 and consisted exclusively of people from Nordfjord in western Norway.

and were among the pioneer settlers that Edward Neill described as "the advance guard of the army of civilization."

Immigrants from the district of Valdres, located east of Hallingdal, were the second large Norwegian *bygd* group in Kerkhoven Township. They, too, had resettled from Goodhue County. The Valdres Prairie settlement north of Lake Monson consisted mainly of immigrants from the Vang parish, reflecting a specific local identity within the larger Valdres district. The Sondrol name especially but also other Valdres monikers like Quamme and Ellingboe are still prominent on recent plat maps showing land ownership. The community in Kerkhoven Township was part of a large belt of Norwegian settlements, mainly people of Halling and Valdres descent, that extended north into Pope County, northeast into Stearns County, and east into Kandiyohi County.[52]

People from the Sogn region of Norway settled most heavily in Six Mile Grove, Cashel, and Swenoda townships. In the first two, many settlers came from the parish of Hafslo on the Sognefjord but also from other parts of Norway. Two pioneers introduced earlier, Lars Christenson and Ole Corneliusen, both arrived in Six Mile Grove in 1866. Corneliusen was twenty-four years old when he took a homestead claim on the west side of the Chippewa River; he had emigrated two years earlier from Modum in the County of Buskerud. In 1869 he married fifteen-year-old Randi Hanson, born in Vikhamar in the city of Trondheim; together they raised eleven children.

Residents of the village of Benson, not surprisingly, represented people of many local backgrounds. Moving into town from the outlying settlements of immigrants hailing from a variety of localities, within the village limits they resided side by side with fellow Norwegians regardless of local identity. Neighborhood concentrations were thus based on nationality rather than on localism. It is, however, possible to identify a clustering of Nordfjordings, many of whom had moved from Camp Lake Township to Benson and purchased adjacent lots. Based on anecdotal evidence, it appears that Norwegian immigrants were more likely to come directly to Benson if no farm settlement of their own *bygd* folk was there to receive them. One such district was Sunnmøre on the northwestern coast of Norway, which early on contributed to the growth of the village although it was not represented among the many rural *bygd* settlements in Swift County. As in the farm communities, the earliest immigrants in the village—from Sunnmøre and other regions of Norway—were later followed by kin and neighbors from their home district.

LIFE ON THE WESTERN PRAIRIE

Ethnic self-segregation and local exclusivity were tempered by the need to make accommodations to new realities. Life on the western prairie was harsh. New strategies were required to cope with the new environment. The immigrant settler accepted a general allegiance to both American citizenship and ethnic adherence, which, as Jon Gjerde writes, may even be "mutually supportive and self-reinforcing." There was, however, a price to pay. The cost of the strain of frontier life should not be overlooked. One is here reminded of *Giants in the Earth*, the classic novel by O. E. Rølvaag, and its depiction of the price in human happiness demanded by the westward movement. Reports of suicide or mental problems graphically described in the columns of the *Benson Times* surely reflect defeat in a struggle to overcome the all-consuming forces of nature and isolation on the western frontier. "A Swede, named Gronerud, living near Holmes City [Douglas County], committed suicide by hanging Dec. 31," was the brief notice of this tragedy. "Sven Nelson, and the wife of Ole H. Sand, of Kandiyohi county, have both been pronounced insane, and sent to the hospital for the insane in St. Peter," the newspaper reported, and later, "A Norwegian named Knute Ardall, living 2 miles south of Benson, became violently insane this week and was brought in and sent to jail for safe keeping until he can be sent to St. Peter." Such tragic episodes were a not-so-infrequent part of the immigrant experience as well.[53]

The strains of migration and settlement were many, and success in the new environment was hardly assured. On the western prairie in Minnesota, the Norwegian immigrant as well as newcomers of other nationalities faced the destructive forces of nature, the unfamiliar landscape, a foreign culture, and the need to adapt to new livelihoods and ways of life. Peter Sather's experience typifies that of many pioneers. His story illuminates not only hardship and courage but also the strategies that created security and progress. Born in Aure in Nordmøre, Norway, in 1845, Sather emigrated together with his wife, Mali Sylte from Surnadalen, and two daughters in 1869. Both infants died midtrip and were buried at sea. The couple moved first to Norway Lake in Kandiyohi County and then homesteaded in Swenoda Township. A son, John, had been born to them while at Norway Lake. It is told that Peter Sather arrived in Swift County with only fifty cents to his name; he worked for other farmers until his small farm gave some returns. First Sather acquired eighty acres; then he added another eighty under the Homestead Act. He later purchased more land so that he owned 160 acres in Swenoda and another 160 in Six Mile Grove, which became the family residence. He survived, though at a heavy loss, the locust invasion that took his grain in 1876 and 1877, the rust that destroyed his wheat in 1878, and the hailstorm that obliterated his crop in 1879.

As was common, the Sathers had a large family; the lives of their children show the opportunities and the dynamics of frontier life. John homesteaded together with his wife on the Red Lake Reservation; eldest daughter Sophia married Ezra Horning and settled on a farm near

Holloway. Other children went farther afield and responded—along with a large number of Norwegian land seekers—to the "great Dakota land boom," which began in 1879. "Norwegian settlement in northern Dakota," as the author states elsewhere, "took on the proportions of a large-scale folk migration." Settlers moved into the Red River country and later westward along the main line of the Great Northern Railway in the northern part of Dakota Territory that in 1889 became North Dakota.[54]

Christ Sather, the second son, was the first to respond to opportunities farther west; he settled near Rugby Junction in North Dakota. Daughter Pauline married Carl M. Corneliusen, a North Dakota farmer; the sixth child, Peter, married and also homesteaded in North Dakota. Ole resided at home and assisted his father; Jennie, like many single rural women, taught in the Swift County public schools; her sister Inger lived at home; and the youngest son, Simon, died in infancy. The Sather family's varied experiences illustrate adjustment to the demands of the western frontier setting. Peter Sather was a member of the Six Mile Grove Norwegian Lutheran Church and also served as chairman of the board of township supervisors, school director, school clerk, and town clerk. No contradiction existed between his undertakings in a Norwegian world and his public activities. Given that in Six Mile Grove there were Norwegians "as far as the eye could see," the distinction between the two—ethnic and public roles—was not, however, sharply drawn. Indeed, in townships where Norwegians formed the vast majority of settlers they had no choice but to assume political responsibility. For example, the organizing meeting of Six Mile Grove on November 1, 1877, consisted entirely of Norwegian settlers, including the county auditor, Knud P. Frovold.[55]

They convened in Ole Homme's home to elect the first township board; Olaf P. Newhouse served as clerk of the meeting and Claus A. Rodal presided as moderator. Lars Christenson was elected chairman of supervisors, who were Hans E. Hanson and Ole Corneliusen; Olaf P. Newhouse became town clerk and John O. Strom treasurer; Henry Johnson and Carl M. Corneliusen were elected justices of peace; Ole Tverstol and Iver Hanson became constables. The minutes were penned in English. The distinctive element of the town meeting in township government educated Norwegian settlers and others on community

*Six Mile Grove Township board, 1905. Pioneer Norwegian settlers were
active in township administration. Three of the four members in 1905 had
Norwegian names. Left to right: Christ Kjornes, Carl Strom, Peder Sather,
William Ohmach*

issues and eased their entrance into public life. As Harvey Walker explains, "Here, once a year at least, the voters of the township gather to
elect the town officers and consider such other questions as may arise for
decision."

In assuming local political responsibility, Norwegian immigrants
were not novices, and it would be wrong to view them as ignorant peasants pulled into the American civic arena. They in fact arrived with
knowledge of and experience in the management of local affairs. Though
the social and political environment was not the same, the 1837 enact-
ment of local self-government in rural communities in Norway likely
facilitated immigrants' acceptance of civic responsibility in America. Village governance differed from township administration; even so, in the

small village of Benson as well as in countywide positions Norwegian immigrants participated from the start. In Norway, a historian has said, the new law made the democratic principles of the Constitution of 1814 applicable to local administration. The ease with which Norwegian immigrants and their children appear to have entered into township, village, county, and, later, more broadly public affairs while simultaneously creating a comforting ethnic milieu speaks to later-day observers of a harmonious process of adjustment to life in America.[56]

STATUS AFTER A DECADE OF GROWTH

Considerable achievements were made during the first decade of settlement: pioneers—immigrants and American born—had arrived in ever-increasing numbers; their numbers would rise further in the following decade. A substantial framework existed to receive them, guaranteeing continued growth.

More than other Nordic groups, Norwegians sought land on the farthest edge of settlement; encouraged by speculators, various settlement promoters, and the railroads, they moved to newly opened lands. They established rural communities and exhibited, as the Swedish American historian George Stephenson notes, a nationalistic solidarity that had no counterpart among the other Scandinavian groups. Their rural communities were regularly based on old-country localism and centered on the local Lutheran church. In Swift County Norwegians were joined by other Nordics, and even while practicing ethnic self-segregation they displayed a Scandinavian mutuality. More distant were their relations with the Irish, German, French Canadians, and other ethnic groups who made their homes on west-central Minnesota's undulating prairie.[57]

A railroad town, the village of Benson—its crude frontier appearance notwithstanding—established itself as a central market through the sale and transportation of farm products, as an administrative and railroad center, and as a place where newspapers were published. An impressive Norwegian business coterie made the village seem like a Norwegian town; historically it may be seen as a corrective to the notion that western country towns were simply Yankee bastions serving a rural immigrant population. In Benson, as in many other marketplaces in regions of Norwegian settlement, it was mainly a Norwegian business community that met the needs of compatriots in the town and in its hinterland. Viewing the pioneer history of Benson, one might agree with Lewis Atherton that the country town provided leadership in the development of the Midwest, in this case, on the prairie in west-central Minnesota and with heavy emphasis on its Norwegian-speaking residents.

Three

Norwegian Small-Town Apotheosis

A NORWEGIAN TOWN

The 1880s were central years in the maturing of the village of Benson; in that decade it secured its firm reputation as a "Norwegian" urban place. Even so, an old-stock elite of bankers and professional people reinforced a traditional view of the country town as a Yankee domain. What, then, made Benson a "Norwegian" town? This chapter seeks an answer by looking at the demographic composition of Benson and selected townships. The statistics document a predominant Norwegian presence and a younger, unmarried, and gender-balanced population in town compared to the countryside. Furthermore, this chapter identifies among these ambitious and youthful townspeople Norwegian immigrants who asserted influence in how the village functioned. The overwhelming majority of Norwegians—men and women—were, however, blue-collar and service workers. And, finally, this chapter shows that residential patterns responded both to ethnic and to socioeconomic forces.

As the previous chapter indicates, Norwegians were most successful in small business enterprise and there dominated the town landscape; business was regularly conducted in the Norwegian language, and Norwegian farmers and townspeople were loyal customers. This chapter considers as well the role of the Norwegian Lutheran church in the new environment as a preserver of the homeland's faith and as a protector of an old-world cultural heritage. Its position is analyzed in the context of the religious strife that marked Norwegian Lutheranism's American experience, its frontier Puritanism and strict moralistic code, and its relationship to institutions of competing faiths. The congregation became a safe ethnic haven.

Ethnic festivals, such as May 17 commemorations, became community affairs with participation by townspeople of all national backgrounds and social standings. Norwegians from the countryside came to town in great numbers to enjoy the festivities. On such occasions Benson exhibited in language and in national symbols a truly demonstrative Norwegian bent. Coextensively Norwegians in Benson and its environs broadly both adjusted to and influenced their American circumstances. By century's end they reached a juncture in their history where there was for the entire region an account of pioneer times to recapture.

Pioneers

Shared historical memories from pioneer days were embraced by Norwegians who had experienced them and in later generations became a source of ancestral pride for all Norwegian Americans. Norwegian Americans continue to celebrate their historical participation in the winning of the West—the great land taking—and the process of putting land under the plow, creating a sense that Norwegians as tillers of the soil helped build America. Even the Norwegian-American Historical Association—whose historical studies from its organization in 1925 were scholarly in approach—in its early publications celebrated a wholesome rural existence and the heroic aspects of the Norwegian pioneer saga on the American frontier.

"Old Settlers' Associations appeared quickly on the agricultural frontier," writes Lewis Atherton, "and had an enormous popularity with elderly people, who sensed the rapidly changing nature of life around them." An exclusive Norwegian Old Settlers' Association (*Settlerforening*) was not organized until 1899; it included the counties of Lac qui Parle, Swift, and Chippewa and, like similar groups, celebrated "our pioneers' labor in the pioneer days." The tempo of change was rapid indeed, from wilderness to farm to neighborhood and thriving trading center. Family strategies created a safe social environment: settling close to kin and having large families provided social security; it was furthermore important—and especially common among German settlers—to place children on land close to the original homestead. The family history prepared by Yvonne Hanson Dewar, "The Hansons of Six Mile Grove," illustrates some of the aspects that Jon Gjerde details in *The Minds of the West:* the private worlds and the challenges that existed in the rural middle west and called for specific strategies, including those suggested above, as well as interaction with the larger American society.[1]

The family character of settlement had implications far beyond the pioneer stage, creating community stability over several generations. The story of the Six Mile Grove Hansons relates the life experiences of two brothers, their families, and descendants. They hailed from Hafslo in Sogn and in Six Mile Grove Township, just west of the village of Benson, became part of a settlement of Sognings, many like themselves from the Hafslo parish. The first arrivals were Ana and Erich Hanson, who together with their five children came to the United States in 1862. They lived in the Sogning community of Lodi, Wisconsin, where a sixth child was born, and moved to a homestead in Six Mile Grove in 1869. Responding to the ever-advancing frontier, Ana and Erich moved to Larimore in Dakota Territory in 1882, following several of their children. The Six Mile Grove farm remained in the family, however, and in 1969 became a century farm, indicating ownership by the same family for one hundred years.

On their way west, land-seeking Norwegian immigrants sojourned in settlements of their own *bygd* folk; there they found rest and guidance in their search for land. Among fellow *bygd* people they strengthened bonds of kinship and local loyalties and their rural orientation found added nourishment. In 1869 the Hansons had traveled to Swift County by way of Albert Lea, Minnesota—another area of strong Sogning settlement— by oxcart and covered wagon. In 1871 Erich's brother Rasmus, his wife Guri, and their five children came to Swift County, first to Swenoda and then to a homestead in Six Mile Grove. They had emigrated in 1865 and stayed in Lodi for six years before moving west; the two youngest children were born in Wisconsin. Son Hans Rasmus, born in Hafslo in 1855, farmed in Six Mile Grove but also was active in civic life, holding township offices and for sixteen years serving as county commissioner. Such involvement represented cultivation of a transplanted heritage within a new reality on the American frontier. Hans married his cousin Britha, or Betsy, Ana and Erich's daughter, in 1875; like Hans, she was born in Hafslo in 1855. This union of first cousins reinforced both ties of kinship and attachment to a local Norwegian cultural world. Betsy's Americanization of her name as well as Hans's public involvement combined with their obvious loyalty to transplanted beliefs and practices suggest what Jon Gjerde calls a complementary identity "that pledged allegiance to both American citizenship and ethnic adherence." These allegiances not only coexisted, Gjerde maintains, but "could be mutually supportive and self-reinforcing." Further illustration of this double identity—or of circles of identity, suggesting multiple means of social adjustment—might be found in the fact that Hans mastered English, became a naturalized American citizen, taught English school, and was active in local politics while he and Betsy operated a farm in an immigrant community and were charter members of Six Mile Grove Lutheran Church, organized in 1872—congregational life serving as an ethnic place of refuge for immigrant farmers. No identifiable contradiction between residing in an ethnic environment while simultaneously delighting in the privileges and obligations of American citizenship seemed to exist—the experiences were instead mutually confirming.[2]

In any consideration of western expansion and its effect on those who took part in it, one cannot ignore the frontier thesis of Frederick Jackson Turner and his idea of the "democracy born of free land." While recognizing the thesis's exaggerations, Merle Curti and his students in their testing of it in western Wisconsin's Trempealeau County, a region with strong Norwegian settlement, determined, with some important qualifications, that "Turner's poetical vision of free land and relatively equal opportunity was for a great many people realized in Trempealeau County." It appears to have been a reality for the Hansons in Swift County as well. One may, however, raise questions about Turner's thesis that "The struggle with the wilderness turned Europeans into Americans, a process, which," as Patricia Nelson Limerick explains, "Turner made the central story of American history." He ethnocentrically omitted Native American claims to the land and, in fact, presented a mythic and legendary West that held sway in the American imagination. Unlike later historians of the West such as Lewis Atherton, Turner did not "give explicit attention to the relative importance of the village and the open country in the process of development from frontier to settled communities."[3]

A generational review of the Hanson family suggests that life in the open country and life in town were interrelated, constituting two different aspects of a strategy for adjusting to the demands of the world in which they lived. Betsy came to America together with her parents in

1862. She related how during the journey from Lodi she had walked alongside the covered wagon: "We didn't sit and ride in the wagon. It was mostly chasing cattle, walking, and sleeping under the wagon." When they arrived in Benson in 1869, the village did not yet have a railroad. St. Cloud was the nearest town of any size; Betsy worked in St. Cloud and in St. Paul before returning to Six Mile Grove to marry Hans. In 1882 they took over Erich and Ana's farm. Hans and Betsy became the parents of thirteen children, seven of whom survived to adulthood. In 1920 they moved, in the manner of many retired farmers, to nearby Benson, and the next generation, Hans and Tillie Hanson Tjosaas, took over the property. Moving to Benson in retirement has been a common practice throughout the town's history, reinforcing relations between the farm population and the town and providing yet another example of how a country town functions as a central place for outlying communities.[4]

AGE, SEX, AND CIVIL STATUS
OF NORWEGIAN IMMIGRANTS

The majority of Norwegian immigrants destined for both rural and urban parts of western Minnesota had earlier been engaged in agriculture. Can one then identify a typology of those who chose the town rather than continue in the field? Some men, like successful Benson businessman Andrew J. Hoiland, emigrated from one of Norway's many small towns and in America naturally sought a livelihood in an urban economy. Norwegian youth with no *bygd* folk or kin in farming might also, as suggested earlier, prefer life in town. In considering immigrants from peasant circumstances, Walter Kamphoefner has found in his study of Westfalians in Ohio and Missouri "suggestive evidence that life-cycle stage was as important as occupation in determining who would settle in cities." He concludes that urban areas "were especially attractive to young, single, and mobile immigrants, with occupation playing only a secondary role."[5]

One may well ask if Kamphoefner's deduction applies equally well to a village environment such as Benson. Comparison with the surrounding "Norwegian" townships will offer contrast between town and country.

Table 4 shows that Norwegian immigrants in Benson, as Kamphoefner deduces for German immigrants in larger urban centers, tended to

TABLE 4

Characteristics of Norwegian Immigrants in Benson Village and Surrounding Townships, 1880

	Benson Village	Torning Township[a]	Six Mile Grove Township	Camp Lake Township	Benson Township	Kerkhoven Township	Swenoda Township
Number of Norwegian Immigrants	95	121	98	159	69	151	62
Percentage of Total Population	20.8	34.0	36.4	42.2	17.0	34.3	31.0
Norwegian Immigrants and Second Generation	36.6	60.1	71.0	74.5	32.3	70.9	56.0
Sex Ratio	1.16	1.24	1.39	1.30	0.82	1.29	1.30
Mean Age (Standard Deviation)	30.3 (11.8)	32.7 (16.7)	32.0 (14.6)	33.1 (15.5)	36.3 (16.3)	32.6 (15.7)	36.8 (16.8)
Males	30.8 (10.4)	33.3 (16.8)	31.4 (14.0)	31.8 (16.7)	41.9 (14.5)	31.2 (14.3)	35.7 (16.1)
Females	29.6 (13.5)	32.0 (16.8)	33.0 (15.5)	34.9 (13.8)	31.7 (16.5)	34.4 (17.3)	38.1 (18.0)
Percentage Ever Married[b]	51.1	70.9	71.8	73.8	68.2	72.1	72.7
Males	46.0	65.5	65.3	63.3	64.5	59.0	62.5
Females	56.8	77.8	80.6	86.4	71.4	89.7	87.0

Source: U.S. Census, 1880

a. Not including Benson Village
b. Of persons over the age of fourteen

be younger and were more likely to be unmarried than were Norwegian immigrants in rural townships. The sex ratios in town, even though men outnumbered women, were more balanced than for the agricultural population. One can thus infer that the Norwegian immigrant population in the village of Benson in general was younger and unmarried compared to that of the countryside. The small gender imbalance that existed, as suggested also in the low marriage rate for men, relates to the arrival of young single male immigrants to the village. Stage of life, as Kamphoefner found, played an important role in whether the immigrants settled in the town or in a farming community.

Marriage rates were higher in rural Swift County—as suggested by the experience of the Six Mile Grove Hansons—because of family strategies. Effective farm operations required the assistance of a wife and children. "The pioneer's wife," as the author writes elsewhere, "might make the difference between progress and ruin" since "a man could hardly put land under the plow alone." The higher sex ratio—percentagewise more men—in rural areas than in the village may be explained by fewer job opportunities for women there. Men found jobs as field workers and in other agricultural labor; women were limited mostly to being country schoolteachers. The marriage rate for women supports this analysis since most women in farming communities were married and there were significantly more single men than women. It is possible to view the lower age of Norwegian immigrants in the village in terms of marriage rates; in town the median age of single individuals was 23.4 while the median age for married or widowed persons was 36.8. The many single immigrants who moved into the village drove down the mean age. And, one might wish to agree with the *Benson Time*'s assessment that, as a consequence, "Benson has more pretty girls to the square inch visiting within her limits than any other town in the northwest." More importantly, the town offered women gainful employment, mostly in domestic and service occupations.[6]

THE VILLAGE OF BENSON IN THE 1880S

Employment opportunities expanded with the growth of population, which itself was greatly increased by immigration. In 1880 the village of Benson could boast a population of nearly 500; by 1890 there were 877 residents in the village and the population of Swift County had grown to 10,161 individuals. The increase in citizens reflected the fact that 1880–90 was the century's main decade of European immigration. Ole Wenaus entered the prepaid ticket market and in the 1880s sold passage by steamship from Europe to New York and then by rail to Benson for a total price of $50.50. "Now is the time to send for your families," he advertised. The *Benson Times* kept track of incoming immigrants and in July 1882 expressed some concern that "Immigration is beginning to slacken" although it was still "quite large enough to be healthful." The following July the newspaper was encouraged by the great number of immigrants arriving, "many of whom had purchased farms in this vicinity . . . mostly foreigners, accustomed to hard labor [who] will work decided improvements in the aspect of the county." In June 1884 the *Benson Times* informed its readers that "A large group of immigrants fresh from Norway arrived at the depot Wednesday noon, and ere night fall, had all found the friends and places in search of which they had crossed the wide Atlantic." The newspaper heaps praise on them by predicting that before the end of the year they "will have transformed into industrious contented American citizens, able to make their way alone and earn their own living in any community." The newspaper's report illustrates the dynamics of immigration and settlement as well as the county's need for new citizens.[7]

The number of Norwegians in Benson as reported in federal decennial counts consistently amounted to about 40 percent of the total population. Benson's ordinances, adopted by the village council following its incorporation in 1877, reflected the prevailing horse culture of the time. The village law enacted by the Minnesota legislature in 1875 produced a degree of uniformity in village government; Benson in its ordinances and governance fell, according to Harvey Walker, "partly under this law." It provided for the election of a president, three trustees, a treasurer, and a recorder who would serve for one year; a justice of the peace and a constable would be elected for terms of two years. As anticipated, citizens of Yankee background had considerable influence in village affairs, but the impact of a predominant immigrant population was notable, and Norwegians were represented in the village administration from the beginning. The village council consisted of the president, the three trustees, and the recorder. Albert N. Johnson, born in Vermont and a

Knud P. Frovold served as county auditor in Swift County in the 1870s.

pioneer businessman, was elected village president; Thomas Knudson, the council's only Norwegian, was a trustee.[8]

The village landscape allotted space for county administration. The first county courthouse, a wooden frame building, was contracted in 1876 and completed the following fall, in "advance of all . . . the surrounding counties," as the *Swift County Monitor* later wrote. Located on the village's north side, the courthouse was an essential part of the physical landscape. The contracting committee consisted of Dane O. F. Bronniche, whose business training let him advance in public affairs, and Knud P. Frovold, born in Eggedal, Norway. Frovold immigrated at age twenty-two in 1866 and attended Luther College and a business school in Decorah, Iowa, before coming to Benson in 1872. His education secured his role in county affairs, as county auditor and in other positions in the auditor's office.

According to local ordinances, no one could ride or drive faster than six miles an hour within the village's fire limits; fines were imposed for violations. In June 1877 Knud Angleson and Even Olson, both obviously Norwegians, drove too fast on newly graded streets, were arrested and fined the considerable amount of six dollars each, and spent a night in jail. A prohibition existed against placing dead animals on sidewalk or street and against the copulation of animals in view of the general population within city limits. Further, the removal of manure from any livery stable or barn was circumscribed to protect public sensibilities. An ordinance also prevented cattle and other animals from running at large in the village streets, suggesting that this nuisance was not an uncommon occurrence.[9]

These ordinances and several others were hardly the signs of urban sophistication, but they regulated village life and set boundaries for proper behavior. The town's Norwegian Lutheran congregations became a force alongside other denominations in advocating adherence to what was defined as a moral life. A strict observance of the Sabbath was ordained so that "no person shall publicly pursue or carry on any vocation, trade, or employment . . . except if the same be for religious purposes." The *Benson Times* decried activity at the Summer Garden, a "resort of questionable morality" south of town, whose customers "think that Sunday, instead of being the Lord's day, is a day, particularly set apart for riot and license." The journal asked authorities to "take steps to prevent any such proceedings within the village limits in the future." The village council in 1877 enacted a ban on "indecent books" and on "public nudity." Evidence of prostitution in a "tar shanty . . . on the northern border of the village" and open solicitation "of young men about town" elicited "strong threats of lynching" toward the man who pimped and ran the brothel. The ordinance's final section imposed a fine of up to the truly punitive amount of $100 plus cost of prosecution, depending on the seriousness of the offense.[10]

Ordinances carrying a strong moralistic content, if not quite in the spirit of the Puritan Congregational New England town, may nevertheless serve as indicators that a community different from the surrounding farming districts was being constructed. At the same time of course, closeness to rural life was made obvious in a number of the ordinances that were passed.

Class distinctions in residential patterns made visible the operation of socioeconomic forces in the village environment, but there was also a tendency to settle among kin and earlier neighbors along national and regional lines. Statistics on income and national origin create a distinct picture of Benson's emerging neighborhoods. Evidently, early on a "colony" of Nordfjordings existed; people with roots in Nordfjord purchased lots next to each other and created a special local flavor in speech and traditions. On the subject of new residential housing, the *Swift County Monitor* reported in 1892 that "The Nordfjording district

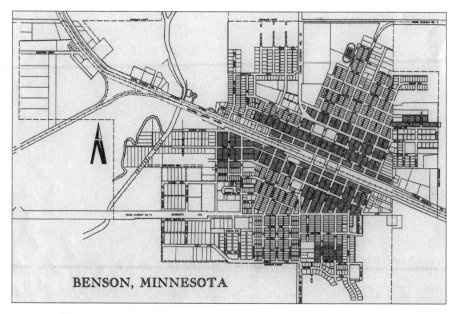

Plat of the City of Benson
Original plat is indicated by darker color.

in the south-western part of town appears to be growing as rapidly this spring as it did last." The federal census, which shows a general spread of Norwegians throughout the village, both on the north and south sides, nevertheless indicates a special concentration in the southwestern corner of town. As later census figures show, twenty-one of thirty-two households on Seventeenth Street South were headed by Norwegians.[11]

Not until 1910, as a result of Benson achieving city status in 1908, did federal census data indicate street of dwelling. Presumably the general pattern of residence established in the 1880s did not change much in the following decades. The 1920 census lists residency and occupation by streets, making it a good source for indicating ethnic and class divisions. Benson's population had by then grown to 2,111 residents. An earlier census would naturally have been preferable; the available figures nevertheless give a clear impression of Benson's general historical characteristics.

The census data validate the evidence given in interviews and in newspaper accounts of a north side and south side division in the city.

The north side had more immigrants and a larger working class than the south side. By looking at heads of household—the census designation—regardless of gender and by excluding the main streets of Atlantic and Pacific, one finds that only 11 percent of residents on the north side of the railroad tracks were Yankees, whereas 17 percent on the south side were. As late as 1920, 49 percent of the north-side heads of household were immigrants, compared to 41 percent on the south side. Heads of household with professional training clustered on the south side—twenty-five; only seven lived on the north side, five of whom were clergy. The fact that nearly half of all heads of household, men or women, were immigrants suggests a strong immigrant influence even in the 1920s. As Table 6— with statistics from 1880, 1900, and 1920—shows, however, the total percentage of immigrants not surprisingly declined while the second generation increased in number. Regardless, the heads of household, many of them immigrants of the 1880s and 1890s, were older and held claim to Benson's economic and political power.

Atlantic Avenue housed a "main street" class largely of Yankee background and persons in professional, managerial, or proprietary occupations, as defined in the census. Pacific Avenue was too sparsely populated to draw valid conclusions. Thirteenth Street South, in the city's exclusive Sunnyside district, formed another Yankee bastion; ten of thirty heads of household were Yankee. A large number of Norwegians lived on this street as well; seven immigrants and three of the second generation made the total Norwegian heads of household equal to the Yankee tally. These successful Norwegian Americans were businessmen and community leaders. In fact, a long- and well-established Norwegian elite resided in

TABLE 5

Population of Benson City by Census Year, 1880–2000

Year	Population
1880	456
1890	877
1900	1,525
1910	1,677
1920	2,111
1930	2,095
1940	2,729
1950	3,398
1960	3,678
1970	3,484
1980	3,656
1990	3,235
2000	3,376

Source: U.S. Census Reports, 1880–2000

TABLE 6

Countries of Origin for Immigrants and Second-Generation Americans in Benson Village/City

	Immigrant	Second Generation[a]	Total
	A. Percentage of Population in 1880		
Canada	2.9	2.2	5.0
Denmark	1.1	2.0	3.1
German Empire	1.3	2.0	3.3
Great Britain	1.5	3.3	4.8
Ireland	4.6	11.4	16.0
Norway	20.8	15.8	36.6
Sweden	2.9	2.4	5.3
Other foreign origin	0.7	1.5	2.2
Non-duplicated totals	35.8	40.6	76.3
	B. Percentage of Population in 1900		
Canada	2.6	4.0	6.6
Denmark	0.5	1.3	1.8
German Empire	0.7	3.3	3.9
Great Britain	0.6	3.0	3.6
Ireland	1.3	7.5	8.9
Norway	14.6	28.3	42.9
Sweden	4.6	7.0	11.6
Other foreign origin	0.1	0.3	0.5
Non-duplicated totals	25.0	54.7	79.8
	C. Percentage of Population in 1920		
Canada	1.6	3.3	4.8
Denmark	0.3	1.2	1.5
Germany	0.5	3.9	4.4
Great Britain	0.4	1.8	2.2
Ireland	0.8	4.2	5.0
Norway	11.3	27.9	39.1
Sweden	4.2	7.0	11.2
Other foreign origin	0.6	1.0	1.6
Non-duplicated totals	19.7	50.3	69.8

Source: U.S. Census, 1880, 1900, 1920

a. Second generation determined by at least one parent born in country of origin

this attractive part of town: only one of those seven immigrants had arrived after 1871.

In considering ethnic residential patterns further, one finds that Swedes were greatly over-represented in the northeastern section of the city. The Trinity Lutheran Church, until 1925 carrying the name Swedish Evangelical Lutheran Congregation (*Svensk evangeliskt lutherska församling*), was originally dedicated in July 1890 "in the eastern part of the city," according to the *Benson Times*. Furthermore, one-third of the heads of household on Thirteenth Street North were Irish, French Canadian, or German. In no other part of the city were they represented in such numbers—the St. Francis Xavier Catholic Church, built in 1882 and located on this street, obviously made the neighborhood attractive to heavily Catholic ethnic groups. The social order within the Benson village community can thus be explained along ethnic, religious, and even class lines.[12]

THE WORKING CLASS

Historian John Higham sees ethnicity and class as organizing principles of the larger social structure as well as within a particular ethnic group, maintaining that "Each ethnic group is likely to have its own class hierarchy that is partly based upon but only imperfectly reproduces the class system of the dominant society." Class distinctions in Chicago's Norwegian colony were well defined, at least if one accepts the Norwegian-language *Scandia*'s analysis. The newspaper identified a Norwegian aristocracy, a middle class, a working class, and a very poor class. Such distinctions were indeed quite visible within the Norwegian population—in residential patterns and social life—even if they were not as severe as *Scandia* would like its readers to believe. Economic disparity nevertheless intensified group identities. Without doubt a strong working-class culture emerged. Wealthy compatriots were not the only models working-class Norwegians could emulate; laborers organized and showed loyalty to trade unions of many kinds, engaged in social activities such as picnics and lodge meetings, and took part in strikes and became the victims of lockouts. Working-class activism in Chicago, including the cause of Socialism, revealed a worker's Scandinavianism among Norwegians, Swedes, and Danes and encouraged a working-class consciousness.[13]

Class distinctions in a village or small-town environment such as Benson could never be as firm or as accepted as in a large metropolitan area like Chicago; neither could ethnic and religious differences separate people to the same extent, although the small-town environment was by no means immune to prejudice or mean-spirited gossip. Social distinctions operated in Benson and placed a distance between people; at the same time, the individual became more visible in small communities. "In spite of latent antagonisms," writes Lewis Atherton, "villagers lived close together and could not avoid influencing one another.... It was a rare boy indeed who grew to manhood solely as the product of one cultural layer." The importance of local news and individual experience is reflected in the country newspapers of the postbellum years, which, as Atherton explains, "dignified the lives of common people by assuming that their activities were important." The columns of the *Benson Times* or the *Swift County Monitor* and other newspapers are filled with vignettes of people's more or less mundane activities, such as "Daniel Desmond is going to work on the farm of Mr. Stocks this summer" or "David Hilt and family went to Hancock Monday for a short visit" or "Mrs. Magnus Pederson entertained the school teachers Saturday afternoon" or "Miss Lilly Lyslo had her tonsils removed at the local hospital Tuesday."[14]

A working-class mentality or solidarity was not much in evidence in the country town, a sharp difference compared to the culture that existed among Norwegian workers in Chicago. Merle Curti, in his study of villages and towns in western Wisconsin's Trempealeau County, has shown that general laborers regularly changed occupation, moving up and down the social ladder, some becoming farm operators, many farmers retiring to town—as was also the case in west-central Minnesota. In tracing social mobility and in measuring economic adjustment for townspeople compared to the farm population, Curti encourages "conventional historical methods." He suggests in his survey that those who made their living in town shared in the initial frontier prosperity—a frontier surge—but did not as a whole do as well as those who made their living on a farm. Benson's rapid growth makes Curti's findings seem applicable to frontier economics. In the 1880s and later Benson nevertheless was essentially a blue-collar town; its population interacted with the surrounding farms to a significant degree; homesteading settlers

TABLE 7

Distribution Amongst Occupational Fields of Females and Working Males[a] Aged 15 to 65 by Ethnic Origin in Benson Village, 1880

| | Percentage of Ethnic Group Working in Occupational Field | | | | | |
| | Males | | | Females | | |
	Norwegian	Other Immigrant	Old Stock[b]	Norwegians	Other Immigrant	Old Stock[b]
Professionals	3.8	10.6	16.3	—	5.5	5.9
Farmers	5.7	4.5	6.1	—	—	—
Managers, Officials, and Proprietors	26.4	15.2	26.5	2.0	1.8	5.9
Clerical Workers	1.9	6.1	10.2	—	—	—
Sales Workers	13.2	10.6	10.2	—	—	—
Craftsmen	13.2	12.1	14.3	—	—	—
Operatives	—	10.6	8.2	2.1	3.6	2.9
Service Workers	11.3	4.5	6.1	39.2	29.1	8.8
Laborers, Including Farm Labor	24.5	25.8	2.0	—	—	—
At School, None, or Unspecified[c]				56.9	60.0	76.5
Total (N)	100 (53)	100 (66)	100 (49)	100 (51)	100 (55)	100 (34)

Source: U.S. Census, 1880

a. Persons with occupations listed as "at school" or "none" or not specified are excluded from tallies

b. "Old stock" defined as native born of native-born parents

c. Also includes "keeps house/housework/housewife"

found supplemental or permanent work in Benson and, as has been seen with Hans and Betsy Hanson, in retirement left the farm for life in town.[15]

Important differences existed between men's and women's occupational distribution. The majority of women worked at home. The 1880 census indicates, however, that immigrant women were much more likely to work outside the home than their Yankee counterparts, mostly because immigrants were less established and had a greater need for income. Norwegian women, both first and second generation, in particular found salaried employment—and did so to a higher degree than women of other immigrant groups. These statistics suggest a greater economic need among Norwegian laborers as well as women's concentration in low-paying service jobs. In 1880, 39 percent of Norwegian women ages fifteen to sixty-five worked in service occupations—as waitresses, domestic servants, and the like; 57 percent stayed at home. In comparison, 76.5 percent of old-stock American women and 60 percent of other immigrant women remained at home.

The occupational picture for men in the same age category is more varied. General laborers, including farm workers, constituted 24.5 percent of the Norwegian male working class, nearly 26 percent for other immigrant groups, but only two percent of the Yankee population. There were many service workers among Norwegian men, in all 13.2 percent, not much different from other immigrants or old-stock Americans. There were in 1880 few Norwegian clerical workers compared to the other two population categories. As many as 5.7 percent of Norwegian men listed themselves as farmers, again not much different from the other groups. Some were in business enterprise or were professional men who, as Merle Curti writes, found supplemental income in farming. In 1880 there were only two Norwegians, first and second generation, in Benson listed as professionals, both pastors, whereas there were seven among citizens of other foreign ancestry and as many as eight Yankees. Since there were fewer old-stock residents, their percentage shows an even greater discrepancy: 16.3 percent as compared to 10.6 for non-Norwegian foreign stock and only 3.8 percent of the Norwegian stock. The statistics indicate that a large percentage of Norwegian men in 1880 and later fell into the general category of common laborers, finding work in blacksmith and machinery shops, with the railroad, in farming-related businesses such as the grain elevators and milling—a flour mill having been erected in 1881—as well as in carpentry and general construction.[16]

PROFESSIONS AND BUSINESSES

Norwegian men in Benson continued to concentrate in working-class occupations. A striking find in the 1880 census, as well as in later ones, is the low percentage of professionally trained Norwegian men. Madison— as will be made clear later—because of unique circumstances diverged from this pattern. In Benson, however, Yankee professionals held a near monopoly in the early years, save for the clergy. The need for medical and dental treatment—the latter offered by resident or visiting dentists in small towns after the Civil War—brought farm families to town. In 1887, for instance, the *Benson Times* announced the regular monthly visit of Dr. C. E. Hale, dentist, who met patients at the Merchants' Hotel. Lewis Atherton tries to assess the social standing of different professions, stating "Like the dentist, the editor of the weekly newspaper ranked below the banker, lawyer, and doctor unless he had an additional claim on community esteem. . . . Teaching was the least distinguished of all professions commonly found in small towns." The first school was taught the winter of 1870–71 by Mrs. Charlotte Knowlton in the Emigrant House, the first hotel, built by the railroad; a one-story frame schoolhouse was erected in 1871 and after 1879 was replaced with a two-story brick building.[17]

As the "high priests of finance" and symbols of material success, bankers enjoyed great respect in the country town. Swift County Bank in Benson was started as early as 1875 with H. W. Stone, of Scotch and American parentage, as president and Z. B. Clarke, born in Licking County, Ohio, and later active in political life, as cashier. Early settler Frank M. Thornton—active in the business community and proprietor of the Farmers' Elevator—also entered banking, founding and serving as cashier of the Bank of Benson, which later became the First National Bank. In 1890 Thornton was admitted to the bar; his elegant home and the brick bank building bespoke his success. Thornton was born in England in 1841 and came to the United States as a child of eight. His service in the Civil War, his participation in the Dakota War, and,

TABLE 8

Names of Selected Norwegian Adults Residing in the Village of Benson and Their Occupations in 1880 as Listed in the Federal Census

Aasen, Knud	laborer	Johnson, Pernille	keeping house
Alm, Frederick	plumber	Johnson, Peter	dealer in flour and feed
Alm, Hans	clerk in bank		
Alsaker, Aagothe	works in hotel	Jorgenson, Gabriel	railroad section foreman
Alsaker, Christian	blacksmith		
Alsaker, Oliane	works in hotel	Knudson, Jessie	servant
Alstad, John	laborer	Lee, Andrew	railroad section foreman
Arneson, Anthon	general store keeper		
		Lee, Betsy	servant
Bergendahl, Bernhard	general store keeper	Myklebust, Ole	railroad section laborer
Bjornson, Gullik	blacksmith	Nilson, Betsy	servant
Bjornson, Helene	keeping house	Norby, Brynjeld	clerk in store
Carlson, Maria	keeping house	Olain, Delia	servant
Christoph, Maria	keeping house	Olsen, Ole H.	laborer
Erikson, John	saloonkeeper	Olsen, Otto J.	saloonkeeper
Erikson, Lizzie	dressmaker	Olson, Barbo	waiter
Frovold, Anbjorg	servant	Olson, Hans	laborer
Frovold, Kari	keeping house	Olson, Thore	saloonkeeper
Frovold, Knud P.	farmer	Opoien, John	laborer
Gunderson, Andrew	clerk in store	Paulson, Jennie	servant
Gunderson, Mary	waiter	Pederson, Helga	servant
Halvorson, Aad	farmer	Rake, Ole	railroad section laborer
Halvorson, Isabel	servant		
Hansen, Theodore	merchant	Rodal, Rachael	servant
Hanson, Jenny	servant	Sanner, Dina	keeping house
Hem, Ole	laborer	Sanner, Peter	dealer in furniture
Hoiland, Andrew	artist	Scherden, Ole	saloonkeeper
Iverson, Lars	railroad yard watchman	Schjerden, Paul	saloonkeeper
		Schjerden, Ragnhild	keeping house
Jacobson, Ingeborg	keeping house	Storeine, Ole	railroad section laborer
Jacobson, Ole	machinery agent		
Jenson, Bernt	laborer	Syverson, Ole	county treasurer
Jenson, Berta A.	keeping house	Teien, Caroline	cook in hotel
Jenson, Torwald	machinist	Thompson, Thom	harness maker
Johnsen, Syver	farmer	Thorson, Maria	keeping house
Johnson, Anders	farmer	Vinberg, Magnus	laborer
Johnson, Bernt	works in saloon	Wangen, Ole C.	watchmaker
Johnson, John	hostler	Wenaus, Olaus [Ole]	register of deeds

not the least, his employment by the railroad brought him to Benson in 1870. These men were joined by other old-stock Americans. Rolin R. Johnson, county surveyor, homesteaded near Swift Falls and traded in bonds and offered loans at eight percent from his courthouse office; his 1917 obituary described him as "descended from staunch New England stock." Benson's first practicing attorney is held to be James Hodgson, who arrived from Dakota County in 1874. Walter A. Foland, of Dayton, Ohio, was a lawyer and prominent civic leader who arrived later in the seventies and for twenty-seven years edited the *Benson Times*; S. H. Hudson, born in Janesville, Wisconsin, of "American parentage," as the *Swift County Monitor* has it, in 1880 established his law office "above T. Knudson's store." Benson was in 1880 served by three medical doctors: C. L. Gates, who advertised himself as a homeopathic physician and dentist and was the first resident physician, arriving in 1874, William Ray, physician and surgeon, with special attention to women and children and the eye, who came in 1876, and J. S. Eaton, physician and surgeon born in Vermont, who moved to Benson in 1879. These men met the financial, legal, and medical needs of the village and its environs and formed a Yankee elite.[18]

Norwegian men found opportunity in commercial activity, and for that reason business enterprise exhibited a different face, one not dominated by a Yankee elite. In fact, Yankees might have been at a disadvantage because of potential customers' ethnic loyalty. According to Edward Neill, there were in the early 1880s "about thirty stores and shops of various kinds . . . in the village, including a bank and two elevators." The village's occupational structure indicates the growth and culture of the community. Most individuals classified under "managers, officials, and proprietors" were owners of small businesses. Later chapters will show that there was a marked consistency in occupational patterns over time, though Norwegians in this particular census category did not increase at the same rate as the total population. Regardless, they were prominent in the business community.[19]

Theodore Hansen's pioneer enterprise has been mentioned previously. In 1892 Hansen was described as "one of the solid men of the town financially" and the small general store he started in 1870, stocking dry goods and groceries, continued to prosper alongside his business dealings in grain elevators and warehouses. Thomas Knudson, another aforementioned pioneer businessman, in 1873 started a general merchandise, dealing in dry goods and clothing, having first opened a saloon—a common progression, as a saloon required less of an initial investment. The enterprising Knudson erected Benson's first brick building for his mercantile business.[20]

Of course, not all commercial enterprise was in Norwegian hands. Irishman Michael Hoban became one of Benson's most prominent businessmen. His mercantile store, opened in 1876, maintained departments for grocery and men's, women's, and children's clothing. Hoban came to America from Kilkenny, Ireland, with his family at the age of two in 1853. He arrived in Benson when twenty-five; his initial intent had been to locate in De Graff in Kildare Township, which then was larger than Benson and Irish and Catholic besides. His Irish identity and strong involvement in the St. Francis Xavier congregation greatly benefited his commercial activity.[21]

Businesses established in the 1880s, in addition to the general stores—which offered a wide variety of wares—were those dealing in hardware, furniture, and farm machinery and agricultural implements. Ole P. Jacobson, "born in Christiansand Stift, Norway, in 1845" according to his obituary, immigrated at a young age and in 1869 settled on a claim near Benson. After farming for four years he engaged in a lumber and machinery business in company with Frank M. Thornton and under the name Ole Jacobson & Co; in 1877 he established his own business in the agricultural implement and machinery trade, advertising seeders, harvesters, mowers, and plows as well as "the celebrated Stoughton Wagon." Another early Norwegian entrepreneur who took advantage of the farmers' needs for implements and machinery was H. B. Strand, who in 1876 became an agent for producers of farm equipment and headquartered his business in Benson. There were other enterprises, too—harness shops, meat markets, tailors, jewelers, watchmakers, photographers, and drugstores. Knud Frovold opened Benson's first drugstore in 1873, Ole Wenaus dealt in jewelry, books, gifts, and sewing machines, and O. C. Wangen advertised himself as a Norwegian watchmaker and goldsmith. There were in 1880 no fewer than seven saloons: five owned and operated by Norwegians, one by an Irishman, one by a Yankee. The latter establishments, frowned upon and even condemned by temperance and church groups, nevertheless reflected rather well the existing market, in Benson

Thomas Knudson erected the first brick building in Benson for his mercantile business.

and in the surrounding farm population. Another prominent Norwegian community member, Otto J. Olsen—who was born in Larvik, Norway, in 1843, but grew up in Gudbrandsdalen—began as a saloonkeeper but then entered political life, finding great success as president of the village council and later as county auditor. He came to America in 1863 after attending school and acquiring skills as a store clerk in the small town of Hammerfest in the far north of Norway.[22]

Andrew J. Hoiland illustrates a different career path. He was born in Egersund, Norway, in 1852, emigrated in 1871, and moved to Benson five years later. He began as a photographer and in the 1880 census is listed as an artist. The furniture store he opened in the early 1880s—from 1888 located on the corner of Kansas Avenue and Thirteenth Street—became, according to advertisements, "the largest furniture company in western Minnesota." Such stores generally stocked coffins and provided funerary service when no local mortician was available; Hoiland soon expanded his business to include an "undertaking establishment." Successful Norwegian immigrants like Hoiland resided in the attractive Sunnyside neighborhood alongside leading Yankee residents.[23]

Norwegian immigrants were well integrated into Benson's business community even though they, unlike prosperous Yankees, might not have the same access to large eastern financial institutions and thus faced greater challenges in supporting their enterprises. In actuality, very few old-stock traders in Benson possessed strong capital credentials. Arnold D. and Luther R. Aldrich, brothers born in Northridge, Massachusetts, and prominent in the hotel business, were among those who had eastern commercial connections and arrived in Benson with accumulated funds to invest locally. Business enterprise was otherwise financed through varying measures. Settling on a claim to accumulate funds or establish collateral for a bank loan from one of the many branches that sprang up on the new frontier was one possibility; bankers, eager to do business, made loans on land or to trustworthy and promising young men, generally at very high rates. Another avenue to acquiring collateral might be to join an established business before moving on to one's own enterprise. A few arrived with some capital saved from hard work and commercial activity at previous locations. The move from modest entrepreneurial activity to business success was often a slow process; a majority of the businesses remained small. The boom in the frontier economy from the mid-1870s, however, increased the value of property and encouraged success. Michael Hoban, for instance, realized great profits by purchasing land with railroad bonds at thirty-three cents on the dollar and used at par value in the transaction; in the boom days the quarter section he purchased could be sold for a good deal of money.[24]

The *Swift County Monitor* in its 1927 reflections on the history of Benson defines three periods: the first extended from the earliest settlers to the coming of the railroad; the second ran until the big immigration, which began in 1876; the third followed through to the *Monitor*'s present. The third period replaced the unstable years of the second period, when, as the newspaper said, "business places changed hands often, people came and in a short time left again, those who stayed put were few." One sign of stability: several hotels replaced the Emigrant House, which the railroad maintained for about five years as a place for travelers to stay; it was then sold and became a regular hotel under the name the Pacific House. The Benson House became the second hotel, built in 1871 or 1872; in 1878 it was purchased by the two Aldrich brothers, who had just arrived from Massachusetts.[25]

Disaster struck Benson in August 1880 when fire laid waste to an entire business block. Supposedly, a careless smoker dropped a cigar butt which rolled through a knothole in the floor of Joe Fountain's saloon and, as the *Swift County Monitor* relates, "after smoldering for a few hours burst forth into flame as the citizens of Benson were eating their evening meal." The establishments destroyed included "Fountain's, Paul Schjerden's and Otto Olsen's saloons, the general stores of T. Knudson and M. Hoban, the drug store of E. R. Bundy, the meat market of Brambilla & Hackett, the harness shop of T. F. Thompson, the law office of Foland & Hudson, and the Benson House." Such fires seem to be a part of most villages' history. They were, however, not entirely without benefit, making way for the construction of substantial brick buildings, creating a building boom, and ridding the town of many simple frame structures. The Benson House—renamed the Aldrich House by its owners—was one of the new structures and "was known as the best hotel west of the [Twin] Cities." An efficient fire department was shortly organized.

Not everyone rebuilt. Thomas Knudson, for instance, was unable to recover the losses his business suffered and instead entered politics fully; he was elected county treasurer, a position he held for twelve years. His prominence in village affairs and his well-established leadership role among fellow Norwegian Americans throughout the county assured his election to public office.[26]

THE NORWEGIAN LANGUAGE

In politics as well as in business Thomas Knudson percipiently fostered an appeal based on ethnicity. It served him well. In rural communities of Norwegians in west-central Minnesota, the Norwegian language in its multitude of dialectal variations represented the first language for immigrants and succeeding generations well into the third; English was for many a foreign tongue seriously encountered only in formal schooling. Country schoolteachers decades into the twentieth century complained about children who "could talk nothing but the Norwegian language" when they arrived in school. At home the peasant vernacular transplanted from Norway was spoken; consequently, business was regularly conducted in the Norwegian language. Immigrant farmers as well as later generations patronized compatriots' stores. They might be reluctant to enter non-Norwegians' establishments, not only due to the greater comfort of doing business with their fellows but also of necessity, lacking facility in English.

The non-Norwegian businesses made great efforts to attract Norwegian customers. English-born Frank M. Thornton, "who now runs a hardware store, lumber yard . . . and elevator," according to the *Benson Times* in July 1877, headed the unusual effort by a non-Norwegian to start a "Skandinavien" [*sic*] newspaper. The *Benson Times*, in wishing the enterprise success, asked facetiously but also realistically, "say don't you want to hire an editor?" Albert C. Clausen edited the *Benson Times* from 1876 to 1877; the 1880 federal census records him born in Charlestown, Massachusetts, in 1849 to Norwegian immigrant parents. Some even tried to learn the Norwegian language, as the *Benson Times* reported in February 1882: "Four of our businessmen have formed a class for studying the Norwegian language. . . . I. L. Preus is to pilot them through the breakers of translation and past the obstacles of Peterson's grammar, to a perfect understanding of good Norsk, as written and spoken."[27]

Michael Hoban might well have been one of these four businessmen; at the least it is known that he owned a Norwegian-English dictionary and made an effort to learn Norwegian. He thought it wiser, however, to attract Norwegian customers by hiring "a clerk who was able to converse with them." Through the years Hoban employed a great number of Norwegians. One example is Martin C. Ostvig, who was born in Trondheim, Norway, in 1845 and immigrated in 1869; he joined the Hoban store in the early 1880s, first as an employee, later serving as a member of the firm until his death in 1918. His close connection to the Norwegian community was clearly an asset.[28]

The main avenue to the Norwegian American community was through the columns of the immigrant press. No separate Norwegian-language newspaper was ever published in Benson, however; local foreign-language papers were difficult to sustain. Norwegians in Madison enjoyed some success in this regard, but an attempt in the mid-1880s to issue a Norwegian-language weekly in Glenwood for Pope County quickly floundered. Another option was to insert Norwegian text into existing English-language newspapers. In 1878, from April 5 until July 19, the *Benson Times* printed part of one page in Norwegian under the title *Benson Posten* (The Benson Post). Thomas Knudson, always active in community affairs, is listed as *Udgiver* (publisher). The column mainly contained reports of activities among Norwegians in Benson and elsewhere in Swift County, accounts of occurrences in Norway, and notices of business activity. Knudson served as agent for the two established Norwegian-language newspapers, *Skandinaven* in Chicago and *Budstikken* (The Messenger) in Minneapolis.

After the merger of St. Anthony and Minneapolis in 1872, the infant metropolis near St. Anthony Falls, with its growing Norwegian population, institutions, and societies, gradually came to function like a Norwegian American capital and commercial center for the widespread Norwegian settlements throughout the Upper Midwest. The politically liberal *Budstikken,* founded in 1873 and edited by Luth. Jæger from 1877 to 1885, had subscribers in Swift County and reported regularly from that part of the state. Such national journals as *Skandinaven* and *Decorah-Posten* in Iowa also had readers in west-central Minnesota. In May 1876 *Budstikken* made an effort to enter directly into the market by offering a joint subscription with the Republican *Benson Times;* the latter newspaper reminded "our Norwegian friends" of "an excellent chance to obtain your state and county paper, both at a very reasonable sum."

The political differences between the two journals made for a short-lived collaboration, however. In the election later that year the *Benson Times* even accused *Budstikken* of being "the refuge of the double-faced hypocrites of that nationality." Nineteenth-century politics were nothing if not scurrilously blunt and divisive. The *Benson Times* naturally wished to appeal to "all intelligent Scandinavians," both politically and commercially. Like later newspapers in Swift County, every issue carried national news from Sweden, Denmark, and Norway.[29]

Reminding potential customers and patrons of a shared nationality expressed a common conviction that ethnicity united. All Norwegian immigrant journals, regardless of place of publication, carried notices for "Norwegian" lawyers, "Norwegian" doctors, and "Norwegian" land agents, presumably to convince Norwegian immigrants that these compatriots could be trusted as honest and efficient professionals in a new environment. There were "Norwegian" hotels seeking a Norwegian clientele and "Norwegian" businesses of all kinds; at times the national designation broadened to "Scandinavian." Being able to communicate in the mother tongue and the comfort of the familiar possessed great appeal.

Even though Benson had few Norwegian resident professionals until after the turn of the century, ethnic signals were obvious in the announcements placed in such newspapers as the *Benson Times* and the *Swift County Monitor*. There was early on a Scandinavian Hotel in Benson. Ole Thorson, born in 1831 in Aurdal in Valdres, Norway, emigrated with his parents in the 1850s and settled in La Crosse County, Wisconsin; the family came to Pope County in 1866. In 1872 Thorson moved to Benson, where he built and operated the Scandinavian Hotel; named in an appeal to nationality, the hotel became a popular meeting place. O. C. Wangen consistently identified himself as a "Norwegian Watchmaker and Goldsmith," and Knud Knudson continued to invite Norwegians to his "Norsk Saloon and Billiard Hall." Thomas Knudson in 1877 married Ole Thorson's youngest daughter, Mary, an example of inmarriage within an emerging immigrant social elite. Until fire destroyed his business in 1880, Knudson had inserted Norwegian into his newspaper advertisements, in November 1877, for instance, as follows: "Thos. Knudson, HANDLER MED Dry Goods, Clothing, Hats and Caps, Boots and Shoes, Skandinaviske Morskabs og Skoleböger GENERAL MERCHANDISE. GODE

VARER OG GODT KJÖB. Call and Examine Goods and Compare Prices with Other Places." No doubt these Norwegian phrases attracted the attention of the people Knudson strove to serve.[30]

THE RELIGIOUS IMPULSE

The Norwegian American author O. E. Rølvaag defined his ethnic identity in terms of the Norwegian language, Norwegian nationality, and the Lutheran faith. The Lutheran church in its conflicting manifestations became the immigrant community's central institution, not only in religious affairs but also in Norwegian American organized social life, which focused greatly on the churches. The main concern of Norwegian American Lutheranism was nevertheless the preservation of the homeland's faith. The transition from the authoritarian, episcopally organized Lutheran state church with automatic membership in Norway to an extreme free-church system based on voluntarism was fraught with difficulty from the start and posed great challenges to religious leaders. In the West it was accomplished in a society where, to quote Jon Gjerde, "political immoderation, economic excess, and inordinate individualism" prevailed. Ray Allen Billington traces an American materialistic attitude, identified by citizens of other lands, in part to frontier affluence as well as to hard work, which he sees as "the gospel of the frontier." "Money," he writes, "was the talisman that would open the door to elevated social status, the key to political influence, the portal to cultural magnificence." Regardless of the fear of political immoderation, excessive materialism, and dangerous individualism—all of which challenged both secular and spiritual authority—church leaders expressed confidence in the survival of their faith. H. G. Stub, an early prominent Norwegian American church leader, spoke of creating a genuinely Lutheran community imbued with religious truth and pure doctrine, "a Lutheran Zion," in a sectarian and free churchly America, liberated from the secular authority of the state church. Gjerde finds in this optimism another example of a complementary identity, "a syncretism that applauded both American freedom and religious truth."[31]

A sectarian America with its competing faiths and religious bodies might indeed seem to present a marketplace of creeds. In August 1876 the *Benson Times* reported that the village's first church edifice was under construction; the Pilgrim Congregational Church, built by the small local Congregational Society at a cost of $1,400, was dedicated in October 1876. The Congregationalists' missionary efforts among immigrants and their ability to submerge denominational lines in the interest of advancing Christian work everywhere gave them entry into the Norwegian American community. The Reverend Paul Andersen, an early Norwegian Lutheran pastor in Chicago, had, as an example, in 1848 entered the Lutheran ministry at the urging of friends at the Presbyterian and Congregational Beloit College where he received his training. Mindful of the religious needs of Scandinavian immigrants, the home missionary society sustained by the two denominations gave his ministry financial support for some years. In Benson as well, the Pilgrim Church displayed benevolence toward the many Norwegian newcomers and gained a few converts. Indeed, the first meeting of the Ladies Aid Society, organized in December 1876 to help maintain "the new Congregational church," took place in the home of second-generation Norwegian Albert C. Clausen, whose Massachusetts childhood and youth likely influenced his decision to join the Congregationalists. A succession of short-term pastors and missionaries indicated the difficulty a small congregation faced in financing church operations.

Prominent Norwegians and Swedes in Chicago had in 1849 cooperated in founding the Episcopal St. Ansgarius congregation. Episcopalians' high social status in American society attracted prosperous Scandinavian immigrants; the denomination's ordained clergy and high church ritual might remind members of practices in the two homelands' state churches. The Episcopalians entered early onto the religious scene in Benson, extending an invitation to Norwegians to become parishioners. But they made little headway among Norwegians in the West; perhaps, as has been suggested, many turned away from the Episcopal Church because in organization and practice it reminded them too much of the Church of Norway and the conditions they had left behind. In December 1876 the *Benson Times* reported that the Reverend D. T. Booth preached in the schoolhouse and a committee had been founded to "erect a house of worship in spring." The original application for permission to form an Episcopal parish in Benson, addressed to Henry B. Whipple, bishop of the Minnesota diocese, is signed by sixteen individuals, many of them husband and wife; they were, among others, Frank M. Thornton, John

Moore, C. A. Dwight, and the Aldrich families, together representing an old-stock social elite, and other socially eminent individuals like German-born congregational secretary F. A. Heebner. In January 1877 Bishop Whipple conducted services in the courthouse, according to the *Benson Times*, to "a spellbound audience." The edifice—Christ Church, a small wood-frame building—was not ready for use until October 1879, however. The congregation remained small, but through its many prominent members and its active social functions, regularly advertised by the Ladies Guild, the church in an Episcopalian tradition became the site of lectures, concerts, and other events.

Other early efforts to create a following by Protestant groups—aside from Norwegian and Swedish Lutherans and including what Edward Neill terms "a Baptist organization and a Methodist class"—did not succeed. Considering the progress that the Methodists especially had on the frontier, if not among Norwegian settlers, their near-absence in early Benson may speak to the strength of the other Protestant creeds as well as, in the opinion of some historians, to a Scandinavian dislike of revivals. Methodism's marked American character—its almost nativistic attitude—might also have alienated Norwegian settlers; American-dominated religiosity kept Norwegian Baptist membership low as well. Both Baptist and Methodist converts were made, but never in great numbers and most successfully in large urban areas. After 1880 an early viable Norwegian-Danish Methodist mission effort became a national conference within the Methodist Church. The center of its activity was Chicago, with a separate theological seminary in Evanston, Illinois, but congregations were broadly organized. By 1900 ninety-one congregations existed, seven in Minnesota. In 1899 a Norwegian-Danish Methodist congregation was established in Swift County's Appleton, with its large old-stock American population, and another small one had been founded in the early 1890s in the strongly Norwegian village of Milan in Chippewa County. It has been suggested that Methodism's use of emotionalism, its simplicity and lack of class consciousness, and its involvement in the everyday lives of the common people—religious as well as mundane secular goings-on—attracted converts. The Milan congregation grew to a membership of forty-five by World War I; the national conference, however, in 1900 had only 4,640 members in "full union."[32]

Greater defections from the Lutheran faith were likely prevented by the Norwegian Lutheran Church's social role and organizational might in farming communities and small towns on the American frontier. A strong ethnoreligious identity, as suggested by Rølvaag's definition, kept Norwegians within the Lutheran fold; in fact, one may claim a nearly symbiotic relationship between Lutheran and Norwegian ethnicity. Conversion to other faiths placed barriers between Norwegians.

Protestant antipathy toward Roman Catholicism made conversions to the Catholic Church in the nineteenth century, and even much later, almost unheard of among Norwegian immigrants. Indeed, historians have identified an intense anti-Catholic prejudice among Norwegian Americans. The large population of Irish and French Canadian Catholics nevertheless made a showing in Benson and more strongly in other parts of Swift County. The first Catholic mass in Benson was held in May 1876, "in Frank Thornton's new building by the Reverend John McDermott." St. Francis Xavier Catholic Church of Benson was, however, not organized until December 1881 and incorporated in January the following year. Michael Hoban, of Irish origin, and Firmin Bedard, the trustee and leader of the French settlement, were members of the parish corporation; ethnically they represented the county's two major Catholic nationalities. The St. Francis Xavier church was built in 1882; the parish that year had only seventeen members; it was served by Father Anatole Oster, resident pastor of Clontarf parish.[33]

Inadequate resources and small beginnings characterized all effort to assure the establishment and survival of the homeland's faith. The Swedish Trinity Lutheran Church had a truly inconspicuous beginning, being organized in a dugout in June 1874. It should be noted that it is not uncommon to find similar descriptions of dwellings that more accurately should be defined as sod huts, which may have been the case here. Nevertheless, it was a primitive and crude home at best. In 1872 Pastor Frank Peter Beckman had, as a traveling missionary, journeyed to Benson by train to see if any Swedish immigrants were in the area. There he met the young Frank Johnson, who took him to his father's farm. In the Johnson dugout, or perhaps sod hut, the church was later organized.

Church services were conducted in members' homes and, later, until a church structure had been erected in 1890, in the Benson schoolhouse and courthouse. Beckman related his impressions following his first visit to Benson: Swedish immigrants "were only a few . . . lived far apart . . . [and] had no houses. . . . Several families were crowded together in dugouts [but] seemed well satisfied, and happy with their homes." Born in Hälsingland, Sweden, in 1822, Beckman came to Red Wing, Minnesota, in 1856, where he met the pioneer Swedish American church leader Eric Norelius, who encouraged him to enter the ministry. Norelius, like Beckman a native of Hälsingland, had assisted in founding the Swedish American Lutheran church known as the Augustana Synod, organized in 1860 as a joint Swedish Norwegian enterprise. The Norwegians departed from the union ten years later and formed a separate national synod, the Norwegian Augustana. Beckman belonged to the Swedish pietists, the so-called *läsare*, literally "readers," with the meaning "bible-readers;" his piety and religious fervor did not suit the adherents of the liturgical high-church traditions of the Augustana Synod. He seems to have met little resistance on this score in his ministrations in western Minnesota, even though Trinity in Benson was a member of Augustana Synod. Organized by ministers trained within the Swedish Lutheran State Church, Trinity adopted its confession of faith and its high-church ritual of worship, far removed from the persuasion of the pious *läsare*

Atlantic Avenue in Benson looking north, 1895. The courthouse can be seen to the far left.

Beckman represented. But, as Swedish American scholars like George Stephenson have pointed out, it would be a historical misconception to consider the Augustana Synod a daughter to the homeland's church, as some have liked to describe the relationship. It was not a state church but a religious institution based on voluntarism and shaped in America's multi-religious, free-church environment.[34]

NORWEGIAN LUTHERANISM IN AMERICA

Norwegian American Lutheranism exhibited a pronounced denomi-nationalism; it was an immigrant church that emerged in the fractious crossroads of transplanted and domestic partisan tensions. Norwegian immigrants participated in founding no fewer than fourteen synods between 1846 and 1900; the term "synod" (*synode*) was used to define each of these ecclesiastical communions, and they all bore the Lutheran name. Historian Laurence M. Larson describes the pioneer church as a militant body; he attributes its many violent controversies not only to religious conviction but just as much to frontier individualism, "for in those days individualism was exceedingly 'rugged.'" Historically, of

Pacific Avenue in Benson, 1895. It marks the more prosperous south side of town.

course, it cannot be denied, as was the case with the Augustana Synod, that it was an American institution, developed on American soil: even as church leaders strove to transplant the homeland's creed, in so doing they entered into a heated, on occasion hostile, discourse concerning the essence of that belief. "In the free environment of the American frontier," writes Eugene L. Fevold, "divergent views that held together in Norway under the broad umbrella of the state church were assuming separate institutional and synodical expression." The main division was between the church of the laity and the church of the clerics—the pietistic low-church and the liturgical high-church persuasions. An intermediate position—a broad-church direction—rejecting both the clericalism and dogmatism of the clergy and the pious extremes and evangelism of the laity, complicated the creation of a single Norwegian Lutheran Church in America.[35]

The two Norwegian Lutheran congregations that were founded in Benson placed themselves in two different synodical camps: one in the liturgical high-church Synod of the Norwegian-Evangelical Lutheran Church in America, organized in 1853, commonly referred to as the Norwegian Synod or merely the Synod; the other in the broad-church Conference of the Norwegian-Danish Evangelical Lutheran Church, formed in 1870 but with roots back to the Augustana Synod in 1860, referred to simply as the Conference.

A brief history of the churches will illustrate the volatility of religious life on the frontier as well as the challenges posed by lack of resources. The Synod Church, as it was consistently referred to in the columns of the *Benson Times,* was the Trinity Lutheran Church of Swift County (*Trefoldigheds menighet*), initiated by a group of men who first met in February 1870 at the farm home of Halvor H. Dahl on the outskirts of Benson; formal organization was made in May of that year. Debate preceded joining a specific Lutheran church body. Not until 1876 did Trinity join the Synod, after Knud Frovold had visited a synodical meeting in Kandiyohi County and reported back that the "Synod was a strong and useful church body in the work of the Kingdom." In 1884 Trinity was divided into two districts, northern and southern, each becoming a separate congregation. Incorporation occurred in 1886: the Northern District in Benson took the name Our Savior's Norwegian Lutheran Evangelical Church (*Vor Frelsers menighet*), with a membership that year of about 150, while the Southern District in Swenoda Township retained the original name, becoming the Trinity Swenoda Church. They had a joint pastorate: the Reverend Christopher Pederson served four congregations from 1881 to 1917 and two until 1924—Trinity in Swenoda Township, Our Savior's in Benson, East Zion in Langhei Township, and West Zion in Hoff Township, the last two in Pope County. Born in Nordre Land, Norway, in 1852, Pederson had immigrated in 1869; he received his training at Luther College and the Synod's theological seminary in Madison, Wisconsin, and was ordained in 1880. As his son later related, Pederson "always kept a team of fine driving horses," which took him to preaching places and churches. Norwegian Lutheran churches of the same synodical body regularly began as one congregation and, as membership grew, later split into two independent congregations, in this case one in the country and the other in town. The same pastor served both rural and village congregations. A distinction between country and town consequently can not be made in regard to religious practice and synodical affiliation, although use of the Norwegian language in worship as well as in everyday speech persisted longer in the countryside.[36]

A constant problem, whether in town or in the country, was securing a place of worship other than members' homes and schoolhouses; the irregular and infrequent visits by pastors who served several congregations posed additional challenges. Our Savior's congregation in 1882 purchased the Pilgrim Congregational Church building and, after remodeling, dedicated it in 1884.[37]

The first permanent meeting place for Immanuel (*Immanuels menighet*), the small congregation of the Conference, was the old public schoolhouse, located on lots north of the courthouse and purchased in 1880 for $400. The church had begun in 1872 as the Six Mile Grove Congregation (*Six Mile Grove menighet*), seven miles southeast of Benson, with members from both the village and the township. They separated into two congregations in 1877, the Benson residents forming the Immanuel Lutheran Church, its membership numbering only about thirty. Earlier the Six Mile Grove Congregation had joined the Lake Hazel Congregation (*Lake Hazel norsk luthersk menighet*) and the Swift Falls Congregation (*Swift Falls menighet*) in applying to the Conference for a pastor. In summer 1877 the Reverend Severin Almklov arrived to

Dedication of Our Savior's Church in 1884. The building was purchased from the Pilgrim Congregational Church in 1882 and remodeled.

serve these churches, including the newly organized Immanuel congregation in Benson. Again one is reminded of the shared origin and pastoral service of rural and village congregations. The fact that a class motive might prevail in the selection of membership—the more prosperous Norwegians being inclined to seek a church home in the Synod—operated within the village of Benson but does not seem to have caused a rural and urban dichotomy in synodical affiliation nor a social division within farming communities. Only in Benson was there a choice between a high-church Synod congregation and a broad-church Conference congregation. The rural churches Almklov served were each, as was the case for the country parish Pastor Pederson ministered to, the community's central institution. Almklov was the first resident Norwegian Lutheran pastor in Benson; he was born in Vanylven in Sunnmøre, Norway, and immigrated in 1874 when he was twenty-four years old. Almklov received his theological degree in Minneapolis at Augsburg Seminary, the Conference's training institution, and then moved to Benson, where he remained until 1887.[38]

Theological debate set boundaries between Norwegian Lutherans. Responding to a call from a party of lay people to clarify the difference between the Conference and the Synod, the pastors Ole N. Berg of Fergus Falls, representing the Conference, and Ole E. Solseth, pastor of Our Savior's, representing the Synod, met on May 8, 1876, in the Benson schoolhouse for a public discussion. The issue first debated—in Norwegian, but fully reported by the *Benson Times*—was the question of justification: Solseth maintained "that the bible taught that all were justified through the redemption of Christ," while Berg, in giving the Conference belief, said he "could not see that the word of God taught all were justified," insisting that "we are justified by faith, when we believe through the redemption of Christ." They then moved on to the old question of slavery—likely more easily comprehended by the audience—where Solseth defended the controversial Synod doctrine "that slavery is not sin," whereas the Conference position declared by Berg was "that slavery is contrary to the word of Christ." Aside from the remarkable decision to introduce the Synod's painful and divisive statement of 1861 on its teachings on slavery—in the midst of the Civil War—Solseth's defense of it some fifteen years later illuminated the Synod's strict Bible-based doctrine of the holy scripture's verbal inspiration and literal inerrancy. Incompatible views on biblical truth were defended by uncompromising men; the dissension was intensified by a nearly undisciplined sense of freedom in the Norwegian laity. The party asking for the debate spoke for this group of Norwegian immigrants; in March 1877 five members withdrew from the Synod congregation because "they did not agree with certain teachings" on slavery and lay preaching.[39]

The Norwegian Synod disapproved of lay preaching, which, as the history of Trinity and Our Savior's churches states, "had a few adherents but failed to gain foothold." Lay preaching was accepted and common in other Norwegian Lutheran synods. In the 1870s the Church of Jesus Christ of Latter-day Saints sought converts in Benson "but failed to cause any noticeable disruption." In fact, the churches acted quickly to counter any potential Mormon influence. Trinity's congregational minutes tell of a meeting in April 1875 in the home of Lars Christenson (Kjørnes), the pioneer settler of 1866, where "the question of Petter Hanson's religious belief was brought up." Petter Hanson's error was to reject baptism of children in favor of "the Mormon baptism as the only right one." Confronted by Pastor Solseth and members of Trinity, he concluded "that the Lutheran, or child baptism, is the only true baptism" and begged the congregation for forgiveness, which "was granted him." Public confession of sinful behavior and doctrinal fallacies were powerful reminders of the nature of religious truth, keeping church members within the fold and setting boundaries against other creeds and nationalities.[40]

Lars Christenson, a deeply religious person, was one of the organizers of the Six Mile Grove Lutheran congregation, which often met in his house during the ten years before there was a church. Christenson was a carpenter, a blacksmith, and a dedicated woodcarver; his best-known work is the wooden altarpiece now in the Vesterheim Museum in Decorah, Iowa. It belongs, as art historian Marion J. Nelson writes, to a transplanted Norwegian folk-art tradition, of which Christenson was a rare practitioner; the altar is a "unified artistic masterpiece," Nelson explains, and shows Christenson's "sense for monumental composition and for the spiritual content of his subjects."[41]

All Norwegian Lutheran churches inculcated a pietistic way of life. The church countered what it saw as lax morality by enforcing strict standards—the observance of the Sabbath, abstinence from alcohol, and rejection of frivolous behavior. At the same meeting in April 1875 in Christenson's home, the first order of business had been "the punishment to be meted out to Thomas Johnson, for his gross misbehavior as a member of the congregation." His transgression might well have been public drunkenness, a common enough offense, but as it turned out it was even more serious. It was decided that he should "be compelled to appear before the congregation and he should ask for forgiveness." The discussion of further discipline was postponed to a later date since Johnson was not present at the meeting. He did attend the annual meeting in June, at which he was asked to confess his sexual misconduct with a girl, Kristiana Christoferson. The minutes record bluntly that "the congregation was not satisfied with his version of the affair and would not forgive him." He was therefore "given church chastisement," whatever that entailed. At the same meeting the majority struck "Gunsten Olson's widow" from the record, finding her, one must assume, unworthy of membership. Church discipline was enforced through austere measures.[42]

Historian Marcus Lee Hansen has proposed the thesis that frontier churches, dealing with people who under the new conditions were tempted to forget traditional morality, were always inclined to be puri-

Altarpiece made by woodcarver Lars Christenson, now in the collection of Vesterheim Norwegian-American Museum in Decorah, Iowa

tanical and that immigrant Puritanism became progressively more pervasive with time. "Discipline became more and more strict," he writes, "one after the other, social pleasures that were brought from the Old World fell under the ban.... Temperance and Sunday observance were early enforced, then cardplaying and dancing were prohibited." Theodore Blegen insists that immigrant Puritanism had deeper roots than Hansen suggests. He believes Norwegian American Puritanism was independent of New England, or American, Puritanism. "It was brought to the West," Blegen explains, "from Norway by the immigrants themselves, particularly by those who accepted and followed the teachings of Hauge, Eielsen, and other apostles of pietism." [43]

Elling Eielsen was the first great Haugean lay preacher among Norwegian immigrants, arriving in the Fox River settlement of Illinois in 1839. As a follower of Hans Nielsen Hauge, the influential Norwegian lay religious leader, he in 1846 established a Lutheran low-church organization which became known as Elling Eielsen's Synod or simply Eielsen's Synod. Organized at the Trinity Lutheran Church in Chicago in 1876, Hauge's Synod—as it was consistently referred to—grew out of Eielsen's church, a church of believers. The emotional form of Christianity encouraged by Hauge's Synod and its evangelization in an American Protestant spirit set it off from other Norwegian Lutheran immigrant churches. But these churches were also greatly affected by an increasingly pervasive Puritanism—a frontier pietistic-puritanical orientation—that harbored a strong distrust of human pleasure. This intense distrust in a pietistic Haugean spirit existed in all Swift County congregations, as suggested by the incidents related above, even though none of them directly affiliated with Hauge's Synod. O. M. Norlie lists fifteen Norwegian Lutheran congregations and one preaching place through 1916 in Swift County; some of these lasted only a few years. It is of interest to note that they were non-affiliated or divided between the Norwegian Synod and the Conference and its successor synods. These two had the greatest success in their efforts to recruit member congregations: the high-church Norwegian Synod gained a dominant position, claiming nine of the fifteen congregations in Swift County. In Pope County as well Norwegian Lutheran congregations all belonged to one or the other of these two church organizations; they were the largest and were both referred to as "the churchly." The smaller Hauge's Synod, the church of the laity, called "the holy," gained a firmer foothold in Lac qui Parle County and there competed successfully with the churchly synods, perhaps because many of the pioneer settlers came from districts in Norway that had experienced pietistic Haugean revivals.[44]

The Puritan spirit expressed itself in the movement for temperance reform. Abuse of alcohol was only one of the many practices of which the church severely disapproved. The temperance cause, however, differs from other moral uplift efforts in that it moved Norwegians beyond the confines of their congregational life to cooperate with non-Lutheran creeds. And it moved them into the political arena as well. At the June 1874 meeting Trinity Lutheran Church of Swift County decided that "when a member becomes intoxicated he shall be chastised." And, to be sure, indulgence in alcohol was by no means unknown among Norwegian immigrants. The *Benson Times* did not hesitate to ridicule the intoxicated publicly. It had this to say about a Norwegian pioneer in Swift County, showing no mercy or compassion: "Ole Homme was in the lock-up again Tuesday night. Ole is one of those misguided individuals who loves to look upon the wine when it is red. Whiskey, however, has greater charms for him than the milder beverage and he not only looks upon it on every convenient occasion, but absorbs vast quantities of it, until he becomes a gibbering, irresponsible maniac." In the following issue the newspaper complained about a group of women "who made such a spectacle of themselves last Friday, by appearing upon the streets in a drunken condition." The saloonkeepers became objects of strong criticism by citizens concerned about the village's morality. In April 1880 the *Benson Times* had all day viewed "men on our streets under the influence of liquor." It warned the "liquor businesses" of dire consequences if they did not better control sales, else the license to operate their establishments might be denied.[45]

From the late 1870s Norwegians were swept along in the American temperance movement. Reports and announcements for temperance meetings appear regularly in the columns of the local press. Norwegians became active community participants. At a temperance meeting in February 1878, Pastor Severin Almklov of the Immanuel Church "in a few words had encouraged the movement, and advocated its espousal by his Scandinavian countrymen." The meeting voted to establish the Order of the Blue Ribbon in Benson to promote the cause of temperance; this Christian order had been founded only the previous year, in 1877, in Pittsburgh, Pennsylvania. In the same March issue of the *Benson Times*, H. J. Heebner, secretary of both Christ Episcopal Church and the local temperance society, announced a meeting the following week where again "Rev. Mr. Almklov is expected to address the Scandinavian citizens."[46]

Norwegian Lutheran pastors like Almklov clearly enjoyed the respect of the local community and were recognized as individuals. In comparison, Merle Curti in discussing social distance between the immigrants and the Yankee element in Trempealeau County, Wisconsin, finds that in the early years the local newspapers only mentioned nationality, not name, when reporting on immigrants. As an example, he notes that in 1878 the *Trempealeau County Messenger* had reported that "the pastor of the Norsk Lutheran church had arrived direct from Norway, without giving his name." Even though there is clear evidence of a social distance between old-stock Americans and immigrants in Swift County, no instance was found in local newspapers where the names and titles of foreign-born priests and pastors were not given. They are consistently treated with the same esteem afforded the clergy in mainstream Protestant churches. The congregations these clergymen served were major ethnic institutions.[47]

In addition to its religious role, the church became the most important social institution established by Norwegians in America. Language, traditions, and food were those from the homeland. Eugene Fevold describes the church as the cohesive social force of Norwegian immigrant communities and the pastors' homes as the chief centers of culture. The pastors became the social and intellectual leaders. The church on the prairies and in the wooded groves of the middle west provided an array of social activities; mutual support in time of need; comforting rituals associated with baptism, confirmation, marriage, and burial; and solemnity and a sense of security in unfamiliar surroundings. Members and spiritual leaders alike gave the church their support under difficult conditions and found a protective sanctuary in the ethnic world of the congregation. Even those who did not directly come under its religious-ethical influence through membership were touched by the church and might on occasion request the sacraments and other ecclesiastical services. It was not, however, their only social reality. Norwegian immigrants, in the manner of other foreign-born residents, moved out into the larger community and cultivated their status as citizens of a new land.

The insightful term coined by Ewa Morawska in her study of Jewish immigrants in the small Pennsylvania burg of Johnstown here comes to mind, even though Morawska is mainly concerned with the creation of an American working class. She introduces the concept of "ascriptive inclusion" to describe a divisive-inclusive process of ethnicization, where ethnic awareness and boundaries are sharpened through "the participation in ethnic organizations and daily activities carried on within ethnic communities that extended from neighborhoods to the workplace." It is thus a process of self-incorporation—and one not entirely free of conflict and tension—into the broader social American environment that may well possess some application to the experience of Norwegian immigrants in west-central Minnesota.[48]

ETHNIC LIFE AND THE COMMUNITY

During the early decades of its existence, the village of Benson gave clear evidence that the Norwegian American temporal sphere more so than the sacred exhibited a nearly spontaneous pattern of incorporation and gained broad acceptance in the public life of the village. Indeed, in the civil arena urban practices set the tone for the entire Norwegian community. The observance of May 17, Norway's Constitution Day, or Independence Day, if you will—the most prominent of all celebratory ethnic events—was, for example, from the beginning a community affair in Benson, though one sponsored by local Norwegian organizations. In large metropolitan areas, such as Minneapolis, Chicago, and Brooklyn, May 17 observances to a much higher degree from the 1880s assumed a role as the major symbol of Norwegian ethnicity and heralded a period of strong ethnic self-assertion. From the middle of that decade a colorful parade by Norwegian societies and clubs marked the day in Chicago, and in time a large program in Humboldt Park in the central Norwegian district became the highlight of the extensive May 17 festivities; a separate children's procession (*barnetog*) became a distinctive part of the Chicago celebrations, adopted from the practice introduced in Norway by the famed author and poet Bjørnstjerne Bjørnson. To quote from *A Century of Urban Life:* "In 1890 an observer wrote from 'the corner of May and Ohio streets' that 2,000 noisily rejoicing youngsters had passed 'with a flag in their hands, a smile on their lips, and joy in their souls, shouting hurrah and singing.'" In Chicago then, the day was observed as an exclusive ethnic event rather than, as in Benson, a community affair, and the Chicago observance had few non-Norwegian elements. Part of the explanation is that in urban Norwegian colonies public life more and more fell under the influence of a rising class of professionals and businessmen. As ethnic leaders—many of them American-born Norwegians—they gained recognition within the larger urban political and economic world. "The American-born generations," as the author states elsewhere, "would have a greater concern for ethnicity than those born in Norway since it for them to a higher degree became a means of interacting with American society and of establishing acceptable credentials."⁴⁹

Circumstances were simpler in the village setting, and the inclusive nature of the festivities, as the day took on a local color and became a regular feature of village life, made an introduction of common American celebratory practices natural. Even so, May 17 persisted in the small-town setting as a recognized ethnic social institution and a part of Norwegian American folkways. The ethnic impulse remained strong, evidenced in the Norwegian societies that saw the light of day during Benson's early history. The Society Norden (*Foreningen "Norden"*) was organized in April or May 1876—in the centennial year of American independence—with an impressive membership of eighty-three in order to arrange May 17 festivities. In the annals of Norwegian American history these festivities would be among the earliest celebrations of shared historical memories relating to May 17; the initial observance in Benson displayed a greater loyalty, as one might expect, to transplanted Norwegian traditions than would later be the case. The omnipresent Thomas Knudson was elected president and reported to *Budstikken* that "Festivities will be very grand to be this far in the West."

Both *Budstikken* and the *Benson Times* gave a full report of this first commemoration of May 17, *Syttende mai,* as Norwegians referred to the day. The latter newspaper explained to its readers, "On that day in 1814, the Danish yoke was thrown off, and [Norwegians] have been a free people since." It described a long procession that marched east along the tracks and then turned and marched back again to a designated grove for the May 17 program outside the village limits: "The American and Norwegian flags, which had floated upon the same breeze all morning from the top of [Theodore] Hansen's store, were borne near the head of the column, and gave quite a military and patriotic appearance." As the procession passed the windows of the newspaper, "they stopped and gave us three cheers." The *Benson Times* estimated that from seven to eight hundred people listened to the prominent lawyer John W. Arctander address the crowd in Norwegian, which the newspaper reporter admitted "we don't forstore [understand]." The main speaker was Ole Syvertson of Big Stone County; Walter Foland, editor of the *Benson Times,* also addressed the assembly. The festivities ended with "a large ball at Hansen's new building"; in the evening "rockets and roman candles were sent on journeys toward the moon." The ethnic emphasis of the day-long observance does not appear to have dampened the community spirit; Knud Frovold reported to *Budstikken* that "the harmony and enjoyment that prevailed during the festivities will long be remembered."[50]

May 17 was observed in some fashion in the following years, but later celebrations were not as consistently grand as the first; the Society Norden appears to have lost some of its initial fervor. In 1881 the *Benson Times* reported an obvious lack of interest, since the newspaper had seen only one Norwegian flag raised on May 17 and no celebration. The devastating fire in August of the previous year may be partly to blame: the heavily damaged business owned by Thomas Knudson, president of the Society Norden, was that spring "closed by his creditors," and the Norwegian community was consequently robbed of its most enthusiastic leadership. The Norwegian Larken Society was organized in 1876. It does not appear to have been active long, but its Grand New Year's Ball that year as described in the *Benson Times* gives vivid insight into early social activity among Norwegians in Benson. Larken arranged the "grand dance" at Larson's Hall, decorated with the colors of Norway and the United States. Bakke's String Band provided the music, and the newspaper insisted that "it has not been excelled by any music we have ever heard at a ball in Benson." Larken also had literary interests, and in January "a large audience" listened to John W. Arctander give "a select reading from the Old Norse." The *Benson Times* commented, "This society is setting a good example and one which we commend to our American citizens, by starting a lecture course."[51]

The Norwegian societies were founded by an immigrant business elite that socialized with Benson's commercial leaders of all nationalities. The local press clearly wished to be on good terms with these influential individuals. Early in the town's history there were women's societies, such as the Scandinavian Ladies Sewing Society, organized in the early 1880s; to raise money for its causes it sold articles of handwork and arranged public oyster dinners. Indeed, oyster, rather than the later ethnic foods of lutefisk and *lefse,* was the most common dish at public events sponsored by churches and societies, regardless of national background. Like the more recent lutefisk suppers, they had fund-raising as a major purpose. "If anybody knows how to get a good dish of oysters it is the Scandinavian ladies," the *Benson Times* reported.[52]

Interest in literary pursuits obviously existed: the Society Fram (*Foreningen Fram*) organized in December 1882 as a literary society. Otto J. Olsen was elected temporary president, later replaced by the inveterate Thomas Knudson; the other officers represented successful Norwegian men of commerce. The society was "made up of intelligent men and women," as the *Benson Times* reported, and was "composed of some of our best and most highly respected citizens."[53]

The Society Fram, meaning "forward," functioned well beyond its literary objectives. Perhaps inspired by the Benson Dramatic Company, which regularly had successful productions, Fram created its own dramatic troupe to present Norwegian plays which were shown in other towns, among these Morris, Glenwood, and Willmar. Its town hall production in 1884 of C. P. Riis's popular *Til sæters* (To the Mountains), with its splendid medley of folk songs and its nationalistic emphasis, was well received. The *Benson Times* reported on all theatrical entertainments, whether in English or Norwegian, but had to admit in its review of *Til sæters* that "We of course cannot understand but a few words of the play, but from the manner in which it was enjoyed . . . by those who could, the Scandinavian auditors . . . may look forward to a pleasant entertaining time."[54]

In 1883 the Society Fram arranged a spectacular May 17 observance on the fair grounds in Benson. From this time, the festivities assume an obvious American slant. Most striking is the participation by prominent Benson citizens with no connection to Norway and the introduction of events more common to July Fourth observances. One might speculate that an unexpressed motive was to promote business by attracting Norwegian rural families to town. Indeed, this concern might, at least in part, have encouraged the broad participation by businessmen of all ethnic backgrounds. Old-stock Americans C. R. Colby and E. E. Stone constituted the reception committee. The Hancock Brass Band played, Benson Fire Engine Company No. 1 entered into the pageant with a horsedrawn fire engine "under the skillful guidance of Luke Keefe," Frank M. Thornton was one of three marshals, and there were sack races, wheelbarrow races—the latter arranged by Italian-born John Brambilla and Norwegian-born Ole Jacobson—and finally a greased pig race. The festivities attracted many from the country so that "crowds of sight-seers with fresh hats and ribbons and holiday dresses could be

seen upon the boulevards and congregated about Stone & Hand's pea-
nut roaster." But of course, it was a *Norwegian* event.

At the fair grounds the Norwegian-born state representative Ole O.
Lien spoke to "the Scandinavian people" and "held forth to them in
the Norwegian tongue for quite awhile." The paper continued: "In the
evening a dance was given in the town hall and the Norwegian ladies
society tendered refreshments." Even though rain had put a damper
on the festivities so that, according to the *Benson Times*, it was not an
"unbounded success," the program and the extensive community participation assumed the semblance of an ethnic festival—a celebratory
exposition much like the patriotic July Fourth festivities regularly sponsored by the village or even like the community character of present-day
May 17 observances—rather than evidence of ethnic self-assertion. A
major difference is the fact that the 1883 celebration was arranged by
first-generation Norwegians—not, as in the current situation, by their
distant descendants—making the original Norwegian impulse stronger and more visible. Even so, the inclusive community accord at this
particular ethnic event may, everything being equal, have more to say
about the dynamics of social interaction in a small town than of ethnicity on parade.[55]

COUNTRY TOWN APOTHEOSIS

The village of Benson can claim to have achieved its essence, its ideal status, as a central urban place for Norwegians in west-central Minnesota
by the end of the 1880s. With relatively larger Norwegian presences,
Starbuck and Madison emerged in that decade to achieve a similar status well before the end of the century.

Though dominant, Norwegians were not the only nationalities to
make these towns and the farming communities they served their home.
During the first two decades of Benson's history a Yankee elite controlled the financial institutions, provided professional expertise, and
had a strong voice in administrative affairs. But that reality was, as this
chapter shows, not the whole story. Benson can obviously be described
as a "Norwegian" town in terms of the large local population and the
central place it constituted for an extensive Norwegian rural hinterland.
And, indeed, Norwegians accepted their civic duty and entered public

office; taking advantage of resident compatriots' needs, they became a dominant force in the commercial landscape. Family stability and ethnic segregation preserved community life, albeit within a larger American matrix that required adjustment to new circumstances and redefinition of the bonds of family, community, and church.

The Norwegian Lutheran church, expressing itself in two competing expositions, influenced greatly the civic morals and virtuous ordinances that set boundaries for public conduct. The church by necessity defined itself as a voluntary organization and thus departed greatly from the homeland's state institution; it expressed its opinions on moral and political issues encountered only in the new environment. Lacking a secular authority to guarantee its official position as a state church, discipline within the congregational fold was achieved through a strict Puritanism imposed by a dominant clergy that saw a threat to the homeland's Lutheran creed, not only in the mix of competing faiths in America's religious marketplace but also from the hostile denominationalism within its own faith. If we should consider, as many have, the Lutheran church among Norwegians in America a daughter to the Church of Norway, it should at least be described as "a vivacious daughter," as Pastor H. A. Preus called the Norwegian Synod as early as 1867.[56]

An obvious ethnocentric strength did not prevent participation in community and civic activities; indeed, American citizenship and ethnic life, as stated earlier, coexisted and mutually benefited each other. They were, as Jon Gjerde writes, complementary identities. The community character of the celebration of May 17, the main Norwegian ethnic festival, suggests the circle of identities in which Norwegians and their fellow citizens maneuvered; it also evidences the emergence of a redefined sense of community and a shared identity based on landscape and place. It has been claimed that people carry within them a sense of place, the images of a geographical landscape engraved from childhood, regardless of distance from the place of their birth. This sense of place provides belonging and comfort. Norwegians certainly harbored the memorable images of the fjord or mountain valley they had left; in time it became an imagined and primordial home that fueled ethnocentric emotions. Even so, their life on the prairie and in the country town, with those unmatched prairie images, was a reality they had in common with the region's other inhabitants and which encouraged a local identity founded on the new place and landscape. Even if the immigrants could not in their hearts abandon the legacy of the dramatic scenery they had departed, they were part of a process that would make Benson and west-central Minnesota the place that gave a shared identity of landscape and place and a secure sense of belonging to generations to come.[57]

Four

Towns of a Common Heritage

A Comparative View

Starbuck in Pope County and Madison in Lac qui Parle County in this chapter enter more systematically and with greater attention to empirical knowledge into an analysis of "Norwegian" country towns in west-central Minnesota. Their strong Norwegian presence becomes a probative of how representative Benson in Swift County is as a country town with a common immigrant heritage. Different ethnic groups, as they spread into the Upper Midwest, became dominant in trading centers located in their regions of heavy settlement. One may therefore speak of "German" towns, "Irish" towns, "Swedish" towns, and the like, each with its own unique ethnic identity. And there were many "Norwegian" towns. Beginning in northern Illinois, from thence to Wisconsin, and onward to Iowa and Minnesota and beyond, small commercial centers sprang up in areas of Norwegian settlement. They became central places and took on a distinct Norwegian coloring.

The three towns under scrutiny consequently fall into a common pattern. Before taking a comparative look at these three "Norwegian" towns, we might illustrate the general situation by broadening the view to include additional examples from western Minnesota. This region is rich in small urban areas with large Norwegian populations. The anniversary histories published to celebrate advancement mostly make little note of the ethnic composition of these hamlets, villages, and cities or of the nationality of the original settlers. The names of pioneers and leading citizens, however, give evidence of immigration's dominant role in their founding and growth. These celebratory narratives, frequently recording bombastic claims to greatness, nevertheless provide precious insights into the drama of nation building on the frontier; adding an interpretive ethnic component will surely further elucidate their past as well as their current juncture in history.

Town boosters harbored great dreams. In early 1871, John H. Brown, editor of the *Willmar Republican*, the first newspaper published in the Kandiyohi County town, reported on the introduction in the state legislature of "a bill for the removal of the capitol from St. Paul to the capital lands in Kandiyohi county," having in an earlier editorial declared, "Fate and fortune have united in pronouncing the unalterable decree that the future capital of the state of Minnesota" is to be located in that county. Settlers were needed, whatever the future held in regard to capturing the state capital; the *Republican* boasted, "we need but to inform the immigrants of the advantages of this location to make Kandiyohi one of the great farming counties of the state in a very short space of time."[1]

Minnesota would continue to be administered from St. Paul. The rapidly growing village of Willmar, having the advantage of being located at the end of the railroad division, instead entered into a bitter fight over the county seat with Kandiyohi Station, the temporary seat, before securing that status in late 1871. In 1880 there were 1,002 inhabitants, a number that by the turn of the century had increased to 3,409. Of the latter, 1,070, or 31.4 percent, were either first- or second-generation Norwegians. The Swedish stock actually surpassed the Norwegian, numbering 1,118, or 32.8 percent of the city's residents. A strong Scandinavian presence is suggested by the names of men active in local politics: the most prominent Norwegian-born persons at that time were likely Andrew Railson, from Krødsherad by Lake Krøderen in Buskerud County, who served in the state House and later in the Senate; Lars O. Thorpe, from Kvam in Hardanger, state senator and prominent businessman; and the prosperous lawyer J. W. Arctander, born in Stockholm, Sweden, of Norwegian parents. The 1870 census indicates that 53 percent of Kandiyohi's 3,161 residents were foreign born; Norwegians and Swedes, listed as a single category, were by far the most numerous, accounting for 86 percent of all foreign-born residents.

Another example is the tiny country village of Sunburg in Norway Lake Township. Sunburg Lutheran Church, organized in 1876 and located in the middle of a large Scandinavian population, was one of the congregations served by Pastor Severin Almklov of Benson. The foreign born in 1870 constituted 67 percent of the township settlers, nearly all Norwegian. If the second generation is added, the 1900 census shows that the township was 95 percent Norwegian in a population totaling 708. Even today Sunburg remains a Norwegian enclave.[2]

The village of Glenwood in Pope County, located east of Lake Minnewaska, was originally laid out—with assistance—by A.W. Lathrop, who arrived there in 1866 and served as county attorney before moving to Benson. Glenwood became the county seat and another center of Norwegian activity. It was only incorporated in 1881 but by 1900 had 1,116 citizens. Norwegian immigrants and their children, the Norwegian stock, numbered 463—41.5 percent of the population. Glenwood adopted its first city charter in 1912, receiving, as the charter states, "all the general powers possessed by municipal corporations."[3]

Granite Falls Village, incorporated in 1879 in Yellow Medicine County and by 1900 extending into Chippewa County, may be included in a list of "Norwegian" towns; of its 578 citizens in 1880 about 37 percent were either Norwegian immigrants or their children. By 1900 nearly half—48 percent—of its 1,213 citizens fell into that category. The village of Milan, incorporated in 1893 in Chippewa County's Kragero Township, had an even greater Norwegian presence: in 1900, 82.3 percent of the town's 396 citizens were Norwegian. According to the state census figures, Chippewa County in 1905 had 1,766 Norwegian immigrants and 4,688 American-born Norwegians; combined they constituted 46.8 percent of the county's 13,356 residents.[4]

How representative are these towns? In fact, any one of these small urban centers in western Minnesota might have replaced Benson as a case study of the Norwegian country-town experience. The list could easily have been expanded to include many other "Norwegian" towns; these, in the manner of other towns on the American frontier, exemplify Ray Allen Billington's vision of a rapidly expanding urban frontier.[5]

THE VILLAGE OF STARBUCK IN POPE COUNTY

Agricultural settlement preceded Billington's urban frontier. Replicating the Swift County story though arriving earlier, Norwegian pioneers were among the first to claim land in the neighboring county to the north. Again, the historical record supports the immigrants' pioneering activities in western Minnesota as they responded to the promises set down in the 1862 Homestead Act as well as to speculators and assorted settlement promoters. "Pope County settlement history began in the spring of 1862 when four Norwegian emigrant families took homesteads near Lake Johanna," declares a historical plaque erected in 1999 in Fort Lake Johanna Historical Park, founded on a small portion of the homestead of one of these pioneer settlers. The first permanent settler in the county, however, is held to be the Norwegian Olaus Olson Grove, "a trapper and hunter who squatted in 1861 on Lot 1, Section 2 in Barsness Township." The pioneers by Lake Johanna were Ole Kittelson Ovretvedt and wife Betsy from Setesdal and John Johnson Sandvig and wife Ingeborg, Gregar Halvorson Stordahl and wife Svanaug, and Salve Oleson Gakkestad and wife Kjersti, all from Telemark. They abandoned their frontier dwellings that fall because of the Dakota War but a few years later returned to the homes they had left in what today is Lake Johanna Township. The same plaque relates that resettlement of the area in 1865 and renewed threat of hostilities resulted in the building of Fort Lake Johanna, one in a series of crude military posts to defend against possible Indian attacks. The fort never saw action and was abandoned after a few months.

A much-celebrated early settler is Urjans Iverson, born in Ulvik in the Hardanger district of Norway in 1833. His odyssey in the New World typifies that of many of his compatriots. He immigrated to Spring Grove, Wisconsin, in 1853 and four years later married Brita Monsdatter Thorsness from Balestrand in Sogn. The two moved to Pope County with their children in 1866; there, close to the present Fort Lake Johanna Park, Iverson built a home with oak logs from the fort. The Iverson family owned land both in Lake Johanna and in neighboring Gilchrist Township; the family moved on in 1868, but the Iverson cabin through the years served as a school, church, and farm blacksmith shop. Restored in 1991, it is a monument to the demands, as well as the crudity and simplicity, of frontier life.[6]

Urjans Iverson and his family arrived the year the county was organized, named for General John Pope of Civil War fame. Organization occurred on September 4, 1866, at Stockholm in Gilchrist Township. In 1868 Iverson became township assessor; under frontier conditions—and in a population consisting heavily of fellow Scandinavians—immigrants

Andrew Andersen Tofte clears land with a team of oxen near Madison, Lac qui Parle County, ca. 1880.

could quickly enter into public life and, in fact, often had little choice but to assume responsibility for local affairs. Stockholm, located on the north end of Scandinavian Lake, never became the county seat as the men who organized the county in a small log cabin above the lake had intended; that honor, granted by legislative action at the 1866 fall elections, came to Glenwood by Lake Minnewaska. Pope County had a small population; in 1870 it was home to only 2,691 residents, a circumstance that gave ambitious men opportunity to advance materially as well as politically.[7]

During the next thirty years the total population grew to 12,577, thanks in large part to immigration. In 1900, 30 percent of its residents had been born outside the borders of the United States; the Norwegian-born were by far the largest group, numbering 19.3 percent of the county's population. Norwegians clustered in clearly defined areas and were a dominant population element. Other ethnic groups were small. The second-largest group, the Swedish-born, formed 5.1 percent of the county's residents; the Canadians as the third largest equaled 2.2 percent; and the Germans, as the fourth-largest foreign-born group, made up only 1.2 percent. If the children of immigrants are included, the Norwegian stock in Pope County, according to the state census of 1905, that year rose to 64.8 percent of the total population.[8]

As in Swift County, the forces of kin and regional cultural loyalties strongly influenced patterns of clustering and settlement among Norwegian homesteaders. The 125-year history of East and West Zion Lutheran churches contains the illustrative and intriguing story of the Aslakson family's immigration from Valdres, Norway, to the American frontier in the years 1868 to 1871, a reminder of the family character of the western movement and the strategies that assured survival and eventual success. Haldor Aslakson, Sr., and his sister Olena arrived in 1868, nineteen and fourteen years old, respectively. They came by way of Quebec and made their way to their uncle in Monroe, Wisconsin. The following year they were able to bring over the rest of the family, including their parents, Aslak Haldorson, age forty-eight, and Ingrid, forty-seven, and their seven siblings, Haldor Jr., Dorothea, Jorend, Knud, John, Ingrid, and Anna. In 1871 the large family moved to Hoff Township in Pope County, where Aslak and Ingrid homesteaded. Their nine children, in accordance with Norwegian practice, took the patronymic Aslakson, and all settled on farms in Hoff and Langhei townships. Eight of the nine children raised families ranging in size from seven to thirteen children for a total of seventy-three—the nineteenth century was indeed "the century of large families." In America land was cheap but labor expensive, making the farmer more dependent on the core family for labor. A large family was consequently a great blessing. The Aslakson clan illustrated the advantage of having many children to assist in farm work as well as an inborn ability to re-create on the American frontier a comforting and secure environment. Having children placed on land close to the original homestead was a reassuring corollary. Many similar examples exist.[9]

A map of Pope County prepared by Calvin E. Pederson of Starbuck indicates *bygd* concentrations of Norwegians, which he describes as a "Norse Invasion" via Norway Lake in Kandiyohi County as well as from other counties to the east and southeast. There were clusterings of people from Sogn in Barsness, Chippewa Falls, and Glenwood townships in the central part of the county and in New Prairie, White Bear, and Walden townships along its western border. Immigrants from Valdres were most heavily settled in Nora, Blue Mounds, Hoff, and Langhei townships, with a Trønder enclave in the latter. Other Trønder settlements existed in Barsness, adjoining a settlement of immigrants from Setesdal in that and adjacent townships; the largest Trønder settlement was found

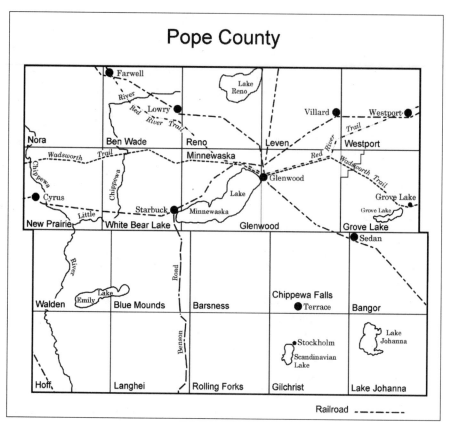

Pope County

Map of Pope County Townships

north of Lake Minnewaska. West and south of the lake settlers from Gudbrandsdalen dominated; eastward along the south shore there were Halling settlements; and Nordfjord settlements extended south to Swift County in Rolling Forks Township. Starbuck, located in White Bear Lake Township at the foot of Lake Minnewaska, was thus founded in a district with large populations of people who hailed from Gudbrandsdalen and Trøndelag.[10]

Trønders were among the first settlers in the Starbuck area, arriving in July 1867 by ox-drawn covered wagons from Iowa. The pioneer party included Nels B. Wollan, Bernt C. Wollan, Anton Holte, and Andrew Schey; their families joined them later. From 1869 until the Northern Pacific Railway arrived in 1882, the community was known as White Bear

Center or the Wollan Settlement on the Wadsworth Trail—which ran from St. Cloud to Fort Wadsworth—about three miles north of the present city of Starbuck in White Bear Lake Township. It was located on the farm site of Nels Wollan, who operated a general store and post office on his property. In all eight Wollan brothers—from the Steinkjer region in Trøndelag—farmed there, giving the settlement its name. Their two sisters joined them and married Norwegian farmers in the area. This farming community largely created of close kin—a step beyond simple *bygd* loyalties—may be seen as a poignant, even dramatic, example of one family's strategy to create security and familiar surroundings under crude frontier conditions.[11]

The village of Starbuck was platted in spring 1882 and incorporated in June 1883. In 1975 Starbuck, retaining the original village charter with its revisions over the years, became a statutory city as listed in the *Minnesota Legislative Manual*. The village continued to be settled by Norwegian immigrants and American-born Norwegians. By 1900 its population had grown to 469: 65.9 percent were of Norwegian stock, 14.7 percent of Swedish, and 1.7 percent of Danish. In comparison, Benson's residents were 42.9 percent Norwegian, 11.6 percent Swedish, and 1.8 percent Danish. Both towns, despite differences in populations and percentages of ethnic residents—Benson being the less Norwegian—obviously were not only immigrant laden but also predominantly Scandinavian.

In spite of Starbuck's greater youth, both towns were by 1900 established communities; their full populations had a nearly balanced sex ratio. Considering only Starbuck's total Norwegian population, there were, as was the case for Benson, significantly more women than men. Employment variables, keeping in mind the solid Norwegian farming communities in Starbuck's upland, may explain the greater likelihood for men to live in the countryside, where they entered farming, and for women to live in town, where they engaged in domestic and service jobs. The men very likely came to town to court the Norwegian women who had moved there. The Norwegian language was maintained in the village and in its hinterland to an equal degree; in this regard there was not the disparity in Benson and its surrounding townships that in time existed between Norwegian townspeople and their country cousins. Even though Norwegians were the largest nationality in Benson, its greater

Eight Wollan brothers and two sisters populated the Wollan Settlement. Nels (Nils) and Casper were prominent ethnic leaders and businessmen. Michael distinguished himself in local and state politics. Their parents, Benjamin and Bereth Wollan, joined their children in America.

cultural and religious diversity compared to Starbuck allowed English to intrude more easily into the daily life of all residents. Starbuck to a higher degree than Benson consequently qualifies as a place defined as "a localization of culture," a notion developed by historian Kathleen Conzen in her study of Germans in Stearns County. Like the Germans, Norwegians in Starbuck and in its hinterland to a great extent chartered the local culture; Norwegian culture may be said to have permeated all aspects of the local community. One might even claim that Norwegian ethnic institutions, habits, and views reshaped and influenced circumstances and values in the broader society.[12]

DEMOGRAPHICS, OCCUPATIONS, AND BUSINESS

The demographic characteristics of Norwegian residents in Starbuck and Benson—as well as in Madison—as given in the 1900 federal census are strikingly similar, with only a few easily explained differences. The clear implication is that by the turn of the twentieth century—demographically speaking—a homogeneous and youthful Norwegian community existed in west-central Minnesota. The Norwegian immigrant generation, viewed separately, had a nearly balanced sex ratio, suggesting that many Norwegians had emigrated as married couples or had been joined by spouses after settling in America. Before 1900 there were thus, as recorded in the federal census, few cases of intermarriage for Norwegian immigrants in the communities and towns under consideration. The two villages showed similar age structures and marriage rates; 61.9 percent of the Norwegian stock above age fourteen in Starbuck were or had been married, whereas the percentage for Benson was 58. The residents were young people and had rapidly growing families, making the overall median age for Norwegians 23.5 years in Benson and 23.6 in Starbuck. If one considers the immigrants separately, their median age was identical in both villages, namely 38.7 years; the majority of Norwegian immigrants had arrived before 1888 and were thus older. Employment opportunities attracted people to town, from the surrounding farming communities and from abroad, and convinced those born in town to seek their livelihood there.

Occupations available to Norwegian men in Benson and Starbuck differed somewhat, though in both cases there was a heavy partiality toward common labor. Timing of arrival may explain the variations that existed. In Benson, 56 percent of Norwegian immigrants arrived in the 1880s, whereas in Starbuck only 47 percent of the Norwegian born came during that same decade. By adding the immigration that occurred the first five years of the 1890s, the main era of Norwegian immigration—1880 to 1894—is covered. Only 8 percent of Norwegian-born residents arrived in Benson in the early 1890s, but Starbuck's percentage rose to nearly 16. The smaller wave of Norwegian immigrants that came before 1874 represented about 20 percent of the Norwegian population in both villages and served as the initial link in a chain migration that exploded in the 1880s. In 1900, because of their large recently transplanted populations, many men in Benson, and proportionately more in Starbuck, were employed in working-class occupations. The disparity between the two villages may be explained in part by the relatively larger arrival of Norwegian newcomers—"greenhorns"—in Starbuck than in Benson in the century's final decade. However, a great number of men in both villages did become craftsmen. Madison, for a variety of reasons to be discussed later, presented a somewhat different occupational profile. Starbuck had in percentages even fewer Norwegian professionals than did Benson, figures explained by its smaller size and more working class–centered farm economy as well as by the more recent immigration; many listed as laborers worked as farm laborers, a category that is larger in Starbuck than in Benson. Furthermore, Benson's status as county seat created white-collar positions for its residents of all ethnic backgrounds.[13]

As in Benson, Starbuck's local businessmen catered to the farming communities in its hinterland: its centennial history explains, "the surrounding country is thickly settled by an intelligent and well-to-do class of farmers, and Starbuck therefore, does an extensive business." Norwegians' active participation in small businesses as managers and proprietors, in Starbuck equaling 23.7 percent of working-age men, indicates, as it does in Benson, the preferences and power of a Norwegian rural and village clientele. This category was, however, in percentages smaller in Benson than in Starbuck, only 15.8 percent of working-age males, which suggests the greater impact—both in every-day affairs and in business—Starbuck's proportionately much larger Norwegian population had. The data gives the clear impression that Norwegians in Benson took part "in the community in more 'back door' ways," researcher David LaVigne suggests, as sales and service workers, whereas a heavily concentrated Norwegian population in Starbuck and its environs assured a greater commercial as well as cultural dominance within village limits.[14]

Pioneer business ventures testified to the farm-directed economy. According to the centennial history, "In 1884 Axel G. Englund was a local agent for Mc-Cormick Deering. He sold farm machinery of various kinds. Later he and Martin Ness had a hardware store. Alfred Nordstrom began to do carpenter work in the village in 1883. Andrew Saglie built the first store and A. P. Nygaard painted it." Three of these pioneers carry Norwegian names and two Swedish. Englund, a colorful character known as "King Swede," was especially prominent in the local business community; besides operating his store in Starbuck he was involved in land business, owned a grain elevator, and installed a printing press; the *Starbuck Times*, appearing in December 1898, was printed on Englund's press.

Other business enterprises to serve the community were launched in the early years, nearly all with a Scandinavian, or most frequently a Norwegian, owner and manager. Glenwood's Fremad Store, also known as the Wollan Store, was a continuation of the modest business Nels Wollan had started on his farm. The store was incorporated in 1874 as the Fremad Association by the entire Wollan clan, the eight brothers and two sisters; for half a century it was Glenwood's main mercantile, a department store carrying a wide variety of merchandise. Nels Wollan moved from Glenwood to Starbuck in 1882 as the Northern Pacific was coming there, and the association opened the Fremad Store in Starbuck. Another prominent pioneer businessman, Aage Peterson, having earlier partnered with Wollan, managed the store. In its very name the store strongly advertised a Norwegian commercial presence; meaning "onward" or "forward," *fremad* is a common ethnic appellation for a variety of societies and organizations.[15]

The Lutheran Church in Starbuck

The Norwegian Lutheran church in the village of Starbuck enjoyed an even greater superiority than Norwegian business enterprise; indeed, it had a near religious monopoly, though it was not unified but in fact split into warring synodical factions. Benson and Madison showed a much greater denominational diversity, while Starbuck became the domain of Norwegian American Lutheranism. The two Norwegian Lutheran churches founded in the village evolved in familiar ways; they became preeminent ethnic institutions with a social as well as a religious function. Beginnings for all Lutheran congregations in the West were consistently modest; growth might lead to divisions and the founding of new congregations, either because of distance or, not infrequently, controversy. In August 1869 the much-traveled missionary pastor Nils O. Brandt held a service at White Bear Lake where eight children were baptized. The Wollan Settlement or White Bear Center just north of Starbuck was, of course, the pioneer community that existed before the village's platting in 1882. The people Brandt had gathered the following year organized the Indherred Congregation, its name indicating the part of Trøndelag—the districts in the inner part of the Trondheimsfjord—that most of the settlers had left.[16]

Indherred Congregation in 1875 joined the Norwegian Synod, which had a strong position in Pope County. Other Norwegian Lutheran churches near Starbuck chose the same synodical affiliation: Immanuel, organized in 1872, St. John's (*St. Johannes menighet*), organized in 1875, and East and West Zion in 1883. The last two resulted from a division of the Zion congregation, organized in 1871, due to distance. All these churches were located within a manageable radius of Starbuck.

Soon after Starbuck's founding, this time within the village limits, competition to the Synod arose from opposing Norwegian Lutheran synods that sought entrance into the area. In 1883 an effort was made to establish Hauge's Congregation of Pope County (*Hauges menighet av Pope County*) in Starbuck, but, according to O. M. Norlie, it was dissolved in 1886. In 1887, however, some of the same adherents to a low-church practice joined with other Norwegians to organize the Minnewaska Norwegian Evangelical Lutheran Congregation with forty members. It did not join Hauge's Synod but instead the broad-church Conference, then in 1890 the newly formed United Church (*Den forenede kirke*), and in 1896 the Lutheran Free Church (*Den lutherske frikirke*). The small congregation in the 1890s shared the services of Pastor Paul Winther with another small congregation in Morris in Stevens County. Winther, born in Hamarøy in Salten in northern Norway in 1862, immigrated in 1882 and, like Pastor Severin Almklov, received his theological training at Augsburg Seminary in Minneapolis. Then the seminary of the Conference, in 1897 Augsburg was linked to the Lutheran Free Church. The renamed Minnewaska Lutheran Free Church thus fell into an extreme free-church arrangement, establishing unrestrained congregational autonomy as adopted by that church body. It has been argued that this attitude reflected Norway's democratic spirit and the Liberal political movement that gained strength in the 1880s. Church leaders in the Lutheran Free Church were also encouraged by the religious awakenings they were associated with in Norway and which they encountered in the spirit of Protestant evangelization in America.[17]

The liturgical mode of Norwegian American Lutheranism expressed itself in the Fron Congregation (*Fron menighet*), a member of the Norwegian Synod and the second church to locate in Starbuck village. The congregation bore the name of the Gudbrandsdalen district from which many members had emigrated. It was nearly inevitable that the high-church persuasion would establish an institutional presence. The Norwegian Synod's orthodox, Bible-based indoctrination of its membership distanced it from the more democratic and liberal stirrings within Norwegian American Lutheranism. The Fron Congregation in Starbuck was founded in 1888, but its history extends back to 1867, when it was part of other congregations, first in Terrace and then in White Bear Lake. Before the actual founding, services were conducted in the schoolhouse by Pastor Magnus M. Koefod, who also served other congregations, including Indherred. In 1887 his brother, Pastor Hans Oluf Koefod, accepted a call to serve the congregation; his ministry lasted from the founding of the Fron Congregation the following year until 1922—a period of thirty-four years. The brothers were born in Kristiansund, Norway: Magnus immigrated in 1869, when twenty-one years old, and received his theological training at the German Missouri Synod Concordia Seminary in St. Louis in 1872–74; Hans immigrated only in 1880 at age thirty-four and in 1880–82 was trained at the Synod's own seminary, fully established in the years 1876–78 in Madison, Wisconsin. The separate training institutions speak to an epoch in Norwegian Lutheran church history in America, when the Norwegian Synod was closely associated with the stagnant theology of the Missouri Synod, an alliance that many have deplored as strengthening conservative attitudes.[18]

Congregational life gathered many impulses from American religious conventions. The early founding of Ladies Aid (*Kvindeforening*), Youth Society (*Ungdomsforening*), Young Women's Society (*Pikeforening*), and Singing Society (*Sangforening*) in the Minnewaska and Fron congregations as well as in other area Norwegian churches bears witness to close congregational relations and social activities, regardless of doctrinal differences. These activities also suggest redefinition of the church's social responsibility within the Norwegian American community. The congregational societies give evidence of common practices adopted in American churches that at the time were absent in the congregations of the homeland's state church. Women's and other religious societies did exist outside the parish churches in the low-churchly meetinghouses and were thus not entirely unknown to Norwegian immigrants. However, the great increase and diversity of such groups in America made visible how the Norwegian Lutheran church responded to the new demands placed on it as an immigrant institution. For its members, the congregation became an ethnic sanctuary; from their Norwegian haven filled with numerous social, educational, and on occasion even commercial activities, it may be presumed that they easily moved beyond its bounds to interact with the larger society.

In the local small-town environment of Starbuck and in the surrounding farming communities, the strong presence of fellow Norwegians blurred, or even suppressed, the cultural differences between the sacred and the profane worlds. The congregation was not an insular cosmos, but through the force of tradition it could influence the lives of Norwegians beyond its member communicants; even non-Norwegians in a Norwegian-dominated town such as Starbuck were subject to its social import. Prominent church members played a significant role in business and in civic affairs. Nels B. Wollan, active in the Indherred Lutheran Church and one of its organizers, exemplifies the convergence of ethnic loyalty and religious belief with social assertiveness. An 1888 biographical sketch says the following about the Starbuck resident and successful businessman: "He has always taken a deep interest in public matters and has at different times held about all of the township and school district offices, and also served for four years as a member of the board of county commissioners, making a most efficient and capable officer." The writer further states that Wollan was active in organizing Starbuck and in securing its village charter and that he "was elected president of the council in 1884, and is now a member of that body."

Timothy Smith's emphasis on the pervasive relationship between ethnic identification and religion among immigrants may provide some insight into the role of the latter. Smith interpreted this relationship as a process by which ethnic groups mobilized to pursue political and economic agendas. In Smith's view, religious leaders were looked upon by adherents as "agents of progress" and change, not simply as preservers of tradition, and, to quote from John Bodnar's explanation, "By intensifying the 'psychic' basis of religious commitment through association with an ethnic past . . . immigrants could believe they were a 'pilgrim people' legitimately in search of education, upward mobility, and their share of American capitalism." Bodnar questions the basic premise of Smith's argument—assumptions that all religious leaders were in agreement, that they accepted the idea of an association between ethnic identity and religion, and, even more telling, that the middle and working classes had identical convictions. He sees these three assumptions as tenuous at best. Nevertheless, Smith's contention that religious leaders held strong positions, whether or not they are viewed as agents of change, has great merit. Evidence, at least as it applies to the Norwegian immigrant group, suggests a significant and prevailing ethnoreligious identity, a nearly symbiotic relationship between Lutheranism and Norwegian ethnicity that showed a continuous strength. In a study of Norwegian settlements in Wisconsin as recently as the 1950s, Norwegian-born sociologist Peter A. Munch concluded, "it is virtually impossible to distinguish 'Lutheran' from 'Norwegian.'"[19]

Norwegians in Starbuck clearly dominated secular and religious life; the village's two churches were both Norwegian Lutheran. Other churches were located beyond the village limits. A Swedish Augustana congregation, the Bethany Lutheran Church—or Bethania in the original Swedish form—founded in 1877, had its own church by Lake Emily in the Swedish settlement some six miles southwest of Starbuck in 1900. The Bethesda Covenant Church broke away from Bethany, dating its beginnings to 1879, and around 1900 similarly had its own church on the lake's north side. The prominent Starbuck physician Carl Rasmus Christenson, of Danish parentage, in 1903 with his wife, Nellie Eleanor

Grant, organized a Congregational Church, since at the time all church services were conducted in Norwegian. The total foreign stock constituted 86.1 percent, making the old stock, or Yankees, who might join the Congregational group 13.9 percent of Starbuck's fewer than 500 residents. And thus, as Christenson's biography relates, "for lack of membership, a resident pastor could not be maintained and the plan of an English-speaking church had to be abandoned."[20]

Conversely, a Norwegian presence was very much in evidence. A localized Norwegian ethnic strength may indeed be said to have permeated the community. Applying the quote to Starbuck and the Norwegian townships in its environs, "Norwegian" might very well replace "German" in the following excerpt from Professor Conzen's article: "The local culture of thrift and non-ostentation . . . and the local standards by which politics were practiced, and honor and status accorded the individual, were molded in a German ethnic matrix, but quickly overflowed its bounds to define the county's values." In Starbuck, the Norwegian language persisted in church and town for several decades, as did a transplanted conservative lifestyle; an imbued striving for respectability and self-reliance—even under severe conditions of poverty and privation—existed, one that is universally present in accounts of Norwegian pioneer life. There was as well a strong culturally defined sense of honesty, personal pride, and integrity in all relationships—"Business was done with a handshake," someone insisted. And Norwegians embraced values of frugality and thrift and a commitment to hard work. A clinician and an anthropologist, both Norwegian American, found in their study of the Norwegian character that in America Norwegians regard social, educational, and monetary success as attainable through hard work and diligence. The two authors also pointed out a characteristic stoicism, a public denial of inadequacy and suffering. Not surprisingly, the study found that emotional expression was strictly controlled and that overt and direct aggression was rare, especially within the family. Family unity and gatherings of extended kin were important, conveying a strong feeling of continuity with the past. This adaptive process, hardly assimilation, extended its influence to local cultural and social values.[21]

In this process of adaptation, the Norwegian Lutheran church in America, in its puritanical zeal, no doubt strove to define what it meant to be a Norwegian American Lutheran and to set boundaries for a proper Christian moral life. The extent to which the church succeeded in its goals—as well as the precise roles of its leaders—is open to debate, but the nearly ubiquitous presence of the church in Norwegian immigrant communities throughout the Upper Midwest is a historic fact, as was the ability of a fractured clergy to engage Norwegians in a debate about the nature of their Lutheran faith, strengthening religious conviction along the way. Starbuck truly qualified as a distinctly Nordic cultural arena, obviously more so than Benson, in which the Norwegian Lutheran church was a conspicuous actor, though on a western American stage. In Starbuck there were the Norwegian places of business, the regular arrival of newcomers from Norway, participation in local political life, and the presence of other Scandinavians—in fact 82.3 percent of Starbuck's citizens in 1900 were either Norwegian, Swedish, or Danish. A local Norwegian cultural world surely existed, even as its habitants and sojourners adapted to the diversity and demands of life in their singular American environment.[22]

TABLE 9

Distribution Amongst Occupational Fields of Working[a] Males Aged 15 to 65 and of Norwegian Ancestry by Village for the Villages of Benson, Madison, and Starbuck, 1900

	Percent Working in Occupational Field		
	Benson	Madison	Starbuck
Professionals	7.5	10.5	3.2
Farmers	2.1	6.4	2.2
Managers, Officials, and Proprietors	15.8	33.1	23.7
Clerical Workers	4.1	2.9	0.0
Sales Workers	16.4	6.4	10.8
Craftsmen	22.6	16.3	25.8
Operatives	4.8	2.9	6.5
Service Workers	8.9	4.1	6.5
Laborers, including Farm Labor	17.8	17.4	21.5
Total (*N*)	100 (146)	100 (172)	100 (93)

Source: U.S. Census, 1900

a. Persons with occupations listed as "at school" or "none" or not specified are excluded from tallies

THE VILLAGE OF MADISON IN LAC QUI PARLE COUNTY

A Norwegian cultural world also evolved in Madison, though the town was less Norwegian than Starbuck, albeit more so than Benson. First- and second-generation Norwegians made up more than half—55.8 percent—of all residents in 1900, when the village had a total population of 1,336, double that of ten years earlier. Its history extended back to the 1880s, when town boosters promoted the village as "The Future Metropolis of Lac qui Parle County." It was located at the county's geographical center on the line of the Wisconsin, Minnesota & Pacific Railroad Company. Hans Andreas Larson has been declared "the father of Madison." He emigrated from the Hønefoss area in the Ringerike district of Norway with his parents, Ole and Maren (Isacsen) Larson, when only four years old; his experience in America, though a native of Norway, was thus that of the second generation. Larson visited the Madison town site area as early as 1868, traveling from the general store

---

TABLE 10

Countries of Origin for Immigrants and Second-Generation Americans in the Villages of Benson, Madison, and Starbuck, 1900[a]

| | Percentage of Population | | | | | | | | |
| | Benson | | | Madison | | | Starbuck | | |
	Immigrant	Second Generation	Total	Immigrant	Second Generation	Total	Immigrant	Second Generation	Total
Canada	2.6	4.0	6.6	0.9	1.5	2.4	0.4	0.4	0.8
Denmark	0.5	1.3	1.8	0.4	0.4	0.8	0.6	1.1	1.7
German Empire	0.7	3.3	4.0	2.0	7.3	9.3	0.4	0.4	0.8
Great Britain	0.6	3.0	3.6	0.4	2.0	2.4	0.2	1.1	1.3
Ireland	1.3	7.5	8.8	0.1	1.1	1.2	0.2	1.3	1.5
Norway	14.6	28.3	42.9	19.2	36.5	55.7	28.4	37.5	65.9
Sweden	4.6	7.0	11.6	2.1	3.4	5.5	5.8	9.0	14.8
Other foreign country	0.1	0.3	0.4	0.2	1.0	1.2	0.0	0.4	0.4
Non-duplicated Totals	25.0	51.0	79.7	25.3	51.2	78.5	36.0	51.2	87.2

Source: U.S. Census, 1900

a. Second generation determined by at least one parent born in country of origin

he operated in Lac qui Parle Village, where he traded with the Native Americans. Larson helped organize the Madison Townsite Company, which in October 1884 filed the village plat. Madison was incorporated the following October; the town organized on a village basis with an elected council and council president. Madison received its city charter in 1902 and elected a mayor, city aldermen, and other officers. As ordained by the city charter, the mayor would not preside at council meetings; Dr. Eric O. Giere was elected to serve as the first city council president. Born in Deerfield, Dane County, Wisconsin, in 1868 to Norwegian immigrant parents, Giere graduated in 1888 from St. Olaf's School—later St. Olaf College—in Northfield, Minnesota, and studied medicine at the University of Minnesota, graduating in 1892. That same year, as a young man of twenty-four, he began his medical practice in Madison.[23]

Madison's founding was, as Benson's, a consequence of the railroad's arrival. Since the track was laid from east to west, it reached Dawson first; Dawson village incorporated in 1884, a year before Madison, and by 1900 had 962 citizens. It exhibited a strong Scandinavian flavor: Norwegians and Swedes made up a large part of the population. In 1900 there were 612 residents of Norwegian stock, 63.6 percent of all citizens, and 101 residents of Swedish stock, 10.5 percent of all residents. Nearly three-quarters of Dawson's citizens were thus Scandinavian. Madison and Dawson competed to become a central place in the county.

The first considerable party of permanent Norwegian settlers into Lac qui Parle County was led by Peter F. Jacobson in 1869. He had emigrated from Hjelmeland in the County of Rogaland together with his parents and siblings to Fayette County, Iowa, in 1857; Jacobson first visited Fort Ridgely "in search of cheap land" in 1867, traveling "with three brothers and some friends." The party he guided two years later consisted of twenty-two heads of families from Winneshiek and Fayette counties, Iowa, mostly, if not all, Norwegians. Martin Ulvestad identifies them as "mainly from the Stavanger and Bergen regions," that is, the counties of Rogaland and Hordaland on the southwest coast of Norway. Jacobson gives an intriguing account of how land for the settlement was selected and how the party fared on the journey west in canvas-covered, ox-drawn wagons. As he preceded the main group to scout for land, he found "The Minnesota river was very high at the time and we got the Indians to take us across the river in their canoes. We walked up the south or east bank of the Lac qui Parle river, examining the country as we went, up to the forks of the river a little below the present city of Dawson. We found the country very satisfactory and I decided to lead the caravan to this locality."[24]

The Jacobson Colony in Section 31, Lac qui Parle Township, on the banks of the Lac qui Parle River attracted many more Norwegians in years to come and, according to Madison's centennial history, also "formed the predominating Scandinavian population in Madison." Lac qui Parle was established as a county by an act of the legislature on March 6, 1871. Its population in 1880 grew to 4,891; fifteen years later, in 1895, to an impressive 12,687; and in 1905 to 15,182. The state census gives only the foreign born for 1895, but in 1905 both foreign born and mixed foreign born—individuals with at least one foreign-born parent—are given. That year the Norwegian stock numbered 9,481, or 62.4 percent of the county population.

Norwegian regionalism dictated patterns of settlement. Immigrants from Stjørdalen in the Trøndelag district of Norway concentrated in Hantho and Cerro Gordo townships and also found their way to Lac qui Parle and Lake Shore townships; in the latter, the Hegre (now Hegra) Church indicates the early settlers' origin. Norwegian politician and amateur historian Jon Leirfall relates that "Goodhue County gradually became a center for the Stjørdalings in America. . . . For a generation, most of them came here and their settlements became a station on their way farther west." Leirfall continues, "Just as people from the same *bygd* had emigrated together they now moved west together, since there was no more free land in Goodhue County for the newcomers or the children of those who had arrived first. [In 1870] many from Stjørdalen went from the old Goodhue County to western Minnesota and took land around Madison." Leirfall identifies settlements that consisted almost entirely of people from specific communities within Stjørdalen.

During the 1880s, these settlements experienced a regular influx directly from Norway; they later served as mother colonies for new communities in the Red River Valley and the Dakotas. Norwegian settlers also dominated in the county's eastern and southern townships, and there was a small enclave of settlers from Valdres and Telemark in Augusta Township near the South Dakota border. Providence and Maxwell townships south of Dawson were heavily Swedish; in the northwestern townships German Catholics settled along the Yellow Bank River; German Lutherans took land farther south and east. Ethnic segregation created separate cultural worlds within the county.[25]

A County Seat War

Living in an ethnic world did not prevent Norwegians from taking active part in local affairs. To the contrary, they became major players in shaping and promoting the welfare of the larger community. The conflict over the location of Lac qui Parle's county seat, with Norwegians leading the battle between the contenders, demonstrates their total involvement in the politics of the country town. As a central place, county-seat towns benefited greatly from the drawing power of administrative functions; as a result, the late nineteenth century was marked by county seat wars. The Norwegian American author and newspaperman Johannes B. Wist in his novel *Jonasville* (1922) gives a lively account of two Red River Valley communities' fight to gain the county seat. What Lac qui Parle County experienced was not fiction but a true western bush fight.

Lac qui Parle Village was the county seat from the beginning of county government in 1871; the small village even had dreams of winning the competition for the state capital. The coming of the railroad through central Lac qui Parle County in 1884 changed its prospects radically, however. Several town sites were established along its line, the most important being the two "boom" towns of Dawson and Madison. These villages, both housing dominant Norwegian populations, engaged in a bitter rivalry to have the county courthouse moved from Lac qui Parle Village to their town sites. Further, both villages, as the county's history notes, had "men of energy and resources to support their respective claims."

Many of these men were, like Hans Andreas Larson, Norwegian-born, and it is easy to imagine both sides of the debate engaging in an acrid exchange of opinions employing the rich Norwegian store of impious language. These men not only took part in the conflict but had initiated it, and they sustained it to a degree that risked an armed confrontation. How the ethnic factor precisely figured in might be a moot issue, but at the very least the situation demonstrates a forceful engagement by Norwegian immigrants in local and state politics. Success

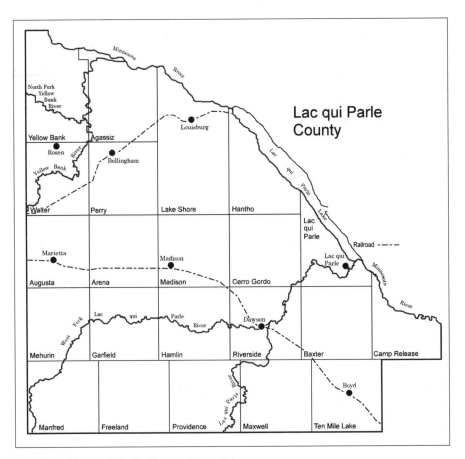

Map of Lac qui Parle County Townships

would assure prosperity and influence. Retaining the old county seat had its supporters as well, and Bellingham, not to be outdone by the other villages, also threw its hat into the ring, though with little chance of success.

The issue of removing the county seat created great excitement and tension, increasing in intensity as the time to determine its outcome drew near. The Madison Townsite Company offered to deed a site for the courthouse and to carry the expense of transfer. Following the November 1886 election, the citizens of Madison took the matter into their own hands and "kidnapped" the courthouse. The *Independent Press,* begun at Lac qui Parle Village but by then moved to Madison, reported that on

Friday morning, November 12, "about one hundred and fifty men and forty teams from this place and vicinity gathered at the court house at Lac qui Parle and took possession of the records and other valuable movable property therein and brought them to Madison, where they now are."

The following day, a second "posse" went to Lac qui Parle and began the daunting task of removing the courthouse. It was hauled on wagons across the prairie, a distance of fifteen miles, enduring a snowstorm and a broken axle, and reached its imposing new site in Madison on November 19, 1886. The removal of the courthouse caused a high degree of tension and anxiety, even talk of "armed conflict." Madison finally won out after the election in 1888; Jacob F. Jacobson of Madison—who emigrated from Ryfylke in Rogaland at the age of eight and became known as "the Norwegian Giant from Lac qui Parle" or "King Jake"—was elected to the legislature on the Republican ticket and took the issue to St. Paul; a new law passed in March 1889 authorized the removal of county seats. Jacobson had earlier led the forcible transfer of the courthouse, according to the *St. Paul Dispatch*, "astride the ridge pole of the kidnapped building." At a special county election in May, Madison won by a large majority. The need to bond a new courthouse renewed the bitter discussion, however, as Dawson again advocated its local site. The bond issue passed in March 1899—by a narrow margin of 163 votes—and ended the acrimonious "courthouse fight." The present stately courthouse rose on the site of the old one. In Madison as in Benson, the courthouse square was a significant physical image, created with countywide financial support and serving as a central destination for county residents.[26]

THE NORWEGIAN CITIZENS

Among Madison's Norwegian citizens the ethnic dimension asserted itself with some strength—distinctive personalities had a decisive voice at the village's inception and during its later growth. In most respects Madison did not differ from the two other villages, though the town did exhibit a few unique characteristics. Norwegians in Benson, and even more so in Starbuck, were more likely to be employed in working-class occupations due to the large number of newcomers that arrived in the 1880s. Starbuck additionally suffered the disadvantage of not being a county seat

The courthouse arriving in Madison. The man on the roof might be Jacob F. Jacobson. Ness Lutheran Church is seen directly behind the courthouse; to the far right is the Madison schoolhouse.

and thus did not benefit from government service. In contrast, Madison had a larger Norwegian professional and managerial class, also explained by the settlers' time of immigration. In Madison in 1900 about 26 percent of the Norwegian population had arrived between 1865 and 1874, compared to 20 percent for the two other villages. Only 37 percent of its Norwegian citizens were immigrants of the 1880s compared to much higher numbers for Benson and Starbuck. Presumably Madison's larger, more established Norwegian immigrant population was not only better equipped to welcome newcomers but also had been able to move fully into professional and proprietary occupations. Even so, Madison housed a large Norwegian class of common laborers, albeit one proportionately smaller than in either of the other two villages.

Similarities in experience and adjustment, despite some notable differences, are the most evident aspects of the lives of Norwegian residents in all three towns. Statistics again provide revealing insights. The median age of first- and second-generation Norwegians in Madison was 24.3; for Norwegian immigrants, if considered separately, the average age rises to 39.7. As in the other two towns, Madison's was thus a young population.

Yet the mean age for first- and second-generation Norwegians combined, as compared to 21.6 in Benson and 24.9 in Starbuck, may seem somewhat high considering that Madison had the Lutheran Normal School with many young Norwegians students. The enrollment, never large, does not appear to have affected the median age of Madison's citizens. In the population as a whole there were more men than women; viewing the Norwegian group separately, however, there were 88 men for every 100 women, compared to 82 in Benson and 93 in Starbuck. The sex ratio attests to the interaction the three towns experienced with the solid Norwegian farming communities in their hinterlands: Norwegian women in the countryside sought employment in the urban environment whereas the men found work in agriculture. For Benson there is a marked change from 1880, when Norwegian men outnumbered women; the marriage rate that year was 51.1, again indicating the presence of many young single Norwegian residents. The higher marriage rates later gave evidence of increased social stability. In 1900, marriage rates among Norwegians in Madison were, however, somewhat lower than in either Starbuck or Benson: 55.3 percent for Norwegians as a whole, compared to 61.9 and 58 for the two other towns respectively. These percentages are still fairly low—since they include the immigrant and the second generations—and indicate that all three towns continued to have many single Norwegian residents. [27]

By 1900 all three villages were statistically speaking well-established communities. A successful Norwegian business community existed in Madison; as in other "towns of a common heritage" it appealed to village and rural residents of its own ethnicity. Larson's General Store, relocating to Madison in 1885, continued to prosper, but several similar stores existed, together with hardware stores, agricultural implement stores, harness stores and livery stables, as well as banking establishments, a number of saloons, and by 1886 no fewer than three hotels.

Madison's most thriving industry before 1900 was the Madison Milling Company, in operation from 1893. Again, Norwegians took the lead. The cousins Nick and Gerhard Herriges and Elling O. Berg—a substantial dealer in agricultural implements born in Wisconsin of Norwegian immigrant parents—pledged the initial funds, but such prominent local Norwegians as politician Jacob F. Jacobson, banker Peter G. Jacobson—born in Iowa of Norwegian immigrant parents—and Einar Hoidale—born in Tromsø, Norway, in 1870, though his family hailed from Sunnfjord, and emigrating to Lac qui Parle County at the age of nine—were all shareholders. A souvenir booklet in 1900 described Madison's citizens as "energetic enterprising hustlers, who, with a determination to succeed, work in unity for the good of the public as well as that of self, being materially aided by the untiring press." It was in this case as a cooperative ethnic enterprise, the creed of all frontier communities.[28]

The relatively large professional class among Norwegians in Madison, in comparison to Benson and Starbuck, may be further explained by additional variables. Norwegians' numerical dominance in a rapidly expanding population in itself provided opportunity for ambitious men; many of them, as described above, either belonged to the second generation or had come to America as children. Their ability to adjust and to take advantage of pioneer conditions was thus greater than that of those who arrived as adults.

Education is an obvious and significant variable in how immigrants and their children met with success in America. The immigrants built educational institutions that played an important role in shaping a town. The different Norwegian Lutheran synods ran academies or high schools to educate youth in a Lutheran setting; they filled a void where public high schools had not yet been established and, thus, were encouraged by town promoters. Glenwood Academy in Glenwood village was incorporated in 1894 by the Norwegian Synod; for many, attendance there led to Luther College in Decorah, Iowa. The academy's broad influence is suggested by the fact that "during the last five years [from 1904] about half of all of Pope County's teachers have attended the academy." It remained active only until 1911. One of the most successful academies was started in Willmar in Kandiyohi County by a private corporation in 1883 as Willmar Seminary; in 1898 it entered into a close relationship with the Norwegian Synod. When the school closed its doors in 1919, more than 7,000 students had been enrolled there.[29]

A NORWEGIAN PROFESSIONAL CLASS

The Lutheran Normal School became a significant community-molding institution. Madison was the location of one of only two normal schools established in America under the direction of Norwegian Lutheran

church bodies. In 1889 the Norwegian Synod opened its teachers' training institution, Lutheran Normal School, in Sioux Falls, South Dakota;
it had begun in 1865 as a Normal Department at Luther College. The
Lutheran Normal School in Madison was the school of the United
Norwegian Lutheran Church (*Den forenede kirke*), formed in 1890. This
church united the Anti-Missourian Brotherhood (*Det antimissouriske
broderskap*), the Conference, and the Norwegian Augustana. The Anti-
Missourian Brotherhood was the name taken by the loosely organized
congregations that in 1887 had left the Norwegian Synod in opposition
to its close ties to the Missouri Synod and in particular to its teachings
on the doctrine of predestination. The United Church embodied the
broad intermediate position in Norwegian American Lutheranism. This
group in 1892 moved the Lutheran Normal School from St. Ansgar in
Iowa, where it had been located since 1890, to Madison; it had begun
in Wittenberg, Wisconsin, in 1887 as a private school supported by the
Anti-Missourian Brotherhood. The prevailing controversy in Norwegian
American Lutheranism is well illustrated by these events.[30]

The history of Madison's Lutheran Normal School (LNS), or *Den
lutherske Normalskole,* shows the influence of a Norwegian American
intellectual and religious elite in a small town with a large and dominant
Norwegian population. It adopted the English word *normal* instead of
a Norwegian equivalent used by some Norwegian American publications, *lærerseminarium.* LNS's purpose was "to prepare teachers to in-
struct the children in Christian education and also to supply Christian
teachers in the public school." In fact, the district school might thus be
conquered from within by its Norwegian Lutheran teachers. LNS's offer-
ings and activities before it closed in 1932 went beyond this initial stated
mission to include foreign missions and preparatory, normal, and parochial courses. Thus it also trained teachers for the Norwegian parochial
school, or congregational schools, meeting the needs of an extensive
number of Norwegian Lutheran congregations. Norwegian language
studies were important in this pursuit, though very few graduated from
the parochial course after 1921 and no one after 1927.

Teachers and students alike were mainly Norwegian. As its first president, Ole Lokensgaard gained influence within the Madison Lutheran
Church—the United Church's local congregation—more broadly in the
synod, and in the affairs of Madison; his weight in community affairs

was proclaimed by the erection of the main building, a three-story brick structure completed in fall 1892, on the northeast edge of Madison, with dormitories and other buildings added later. Lokensgaard had emigrated from Hallingdal, Norway, with his parents at age three in 1857, settling in Rice County, Minnesota, where his brother Knute Lokensgard—who later dropped the second "a" in his surname—was born in 1860. In 1893 Knute became a professor at LNS and in 1907 its third president. Thirty-three students enrolled the first year and the school reached its maximum enrollment of 184 in 1910–11. The influence of the school and "The Lokensgaard Brothers," as they were referred to in the local press, expressed itself as well in their agitation for temperance: the *Western Guard* reported in 1895 that the brothers had just "returned . . . from a lecturing tour through Redwood, Brown, Cottonwood, Renville and Yellow Medicine counties." They had, the newspaper reported, "been at work in the temperance cause, and at the same time been making friends for the Lutheran Normal School here."[31]

The Norwegian Lutheran church supported professional medical service; as a result Madison had trained resident physicians although no hospital existed before 1901. Norwegian Lutheran involvement—providing health care on an interdenominational basis—began with a mass meeting in Madison on February 20, 1901, to consider establishing a hospital. Already on March 4 considerable progress was made in the incorporation of the Lac qui Parle County Norwegian Lutheran Hospital Association at Madison. Significantly, all Norwegian Lutheran congregations regardless of synodical affiliation were invited to join and to make donations. The Reverend A. O. Utheim and the Reverend A. O. Oppegaard, both pastors in Hauge's Synod, were elected president and vice president, respectively; the Reverend Iver Tharaldsen of the United Church became secretary. The Ebenezer Hospital, now the Madison Hospital, opened its doors in 1902 as the only hospital, it proudly proclaimed, between Minneapolis and Watertown, South Dakota. Doctors Eric O. Giere and Marcus Thrane—born in Eau Claire, Wisconsin, in 1876 and grandson of the Norwegian pre-Marxist socialist Marcus Thrane—were the first members of the hospital staff. Ebenezer Hospital was operated under the auspices of a Lutheran board of directors that represented the conflicting directions within Norwegian Lutheranism in America. From 1915 until his death in 1950, Dr. Nels Westby served as chief of staff; he was active

Reverend Ole Lokensgaard,
president of the Lutheran Normal
School in Madison

in public life, serving as mayor of
Madison, and influential in the
Madison Lutheran Church. As
his daughter related, Dr. Westby,
trained in America, made a point
of being Norwegian and spoke
Norwegian with his patients. [32]

Perusal of the Norwegian-language *Madison Tidende* (Madison
Times) for 1895 indicates Norwegian professionals' direct appeals to their
compatriots; there are Dr. C. A. Anderson, Norwegian doctor (*Norsk
Læge*), born in Minnesota in 1867; Miss Ida Kaastad, Norwegian-trained
midwife (*Jordemoder*), midwifery being a female specialty; Dr. M. O.
Teigen, Norwegian doctor, who visited Madison only infrequently; and
Dr. Eric O. Giere, Norwegian doctor. Kristopher O. Jerde, Norwegian
lawyer (*Advokat*), was born in Lyngdal in Numedal, Norway, in 1856 and
at age twelve came to America with his family, settling near Madison,
Wisconsin. After earning a law degree in 1880, he became Lac qui Parle
county attorney in 1884. Clearly, the strong institutional base of the
Norwegian Lutheran church in a mainly Norwegian village and coun-
try population, combined with the influence of the Lutheran Normal
School, attracted professionally trained Norwegians to the area.

Yankees and individuals of other ethnic backgrounds also appealed
to the large Norwegian population—and reflected its power—by announcing their services in *Madison Tidende* and using Norwegian
equivalents of their professional titles, albeit without the added en-
ticement of shared nationality. Serving Madison and surrounding villages were W. E. Todd and Henry W. Gammel, both physicians and
surgeons; an amazing number of men in legal practice, J. H. Driscoll,

H. L. Hayden, Frank Palmer, J. D. Kelly, T. J. McElligott—all attorneys at law; and German-born John F. Rosenwald, real estate and farm loans. Norwegians, then, constituted an ethnic vocational elite alongside an influential old-stock professional class.[33]

MADISON'S NORWEGIAN PRESS

The higher percentage of professional Norwegian men, as well as of managers, officials, and proprietors, in Madison than in either Starbuck or Benson resulted largely from ethnic institutional developments there. Newspaper publishing gave further evidence of ethnic strength: the Norwegian-language *Madison Tidende* was founded in 1894. The most interesting person in its history was Adolf Bydal, from 1897 editor and sole owner. In August 1897 he purchased the subscription list of *Minnesota Folkeblad* (Minnesota Newspaper for Common People), published in Canby as a local Norwegian-language newspaper for Yellow Medicine County from 1892 until 1896. With the broader focus of his new mailing list, Bydal changed the name from *Madison Tidende* to *Minnesota Tidende*. Many obstacles faced the foreign-language press, and the newspaper folded in 1899, but Bydal, born in Kristiansand, Norway, in 1856, and emigrating in the late 1870s after university studies in law and classical and Germanic philology, continued in the service of the Norwegian American press he had begun shortly after his arrival.[34]

Bydal's political involvement on the side of the Farmers' Alliance might have hastened the demise of *Minnesota Tidende;* his aggressive editorials against the corrupt machinations of a political ring in the county likely increased his popularity among Norwegian farmers, but it simultaneously exposed him to a determined, stalwart opponent. Another alliance organ, the *Western Guard,* had been established in 1891, however, and like *Minnesota Tidende* it in many ways expressed the concerns of the Norwegian farming population. Einar Hoidale published the first issue in Dawson, dated January 5, 1891, but already that fall, after becoming the official organ of the alliance of Lac qui Parle County, the *Western Guard* moved to Madison, "a Move to the Center," as it was announced in the newspaper's columns on October 28, 1891. Political implications will be considered later, but it is obvious that the *Western Guard* launched Hoidale's distinguished career in state and national politics. He earned a law degree in 1898 and later opened an office in Minneapolis. In keeping with a treasured American icon, Hoidale invoked Lincoln's "log cabin" image, claiming in a 1929 autobiographical sketch, "My story is that of an ordinary lad who spent his boyhood days upon the frontier prairies of our great state."[35]

By simply considering the editors' nationality, it is easy to conclude that the *Western Guard* as a farmer's newspaper to a great extent functioned as a Norwegian voice. Indeed, the publishers themselves described it as a "little Norwegian paper"; obituaries—even through the 1930s—and particular news items might be printed in Norwegian. The latter might, however, also appear in its competitor, the Republican *Independent Press*. Hoidale was succeeded at least through the 1940s by editors bearing Norwegian names. Lokensgard purchased the *Western Guard* in September 1903 and served as its editor; in 1904 ownership and editorial duties fell to his son Henry L. Lokensgard, who operated the business until February 1911. The newspaper thus was strongly tied to Norwegian Lutheranism and its religious biases. Indeed, an expert on Madison's history, Jon Willand, and Father Eugene Hackert, who grew up in the German Catholic enclave by Rosen in Walter and Yellow Bank townships in the western part of the county, both agree that the *Western Guard* harbored a strong anti-Catholic bias. It had, according to anecdotal evidence, no subscribers in the county's German Catholic areas.[36]

PROTESTANTS AND CATHOLICS

Mutual prejudice between Catholics and Protestants, in this case Norwegian Lutherans, existed widely where they encountered each other. Tensions seem to have run particularly high in Madison, however. Some have even suggested that the town was divided into a minority Catholic and a majority Lutheran world. The *Independent Press* for January 3, 1896, lists four congregations in Madison, two Catholic and two Lutheran. There were St. Michael Catholic Church, established in 1885 and served by German-born Father Peter Rosen, for whom the nearby town was named, and the Congregational Church, served by the Reverend E. A. Powell, dating in Madison from 1886. The two Norwegian Lutheran congregations included the First Lutheran Church of Hauge's Synod, then served by the Reverend A. O. Oppegaard. Organized in January 1879—as its pious seventy-fifth anniversary history describes—by "six of the pioneer settlers gathered at the sod home of Johannes Nelson, 4 miles northeast of Madison," its original name was Ness Evangelical Lutheran Congregation, changed to First Lutheran Church only in 1943. It moved to Madison in the mid-1880s.[37]

The strength of the pietistic low-church Hauge's Synod among Norwegians in Madison and Lac qui Parle County, the so-called holy, may at least partly be explained by the origin of many of the pioneer settlers, in particular the Jacobson Colony, from areas of Norway that had experienced Haugean religious revivals. They rejected the formal ecclesiastical ritual of the high church—centering on the elevated altar, administered by a pastor dressed in black vestments with a ruffed white collar—and instead embraced the simplicity associated with the modest Norwegian meetinghouse, or *bedehus*, literally "house of prayer." The low- and broad-church directions in Norwegian American Lutheranism made the most progress in gaining member congregations; the high-church persuasion had fewer converts.

The Reverend Peter Thompson (Sandve) had been a member of the Jacobson Party in 1869; he emigrated in 1843 at age twenty-eight from the Karmsund district in the County of Rogaland; in America he became a pastor in the pietistic low-church Eielsen Synod. The first Sunday in June, the day the Jacobson Party arrived, he conducted what is considered to be the first Christian religious service in Lac qui Parle County—aside from those earlier at the Indian mission—in a grove on the banks of the Lac qui Parle River. Later forceful guidance was given by religious leaders like Pastor Oppegaard. Born in 1841 in Toten, Norway, he was a tailor and a zealous lay preacher for nine years before emigrating in 1869; in America he became a pastor in Hauge's Synod and was active in the church's Home Mission.

The second Norwegian congregation was the Madison Norwegian Evangelical Lutheran Church, which had been established in 1885 and carried the name St. Peter's Norwegian Evangelical Lutheran Church of Madison until 1887. In 1926 it became Madison Lutheran Church. The congregation joined the United Norwegian Lutheran Church when the body was organized in 1890; in 1896 it was served by the Reverend

Ole Lokensgaard, who in addition to being president of the Lutheran Normal School served Garfield Norwegian Evangelical Lutheran Congregation, organized in 1892 six miles south of Madison. By 1916, according to O. M. Norlie, thirty-five Norwegian Lutheran congregations had been organized in Lac qui Parle County, many of which dissolved after a few years. There was an equal number of congregations adhering to the low-church and the intermediate synodical bodies—fifteen congregations each; even the small pious Eielsen Synod was represented.

The Norwegian Synod, which had only five congregations of the thirty-five, compensated for its weakness in Lac qui Parle County with a strong position in both Swift and Pope counties. Lowell Soike in his discussion of anti-Catholicism points out that after 1890 Norwegian American Lutherans "were divided mainly among churches of the liturgical Norwegian Synod, the moderately pietist United Norwegian Lutheran Church, and the highly pietist Hauge's Synod." High-church liturgical Lutheranism in Madison was limited to German Lutherans who organized St. John's Lutheran Church of the Missouri Synod; it dated its beginnings to 1899 but was not formally established until 1904. Only 9.3 percent of Madison's population in 1900, Lutheran and Catholic, was German: a minority indeed in a town dominated by Norwegian Lutherans—but one that would continue to grow.[38]

The Norwegians' strong institutional base as well as religious leaders' deep conviction might go some way in explaining the obvious schism that prevailed between Madison's Catholics and Lutherans. The roots of anti-Catholicism, as Ray Billington shows in his classic *The Protestant Crusade,* were deeply embedded in American society. Antipapal prejudice and nativistic movements burst out with renewed force in the 1840s but were "grounded before the first English settlement and . . . fostered by the events of the entire colonial period." Norwegian Lutherans found support for their negative attitudes toward Catholics among German Lutherans; however, the Missourians would, according to their own belief statement, not engage in any ecumenical activity with the Norwegian Lutherans represented in Madison. Whether the fact that St. Michael to a large extent gathered German Catholics—whereas members of St. Francis Xavier Catholic Church in Benson were mainly French Canadians and Irish—somehow intensified negative attitudes among Lutherans in the former city would be difficult to determine, as would the strength of the Norwegian Lutheran low-church movement in Madison as an explanatory factor.

The general attitude of the clergy as religious leaders—on the Catholic as well as the Protestant flanks—might be a more significant factor in explaining interdenominational conflicts. Robert Joseph Dineen, born in 1927 on a farm north of the heavily Irish village of De Graff in Kildare Township, Swift County, recalls, "You were instructed by parents not to interact with those Lutherans." Considering only the Lutheran situation, tales of pastoral relations with congregants suggest strongly that Norwegian Lutheran pastors, regardless of synodical affiliation, might strive to assume the social superiority and authoritarian outlook present in the homeland's state-appointed clergy. The high-church Norwegian Synod did not have a monopoly on religious arrogance: Lutheran ministers, in spite of excessive partisan bickering about the nature of the true Lutheran faith, instilled a common Lutheran confessionalism in their flock and placed a distance between it and non-Lutheran denominations. Ethnoreligious historians have concluded that a liturgical-pietist division did not create an anti-Catholic animus; it was instead an attitude that cut across all Norwegian partisan loyalties. On the other hand, as has been seen, Catholics and Lutherans might cooperate in commercial ventures and in the public arena.[39]

AT THE DAWN OF THE NEW CENTURY

Benson, as well as Madison and Starbuck, met the new century with the gadgets and innovations that defined it. By the mid-1890s telephone lines extended into western Minnesota; in 1904 the Swift County Telephone Company incorporated and took over the existing system. All three towns had municipal electric power plants by 1900; rural communities had to wait another forty years or so before power lines reached their scattered homesteads and they were lifted "Out of the Dark Ages," as the history of Benson's Agralite Cooperative has it. Ada Olson, born in 1896, the youngest daughter of Adam Olson, relates in her memoirs that hers was the second family in Benson, after the Hobans, to get electricity. Ada Olson proudly brought in all the neighborhood children to see the lights being turned on. The difference between town and country was made manifest by these early municipal improvements, which also demonstrated that towns operated under a separate governance—county commissioners tended to the needs of the agricultural population.[40]

On the streets of these small western Minnesota towns were seen the first automobiles, signaling that the horse culture was weakening and would eventually be replaced by the automobile culture. In Benson there was in the mid-1890s the Motor Club, which arranged bicycle races and distance contests; in 1910, indicating radical changes in transportation, the Benson Automobile Club was organized. These fundamental shifts suggested to Lewis Atherton that the city was coming to "Main Street." Olson states that her father was generally the first man in town to make improvements—he took pride in being ahead of his neighbors. The Olsons thus had the first furnace, the first plumbing, the first washing and sewing machines—and the first automobile.[41]

By 1900 Benson had become a fair-sized little city of 1,525 with a large number of business interests; its first water tower was built in 1897, announcing the modernization occurring within village limits. Yet the distance to rural life was not great. One may again consult Ada Olson's observant memoirs for details. Her father, Adam Olson, had emigrated in 1879 from Syvdsbotn in Sunnmøre, Norway, at sixteen and came to Benson that same year. A hardware merchant and the proprietor of the Olson Hardware Company, he developed the career of a prosperous American entrepreneur. Olson had begun as an employee of another hardware merchant and then in 1888 started his own business in partnership with G. M. Peterson, a business that was housed in a brick building located on the town's main street and of which Olson eventually gained sole ownership. The family's large two-story frame building on the south side was only a mile from the first farm outside Benson. And, as Ada Olson relates, "Behind the house was a barn for the two horses and the cow and a windmill to raise water for the animals. Next to the barn was the chicken house." Her description offers a view of Benson before more modern conveniences became commonplace.

A close economic relationship with the surrounding agricultural communities naturally continued even after urban modernization. This interdependence might be illustrated by Adam Olson's brother, Ole Olson Sordahl (Sørdal), who, retaining a form of the farm name in Syvdsbotn, joined his brother in Benson in 1884; eventually he accumulated sufficient funds to start his own general merchandise store, and he appealed to the farm population to become his patrons. In 1909, for instance, he announced in the *Benson Times*, "We are prepared to take all kinds of FARM PRODUCE in exchange and at the Highest Market Price. Bring in your Butter and Eggs and do not forget the right place." This common practice benefited the merchant as well as the farmer.

The entire county invested in building the courthouse; a significant landmark in the Benson landscape, it became a visible indicator of government functions that had great drawing power. The citizens of Benson dedicated their new brick courthouse on June 11, 1898. Judge Gauthe E. Qvale offered the principal speech. Born near Haugesund, Norway, in 1860, he emigrated with his parents in 1878 and settled in Willmar. In 1882 Qvale was admitted to the bar; in 1897 he was appointed to the office of district judge in the twelfth judicial district, which included Swift County. Qvale served for nearly fifty years in this position and enjoyed high social status and respect. His death in 1951 became front-page news, announced in large boldface print.[42]

Men like Judge Qvale were visible proof that immigrants could succeed in the professions and even, as Qvale had, reach the pinnacle in their vocation. One might by 1900 have expected a greater professional presence by Norwegians in a county-seat town like Benson, with its large number of Norwegian citizens. In the main, Benson's professional elite, especially in medical services, continued to be old-stock American. Dr. Charles L. Scofield, born near Cannon Falls, Minnesota, in 1865, arrived in Benson in 1890 and became one of the town's most prominent men of medicine, especially in public health; it remains a badge of honor to claim that you were "delivered" by Dr. Scofield. His interests included the town's early history, and his accounts were published in the local press. The Swift County Hospital, established in Benson as a public institution in 1912, created a need for medical staff. Dr. Scofield's Norwegian connection was his wife, Bertha Arnesen Scofield, whom he married in 1892. She had come to Swift County from Kristiansand, Norway, in 1880 with her parents.

However, in 1900 only eight Norwegian immigrants and only two in the second generation qualified as professionals; they were mainly clergy, educators, and pharmacists. The 1900 federal census lists three Norwegian-born druggists in Benson. Two of them, Ernest Meyer and L. M. Koefod, started the Lion Drug Store. In a common Norwegian

TABLE 11

Number of Males Aged 15 to 65 and of Norwegian Ancestry by Occupational Field in the Villages of Benson, Madison, and Starbuck, 1900

| | Number of Individuals | | | | | | | | |
| | Benson | | | Madison | | | Starbuck | | |
	Immigrant	Second Generation	Total	Immigrant	Second Generation	Total	Immigrant	Second Generation	Total
Professionals	8	3	11	12	6	18	2	1	3
Farmers	1	2	3	8	3	11	2	0	2
Managers, Officials, and Proprietors	20	3	23	32	25	57	11	11	22
Clerical Workers	4	2	6	1	4	5	0	0	0
Sales Workers	14	10	24	5	6	11	7	3	10
Craftsmen	23	10	33	19	9	28	20	4	24
Operatives	5	2	7	3	2	5	4	2	6
Service Workers	10	3	13	2	5	7	3	3	6
Laborers, including Farm Labor	18	8	26	21	9	30	16	4	20
At school, none, or unspecified	1	12	13	16	33	49	4	1	5
Total	104	55	159	119	102	221	69	29	98

Source: U.S. Census, 1900

practice they gave it an animal name, which later non-Norwegian proprietors retained. H. G. Swenson advertised his business as *Skandinavisk apothek,* that is, "Scandinavian pharmacy."

The potential of serving compatriots in Benson and environs had not totally escaped the notice of Norwegian-trained doctors even before the turn of the century. As early as the mid-1870s, Dr. Karl Bendeke from the by then bustling city of Minneapolis, advertising himself as *Norsk Læge,* "Norwegian Doctor," visited Willmar and Benson "to receive patients." Regulation of medical services was at that time lax and would continue to be so for some time. Medical training, even when given at a reputable institution, was by today's standards not extensive. Norwegian immigrants had most confidence in medical doctors who had graduated from the university in Oslo (Christiania). A Norwegian-trained doctor could consequently establish himself with some ease among his emigrated compatriots.

In 1898 the *Swift County Monitor* announced the arrival of a Norwegian-trained medical doctor, Dr. James Lee, even indicating where he would have his office, but he seems not to have moved to Benson, despite "the best of recommendations." The first Norwegian-born physician in Benson was Dr. Nils Juell, listed in the 1900 federal census; Dr. Juell came to the United States at age twenty-two in 1882. About 1902 he was replaced by Norwegian-born Dr. E. B. Johnson, who in turn was succeeded in 1904 by Dr. Thore Nils Thoresen, who proudly advertised his medical training at Christiania University. By 1910 there were sixty-four physicians with Norwegian medical training practicing in America, hardly a sufficient number to meet the needs of fellow immigrants. But Norwegian doctors who received their training in America, as did Juell and Johnson, and Norwegians in a variety of other professions could also claim a shared ethnicity and gain the trust of their fellow immigrants. Benjamin Castberg—Norwegian born but trained at the University of Minnesota law school—thought it good business to advertise himself as *Skandinavisk Advokat,* or "Scandinavian lawyer." An appeal on the basis of nationality persisted as a means of attracting patients and clients.[43]

Benson received relatively few Norwegian immigrants in the first two decades of the twentieth century. The Norwegian community, well established by 1900, continued to assert itself. Considering the situation in 1900 forms a basis to measure later changes and growth. Table 11 gives the number, rather than percentages, of male occupations in 1900; there was a tendency for persons of Norwegian stock to seek employment in managerial, sales, crafts, or labor jobs. Examples presented in Table 12 suggest how ordinary Norwegian Americans in Benson made a living; they also indicate a common practice of seeking U.S. citizenship, bearing witness to a new loyalty visible at all levels of Norwegian American society. The major occupations listed in the table continued to predominate among Norwegians, but as the city grew their employment in other fields increased. Looking back to 1880 and 1900, the Norwegian immigrant population, rather than the second generation, showed a clear dominance in managerial and proprietary fields as well as in other occupations. The children of the immigrants would establish themselves more forcefully in the new century.[44]

TABLE 12

Selected Norwegian Adults Residing in the Village of Benson and in 1900 Employed in Working-Class Occupations

John L. Nelson, age 37, married, barber
Emigrated from Norway in 1883 (naturalized citizen)

Jacob Andersen, age 36, married, bartender
Emigrated from Norway in 1882 (naturalized citizen)

Christian R. Alsaker, age 46, married, blacksmith
Emigrated from Norway in 1875 (naturalized citizen)

Anthon Christofferson, age 63, married, boardinghouse keeper
Emigrated from Norway in 1870

Peter F. Hamre, age 50, married, carpenter
Emigrated from Norway in 1880 (naturalized citizen)

Nicolas Isaksen, age 66, married, day laborer
Emigrated from Norway in 1867

Lars S. Hole, age 32, married, janitor
Emigrated from Norway in 1892 (naturalized citizen)

Marie Nelson, age 35, widow, laundress
Second-generation Norwegian from Wisconsin

Ben Skapple, age 21, single, machinist
Emigrated from Norway in 1885

Charles O. Haugen, age 65, married, railroad section hand
Emigrated from Norway in 1886 (naturalized citizen)

Caroline Oldervick, age 34, widow, domestic servant
Emigrated from Norway in 1889

Thore Knutson, age 46, married, stone mason
Emigrated from Norway in 1883 (naturalized citizen)

Anna B. Lere, age 38, widow, washerwoman
Emigrated from Norway in 1887 (naturalized citizen)

Dora (Mrs. Knut) Knutson, age 35, married, no occupation
Emigrated from Norway in 1884

Lovisa (Mrs. Hans) Pederson, age 41, married, no occupation
Emigrated from Norway in 1884

Mathilda (Mrs. Michael) Romstad, age 39, no occupation
Emigrated from Norway in 1868

A COMMUNITY VIEW

Growth and change were at times mixed blessings. The intimate character and the sense of "togetherness" was, according to Atherton, altered as "midwestern country towns" became "more and more like cities," yielding a social loss for their citizens. Large ethnically inclusive community festivals, as for instance May 17 celebrations as well as July Fourth festivities, were more common in the early pioneer years. The rural population came to town in large numbers to take part. The *Benson Times* reported in 1880 that due to rain the July Fourth parade was small, "consisting of the Benson Cornet Band, and a few carriages containing the speakers and others," but the country people came in force to witness the horse races at the racetrack. The many Norwegians among them encouraged Pastor Severin Almklov, the last speaker at the Independence Day exercises, to address the audience in "the Scandinavian language." According to the newspaper, even those who did not understand him "pronounced the speech as an exceedingly fine one, bespeaking a learned orator." A sense of community fellowship existed; it even allowed for ethnic representation. Atherton describes a real country town as "a community in which people speak to one another as they pass along the street and a stranger is recognized as such the minute he arrives."[45]

This sense of community was being threatened. Atherton blames the loss of "togetherness" on the great number of social clubs that came into being, encouraging exclusivity. Organizational life created a split between religious institutions and secular societies; it was especially manifest in the growth of lodges inspired by Freemasonry. Still, evidence suggests that the social informality of small-town life and other established attributes persisted, even under changing conditions. Rural towns had, as one example, fewer organizational activities for children. For young people this reality made informal, spontaneous get-togethers, even, again to cite Atherton, "having a coke at the local drug store," a major social event. Further, country towns, "as the home of old people . . . have been slow to abandon the more informal life of earlier days." Many who left farming and moved to town in retirement cherished the common conventions formerly associated with country towns.

Nevertheless, if the club movement indeed was devastating to small-town solidarity, it also quite clearly adversely affected social interaction between villagers and the farming population. According to a University of Minnesota report on the city of Ada in western Minnesota's Norman County—49 percent first- and second-generation Norwegian in 1910—there was in 1915 "very little social intercourse between the village and the country." The report called "the splitting up into groups" that had developed "unfortunate."[46]

Other factors than the many clubs of course may have played a part in the decline in community social activity—factors such as the growth of the town, which made communitywide participation in hastily planned activities more difficult to achieve, and the departure of young people who sought opportunity elsewhere, which deprived the town of many of its most invigorating citizens. However, the broader interest created by membership in national and international organizations clearly affected the character of communal life. American service clubs, fraternities, and secret societies entered early into west-central Minnesota's small towns. The secret lodge of the powerful Masonic Order, as Catherine McNicol Stock states, "often stirred embittered criticism, sometimes out of fear for the nature of its secret rituals but also because its membership wielded great power within towns and villages across America." Its exclusive male membership represented social elites.

The Geneva Lodge No. 196 of the Masonic Order was constituted in Madison in 1891; the Masons came to Benson as early as November 1876 as Swift Lodge No. 129, A. F. & A. M. Norwegian American Albert C. Clausen, then editor and part owner of the *Benson Times* and also grain buyer for the Northwest Elevator, was one of the main instigators to form the lodge, which was organized under a dispensation granted by the Grand Lodge of the State of Minnesota. The membership gathered influential men in the village of Benson, including Z. B. Clarke, banker, politician, and for a time editor and publisher of the *Benson Times,* and H. W. Stone, businessman, founder of the Swift County Bank, and state politician.[47]

Secret societies, greatly at odds with religious leaders, established a pattern for ethnic organizations such as the Sons of Norway, which began in Minneapolis in 1895 as a mutual aid society, the most common type of ethnic organization. Its roots can be traced to similar organizations in Chicago. Inspired by American fraternalism, the order like the Masons adopted secret membership ceremonies and passwords to meetings, and members called each other brothers. It became by far the largest secular Norwegian American organization, with a supreme lodge headquartered in Minneapolis and in time lodges from coast to coast. Sons of Norway gave small-town and urban Norwegians a voice outside the domain of the Lutheran church. The fraternity imposed male and Norwegian qualifications for membership and placed itself in the morally uplifting tradition of the fraternal movement, which reflected the moralistic attitudes of contemporary urban reformers. Applicants had to provide proof of moral worthiness. The Sons of Norway began as an idealistic organization of young Norwegian men; temperance was strictly enforced—persons engaged in "the liquor trade" were barred from joining. Unlike the Masons, it had a largely blue-collar membership, though some leaders might also be part of a Masonic lodge. The local lodges became the main venue for Norwegian American activities.[48]

Bjørgvin Lodge of the Sons of Norway was organized in Benson in 1902; the Mason connection was suggested by the fact that one of the founders and first president, Adam Olson, was active in that organization. In 1905 Nornen Lodge was formed in Madison; in 1916 Gimle Lodge in Starbuck and Mjøsen Lodge in Glenwood were formed. As social institutions and promoters of Norwegian American events and festivals, Sons of Norway lodges competed with the local Lutheran congregations; however, their influence in west-central Minnesota falls entirely into the twentieth century.[49]

In Starbuck, the strong position of the Lutheran church and the late founding of a Sons of Norway lodge gave an advantage to the church people. Consequently, May 17 was observed in Starbuck and surrounding communities under the auspices of church groups, such as the Young People's Society in the Indherred congregation. In 1903 the observance was limited to a Sunday evening program "appropriate for that day." In 1908 the arrangement was more ambitious: the Starbuck Cornet Band played and there were "speeches, singing, reading"; much like at a church picnic, "the ladies [were] requested to bring baskets and cups." The centennial history of Starbuck gives 1913 as the earliest record of a *Syttende Mai* celebration, also presented by church youth groups, this time at the west end of Lake Minnewaska, with "music and speeches, all in Norwegian."[50]

Given the large Norwegian population, the modest and historically late observance of the homeland's Constitution Day in Starbuck may seem at odds with expectations. No secular society or committee outside the Lutheran church before the founding of Gimle Lodge assumed responsibility. Secular societies and groups had mainly arranged public commemorations of the day in Madison and Benson. But the Lutheran clergy was not left out: it was important to recognize Lutheran pastors as the natural leaders in the Norwegian American community. Celebrations never attained the broad and enthusiastic community participation that characterized the early observances in Benson, however. The day became, as was obvious in urban areas such as Minneapolis and Chicago, a more exclusively ethnic marking. The May 17 celebrants in Madison in 1898 met in a hall, "crowded to overflowing," with a program of addresses, songs by a male choir, and band music and concluding with the inevitable supper served by the local "Ladies society."[51]

Benson had arranged large July Fourth festivities in the 1870s, but these were fewer and smaller or even cancelled in the 1880s, and the American holiday was only minimally recognized. People engaged in agriculture might be otherwise occupied in July; the lack of large public observances may also, as suggested above, represent a gradual decline in community activities. Nevertheless, it can be claimed that May 17 and July Fourth observances both celebrated the liberties of America. In 1898, during the Spanish-American War, the *Western Guard* in Madison defended "the propriety of celebrating the independence day of Norway"—criticized by some because "our nation is engaged in a struggle with a foreign foe"—on the grounds that "the observance of the day is a tribute to the spirit of freedom, patriotism, liberty, and independence—the same in Norway, in the United States of America and in Cuba." The American Independence Day surely also symbolized nationalism and immigrant adjustment to a new society; it is yet another example of ethnicity and American ideals being mutually reinforcing. And public celebrations, even if their vibrancy was inconsistent, had not gone out of style.

The central event at a grand July Fourth celebration arranged in Benson in 1892—a tug-of-war contest between various ethnically based teams—illustrates not only recognition of an ethnic dimension in such observances but also a prevailing competitive spirit among the ethnic groups themselves. German, Irish, Norwegian, Swedish, French Canadian, and American teams were organized, identifying rather well the town's ethnic composition. In the contest, with encouraging shouts from intensely partisan throats, in a confusion of national vernaculars, the Irish team claimed first prize and the Norwegian won second. One may fairly conclude that this friendly interaction among ethnic groups was not simply a show of strength but just as much an event demonstrating a shared identity as citizens of the village of Benson.[52]

A COMMON HERITAGE

The early histories of Benson, Starbuck, and Madison suggest that a transplanted Norwegian cultural heritage manifested itself in unique ways and with varying visibility and strength contingent on local circumstances. All three villages, even considering local differences, nevertheless were imbued with a common spirit as heirs to a shared Norwegian cultural and religious legacy, a unifier across the generations. Similarities in adjusting to the new setting were more obvious than dissimilarities. The analogous as well as divergent experiences of the immigrants and their progeny were both influenced by a number of variables, such as disparate local opportunities, the shifting vigor of ethnic and religious loyalties, time of immigration, ethnic numerical strength, and the vagaries of historical forces and events.

Sheltering substantial Norwegian populations, Benson, Starbuck, and Madison all enjoyed extensive interaction with large Norwegian farming communities in their hinterlands. Their location on the western prairie placed them in a unique environment with its own call into action. The story is thus one of challenge and adjustment by a peculiar people lodged in a transplanted old-world heritage and determined to succeed in a world in which they by choice became active members. The pioneer generation's group and family strategies created security and in time economic progress. Madison, by its industries and with a Lutheran normal school, was a more sophisticated community than Benson. Furthermore, its Norwegian population was larger and, in spite of the village's late founding, a greater number of Norwegians had arrived at an earlier date than in either Benson or Starbuck and were thus better established in business and public life. American-born children of Norwegian immigrants were also on the scene and provided leadership. These factors explain Madison's proportionately larger professional and proprietary class, although second-generation dynamics also operated in Benson and a few professionally trained Norwegians aside from clergymen arrived there before the turn of the century. Despite its large and heavily concentrated Norwegian population, Starbuck, due to its smaller size and large number of newcomers, had a proportionately smaller professional class than Benson and a more working-class, farm-centered economy than either of the two other villages.

Madison and Benson both benefited from the drawing power of being county seats, which offered men—whether Norwegian or of other nationalities—greater opportunity for public service. Even so, the smaller Yankee populations constituted a visible social elite in both towns and furnished essential financial and professional services. All three towns were, however, central places to large and concentrated Norwegian farm populations. The towns provided employment, notably for rural women, thus creating a gender imbalance among Norwegians in town; the agricultural settlements, regularly displaying a local *bygd* culture in speech and traditions, sustained the many small and a few larger commercial undertakings by Norwegian townsmen.

The Norwegian Lutheran church in its contending visages was a major link between Norwegians in town and in the countryside, generally sharing pastoral services. The different synodical bodies vied for converts and for congregational affiliation. The predisposition of early Norwegian settlers in Lac qui Parle County favored Hauge's Synod, the pietistic church of the laity, although the intermediate and largest orientation, from 1890 expressed through the United Church, gained entry and through active leadership asserted great influence in community affairs. The other denominational persuasion, the Norwegian Synod, the liturgical church of the clergy, had greater institutional influence in Swift and Pope counties. Starbuck in fact became a Norwegian Lutheran domain, though not surrendering to one denominational color; Norwegian Lutheranism in Starbuck, while adapting to the voluntary free-church practices in America, became a dominant force in the whole of local society, and men active in its service excelled in business and political positions. Secular interests were stronger in Madison and Benson; the two towns in addition enjoyed a diversity of religious faiths that was completely absent in Starbuck. Interdenominational tensions fostered anti-Catholic prejudice, most visible in Madison, influenced, one must conclude, by the numerical strength of the Norwegian population and the dominance of Lutheran institutions.

Toward the end of the nineteenth century, as modernization proceeded, a decline in community social activity became evident and ethnic festivals assumed a greater exclusivity. In Benson, the early enthusiastic community celebrations of May 17 were replaced by smaller observances under the auspices of secular Norwegian societies such as the Sons of Norway, which after 1900 was represented in Benson by the Bjørgvin Lodge. On the other hand, Norwegians continued the reinvention and re-creation of a Norwegian cultural heritage from one generation to the next, as did all ethnic groups; by their strong presence they added color and had a cultural impact on the social fabric and political structure of all three towns. While interacting with fellow citizens of other national and religious backgrounds, Norwegian Americans became major actors in village and county affairs.

Five

In the American Matrix

THE PROGRESSIVE FRAMEWORK

Benson became a city in 1908, adopting a city charter on February 25 under the Minnesota municipal home rule statute; the charter made Benson almost entirely self-governing and gave the office of mayor a predominant position. J. N. Edwards, president of the village council, was elected mayor in the first city election April 7. Municipal home rule represented, William Anderson explained in 1922, a system that can be traced back to traditions of local self-government carried over from England and a system of almost completely decentralized government in modern-day America. Minnesota's constitution provides that "any city or village in this state may frame a charter for its own government as a city consistent with and subject to the laws of the state." That year, 1908, Benson was divided into two wards, and a divergence in political affiliation became apparent. The more populous second ward, including the exclusive Sunnyside district, showed a stronger Republican party loyalty than the first ward north of the tracks—likely a question of class as much as of ethnicity. The local powers were in any case vested in the people of the City of Benson. "Every home rule city may have," Anderson writes, "the form of government and the range of powers and functions which the people of the city desire to have."[1]

In its evolving social and political structure the city of Benson became a microcosm of the many changes that were occurring in town and country in west-central Minnesota after the turn of the century. Norwegian farmers, with their extensive landholdings, obviously had a stake in the country; in the public arena they acted to ensure their economic self-interest. In this regard farmers and townspeople might display conflicting agendas. The early and persistent political involvement of the Norwegian community, in many elections exceeding the state average in voter turnout, spoke to a strong civic commitment. Electoral politics in local, state, and national elections are the main focus of this chapter. Ethnocultural prejudices such as anti-Catholicism and temperance convictions—heavily swayed by the Norwegian Lutheran church—predisposed Norwegians to vote Republican, but toward the end of the nineteenth century they also moved into Democratic and Populist political camps and in west-central Minnesota by the 1920s to a great extent embraced the Democratic-Farmer-Labor reform movement.

A Norwegian American national subculture flourished during the years covered by this chapter. On the western prairie ethnocultural strength and its broader impact were made visible in the introduction of Norwegian language instruction in the Benson high school and in the formation of cultural and social organizations, in theater performances and festivals, in visits by prominent Norwegians, and in a cultivation of such Norwegian fortes as ski jumping and winter sports. Ethnic loyalties and values, the Lutheran faith and its mores, and festive and mundane preferences in ethnic celebrations, cuisine, and social conventions were living traditions, reconstituted in the new environment, strengthened by Norwegian American activities, and given a content that bespoke ethnic credentials acceptable to American neighbors.

THE EDUCATIONAL COURSE

Education gave access to American society and eased adjustment to the demands of shifting circumstances. For some Norwegian immigrants and for their children, education secured rapid social advancement. Most gained skills to help them prevail in the everyday challenges faced by ordinary citizens. The significance of public education was in all cases obvious to people in town and in the country: it consequently became one of the major functions and responsibilities of township school boards and of village and city governments.

The Benson public school, District 6, was organized March 9, 1870; the next year a one-story frame building was erected on the northeast corner of the courthouse block. It has been claimed that the small-town church, school, and home "furnished education for *heart* and *mind*," establishing "a process which involved the teaching of an extensive code of morality"—a dominant middle-class view of ideals and moral behavior. All existing village ordinances were retained in 1908 and, as stated in Section 3 of the Benson city charter, "shall be in full force and effect until repealed." These and new city ordinances all reflected the values and mores of a churchgoing, middle-class society. In arranging May 17 festivities, in 1903 Bjørgvin Lodge of the Sons of Norway had, as noted in the *Benson Times*, "With the Norwegians' time-honored respect for the Sabbath . . . decided to remain passive on Sunday the 17th and to celebrate the occasion on Monday"—a considerable concession to piety and middle-class religious practices. At the April 7, 1908, election, Benson voted to be dry; the saloons closed their doors. "For the first time in 32 years you cannot openly buy a glass of liquor in Benson," the *Benson Times* reported. The election the following April, however, reversed the decision and allowed for the licensing of saloons. In a city such as Benson, there were many departures from the dominant code. Catholics might clash with middle-class Protestant sentiments in regard to intoxicants and recreation on Sunday; immigrants of varied national and cultural backgrounds offered their own interpretation of proper moral behavior, as did the many city dwellers from all ethnic groups who "simply ignored the middle-class code of respectability and religious observance." In considering the small-town culture of Benson, it is important to recognize the diversity in beliefs and ideals that existed, in spite of the fact that ethnically the city continued mainly with its cultural roots in a Yankee and northwestern European heritage.[2]

Benson High School was organized as a state high school in 1890; its first graduate that year was Hans Bronniche, son of Danish-born Thomas Bronniche, village treasurer. The number of graduates increased gradually, though there were none in 1894 and only eight in 1897. The high school's district stretched far beyond Benson; country youth also attended. The first double-digit graduating class of eleven students received their diplomas in 1904, and that year the high school building was constructed on the north side of town. In 1909 the *Swift County Review* printed the names and graduation year of all graduates; 152 students up to that time had earned a high school diploma. Beginning in 1923 and finishing out the decade, graduating classes averaged about fifty annually.[3]

Hans S. Hilleboe—born in 1858 in Roche-a-Cree, Adams County, Wisconsin, to Norwegian immigrant parents from the Hardanger region of Norway—was likely the most prominent superintendent of Benson schools, serving two five-year terms between 1899 and 1912. He had in 1894 been gubernatorial candidate on the Prohibition ticket and edited the prohibition newspaper *The Hammer*. Before coming to Benson he, among other educational achievements, earned an AM degree from Luther College and taught and served as principal in the Willmar Seminary; he left Benson to become the first president of Augustana College in Sioux Falls, South Dakota. Hilleboe thus had a strong association with liturgical Norwegian Lutheranism and with the temperance cause; no doubt a middle-class Protestant-inspired morality was safely kept and promoted by him.[4]

Members of the Benson school board were also men of prominence in the community. Influential businessmen such as Norwegian-born Andrew J. Hoiland and Adam Olson served and were, like Hilleboe, members of Our Savior's Lutheran Church in Benson and active in the Synod's affairs. And there were also men like Dr. C. L. Scofield and Irish-born P. S. Gallagher, a schoolteacher by education, justice of the peace, and in 1908 along with Hoiland and Scofield a member of the city charter board.[5]

Benson High School had a teacher-training department open to its best graduates, intended "to prepare [them] for teaching in the rural schools." Beginning in 1871, when eight country school districts were organized, and until 1912, ninety-four school districts existed within Swift County. Ole Jacobson, the later owner of Ole Jacobson & Co. in Benson, and nineteen others on April 3, 1871, organized District 7 near Benson by petition; the schoolhouse was built in Section 34 in Six Mile Grove Township and also included Swenoda Township, neither township having been organized at that time. The many one-room schoolhouses operating under township school boards educated the young and relied on the skills of a single person who daily dealt with American-born children who spoke only the language of immigrant parents. The names of many of these teachers suggest that they, like their students, had grown up in a home where English was not spoken. The majority were single women, with Norwegian names from the 1880s like Sophia Sather, Marie Skibness, Ragna Hatlid, and Cora Corneliusen, but also names of other national origins such as Libbie Carny, Mita Rietsch, and Libbie Fleming. Robert Bly, famed poet from Madison, reminisces about his attendance at a one-room country school there; he and his older brother James usually walked the one mile to school "or they rode two on a thin mule." There were two teachers in eight years: "Esther Kemen, calm and affectionate," who "kept a pan of water on top of the coal stove in case we wanted to heat our cocoa for lunch" and "For seventh and eighth grade . . . Marie Skulborstad, excitable and full of energy." Men might also serve as country schoolteachers: in 1899 the *Swift County Monitor* noted, "Hans H. Bakken closes his last term of school at Lake Hazel today. After having taught eight and one half month, during the past year."[6]

Efforts were made to teach young immigrants English. In 1883 Alex M. Utter, the first county superintendent of schools, appointed in 1870, opened a room in the Benson "public school building for the benefit of those who could not speak English but who desired an English education." The *Benson Times* reported that most of the thirty who enrolled were Norwegian. Since the majority knew no English, the direct method was employed with familiar objects, "for instance the word 'cow' with a picture of the animal shown them." Utter described how "one young man . . . who had come from Norway a little over two months ago, began coming to school when he could not speak a word of English. Although only two months in school he is now almost through the second reader." Utter clearly wished to showcase his success in turning immigrants into Americans.

Counterefforts were at work, however—not to discourage learning English but rather to preserve a Norwegian cultural heritage alongside the one encountered in America. Norwegian leaders' influence and their wish to retain a cultural bond to their past and pass it on to their children were reflected in educational programs. A school to teach the Norwegian language as well as Lutheran dogma was started in June 1902 in the north side school building. The Norwegian Religion School or Congregational School had long roots, generally meeting during the summer months but occasionally also at other times. On December 8, 1879, Trinity Lutheran Church in Six Mile Grove decided to hold two months of Norwegian religion school, "one on either side of Röveren," as "the river," rather than the Norwegian equivalent *elven*, is rendered in the hybrid Norwegian English language of the minutes; a school committee

*A rural school in District 55, Ten Mile Lake Township, near the village of
Boyd, Lac qui Parle County, 1901. The teacher was Sarah Egdahl. Six school
board members, five with Norwegian names, are visiting students who were
likely nearly all Norwegian.*

had been elected as early as October 1876. Either the entire congregation
or school districts within the congregation assumed responsibility for the
school. The minister and the congregation carefully examined prospec-
tive instructors in the teachings of the Lutheran faith and in their own
Christian conduct, to assure "with the greatest care that one can give
the children a true Christian upbringing." The Congregational School, or
Norwegian parochial school, became a fixture in Norwegian American
Lutheran churches into the 1930s and lasted even longer in some rural
communities.[7]

The Norwegian language might assume near-sacred standing for those
who grew up in a Norwegian American community, powered by the con-

secrated usage of the formal Dano-Norwegian literary forms in religious services and the warmth of family togetherness conveyed by a multitude of local vernaculars. Both ethnic influence and assimilative progression among Norwegians in Benson is reflected in the remarkable fact that for some years before, during, and after World War I, Benson High School offered instruction in Norwegian. Passing on the old country language to American-born generations posed greater problems in town, where the forces of assimilation and multiethnic interaction functioned more freely than in isolated single-ethnic rural communities. Teaching Norwegian as an academic subject to American-born children thus gained importance among leading Norwegians. Norse, as it was listed, was taught for the first time in academic year 1912–13; all the students who enrolled had Norwegian surnames. In May 1916, as reported in the local press, the Norse class was busy reading Bjørnstjerne Bjørnson's peasant tale *En glad Gut* (A Happy Boy). Adelia Winther of Minneapolis is listed as teaching Norse in 1916–18; Alma Gjertsen of Madelia was hired as high school principal and assumed responsibility for the course in 1918.

One of the students enrolled in the Norwegian class, second-generation Ada Olson, relates how she struggled in the Congregational School to learn Luther's Little Catechism in Norwegian, "since she knew no Norwegian at all." She studied German and Norwegian in high school; the teachers were respectfully addressed as "Professor." Her father, Adam Olson, an active member of the school board, might have had a hand in introducing Norwegian language instruction. The local library carried a fair selection of Norwegian titles. In 1909 the *Swift County Review*'s published list of new library books "in the Norwegian language" purchased from Norwegian American publishing houses contained mainly popular literature, some translated from Swedish and German; historical narratives; and one novel by a Norwegian American writer, Hans A. Foss, *Livet i Vesterheimen* (Life in the Western Home).[8]

"Life after [high] school for most of Benson's students," Ada Olson concluded, "did not include college or professions." As she relates, the farm or jobs awaited the boys and homemaking the girls. High school prepared its students for this life, in the classroom and in school-sponsored events focusing on agriculture and domestic sciences, although a fair number of academic subjects were offered as well. And while university and professional training lay beyond the reach of the majority, the *Benson*

Times in September 1905 nevertheless was able to list the names of "scholars to different institutions" from Benson. Thirteen were at the University of Minnesota; as expected, they were for the most part the sons and daughters of leading citizens. Among them were second-generation Norwegian Americans: Burke Arnesen, Thorvald Hanson, Angell Hoiland, Richter Ostvig, and Ole Sneide. Education represented an expedient and well-trod path to realizing the American dream. The American-born generation could most easily avail itself of the success specialized education promised.[9]

NORWEGIAN CULTURAL LIFE

Higher education did not negate loyalty to an ancestral heritage. Indeed, counting the immigrants and their children, it was a mature and large Norwegian community that interacted culturally, socially, and politically with a multicultural America. A Norwegian America—a popular romantic concept of the Norwegian immigrant culture—blossomed between 1895 and 1925. The federal census shows that in 1910 every third Norwegian, counting only the immigrants and their American-born children, resided in the United States. They numbered more than a million; the Norwegian born—reaching its peak that year—were 403,857 strong. More than 80 percent still lived in the states of the Upper Midwest.

The Norwegian stock in Minnesota—not counting generations beyond the second—comprised a community of 279,606—nearly 19 percent of the state's residents. There was thus a large and concentrated Norwegian-speaking population in the state. This population, rapidly moving into the middle class, engaged, first, in preserving the culture and faith of the homeland, reinvented in the new environment, and, second, in becoming uniquely Norwegian American. Its numerical strength assured success in fostering cultural values, in newspaper publishing, in creating an immigrant literature, and in organizational life. In the prewar years many of its members expressed faith in a permanent Norwegian subculture in America.[10]

Winter sports were a Norwegian forte and a romantic national symbol; in particular, cross-country skiing and ski jumping were developed in the 1880s by Norwegian immigrants. The former had utilitarian beginnings and continued as a mode of travel during pioneer years. There are numerous tales of pioneer farmers carrying heavy loads on their backs while skiing to their individual homesteads, and even of early itinerant Lutheran pastors for whom skis offered a winter conveyance as they visited their dispersed flock.[11]

Of the three towns, only Starbuck was home to a ski jump; the prairie landscape offered few suitable heights. On February 17, 1909, the hill one mile north of the village was the site of the first interstate ski tournament west of Minneapolis. "Following jumps by professionals," the history relates, "local boys were given an opportunity to try out the ski jump." The longest jump was ninety-two feet. The *Swift County Review* reported after the first tournament, "1500 people bought tickets to see the ski tournament at Starbuck last week" and "the Starbuck people are quite enthused over the affair and are planning to improve the slide and give a large tournament next year." After 1922, the tournaments were moved to Glenwood, where the terrain allowed for a higher jump.[12]

Glenwood, Starbuck, Madison, Benson, and most other small towns in western Minnesota regularly hosted performances of many kinds. As venues for lectures, exhibitions, celebrations, and musical entertainment, town halls and courthouses in small midwestern municipalities were replaced by so-called "opera houses." This rather unusual name was adopted, Lewis Atherton explains, "because the word 'theatre' was

The second interstate ski tournament north of Starbuck, February 16, 1910

in bad repute." All progressive towns wanted one, and nearly all of Swift County's trading centers had one. In 1895 the Benson Opera Block was built on Pacific Avenue; it was destroyed by fire in 1906 and a new opera house constructed on the same location the following year. It had an active program of visiting performers who entertained with dramatic productions, comedies, vaudeville, and concerts; in addition, local amateur groups were featured and dances regularly arranged. Some programs appealed directly to Norwegian citizens. In November 1904, a visiting eastern dramatic company presented Henrik Ibsen's controversial *Ghosts*. The *Benson Times* reviewer conceded, "The play was peculiar and above the comprehension of many in the large audience and its nature not what everyone would admire." In December of the previous year, Hans Seland, noted Norwegian author, then on a tour of the United States, had appeared at the opera house and entertained in Norwegian with his own humorous stories that would, as the local press had it, "make one laugh" but "also teach a lesson worth hearing." Visits from the homeland were evidence that official Norway as well as a Norwegian cultural elite had discovered their compatriots in the western home.[13]

Occurrences in Norway encouraged patriotic responses in the Norwegian American community. Two events in particular inspired increased ethnic enthusiasm: the end of the joint Swedish-Norwegian monarchy in 1905 and the centennial of the Eidsvoll Constitution in 1914. There can be little doubt that the first event—the dissolution of the ninety-year Swedish-Norwegian Union—had a rejuvenating effect on Norwegians in America and strengthened patriotic feelings toward the homeland. The *Benson Times*, mindful of Norwegian subscribers, kept its readers abreast of the dramatic and threatening political events on the Scandinavian peninsula as a possible armed conflict between Sweden and Norway loomed. The struggle culminated in the unilateral June 7 declaration by the Norwegian *Storting* (Grand Assembly) of the dissolution of the Swedish-Norwegian Union; thereafter a peaceful resolution of the conflict was achieved. The Norwegian-language *Decorah-Posten*, with its many subscribers in Swift County, announced: "Norwegians Rule in Norway. The Union between Norway and Sweden is Dissolved. King Oscar [the joint Swedish-Norwegian king] is Removed by the Norwegian Storting." For some time, June 7 competed with May 17 as the "key symbol" of Norwegian American ethnicity.[14]

In 1906, a member of the *Storting*, Erling Bjørnson, visited Benson and gave an address "upon Norway past and present and its struggles for independence." The speaker was the son of the celebrated Norwegian author and father of the Norwegian national anthem, Bjørnstjerne Bjørnson. The bombastic patriotism of the anthem, composed in 1859 and emblematic of nineteenth-century nationalism, hallowed the second major historical event: the centennial of the signing of the Norwegian constitution at Eidsvoll on May 17, 1814. A sample rendered in English might read as follows: "Norsemen whatsoever thy station thank thy God whose power willed and wrought the land's salvation in her darkest hour. All our mothers sought in weeping and our sires in fight God has fashioned in his keeping till we gained our right." The fulfillment of national aspirations in 1814 re-established the Kingdom of Norway, even though that fall the European powers forced the country into a personal union with Sweden. According to the Act of Union the following year, there was to be full equality between the nations joined in the Twin Kingdoms of Sweden and Norway under a common king. However, the much larger Sweden's dominance within the double monarchy, particularly regarding foreign policy, led to Norwegian dissatisfaction and the union's eventual dissolution. A national Norwegian monarchy in 1905 symbolized the homeland's full independence.

A decade of nationalistic outpouring among Norwegians on both sides of the Atlantic led up to the constitutional centenary jubilee in 1914. These years furthermore carried the final wave of Norwegian emigration; the American economy prospered after 1900, and its great expansion pulled laborers from all parts of Europe. This third Norwegian mass exodus swelled Norwegian urban colonies. The ethnic impulse was fresh and strong. The main Norwegian centennial celebration on May 16–18, 1914, was held in the Twin Cities of Minneapolis and St. Paul, which long before had replaced Chicago as a Norwegian American capital.

Reporting on the festivities, the *Swift County Monitor* described it as the "Greatest Gathering of That Nationality." The newspaper's estimate of 100,000 "American Norsemen" might be somewhat high; it is actually a near doubling of most other estimates. Nevertheless, there is no doubt it was the largest Norwegian ethnic assemblage ever gathered. The spectacular three-day celebration, with its colorful parading of ethnicity, no doubt reinforced ethnic maintenance, but there was evidence of engagement in American life as well. The twenty-two gray-haired veterans of the Fifteenth Wisconsin Regiment who responded to the roll call attracted special attention. Two parades moved to the fairgrounds: one from St. Paul, the other from Minneapolis. Alongside flags, banners, bands, and women dressed in festive peasant costumes (*bunad*), the processions included floats with such idealized features of a shared national history as a Viking ship with bearded Norsemen, a portrayal of the founding fathers of the 1814 Eidsvoll assembly, and even reflection of a contemporary political issue, woman suffrage, with the proclamation, "Women can vote in Norway."[15]

Special trains carried thousands of people to the festivities; many traveled from Benson and other points in western Minnesota. American capitalism recognized the great community appeal of an ethnic celebration: train fares were regularly reduced on May 17 to allow people living out state to attend the large observances in Minneapolis. In 1914 people from afar took part in presenting how Norwegian Americans defined themselves in terms of ethnicity. There were, however, divergent concerns. The many organizations known as *bygdelag*—"old-home societies"—which represented a rural heritage and thus a challenge to promoters of an urban and culturally refined ethnic identity, united and took the initiative to arrange the centenary jubilee. Those who spoke for Norway's "high culture," mainly middle-class men, rejected the idea of being seen as hailing from a nation of peasants. "The peasants are coming! The peasants are coming" the Norwegian-language *Scandia* of Chicago warned in 1912, accusing the *bygdelag* committee of planning a celebration for "the glorification of the *bygder* [rural communities] and of Lutheranism." Not until the final year of planning did the *bygdelag*, under threat of a competing celebration, agree to expand the committee on arrangement to include a broader civic and cultural representation.[16]

The *bygdelag*, though claiming to represent the Norwegian population as a whole, in reality sought to legitimize their rural cultural heritage as an accepted and respected expression of ethnic identity. These organizations highlighted yet another major divide among Norwegian Americans. Appearing at the turn of the twentieth century, as a historical phenomenon they were basically a first-generation activity, assembling immigrants from isolated rural environments in Norway into nationwide American organizations; the majority of the members were rural, midwestern, Lutheran, and Norwegian born. To quote from an article by the author, "Their identity was tied to the home and geographical place they had left behind, making the *bygdelag* a strategy to enable them to return to a pre-modern rural world and the sense of permanence of place and identity it accorded." Since these societies in general spoke for an earlier generation of immigrants, newcomers from an increasingly modernized Norway might feel alienated and view them with some disapprobation.

Each society represented a particular community or group of communities or a general district, fjord region, or valley. The relationship to landscape provided a feeling of belonging and encouraged a primordial sense of identity. At annual reunions, termed *stevne*, members in a sense re-created in a festive and celebratory manner the Norwegian ancestral *bygd*, or rural community. The Norwegian Lutheran clergy, natural leaders of the rural population, became an obstacle to a broad presentation of Norwegian folk culture. Urban culture became a factor as well. Even though a localized rural Norwegian American culture did not disappear, it was greatly influenced by urban practices and tastes that invaded the many segregated agricultural communities and gradually posed a threat to transplanted age-old rural practices.

Between 1899, when the first society, *Valdres Samband* (Valdres Union), convened and 1913, all major *bygdelag*, thirty-one total, had been organized. They bore regional appellations like Hallinglaget and Telelaget (both formed in 1907), Sognalaget and Trønderlaget (1908), Vosselaget, Gudbrandsdalslaget, Setesdalslaget, and Nordfjordlaget (1909), and the large Stavanger Amt Laget (1911). The degree of piety varied greatly from one society to the next, though the entire movement was given a pietistic flavor. Lutheran pastors considered many common peasant practices sinful and damaging to the group's reputation; consent to American middle-class values thus dictated a sanitized and appealing interpretation of the old-country background.

The individual *bygdelag*, as they met on the fairgrounds on the first day of the 1914 jubilee observances, thus celebrated a selective heritage, evidenced in parochial cultural expressions and folkloristic idioms. On display were the unique peasant vernaculars, regional festive peasant costumes, local specialties in food and music, and traditions that evolved in each *bygd* group.[17]

Norwegian regionalism was well represented in western Minnesota. The national Nordfjordlaget, with members in the city of Benson and in the Nordfjord stronghold of Camp Lake Township, in June 1915 conducted a three-day *stevne* in Benson. The *Swift County Monitor* printed a detailed account. Local interest, then as more recently, might also relate to the commerce the reunion would bring to town. Viewed externally, ethnicity on such occasions might be said to express itself as a commercial commodity. A colorful parade through the streets "was headed by the banner carried by two girls dressed in national costume. They were followed by the Swift Falls band; then two men carried the American and Norwegian flags. Next came thirty young girls attired in national costumes, followed by the guests of which there were quite a number in line." In the evening, "the ladies of the Synod church," as Our Savior's Lutheran Church was consistently referred to, served a banquet "consisting of many Norwegian dishes" in the church basement.

Culinary loyalties were significant ethnic markers. Church lutefisk suppers, functioning as a means to raise funds for the congregation, became emblematic of Norwegian ethnicity. Introduced before the turn of the twentieth century, they evolved and became commonplace in the 1920s. The Ladies Aid of Our Savior's, as noted in its minutes, decided in 1914 "to hold a Ludefisk Supper November 13" and made a profit of $136.71. It was not the first: in October 1905 the *Benson Times* noted, "The ladies of the Synod church will have a Ludefisk supper . . . in the church basement Thursday and Friday." Norwegian wholesale traders and importers, men like Ole A. Thorpe of Chicago, enabled P. J. Larson of Benson to offer *Norske Retter* (Norwegian Food Items) for sale in his general merchandise store. In 1908 Larson advertised lutefisk at eight cents per pound, Norwegian herring, anchovies, *pultost* (sharp cheese of sour, skimmed milk), *primost* (cheese made of whey), fish balls, and lingonberries.[18]

World War I and its nativistic "100 percent Americanism" parole had a destructive impact on the marking of ethnic loyalties. In 1917, in the midst of the anti-hyphenist campaign, Nordfjordings in Benson nevertheless organized a local society, which regularly arranged picnics in

Our Savior's Lutheran Church on Benson's south side, built in 1912 after an earlier church was destroyed by fire

Swift Falls or Benson on July Fourth. Changes in political climate as the United States entered the European conflict made it prudent for the Nordfjordings and for other ethnic groups to demonstrate, as the local press reported, that they "were true and patriotic Americans" by making their picnic, though featuring ethnic dishes, a celebration of America's Independence Day. In 1918 the picnic gave evidence of "By Americans and for Americans" throughout the program. During the hysteria of the war years, the loss of cultural transplants was increasingly evidenced in language, in other cultural products, and in festivals. May 17 observances, for example, were either totally cancelled or became patriotic rallies.[19]

May 17 celebrations had earlier experienced a transition by becoming symbolic markers of a positive and exclusive ethnic self-identity. Sons of Norway lodges assumed responsibility. Mons O. Hauge, a charter member of Benson's Bjørgvin Lodge, in his activities transcended the Lutheran clergy's suspicion of the fraternal order as a secret society.

Born in Langedal, near Bergen, Norway, he immigrated to the United States as a child of two in 1871; following student days at Luther College in Decorah, Iowa, he came to Benson in 1896 as a parochial instructor in Our Savior's Lutheran Church. An "active promoter of Norse culture in America," according to his obituary, he organized and directed the Bjørgvin Singing Society.[20]

Concerts by the Bjørgvin singers, regularly held at the Benson Opera House, became an integral part of May 17 celebrations. In 1904, for instance, the *Benson Times* declared, "The celebration of the 17th by the Bjørgvin Singing Society was a pleasant and successful one." At the end of the program, certainly to the dislike of custodians of the homeland's faith, "the floors were cleared and the dancers took possession till 3 o'clock in the morning." In other respects, of course, Bjørgvin Lodge, like Sons of Norway lodges in general, consisted mostly of laboring people and shared many of the Norwegian Lutheran church's moral tenets, such as the fraternity's moral uplift philosophy, a prohibition against intoxicants, and an idealistic concern for Norwegian cultural heritage.

Republican congressman Frank M. Eddy, who served as U.S. representative from 1895 to 1903, "delivered an excellent address of an hour on Norway and the Norwegians . . . tracing the influence of northern blood through Norman-French and English to the landing on Plymouth Rock." These weighty historical vistas, if not politically motivated, at least placed Norwegian Americans within the democratic ideals of their adopted country. Such romantic claims also speak to the role of the homeland in creating acceptable credentials. Norway and a Norwegian American past served the specific purpose of adjusting to a multicultural America; the core values of a Norwegian ethnoculture were protected while their compatibility with American national norms and ideals were demonstrated. Missing from this and later May 17 observances was public display and community participation. In 1907 a writer to the *Benson Times* complained that "quite a number of people were in town the 17th, but no demonstrations of any kind were held except in the evening by the Bjørgvin Singing Society." The day and the events it symbolized had become a key cultural symbol of a unique ethnic heritage. The historical memories and myths associated with May 17 were well suited to bestow positive ethnic attributes to Norwegian immigrants and their American-born progeny within an American matrix.[21]

A Stake in the Country

Norwegians in west-central Minnesota, like their immigrant neighbors of other nationalities, might, as sociologist Mary Waters has noted, attribute common American middle-class values such as love of family, emphasis on hard work, and belief in education to their specific nationality. Middle-class values were thus passed on to later generations, not with a middle-class label but instead as "Norwegian values." This label carried, Waters insists, "emotional and social resonance" not available in other identifications and "link[ed] the individual and family to a wider collectivity." A self-conscious and positive ethnic self-perception was clearly an important attribute as Norwegians competed in the political arena; self-interest as major owners of land was a concomitant force and encouraged political activity. The large tracts of farmland owned by Norwegians in Swift County established a strong presence but also suggested their social and political influence, certainly in the areas they dominated but also in the entire county. This expansive land ownership illustrated the ethnic isolation possible in the West and also encouraged ethnic cultural maintenance. Ethnic isolation did not, however, preclude embracing American cultural forms.

One is here again reminded of both Jon Gjerde's *The Minds of the West* and Kathleen Conzen's idea of a localization of cultures, earlier applied to the situation in Starbuck and its environs. The localized rural ethnic cultures did not disintegrate: they continued, as Gjerde and Conzen agree, to evolve and develop a locally hegemonic culture and identity while, as Conzen writes, responding "to the transforming pressures of modern life on a parallel trajectory of their own." In the present study much evidence was found, especially in personal interviews, to support their contentions. Writing about an existing consciousness of collective identities, Gjerde claims, "When those of other cultural traditions encroached on their enclaves, they ignored the outsiders." Striking—on occasion humorous and literal—instances suggest a generational transfer of identity as well as its potent reinvention in the American born. During an interview with third-generation Leonard Mitteness of Nordfjord background in Parkview Manor, a senior housing complex in Benson, a woman entered the room and implored us not to forget the Swedes, whereupon Leonard in pure Nordfjord vernacular ordered,

perhaps facetiously but nevertheless with a strong sense of who belonged, *"Ha deg ut! Her er vi berre nordfjordingar"* (Get out! Here we
are only Nordfjordings).[22]

The many interviews conducted as part of research in Swift and neighboring counties give ample evidence of the creation of local Norwegian
cultural worlds, frequently based on Norwegian localism, while adjusting
coextensively to the demands dictated by a move toward modernization,
by political participation and by new American cultural structures. The
need to learn English while retaining the old-country speech transplanted

TABLE 13

Townships Showing Percentage of Norwegian-Owned Acres
in Swift County, 1907[23]

Township	Total Acres	Norwegian Owned	% of Total
Kerkhoven	23,127.15	20,426.38	88.3
Swenoda	22,726.93	17,162.76	75.5
Camp Lake	22,801.64	14,984.48	65.7
West Bank	22,856.67	14,631.12	64.0
Torning	22,222.78	13,157.34	59.2
Hegbert	21,075.95	11,164.83	53.0
Hayes	22,706.50	8,937.49	39.4
Six Mile Grove	22,982.49	8,768.69	38.2
Benson	21,627.42	7,375.09	34.1
Cashel	23,514.41	5,439.90	23.1
Pillsbury	21,728.97	3,682.88	16.9
Edison	22,989.35	2,701.43	11.8
Shible	21,417.46	1,772.99	8.3
Clontarf	22,524.15	880.00	3.9
Kildare	22,082.83	661.24	3.0
Appleton	21,037.33	593.66	2.8
Dublin	22,519.11	585.83	2.6
Marysland	23,008.96	581.60	2.5
Tara	23,298.12	400.00	1.7
Moyer	22,934.29	232.30	1.0
Fairfield	22,701.25	0.00	0.0
All Townships	471,883.76	134,140.01	28.4

Source: Gary G. Erickson

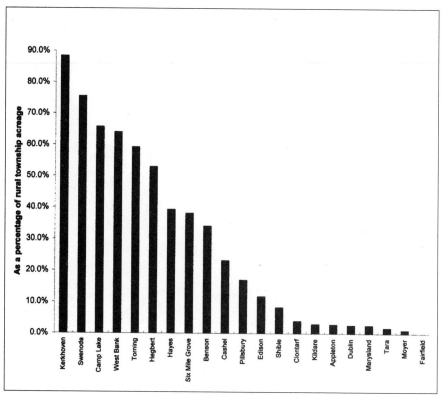

Chart of Norwegian Land Ownership in Swift County, 1907

on American soil suggests response to cultural realities, both those in the tight-knit rural ethnic community and those in the world beyond it.

Ellsworth Smogard, Philip Nygard, and Philip Greseth, all men in mature years now residing in Madison, related in an April 2003 interview that when they get together they speak Norwegian learned in their childhood immigrant homes. Ellsworth Smogard tells of his experience in Cerro Gordo Township, where—like his grandfather Peder Smogard, who had taken land there in 1868—a large percentage of the settlers hailed from Stjørdalen, Norway. The three men grew up in rural Lac qui Parle County and in their Norwegian neighborhoods witnessed boundaries against other ethnic groups and faiths. "The accepted thing was to stay away from Catholics," Greseth volunteered, explaining how "people stuck in clusters." Regular attendance at the Norwegian Lutheran Church

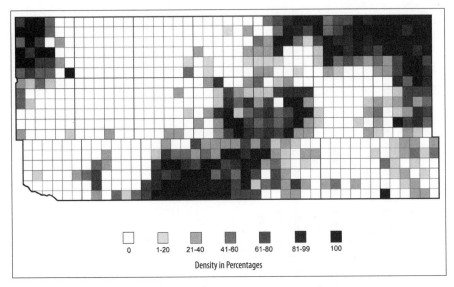

0	1-20	21-40	41-60	61-80	81-99	100

Density in Percentages

Map of Norwegian Land Ownership in Swift County, 1907

was taken for granted; it was the main social center. Hantho Township, where Nygard grew up, "voted dry every election." He belonged to the Hegre Lutheran Church with its roots in the pietistic Hauge's Synod. Ingrained moral values and a moral lifestyle, as defined by the Lutheran clergy, carried over to the community; the congregation enforced strict church discipline (*kirketukt*), which their parents recalled as being severe. Venerable traditions brought over from Norway required that women sit on the left and men on the right in the church edifice; the practice lasted into the 1930s, long after it had been abandoned in the homeland. As members of such ethnic enclaves with their strong collective identities, immigrants responded to modernization and American cultural forms on their own terms. The latter adjustment might well, as Conzen suggests, have traveled in a parallel course.[24]

SWIFT COUNTY INTERVIEWS

Individual life experiences of American-born Norwegians illustrate the process of adjustment in a generational perspective. People of Norwegian descent were born into a rural ethnic world and became immersed in a transplanted cultural environment. Their accounts give evidence that these localized rural ethnic cultures did not disintegrate but instead responded to the challenges posed by modernization and shifting internal and external demands. A segregated rural ethnic world was in terms of personal experience different from the adaptation that occurred in a commercial center like Benson.

The early experience and family history of Ernest Anderson is a common immigrant narrative of the reality of life in a Norwegian rural community. He was born in 1932 and grew up on a 240-acre farm near Swift Falls in Camp Lake Township—with its nearly 66 percent Norwegian ownership of farmland—in a solid settlement of people of Nordfjord origin. His grandparents had settled there after emigrating from Norway; Ernest's parents were both born in the area; they had nine children. "English is my second language. I didn't learn English until I went to school," Anderson relates. It helped that Clara Hagen, his first teacher at the country school he attended for eight years, knew Norwegian. In totality, the situation offers strong testimony to the process of redefining bonds of family, church, and community and to the ethnic separateness— and, thus, maintenance as well as reinvention—of transplanted cultures that was possible on the immense prairie landscape. Anderson attended Norwegian parochial school in summer—at a late date in the schools' existence—and learned Luther's Little Catechism in Norwegian; he had only a few friends who were not Nordfjord Americans.

As Walter Kamphoefner suggests for the Germans in Missouri, an ethnic cuisine required that Norwegians raise a lot of potatoes alongside common American crops like corn, soybeans, and wheat. Potato *klubb*, or "dumpling," together with *rømmegrøt*, "cream porridge," and other dishes made from milk and flour were daily fare; at Christmas there was lutefisk, *lefse*, and pork ribs. The main shopping was done in Benson, where the family would bring eggs and butter to the S & L General Store and exchange them for groceries and clothing. The Andersons attended the St. Pauli Lutheran Church, organized in 1877 within the liturgical tradition of the Norwegian Synod two miles south of Swift Falls; there the pastor conducted services in Norwegian as late as 1942. "In personal contacts," as Kamphoefner writes about the Germans, they "preferred to keep to themselves in their own families and their own church parishes." And at work, Ernest Anderson recalls, during the busy harvest season eight families cooperated in the threshing, going from one farm to the next, and thereby established a special bond among people of a common local heritage from Norway.[25]

Ginter Olander Rice related earlier recollections about life in a Norwegian rural neighborhood. In 1918 he was delivered by a Norwegian midwife in his parents' home on a 120-acre farm in the northeastern part of Camp Lake Township; later the family rented a larger farm in Kerkhoven Township, which claimed nearly 90 percent Norwegian ownership of land and was thus truly an ethnic place. As Rice tells it, the many small-town banks were "anxious to loan out money to local farm boys" during good economic times, which encouraged his father, Oscar Rice, to enter farming in 1916. Ginter Rice started country elementary school knowing only Norwegian, despite the fact that on his paternal side he was fourth-generation Norwegian American and on his maternal, third. Rice views this situation as "an historical example of how Norwegian families tried to remain faithful to their ethnicity." Giving support to Kamphoefner's contention, Rice observed that people stayed in cliques because "they didn't speak good English and so preferred to be with locals." He was confirmed in Norwegian in 1932 at the Spring Creek Norwegian Evangelical Lutheran Church, organized in 1906 in the United Church, a few miles from the family farm.[26]

In her interview, Verna Gomer gives insight into how town life differed from living in a farming environment. She was born in 1918 in the city of Benson and has clear recollections from her childhood and youth there: "Benson was a good place, because all my father's family was there, and we grew up with cousins being more like brothers and sisters." Her father, Rudolph Johnson, was of Voss background; her mother, Ida Hanson Sagedalen, of Valdres and Halling ancestry. Both were second-generation Norwegian Americans who had mastered Norwegian; Gomer recalls them conversing in Norwegian, especially "when they didn't want anyone to know what they were talking about." She herself did not learn Norwegian and admits that when she was growing up she "didn't like to go with anyone with a Norwegian brogue. . . . In Starbuck they all still talk like that." Living on Benson's north side, she "felt inferior to the people on the south side of town." The latter belonged mostly to Our Savior's Lutheran Church with its high-church background; those on the north side were mainly members of Immanuel Lutheran Church of the more pietistic broad-church persuasion. The important people in town, as Gomer saw it, were the bank president, business people, and the law-yers and pastors. She attended high school with storekeeper Michael Hoban's granddaughter, who "had beautiful clothes. . . I suppose I would have liked to have some of the things she had."

Rudolph Johnson worked for Olson's Hardware Company on Atlantic Avenue; in 1939 he and brother Bert Johnson purchased the business and changed the name to Johnson Hardware Store. Gomer was employed in the store. In order not to offend anyone and thus lose customers, her father remained neutral in political matters. He was very religious, Gomer relates, and she spent much time in church. Pastor Herman E. Jorgensen, who had come to Immanuel as a professor at the Lutheran Seminary in St. Paul, "was a better teacher than a preacher," she recalls. At confirmation preparation he outlined clearly the sins of dancing and drinking, "playing cards for money," and of course premarital sex—"that was terrible." He conducted Norwegian services in the afternoon, and Gomer's very musical mother played the organ because the regular or-ganist "did not understand Norwegian and did not want to play."

The transition to all-English services, accomplished earlier at Our Savior's, was thus nearly complete in Immanuel. But in 1943, when Verna married Edwin R. Gomer, she entered a Norwegian-speaking farming community north of Benson and joined Lake Hazel Lutheran Church. She resided there for twenty-two years until she moved back to Benson. Pioneer settlers had transplanted the local vernacular from Gudbrands-dalen. "Even the Swedes up there spoke Gudbrandsdaling," Verna Gomer insists. Her husband, with ancestry in Sweden and in Gudbrandsdalen, spoke the rural dialect so well that when they visited Norway people asked, "How are things in Gudbrandsdalen?" Although Verna Gomer did not learn Norwegian, she does prepare ethnic dishes: "I make a lot of *klubb.*"[27]

POLITICAL ACTIVISM AND NATIONALITY

Persistent Norwegian American ethnocentric qualities, as evidenced in historical analysis and contemporary interviews, maintained traditions and cultural expressions. One may well ask how identifying with an eth-nicity that was continually being re-created and reinvented from one gen-eration to the next—as were all ethnic groups—influenced Norwegians'

The Olson Hardware Store, ca. 1912. From left to right: Rudolph Johnson, clerk; Adam Olson, owner, two unidentified customers

entry into American politics. In his careful investigation of Norwegian American political life in Wisconsin, Iowa, and Minnesota between 1880 and 1924, Lowell Soike tests the limits of an ethnocultural and ethnoreligious interpretation of a manifest Norwegian American reformist and third-party inclination. One might, as Soike does, consider Lee Benson's classic 1961 work *The Concept of Jacksonian Democracy*, which rejects the traditional economic determinist interpretation of American voting behavior as well as the "proposition that socioeconomic cleavages" can explain how individuals vote and offers instead a sweeping generalization "that at least since the 1820's, when manhood suffrage became widespread, ethnic and religious differences have tended to be relatively the most important sources of political differences." Soike finds in 1991 that the prevailing view among historians "seems now to be close to what Lee Benson suggested."[28]

Western Minnesota's special environment constituted a second explanatory factor to ethnic and religious peculiarities. Scandinavian politicians and voters in the Upper Midwest were clearly reform minded, and they frequently joined third-party movements. Theodore C. Blegen sees the reformist political bent as a result of Norwegians' tendency to move out on the frontier. In 1890 more than half of all Norwegians in Minnesota lived in the western counties. There, Blegen explains, they became involved in political movements to redress the special problems faced by wheat farmers. That is of course not the whole story: Norwegians took part in shaping several political cultures, and many could be found in conservative and traditional Republican camps.[29]

Paul Kleppner in *The Cross of Culture* basically sees politics as a conflict between opposing social groups; he considers, among other factors, the Norwegian American divergence of "pietists versus ritualists" and finds that they regardless of differences "shared the Haugean's antipathy to the use of alcohol and the desecration of the Sabbath"; this pietistic conviction, he concludes, became a determinant in political affiliation. Arguing that reality was more complex, Soike instead concludes that nationality and differing Lutheran positions—from the pietistic Haugean to the liturgical Norwegian Synod persuasions—were at best unpredictable determinants of political reform action.[30]

Regardless of one's preferred interpretive scheme, it remains undeniable that Swift County was built by the interaction and commingling of immigrant and Yankee populations; ethnicity thus surely played a significant part in the region's history and human experience. Sten Carlsson in his investigation of Scandinavian politicians in Minnesota between 1882 and 1900 concludes that there existed, as the political history of Minnesota illustrates, "a tangible Scandinavian self-consciousness, which hardly can be reconciled with a common perception of rapid assimilation into American society." It manifested itself from the 1880s, according to Carlsson, "in an especially pronounced Scandinavian advance to elected state offices when the much larger German population is considered." Before 1900 no German was elected governor whereas two Scandinavians held this high office. Norwegian immigrants, like those of other nationalities, arrived in America with an array of attitudes about class, economic status, and religion, with local cultural loyalties, allegiances, and predispositions; the major issue thus becomes which of

and how these survived and interacted, as Soike has it, "in American political issues and social conditions, and in the institutional arrangements
they fashioned." Unique attitudes and characteristics may be attributed
to all ethnic groups and viewed in the context of the resourcefulness
with which they met their new situation and created a new cultural
world different from the one they had left behind.[31]

A pietistic condemnation of alcohol was one of the moral tenets carried across the Atlantic and reinforced in the new setting. The issue of
temperance thus became a major concern in Norwegian American communities. Some ambivalence did exist, in the form of a pietist-liturgical
division: Norwegian areas with predominantly pietistic congregations,
those belonging to Hauge's Synod and the United Church, supported
temperance legislation while Synod townships were more reluctant to
vote for restrictive measures. However, as Soike reminds us, the Republican Party's strong move toward "dry" legislation from the 1870s to the
1890s was less pronounced in Minnesota than for instance in Iowa due
to opposition from large voting blocs like the German Lutherans and
the Catholics. Haugean pietists took with them from Norway a strong
condemnation of intoxicants and to a high degree represented the lower
social groups, whereas the Norwegian Synod was more in tune with
the culture of the middle and upper classes. The latter might approve
of social enjoyment of alcohol, but, as Kleppner contends, a shared religious perspective made Norwegian Synod Lutherans "unite with native
pietists, and other immigrant pietists, to espouse the cause of temperance and the 'Puritan Sunday,' and to oppose the 'Catholic party,'" as
immigrant pietists viewed the Democratic Party. J. L. Nydahl in his
1896 history of the temperance cause seems to support Kleppner's view,
claiming that "a large part of our Norwegian-Lutheran pastors in this
country are now temperance men and almost no one takes a strong position against" temperance. In an 1879 resolution, however, the Synod
leadership had shown its displeasure with organized temperance work;
while condemning drunkenness, it had warned Christians against joining temperance societies "since the congregation is for Christians the
right and completely adequate temperance society."

There were obviously ulterior motives involved in the Synod's opposition to temperance societies. The Synod clearly feared organizational
movements that it did not control, ones that might even pose a threat

to the Synod's religious mission, since the secular temperance societies would bring people into contact with non-Lutherans and nonbelievers. Norwegian Lutherans could hardly, as Kleppner elucidates, visit the Lord's table on Sunday and vote for a Democratic candidate on Tuesday. This strong anti-Democratic sentiment among Norwegian Lutherans, he claims, became a major factor in their long-standing loyalty to the Republican Party. Soike basically agrees and even suggests that strong anti-Catholic and anti-Democratic sentiments might cause political realignment in third-party coalitions as Norwegian voters became dissatisfied with the policies of the Republican Party. As will be seen, however, Norwegian politicians and voters in western Minnesota, in spite of Republican loyalty and a penchant for third-party movements, did not completely reject the Democrats even before the politically turbulent 1890s. And one may at least moderate the role of anti-Catholicism in the formation of third-party movements. Statewide, of course, the Democratic Party, dominated by a distained Irish minority, was to a high degree irrelevant; the only avenues open to discontented Norwegian farmers were the agrarian and anti-party movements of the late nineteenth century. Thus, it might be argued that the weakness of the Democratic Party, as much as anti-Catholicism, alienated Norwegian voters.[32]

Another circumstance must be weighed in any evaluation of the Lutheran impact on political behavior. Only a minority of Norwegians in America ever sought membership in a Norwegian Lutheran Church or in any other denomination. The church, of course, exercised great influence beyond the congregational fold through the force of tradition and its social engagement. In the countryside and in small towns membership was much higher than in large metropolitan areas. A general perception holds that in a small town everyone belonged to a church; membership provided not only a religious identity but frequently an ethnic one as well.

Even though Norwegians in America clearly constituted a peculiar people, whatever explanation one finds for their political attitudes and behavior must take into account the divisions that existed within the group. Norwegian Americans harbored an ethnoreligious sense of identity; "Lutheran" and "Norwegian" might indeed have been the same for most. Even so, Norwegians did not constitute a homogeneous population in Lutheran confessional practices; inroads—albeit relatively small—were also made by other faiths. In political activity as well they did not think with one mind but joined several partisan camps. Their early loyalty to the Republican Party can be easily understood: in postbellum Minnesota, Norwegian immigrants entered a political situation where the Republican Party held a near monopoly; they consequently were encouraged to give their vote to the party supported by their compatriots who had arrived earlier. The Protestant morality and social norms espoused by Republicans also attracted Norwegian voters and influenced their ideas about good government. Major departures from the Republican fold came later.

Norwegian and other ethnic groups, regardless of internal divisions, were frequently regarded as voting blocs. In 1910 the *Benson Times* remarked somewhat tongue-in-cheek that Bendick O. Leitte, who had immigrated with his parents from Haugesund, Norway, at the age of eleven in 1871—first local barber and later owner of Leitte's Diner—"is fixed to work or talk politics in all the languages current here . . . himself looking after the Norwegian." Petitioning Norwegians as a single voting bloc was more serious at an earlier date, when mastery of the Norwegian language by political leaders might appeal to ethnic sensibilities. In the November 1886 election *Benson Times* founder Edward Thomas wrote a letter for support as an independent candidate for register of deeds, giving as part of his credentials: "I speak English and German, and understand quite a good deal of Norwegian, and feel myself able to transact business personally with any one who comes to the office." Nationality became a means of securing votes. Newspaper publishers and editors regularly entered elected public service, printed partisan political opinions, and wielded influence as party leaders. In this process, ethnic politics played a significant part at least to the end of the century and vestiges of it lingered much longer. The local press appealed to and critiqued the ethnic vote up to the end of the 1920s. Ethnicity thus appears to have played a part, though of a much less militant nature than earlier, in the political life of western Minnesota until that time.

THE VAGARIES OF ETHNIC POLITICS

The ethnic politics engaged in by Norwegian-born Ole O. Lien, a resident of Big Bend in Chippewa County, suggest existing tensions between immigrants and old-stock Americans that went beyond political differences. Lien became state representative in 1878 and served several terms, in 1883 even speaking at the grand May 17 festivities in Benson. As a Democratic candidate in 1876 he had, however, lost the election. The Republican *Benson Times* commented on his "vituperative attacks against us" printed in Norwegian in the Minneapolis *Budstikken* by stating that the legislative district, which then encompassed Kandiyohi, Swift, and Chippewa counties, was spared a representative who could not "answer a fair argument in English," stating further that "possibly he can 'snakke' English, and was only endeavoring to excite our irascibility, by abusing us in a language we couldn't understand." Lien continued to introduce nationality as a platform issue; he attacked in particular the liberal Republican and later Populistic politician Ignatius Donnelly in response to Donnelly's disparaging "flagitious attacks" on him and the "Scandinavian crowd."

The basic motivations of ethnic politics were the awards given in the form of political appointments and, of course, the opportunity to run for political office as well as to vote for candidates of one's own nationality. Appeals were regularly predicated on such attractive inferences. It must be borne in mind that prior to political reorientation in the 1890s, the Democratic Party was a conservative party, indistinguishable on most issues from the Republicans. Donnelly was at the time of the controversy with Lien state senator and by then had distanced himself from the Republicans to become the most eloquent orator of Minnesota's farmers and laborers. Before the 1877 election Lien contended that the American opponents "have already kicked to our nationality as to an ass" and promised that "my countrymen will, on the day of election, throw the opposition entirely out of the field and create to them a political Waterloo on the plains of the west." Powerful ethnic sensibilities were brought into play. In his diatribes, Lien referred to Donnelly as "a lineal descendant of Balaam's ass" and described his *Anti-Monopolist* paper, which Donnelly had begun publishing in 1874, as a "filthy guerilla sheet." Lien was ridiculed by the *Swift County Advocate*—established in Benson before the 1877 election as a competing Republican organ by Z. B. Clarke, who was elected state senator on the Republican ticket in 1883—which proclaimed that: "The political campaign now commenced will be a fight between the Skandinavians [*sic*] and the Americans." Lien this time rode to victory, proving that a Norwegian Lutheran Democrat could win, as the official voting record suggests, on the shoulders of his compatriots—though it might be the exception. Norwegian voters would not likely have voted for an Irish Democratic candidate, however. In Swift County Lien carried the "Norwegian" townships and the village of Benson.[33]

THE REPUBLICAN PARTY AND ITS CHALLENGERS

Norwegians took part in civic life to a higher degree than did other populations in the state. Both ethnic proclivities and the special issues Norwegians championed may give insight into why. Eligible voters in Minnesota's Norwegian settlements showed high voting records; in all gubernatorial elections until the end of World War I Norwegian areas exceeded the state average in voter turnout. In Minnesota's franchise requirements, enacted in the bill establishing statehood in 1858, an immigrant could vote after taking out his first paper certifying his intent to become an American citizen, a policy that encouraged voter participation. The unusual extent of Norwegian civic involvement is by some scholars attributed to both ethnic traits and experience. Kendric Charles Babcock in his 1914 study claimed, "The Norwegian, of all men of the Northern lands, has the strongest liking for the political arena." He attributes this advantage both to "their political training at home" and their early settlement in the Upper Midwest, "ten or fifteen years before the Swedes, in the formative period of Wisconsin, Minnesota, Iowa, and Dakota."

National and state voting might deviate from each other. On the national front, Western Minnesota generally adhered to the state's traditional Republican stand. "In national politics," Stanley Anonsen wrote in 1929, "Swift County has been consistently republican, losing votes, only in periods of schism or agricultural depression." The record shows that until the 1920s Republican presidential candidates enjoyed pluralities in Swift County, with only two exceptions: in the 1892 presidential election James B. Weaver, the Populist candidate, won in Swift County, and in 1912 the voters there—along with the entire Minnesota electorate— gave a majority to Progressive Republican Theodore Roosevelt, the Bull Moose candidate. From 1860 to 1932, it was the single exception to Minnesota's steadfast loyalty to national Republican traditions.

TABLE 14

Election Returns for Governor by Townships and Villages/Cities in Swift County, 1892–1924

Townships											
	1892				1896		1924				
	R	D	PP	P	R	D&PP	R	D	FL	S	PR
Appleton	139	101	43	19	142	153	334	22	314	0	0
Benson	18	26	17	7	29	55	12	0	133	0	1
Camp Lake	42	7	50	7	69	50	16	2	164	0	0
Cashel	8	29	26	0	20	59	10	2	86	1	1
Clontarf	11	50	3	0	22	45	6	2	49	0	2
Dublin	3	34	3	2	19	49	30	5	44	1	1
Edison	31	35	7	7	82	19	24	7	90	0	0
Fairfield	7	36	8	1	87	50	12	0	143	0	2
Hayes	22	3	60	2	48	83	25	6	176	0	2
Hegbert	27	10	25	12	17	87	34	1	117	0	0
Kerkhoven	39	1	54	5	50	76	30	2	210	1	0
Kildare	21	76	11	2	28	115	30	16	52	0	0
Marysland	6	10	32	0	24	76	18	5	70	1	1
Moyer	30	24	6	2	79	18	6	1	80	0	1
Pillsbury	64	35	6	13	91	72	67	1	68	0	0
Shible	32	20	13	2	48	20	2	0	134	0	2
Six Mile Grove	21	12	32	2	23	61	18	2	87	2	0
Swenoda	18	15	29	2	45	53	5	0	156	0	0
Tara	3	49	10	0	5	64	5	1	105	0	2
Torning	13	15	48	6	15	67	54	5	124	0	0
West Bank	37	13	24	3	48	22	40	0	142	0	0
Total Townships	592	601	507	94	991	1,294	778	80	2,544	6	15
Villages/Cities											
Benson	108	54	44	4	101	156					
Ward 1							148	22	185	3	3
Ward 2							253	27	271	2	6
Clontarf							12	15	36	0	0
Danvers							36	5	29	0	1
De Graff							39	18	33	0	3
Holloway							23	0	92	0	0
Kerkhoven							170	24	44	0	0
Murdock	17	21	12	1	24	49	78	28	55	0	6
Total Swift County	717	676	563	99	1,116	1,499	1,538	219	3,369	11	34

Source: Published official election returns. Bruce M. White, et al. *Minnesota Votes.* St. Paul: Minnesota Historical Society, 1977, 153–88

R: Republican   P: Prohibition   PR: Progressive
D: Democrat   FL: Farmer-Labor   S: Socialist
PP: Populist (People's)

TABLE 15

Countywide Election Returns in Swift, Pope, and Lac qui Parle Counties
in Selected Minnesota Gubernatorial Races, 1883–1924

Year	Party	Candidate	County			Elected
			Swift	Pope	Lac qui Parle	
1883	R	L. P. Hubbard	680	361	614	L. P. Hubbard, 1882–87
	D	A. Bierman	638	236	219	
	P	C. A. Holt	7	10	9	
1892	R	Knute Nelson	592	1,070	1,202	Knute Nelson, 1893–95
	D	D. W. Lawler	601	205	375	
	PP	Ignatius Donnelly	507	491	653	
	P	W. J. Dean	94	95	67	
1896	R	David M. Clough	1,116	1,527	1,230	David M. Clough, 1895–99
	PP&D	John Lind	1,499	865	1,363	
	P	W. J. Dean	34	45	58	
	I	A. A. Ames	17	11	18	
	SL	W. B. Hammond	4	1	4	
1904	R	R. C. Dunn	1,027	925	975	John A. Johnson, 1905–9
	D	John A. Johnson	1,215	1,045	1,229	
1916	R	J. A. A. Burnquist	1,633	1,984	2,166	J. A. A. Burnquist, 1915–21
	D	T. P. Dwyer	533	301	352	
	S	J. O. Bentall	83	37	101	
	P	T. J. Anderson	157	234	222	
	IL	J. P. Johnson	34	49	18	
1924	R	Theodore Christianson	1,538	2,116	3,087	Theodore Christianson, 1925–31
	D	Carlos Avery	219	125	46	
	FL	Floyd B. Olson	3,369	2,501	2,754	
	SI	Oscar Anderson	11	12	10	
	PR	Michael Ferch	34	18	16	

Source: Published official election returns. Bruce M. White, et al. *Minnesota Votes.* St. Paul: Minnesota Historical Society, 1977, 153–88

R: Republican	FL: Farmer-Labor	S: Socialist
D: Democrat	I: Independent	SI: Socialist Industrialist
PP: Populist (People's)	IL: Independent Labor	SL: Socialist Labor
P: Prohibition	PR: Progressive	

The Republican Party did not do as well in state and local politics for a variety of reasons. Swift County appears to have had many independent Republican voters willing to support strong Democratic candidates. Swift County's Democratic profile was augmented by the fact that the "Irish" townships voted solidly Democratic. Only fourteen of twenty-eight Republican candidates for governor between 1873 and 1928 had pluralities in Swift County; in other cases, seven Democratic candidates, five Farmer-Labor, and two Farmers' Alliance and the Populist Party beat the Republican running for office. Norwegian farmers might view local needs in a different light than they did national politics, giving their support to political constellations with a greater concern for their particular economic and social circumstances. The Farmers' Alliance, launched in Chicago in 1880, gained strength in Minnesota with local alliances and a state organization. In Swift County it had locals in all townships, and Norwegian farmers joined in great numbers in order to advance their social and political interests. Thus the alliance exercised considerable local political influence throughout western Minnesota.

Practically all state representatives and state senators were Republican, however, with few exceptions, such as Ole O. Lien, until the second decade of the twentieth century. Elected state officials represented a district larger than Swift County; between 1881 and 1897, for instance, the counties of Swift, Lac qui Parle, and Chippewa formed one state senate district and from 1881 to 1888 had two state representatives and later, three. The Republican strength was greater in Lac qui Parle and Pope counties than in Swift County for some of the reasons suggested earlier. By the 1930s Swift and its neighboring counties had earned their reputation as a stronghold for the Democratic and Farmer-Labor parties, however, as these progressive political units became advocates for farmers' rights.[34]

The selected election years in Tables 14 and 15 suggest a clear evolution in the political life of Swift, Pope, and Lac qui Parle counties. Gubernatorial elections—until 1962 for two-year terms—may serve as a weather vane to track shifting political winds. The ethnic mix, with a dominance of Norwegian residents, influenced the political course of events. In the region's early history, however, Yankees and their political convictions dominated local politics. The Republican Party, as described above, held sway and controlled most elected county-level positions as these expanded along with the population. In the words of historian Jennifer Delton, Minnesota Republican Party dominance was based on it being "The province of wealthy Yankee industrialists, grain dealers, and railroad magnates" and because "the party also attracted the votes of Norwegian and Swedish farmers, two of the largest immigrant groups in the state." In its first election for governor in 1871, Swift County gave 144 votes to Republican candidate Horace Austin, who was elected, and only 23 to the Democratic contender. The Republicans held the lead in Swift County and Benson, but not with a consistently wide margin. The 1883 gubernatorial election, for instance, showed a close race between Republican Lucius F. Hubbard and the Norwegian-born Democratic candidate Adolph Bierman in Swift County but a much more comfortable Republican outcome in Pope and Lac qui Parle counties. Swift County's Catholic Irish townships and the heavily German Lutheran Fairfield Township gave Bierman their votes, as one would expect, but so did the heavily Norwegian townships of Swenoda, Camp Lake, and Torning, likely influenced by his ethnic origin.[35]

The Yankee population had the greatest access to local political offices, but immigrants, many having arrived as children, and to an even higher degree second-generation Norwegian Americans were engaged in public service. As suggested earlier, they entered township and village positions with some ease where they constituted a majority of the residents. But they also attained higher county offices: Norwegian-born Oley Thorson served as the first judge of probate in Swift County in 1871; Thomas Knudson became Swift County's first sheriff in 1872; Ole Wenaus held the office of county treasurer from 1873 for a decade; and Knud P. Frovold became county auditor in 1874.

In a large Norwegian population it is possible to prepare a long list of Norwegians who held county or village and city office; a few names will suffice to suggest an active participation. Many moved from teaching or business enterprise to elected political office. These individuals had through their social position earned the respect of their compatriots, who gave them their vote, but in order to win elected office they reached beyond their ethnic constituency. They obviously enjoyed the trust of their neighbors of other national origins. Hans C. Odney's political career is a case in point. An immigrant from Telemark, Norway, and a resident of the village of Kerkhoven, where he owned an imple-

ment store, Odney filled the position of county register of deeds for sixteen years from 1907. Michael Romstad, an emigrant at age four from
Steinkjer, is yet another example: he served as county auditor and city assessor in Benson, elected the first time in 1902; his original vocation had
been teaching. Men in less prestigious occupations might also succeed in
the political arena. Christian R. Alsaker, born in Nordfjord in 1853 and a
resident of Benson from 1875, worked at his trade as a blacksmith, gained
social status by amassing considerable property, and served as president
of the Benson village council for two years and as county commissioner
for twelve.

Norwegian Democratic politicians vied for elected office alongside
Republicans. Alsaker ran for local offices in the Democratic Party and
won; in 1908, the year before his death, he unsuccessfully sought a state-
level position on its ticket. Statewide political office regularly fell into
the Republican column, and political success for Democratic and third-
party groups continued for some time to be confined to county and local
offices. Another example is Norwegian-born I. B. Anderson, a Camp
Lake Township clerk who was elected county treasurer in 1900 as the
People's-Democratic candidate and served for several decades.

There was in the new century evidence of an increasing influence of
progressive politics. Norwegian voters in west-central Minnesota moved
into the reformist camp in large numbers. The political career of Julius
Thorson, one of Benson's most prominent politicians after 1900, gives evidence of emerging progressive politics statewide. Born in Rolling Forks
Township, Pope County, in 1868 to Norwegian immigrant parents but
a resident of Benson from childhood, he gained notoriety as a state and
local Democratic politician and co-owner and editor of the *Swift County
Monitor.* At the time of his death in 1928, he was Benson's mayor, a role
that highlights the advance of Democratic and Farmer-Labor forces during that decade.[36]

Nationality might have outweighed party affiliation in the early history of Swift County and may have influenced later voting behavior as
well. In fact, even at present a Norwegian moniker might well win votes,
and Norwegian American politicians continue quite deliberately to attend Norwegian events and gatherings to remind potential voters of a
shared heritage. In ethnic terms Norwegians along with other Scandinavians in Minnesota have shown political overrepresentation. It was

a gradual development, but with the Populist revolt and a persistent temperance crusade drawing much of its leadership and strength from the Norwegians and Swedes, their political engagement increased rapidly. From 1893 to 1940, as Theodore C. Blegen reminds us, "some ten or eleven out of fourteen governors in Minnesota were of Scandinavian origin." In comparison, because of the distrust of political parties and the pessimistic view of society that existed within the German Missouri Synod, as Richard Jensen observes, "Remarkably few American politicians ever emerged from the Missouri Synod, despite its size, intelligence and wealth." Religious conviction and ethnic peculiarities thus obviously affected political behavior, whether one was a German Missourian or a Norwegian Lutheran.[37]

The Populist Interlude

A reformist bent appeared for some time to have distinguished Swift County from other west-central Minnesota counties. Contributing factors were the strong presence of Irish Catholics and, as the record shows, support in traditional Republican townships. In the 1886 election Democratic and Populist candidates made significant gains in Swift County: the Democratic candidate—the popular but notorious Minneapolis political boss Albert A. Ames—narrowly beat Republican Andrew A. McGill, who gained the governorship supported by the electorate in Swift's neighboring counties of Kandiyohi, Chippewa, Lac qui Parle, and Pope. They all gave McGill pluralities and, like Swift County, had large Scandinavian populations. Ames earned pluralities in Swift County's "Irish" townships, but he also received a majority in the "Norwegian" township of Six Mile Grove and a fair showing in the village of Benson. Politically, Swift County thus appears to have been an anomaly when compared to the "Scandinavian" counties that surrounded it. At the time those counties were heavily Republican while Swift chose more of a middle ground, especially in state and local affairs, and in later years became a leader in progressive politics. Even when the Republican Party triumphed in the county, it tended to do so with a much smaller percentage than in neighboring districts.[38]

The 1890 election signaled, as Blegen has it, "the emergence of third-party protest on a large scale in the traditionally conservative state." In the governor's race the Democratic, Farmers' Alliance, and Prohibitionist candidates combined to far out-poll the Republican victor. Agrarian dissatisfaction was at the root of the change, and its stronghold was in the western portion of the state, in particular among Scandinavian, especially Norwegian, farmers. The large Norwegian land ownership in Swift County—replicated in neighboring counties and throughout the Red River Valley—had obvious political reverberations. In 1907 Norwegian farmers owned in excess of 28 percent of the total acreage in Swift County and from 23.1 to 88.4 percent in ten of the twenty-one townships. Through political action the farmers sought control over the marketing of their products as well as to diminish the power of the railroad companies and to establish a better credit arrangement.

The Populist candidate for governor, Sidney M. Owen, won handily in Swift County and finished second in the village of Benson behind the Democratic candidate. Save for Kandiyohi, where he lost to the Republican candidate, Owen enjoyed pluralities in the surrounding counties. His support was especially strong in Lac qui Parle, where the politician Einar Hoidale in early 1891 started publishing the Farmers' Alliance organ the *Western Guard*, which exercised considerable influence among the county's Norwegian farmers. Following the election the pro-Democratic *Swift County Monitor* declared, "In this senatorial district the Farmers' Alliance and the Democrats combined to carry everything. It is but just to the Republican candidates to say that no one could have been nominated by that party in this district who would have stood any show for election." Democratic or Populist candidates won every state and county office in Benson and in Swift County, with one exception: in Benson the popular Dane, O. F. Bronniche, a Republican, retained his position as judge of probate. In a relatively small electorate, there was some tendency to vote for familiar individuals, regardless of political color.[39]

The 1892 election saw the ascendancy of Norwegian-born Knute Nelson to the governorship on the Republican ticket. Nelson, who arrived in America from Voss, Norway, in 1842 at age seven with his unmarried and destitute mother, moved from great poverty through the American political system to represent the ultimate success story. He became the object of great ethnic pride and boasting. He spoke "the good Vossa tongue" and cultivated his ethnic connections. In his visits to Benson he was entertained by the Bjørgvin Singing Society, which performed both the "Star-Spangled Banner" and Norwegian songs. Exhibiting ethnic heritage in political events and rallies was perhaps a less direct means of appealing to the ethnic vote. Rural discontent among Norwegian farmers came to Nelson's aid as he voiced their grievances. Nelson had to gain support beyond his ethnic base in order to be elected; thus he could not play the nationality card without regard for his other constituencies. In Swift County he had majorities in the "Norwegian" townships, losing only Torning but winning in the village of Benson. Even so, Nelson lost Swift County: the Democratic and Populist candidates combined to out-poll him by a wide margin, and the Democratic candidate received the most votes. Nelson had, however, large majorities in Pope and Lac qui Parle counties, again attesting to a stronger Republican position in those counties than in Swift.[40]

Reformist forces were, however, much in evidence in all counties in west-central Minnesota. The colorful and versatile Ignatius Donnelly, the Populist candidate, had a fair share of the votes in 1892 and in both Pope and Lac qui Parle counties did better than his Democratic opponent. Nevertheless, indications are that the earliest example of progressive politics in the three counties had run its course. The 1894 election signified more clearly the changing political winds. The *Swift County Monitor* lamented a huge Republican victory in state and national elections, ascertaining, "One of the surprises of the election was the weakness shown by the populists. It was supposed that they would make great gains everywhere, but this prediction was not verified by the results . . . The verdict of the people would indicate that they believe there is room for only two parties in this country—and the populist is not one of these."[41]

The fleeting character of the Populist Party notwithstanding, it had a lasting impact as a harbinger of reform and the weakening of the Republican Party in Minnesota. John D. Hicks, one of the foremost historians of the period, finds in Populism the roots of twentieth-century reforms that culminated with the New Deal.

It is evident that Minnesota's Populist Party, even with its limited success at the polls, helped maintain the continuity of the state's tradition of reform. Scandinavian voters and politicians were greatly involved in the reform movement. A historic political change took place in the 1896 election; the resulting fusion between the Democrats and the Populists represented a major political realignment. The Democratic Party in alliance with the Populists mobilized small farmers and urban laborers, abandoned its earlier laissez-faire conservatism, and promoted economic radicalism. The fusion party's Swedish-born gubernatorial candidate, John Lind, had a majority in both Swift and Lac qui Parle counties but lost in Pope to the conservative David M. Clough, who gained the governorship. In Swift County the Scandinavian as well as the Irish townships gave Lind their vote. His support trumped the Republican Party's strong position and might be attributed to nationality, prominence, and the reformist platform of the fusion party. In the 1898 election, following service in the Spanish-American War and vigorous attacks against the conflict's imperialistic implications, Lind was elected governor as a fusion candidate. It was the first time after the Civil War that a Republican had not won the governorship of the state.[42]

LOCAL INTEREST AND NATIONAL POLITICS

Judging by election returns, the Democratic Party's historic reform and alliance with the Populist Party during the politically stormy 1890s did not displace the Republicans in Swift County. Party loyalty may even have strengthened at the expense of nationality. Norwegian voters appeared diverse politically, embracing several political parties, whereas the Irish showed great allegiance to the Democratic Party and the Yankees to the Republican. Nevertheless, Republicans typically gained support in Scandinavian districts as well. In the 1908 state and federal elections, for instance, the Democratic candidates won in townships and towns with large Irish populations and Republican candidates won in Scandinavian precincts. In Benson, ward 1—the north side, with its Irish and working-class composition—gave a plurality to the Democratic candidate, Swedish American John A. Johnson, who won the governorship, whereas ward 2—the more affluent south side—supported the Republican contender. Johnson had a majority in Swift County but lost in Lac qui Parle and Pope counties, both of which polled large Republican majorities.

There were, however, serious cracks in the Republican Party. "The wearing of the Democratic label by respected Scandinavians, like John Lind and John A. Johnson . . . strengthened . . . insurgent tendencies," historian Carl Chrislock maintains. In 1912 Theodore Roosevelt, presidential candidate for the newly formed Progressive Party—the reformist Bull Moose movement—carried the city of Benson and the county whereas William Howard Taft, the Republican candidate, finished a distant third. Woodrow Wilson, elected on the Democratic ticket, was a close second, only about one hundred votes behind Roosevelt. The surrounding counties of Chippewa, Kandiyohi, Lac qui Parle, and Pope gave large majorities to Roosevelt as well.[43]

Political reform and ethnic loyalty were both placed in danger by the European war. "By the autumn of 1914," Chrislock notes, "the opposing armies of World War I were slaughtering each other on a scale unprecedented in world history." The Nordic homelands of Scandinavian immigrants maintained neutrality throughout the conflict, sparing them the most severe questioning of their loyalty to America. The United States did not enter the European conflict until April 1917, but the issue of patriotism was raised earlier. Beginning in 1915 and for the next several years a campaign was launched against hyphenate subcultures, especially the German American, although no immigrant group was spared; "anti-hyphenism stridently challenged manifestations of ethnic separatism within American society," Chrislock writes. A major issue is the impact on political life of, as John Higham describes it, "the most strenuous nationalism and most pervasive nativism that the United States has known." The Minnesota Commission of Public Safety appointed the Norwegian-born Republican newspaperman and diplomat Nicolay A. Grevstad overseer of the Scandinavian American press; he would monitor the content of non-English-language newspapers "to correct misinformation, supply needed information, repress disloyalty where it may be found, and . . . convert passive loyalty into wholehearted, strong and active support of the administration and its war effort."[44]

How did the large Norwegian-speaking communities in western Minnesota respond to the call for "100 percent Americanism" and the demands of American war policies? James Youngdale answers that many questioned "involvement in the old feuds of Europe." This antiwar sentiment was reinforced by the continuous deflation of farm prices from the agricultural depression of 1913–14. A renewed agrarian outburst became evident with the emergence of the Nonpartisan League, a farmers' organization inspired by the message of the American Socialist Party led by Eugene V. Debs, though as a presidential candidate in 1912 Debs polled only one hundred votes in Swift County.

The league's founder was A. C. Townley, who advocated political action under such socialist reforms as "state ownership of elevators and mills, state inspection of grain and dockage, state hail insurance and state rural banks." As Robert Morlan suggests in the title of his history of the league, it swept like "political prairie fire" through rural areas of North Dakota—where it emerged in 1915 as a faction within the Republican Party—and through Minnesota and a dozen other states. The party and its leaders were accused of being unpatriotic. Morlan claims that the league was anti-war before U.S. entry into the hostilities and that "it accurately reflected the sentiments of the bulk of its membership and of the people in the area in which it operated." When the league in 1920 endorsed Norwegian American Henrik Shipstead of Glenwood for governor, he out-polled both his Democratic and Republican opponents in Swift County, winning all "Norwegian" townships but losing the city of Benson to the victorious Republican Jacob A. O. Preus. Preus, a third-generation Norwegian American and scion of a distinguished Lutheran clerical family, represented the prevailing conservative business philosophy.[45]

After actual entry into the war, the league formally, if not enthusiastically, backed the war effort but continued its demand for the conscription of wealth as well as of manpower to finance the war. The citizens of Benson and Swift County—regardless of ethnic background—joined their fellow Americans in a show of patriotism. Even before U.S. involvement, *Minneapolis Tidende* and other major Norwegian-language journals had shown a pro-Ally slant, although some members of the Norwegian American press, such as *Fram* of Fargo, a Nonpartisan League organ—like the German and Swedish American newspapers—expressed sympathy for Germany, being mindful of a shared Lutheranism and the admiration of "German civilization" harbored by many leading Norwegian Americans. Once America engaged in the hostilities, however, they all, as one would expect, unstintingly supported the nation's war policies.[46]

In 1918 the *Starbuck Times* announced that Magnus Grondahl had died on the western front in France, the first local man to fall in battle. Casualty lists constitute the most poignant comments on war's dire reality. In December 1918, following German capitulation in November, the *Swift County Monitor* listed the names of wounded and fallen soldiers of Swift and adjoining counties. Benson had witnessed its first military funeral in April 1918, when Andrew G. Gusdal was buried from Our Savior's Lutheran Church.

Details of drafted men were sent off to training camps with parades, music, military balls, and patriotic addresses. The *Swift County Monitor* called the men "our best young manhood," who will "fight in a grand and noble cause and for a nation that deals most generously with her brave defenders." Governor Joseph A. A. Burnquist—serving from 1915 to 1921, of Swedish background with a reputation as a progressive Republican—made visits to western Minnesota, including Benson, and gave stirring patriotic speeches. In 1918 these stops became a part of his re-election campaign, first in a bitter fight for the Republican nomination against the Nonpartisan League candidate, Swedish-born Charles A. Lindbergh, and later in a victorious election race. The loyalty question was raised against his political opponents as Joseph "All-American" Burnquist—taking liberty with his middle initials—established himself as a man with "grand Americanism" who must "not be replaced by one whose loyalty and patriotic Americanism lacks very much of being the 100 percent brand." In a state where 70 percent of residents were immigrants or the children of immigrants, the ethnic factor was given high priority. Burnquist's strong endorsement by Senator Knute Nelson won him favors among Scandinavian voters.

Campaigns to label Townley and the league and its supporters disloyal might advance individual political careers, but they were patently unfair to Minnesota's ethnic populations and to the military men they contributed. Looking only at the lists of Swift County recruits and volunteers who served in the armed forces, one finds that they represented an ethnic cross section of the county's residents, with English, Irish, German, Norwegian, Swedish, and other national names. Minnesotans, as Blegen writes, "gave wholehearted, generous, willing, loyal, eager, and patriotic support to the state's effort and to American success in the war."[47]

THE POLITICS OF THE 1920S

Progressive politics gained strength in the years after the armistice. By the 1920s the Scandinavian and Irish electorates were aligned, united around a rural commitment to progressive politics. However, policies intended to relieve the problems of farmers created a political dichotomy between the city and country, between laborers and the agricultural population.

An agricultural depression in 1920 affected farmers severely, again attracting support to the Nonpartisan League. Its influence declined thereafter, and only with the Depression in 1929, as James Youngdale writes, "did radical movements again surge forward." The Farmer-Labor Party, founded in Minnesota in 1922, united many protest groups in a radical third-party movement, producing an alliance that embodied "the long struggle and deep hopes . . . for ordinary people." Tensions surfaced between its rural and labor wings, however; their separate missions threatened to divide the new political party. The party's Scandinavian American connection was strong and intimate. Three major political shifts may be identified in the 1920s. One major reform was the enfranchisement of women, which Ida Simley Kvale—wife of Ole J. Kvale, a dominant political figure in Benson at the time—explained to the *Swift County Monitor* would have "a purifying influence in politics, especially in those departments which affect children and the home." Even as women quickly entered into both state and national politics, it would, however, be difficult to show that women's voting rights gave politics a new projectile; the major reform issues were already in place. Secondly, emphasis on county politics—the party designation of candidates frequently ignored when publishing election results—moved toward concentration on the state and national political scene; there emerged an intense interest in the races for Minnesota governor and congressional senators and representatives. Finally, there was the third-party development and a major shift toward progressive politics at a countywide level, the latter departure yielding an apparent separation between rural and city voters.[48]

The 1922 and 1924 races gave evidence of a progressive wave that affected both the urban and the agricultural electorate. In 1922 the Farmer-Labor candidate Shipstead beat Republican Frank B. Kellogg in both Benson and Swift County and was elected to the U.S. Senate. On the same ticket, Swedish-born Magnus Johnson, while losing the governorship to Preus, defeated him at both levels. Johnson was, however, elected U.S. senator in a special election in 1923. The Farmer-Labor Party's two senators, both from rural areas, aligned with western Republican progressives in the Senate, distancing themselves from the class consciousness promoted by the party's labor wing. Ole J. Kvale filed for Congress as an Independent in the Seventh District, which included Swift, Pope, and Lac qui Parle counties, and was elected. He was re-elected on the Farmer-Labor ticket until his death in 1929; like his Senate colleagues he favored his rural constituency. The *Swift County News* in 1922 declared on its front page, "the nation has experienced one of the greatest turnovers in recent years."[49]

Born on a farm near Decorah, Iowa, Kvale was a second-generation Norwegian American and a Lutheran minister by training and vocation. In 1917—the year of the major merger that created the Norwegian Lutheran Church of America (*Den norsk lutherske kirke i Amerika*)—he was called to serve Our Savior's Lutheran Church in Benson. His sympathy for the reform policies of the agrarian Nonpartisan League convinced him to enter political life. In 1924 the progressive spirit prevailed locally to an astounding degree. In the presidential race Robert M. La Follette, running as a third-party candidate and a progressive politician favored by Norwegian American voters, won Swift County with a wide margin but lost in the city of Benson and the village of Kerkhoven to Republican Calvin Coolidge; Floyd B. Olson, of Norwegian and Swedish background and running for governor on the Farmer-Labor ticket, won Swift County as well as the city of Benson, though with a small margin. The Norwegian, Irish, and German townships were united in their support. Olson was victorious in Pope County; he polled a respectable vote in Lac qui Parle but lost to favored son Republican Theodore Christianson of Dawson, who won the governorship. Christianson, born to Norwegian American parents on a farm near the village of Lac qui Parle, a lawyer by training and publisher of the *Dawson Sentinel,* was well positioned for a successful political career. Christianson was one among other examples of the ability of small towns to produce political leaders who moved from local, to state, and even to national elected office. The emergence of Theodore Christianson as governor of Minnesota in 1925 signaled, as Theodore Blegen states, "a continuation of Republican dominance" at the state level.

The fact that Calvin Coolidge won in the city of Benson but lost in the county suggests the divide that progressive politics engendered be-

tween farmers and townspeople. Benson voted much more conserva-
tively than did the countryside, although in comparison to the county's
two other main towns—Appleton and especially Kerkhoven—Benson
was relatively liberal. The north side—ward 1—for instance, gave a slight
majority to La Follette. A division becomes even clearer in the 1926 election, when Swift County showed preference for only one Republican
candidate in state and national elections while conversely Benson gave
victory to only one Farmer-Labor candidate—favored son Ole J. Kvale—
and instead supported Republicans. The politics of rural voters and
residents of Benson city clearly diverged. The progressive focus on the
agricultural community's welfare did not sufficiently respond to urban
commercial self-interest; it also reveals the rifts that existed between
the two dimensions of the Farmer-Labor Party.[50]

"Demon Rum"

Progressives regularly blamed alcohol and saloon owners for the social
evils they saw. It was precisely the fight against drinking that as a leading
issue pulled many Norwegians into the Progressive movement and gave
Norwegian politicians an edge as they promised to keep the sale of alcohol out of the community. Thus, this chapter in Norwegians' American
experience deserves special attention. "The saloon can be eradicated,
but cannot be regulated," became, according to J. L. Nydahl, the parole
of the temperance people. He claimed that "drunkenness was bad in
Norway" but got worse in America "because of the new circumstances
and easier access to drink." He continued, "It is . . . a humiliating fact that
there are few nationalities which suffer from the evil of drink as much
as ours, and there thus is a much stronger encouragement to gather our
strength against it." Jon Willand reminds us, "Saloons . . . were the common men's social clubs, democratic in that respect but excluding women
by unwritten rule." Nydahl is certainly correct in stating that "the saloon became a political issue," but as an eager advocate of temperance
he might be faulted for exaggerating the abuse of liquor among his fellow Norwegians. In any case, Norwegians and other Scandinavians did
indeed earn a reputation as heavy drinkers. In Starbuck—in a case of biased stereotyping—the term "Langhei Indians" was used to describe "a
tribe of Scandinavians south of Starbuck and Glenwood" who came to

town to get drunk "and staggered about the streets yelling like Indians." Pastor H. O. Koefod of Starbuck's Fron Lutheran Church even complained in a letter to a local rural church that some of its members "get drunk and wander about the streets." It might indeed be public drunkenness, rather than excessive consumption, that earned Norwegians a reputation as "hard drinkers and brawlers." Those who did represented but a small minority among their compatriots.[51]

A respondent in Lac qui Parle County insisted that, even so, "a 'nip' was very much appreciated by most dry Norskies" since they "voted their beliefs and drank their wants." A respondent in Benson quoted the Irish complaining after Norwegians voted down off-sale liquor: "Those damn Norwegians, they vote dry and drink wet." Be this as it may, there was in any case a general religious condemnation of drinking, as Koefod's actions suggest, and a feeling that imbibing alcohol was not simply a deplorable vice but a sin against the word of God. Ada Olson relates her reaction and Magnus Pedersen's sense of guilt when she happened to see him coming out the back door of a Benson saloon carrying a pail of beer: "He looked like he didn't want to be seen. I was shocked. The minister's brother in the saloon!"[52]

The saloon period for Lac qui Parle County lasted until about 1915, according to Willand; however, that year has a much wider applicability. In Swift County the local optionists won a large majority in a special election even as most of the Irish and German precincts, as well as the villages of Holloway and Clontarf, opposed the policy. Locally, then, the new regulation might clearly be viewed as a "Norwegian" law. County option in fact became state law on March 1 of that year, heavily endorsed by a Scandinavian electorate. The city of Benson supported the reform; the previous April in the annual city election it had voted to discontinue the licensing of saloons. Cities such as Benson could through provisions in their charters enjoy local-option rights; by legislative action in 1913 municipal local-option laws were made applicable to *all* urban areas of less than 10,000 residents. Credit for the grand victory in Swift County, the *Swift County Monitor* writes, "is largely due to the clean and effective campaign conducted by both the Benson Temperance League and the local branch of the WCTU" —the Woman's Christian Temperance Union. The newspaper editorially urged that "all good law-abiding citizens should unite in assisting the incoming administration to enforce

Ole Halvorson and Joe Ward outside the Starbuck Saloon, 1900. The saloon period lasted until about 1915.

the laws." It was precisely this challenge that had failed in the past and would continue to do so.[53]

Dr. Saxe J. Froshaug, a "prominent physician and progressive citizen," became a major county option spokesman. He was born in Lee County, Illinois, in 1867 to Norwegian immigrant parents, Dr. John O. and Caroline Froshaug, and opened his medical practice in Benson in 1907. In 1910 he announced his candidacy for state senator for the legislative district encompassing Swift and Big Stone counties, his main plank in his platform being, "A county option measure by which the people shall control the liquor traffic and not be controlled by it." Froshaug was elected on the county option ticket and served four years.[54]

Froshaug, who cultivated close connections to his Norwegian heritage, typified many, Norwegians and others, who joined antiliquor and antisaloon movements. As a member of Our Savior's he was influenced by the prevailing Norwegian Lutheran condemnation of alcohol. County option was only one of two antiliquor measures under consideration by the Minnesota Legislature; the second was statewide prohibition of the sale of intoxicants. The prohibitionists had the most sweeping success, but the ground had been prepared by the local optionists and the several temperance and prohibition organizations and political constellations that agitated against the evil effects of alcohol. Several Norwegian temperance societies in Minnesota were in 1885 united in the Minnesota Total Abstinence Society (*Minnesota Totalafholdsselskab*)—the name later changed to the Scandinavian Temperance Society of Minnesota. Dominated by the Norwegian Lutheran clergy, in 1914 the society had 125 local lodges and the zealous temperance agitator Reverend Ole Lokensgaard as its president.

The Good Templars also had Norwegian lodges in the state, many members having belonged before emigrating, and Norwegian women were active in the WCTU. Norwegian-born Ulrikka Feldtman Bruun traveled for the WCTU; from its headquarters in Evanston, Illinois, she visited Minnesota and other midwestern states to organize "unions" of Scandinavian women. Women's temperance work moved them into the political arena; voting rights for women was the WCTU's stated goal. By the time of national prohibition enacted in 1919 by the Eighteenth Amendment to the Constitution—the Volstead Act—and in effect January 1920, sixty-three out of the state's eighty-six counties were "dry."[55]

U.S. congressman Andrew J. Volstead sponsored the National Prohibition Enforcement Act to implement the Eighteenth Amendment, which he had authored, thus bestowing his name on the measure. Born in Kenyon, Minnesota, in 1860 of immigrant parents from Telemark, Norway, Volstead enjoyed a long and distinguished political career, beginning at the local and county level in Granite Falls and Yellow Medicine County. He was first elected to Congress in 1902 from the Seventh Congressional District on the Republican ticket as a progressive. He gained large majorities in all fourteen of the district's counties, including Lac qui Parle, Pope, Swift, Kandiyohi, Chippewa, and Yellow Medicine. Volstead served in the House of Representatives until 1923. In his re-election bid in 1920, Ole J. Kvale defeated him in the primary election, but Kvale was disqualified by the district court for having called Volstead an "atheist," thereby prejudicing the electorate. Swift County newspapers were filled with the controversy. Later, of course, Kvale ran successfully on the Farmer-Labor ticket. Republican senator Knute Nelson, by then enjoying the status of a senior statesman, deplored the fact of "Norwegians fighting Norwegians in a vituperative & most malignant manner."[56]

Drinking continued in violation of state and federal laws, evidenced by a great increase in arrests for drunkenness and by the confiscation of large quantities of liquor. Bootleggers made a hefty business in the illicit sale of alcohol. As early as December 1920, the local WCTU charged Benson with "fast becoming the most 'widely open' city in this section of the state," even suggesting that "blind pigs" were receiving the protection of the authorities. Evidence was found, the charges pointed out, in the "number of intoxicated people on our streets every Saturday night." These accusations were immediately rejected as false by the chief of police and the mayor. Nevertheless, stories of bootleggers are legion; there were regular reports of the arrest and release of moonshiners, some several times. In 1921 Gayhart Larson of Minneapolis, who made periodic visits to Swift County, was arrested in Kerkhoven for selling liquor at thirteen dollars per quart. He was further accused of adding strychnine to the moonshine, causing the deaths of two farmers near Murdock. Municipal court books are excellent sources for finding violators. Willand cites the particularly illustrative example of Mrs. Azalia Nicholson and her "chronic den of iniquity" in her home east of the river in Dawson: "It seems to have been visited by bootleggers and petty criminals of all sorts." The *Dawson Sentinel* reported on her arrest and conviction in December 1923: "Mrs. Azalia Nicholson, whose place across the river has for some time been a disgrace for the city of Dawson and a source of scandal throughout the county, was sentenced to spend ninety-five days in the county jail after a jury had found her guilty of maintaining a disorderly house."[57]

National Prohibition was clearly not the solution, neither in removing the issue from politics nor in the sale and consumption of intoxicants. In October 1921 the *Swift County Monitor* published an article predicting that prohibition "is yet to come back as one of the big issues of our political and social life." The article continued, "Prohibition these days is being blamed for more than the intemperance of the saloon days, and these include everything from moral issues to the accusation that the sale of moonshine is the cause of the present financial depression." Enforcement of prohibition measures was viewed as nearly impossible, and illicit consequences were everywhere evident. Not until

1933, however, was the prohibition amendment repealed. Swift, Pope, and Lac qui Parle counties under county option still voted "dry" in 1943; they had all voted "dry" in the 1933 referendum regarding the Volstead Act, although the city of Benson had voted for its repeal. Under local option, Swift County in an October 1947 special election voted "wet," permitting municipal liquor stores. Legal sales were approved by a vote of 3,373 to 1,745. Arguments for and against preceded the vote, the wets arguing that Swift County was "the wettest 'dry' county in the State of Minnesota" and the temperance forces citing a larger number of revocations of driver's licenses in "wet" than in "dry" counties.

During the postwar years the temperance movement still retained strength in the Norwegian farming population; only Six Mile Grove of the heavily Norwegian townships voted "wet." Such typically "Norwegian" townships as Benson, Camp Lake, Kerkhoven—as well as Kerkhoven village—Hayes, Hegbert, Swenoda, Torning, and West Bank all produced "dry" majorities. The city of Benson waited until an election in April 1948 to approve by a large majority the operation of a municipal liquor store in the city. It was, in the *Swift County Monitor*'s judgment, "The biggest transition in Benson" since the legal sale of "intoxicating liquor . . . had been prohibited since 1913." The "drys" were even more entrenched in the Norwegian and Lutheran stronghold of Starbuck, where the "liquor issue" continued to fail "by considerable margins" at the polls; only in the 1976 general election—and then with a narrow *two vote* margin—was the issuing of liquor licenses approved. A city ordinance was finally drawn up to govern the sale of liquor. The strong rejection of licensing the sale of intoxicants might be viewed in the deeper context of the persistent strength of Norwegian ethnoreligious loyalties and morality.[58]

THE NORWEGIAN AMERICAN MOMENTUM

What, then, was the impact of a dominant Norwegian American population on the political, social, and cultural structures in towns like Starbuck, Benson, and Madison? How did town and country differ? During the golden age of Norwegian America, the thirty years between 1895 and 1925, Norwegians in west-central Minnesota demonstrated their cultural loyalty to an ancestral homeland while becoming enterprising actors in shaping their social and political footing. In this regard, culturally as well as politically, the distinction between town and country sharpened. Among the second generation in the urban environment Norwegian cultural idioms were in jeopardy of disappearing and special efforts were introduced to preserve a transplanted heritage, while in the segregated agricultural communities the old-world vernacular was seemingly transferred from one generation to the next as a matter of course.

In both town and country the Norwegian language, in its refined Dano-Norwegian literary form, resounded in Norwegian Lutheran houses of worship. In town, however, the English work intruded into congregational life in the early decades of the new century. Norwegian American Lutheranism gained added resources by the 1917 union of competing Lutheran synods—the United Church, Hauge's Synod, and the Norwegian Synod—to create the Norwegian Lutheran Church of America. Increased secularism might weaken its effective teaching of Protestant morality, yet the Lutheran congregation persisted as a strong moral force that affected the community beyond its membership. The evil of alcohol and the church's pietistic condemnation became a strong tenet of its faith; in its fight against the legal sale of intoxicants the church moved into the public arena.

The drive for total abstinence, with enthusiastic support from Norwegian voters, pulled many Norwegians into the Progressive movement and promoted the election of politicians of their nationality. In fact, Norwegians demonstrated a special zeal for public office and political involvement. They were willing allies in the vagaries of ethnic politics, which though in decreasingly belligerent form visibly persisted until 1930. Agrarian discontent loosened the Republican Party's hold in western Minnesota and inspired Norwegians and other Scandinavians to join reformist movements; their large land holdings were motivating forces. In the 1920s strong reform and third-party successes for the Democratic and Farmer-Labor parties, as the Nonpartisan League had enjoyed earlier, characterized the political climate. The shift toward progressive politics favoring the farmer created tensions between rural and urban voters, however. Universal woman suffrage and Prohibition represented liberal legislation at the national level, though the restrictive measures of Prohibition were destined to fail. Still, opposition to licensing the sale of liquor, supported by strong Norwegian constituencies, continued for decades after Prohibition's repeal.

Responses to a national Norwegian monarchy in 1905 and the festive centenary jubilee of the Eidsvoll Constitution generated passionate ethnic sentiments and convinced some leading Norwegians that a permanent Norwegian American subculture could exist. A debate about its nature surfaced with the formation of old-home societies, the *bygdelag,* which sought legitimacy for the rural Norwegian heritage. But demands placed on all Americans with the nation's involvement in the European conflict dashed hopes for the permanency of a Norwegian America. Indeed, most Norwegians had not harbored such expectations and might in fact not have wished for a separate ethnic existence. But loyalty to an inherited transplanted heritage was cultural, for Norwegians and for all immigrant nationalities, and they did not see a conflict between an ethnic identity and patriotic loyalty to American citizenship. It was World War I that called into question a hyphenated identity, even as young men of varied ethnic backgrounds were brought into or volunteered for military service.

Six

The Persistence of Ethnicity

AN ABIDING ISSUE

The persistence of a separate Norwegian American community may have been in some question in the postwar years. Ultimately, a structural ethnicity and ethnic boundaries dissipated and a sense of a national Norwegian American community weakened.

Norwegian immigration was greatly reduced, though there was a smaller wave in the 1920s; the Great Depression caused many more people to return to Norway than move to America. The continuation of an earlier exodus resumed after World War II but declined quickly. By the end of the twentieth century the tradition of going to America had largely become a part of history. As a result the Norwegian American community was not replenished to a degree sufficient to maintain a viable ethnic subculture. The situation highlighted the problem of transferring a cultural loyalty to generations born in America. Shifting social attitudes in the host society played an important role in whatever efforts were initiated to create pride in ancestry and to transmit a cultural heritage.

During World War I American nativism and xenophobia had subjected immigrant populations to a downgrading and humiliation of their ancestral heritage and national background. Little effort was made to distinguish between cultural and political loyalty. After the freedoms of speech and organization were restored, a naturally strong reaction rose in these same ethnic groups. The simple question they posed might be: "Can we as Norwegians speak Norwegian and still be loyal Americans?" Professor Knute Lokensgard of Madison, then president of Hallinglaget—organized in 1907 to assemble Hallings in America—published a report where he gave a forceful affirmative answer: "We . . . demand recognition as a part of the nation, and we do not tolerate the fact that we are viewed as a pack of strange aliens because we know a language besides English." As the statement was written in Norwegian, it was intended to encourage Norwegians to promote their Norwegian identity, to affirm that they had given to America as much as they had received and thus had no need to feel eternally grateful, and to support efforts to retain their cultural values and Norwegian heritage. "We will continue to build our country," Lokensgard concluded, "but we will do it as Norwegian Americans."[1]

In 1920, still in a patriotic mode, Bjørgvin Lodge of the Sons of Norway in Benson "celebrated their mother country's national holiday . . . with a banquet and a ball, the lowering of the order's service flag and the unveiling of a memorial bronze tablet upon which is inscribed the names of 20 members of the lodge who served in the world war." The following year Bjørgvin Lodge, joined by Lærken Lodge of the Daughters of Norway—organized in Benson in 1916—made the arrangements, attracting "the largest crowd which has ever attended a previous celebration of the birthday of Norway's independence."[2]

Beyond such public displays of ethnic fervor, one may well ask what other indicators of a persistent ethnic loyalty, what sociological evidence of internal cohesive forces, existed. The present chapter will consider on a historical backdrop, sketched over three-quarters of the century, the expressions and changing definition of a Norwegian American heritage, the socioeconomic situation, and the unsteady lot of small towns and farming operations in west-central Minnesota. Popular culture invaded the place Norwegians and other ethnic groups called home and became an additional competitor to transplanted ethnic cultures. A decline in the local agrarian society deepened by the Great Depression further complicated social developments; social concerns were, however, fortified and expanded. World War II in some significant ways became an antidote to ethnic decline as Norwegians united in their assistance to an occupied homeland. Within the local Norwegian American population a high rate of endogamy seemed to contradict fear of "the flight of the second generation," as did living traditions in ethnic cuisine and social conventions. These traditions became a part of a revived enthusiasm as ethnicity manifested itself as a festive culture—celebrated and accepted as an expression of ethnic identity and pride in heritage.

THE NORSE-AMERICAN CENTENNIAL

The immigrant generation exercised great influence—though later generations of American-born Norwegians were much in view—in the largest festival arranged by Norwegian Americans in the 1920s. They celebrated their own past and present in America. In 1925 it would be one hundred years since the arrival of the *Restauration*—landing on the American shore on October 9, 1825—with the first boatload of Norwegian immigrants. The Norse-American Centennial became a magnificent expression of Norwegian ethnicity; it represented an ethnic counteraction during the intolerant 1920s. The joint Council of Bygdelags (*Bygdelagenes Fællesraad*), the cooperative body of the *bygdelag* formed in 1916, took the initiative, but they had learned their lesson from the 1914 event and invited Norwegian civic groups to join them. A four-day festival, June 6–9, headquartered on the state fairgrounds between Minneapolis and St. Paul, highlighted the commemoration.[3]

One might disagree whether the celebration interpreted Norwegian Americans, or, as April Schultz states in her thesis, invented them, but obviously there was a positive portrayal of the people and their century of history. Actually, the program organizers extended history back to the very discovery of America, to the heroic age of the Vikings and the explorations of the brave Norseman Leif Ericson around the year 1000. President Calvin Coolidge, having carried Minnesota in the 1924 presidential election, accepted an invitation to attend. An estimated 100,000 enthusiastic Norwegian Americans heard him speak at the open-air meeting on the fairgrounds on June 8—the high point of the celebration. His speechwriter and expert on Norwegian American history was undoubtedly congressman Ole J. Kvale of Benson. The president endorsed Ericson's claim as the first European to discover the New World. The ethnic conflict surrounding the question of discovery was much more animated than one might assume today. When Coolidge not only established Norwegian kinship with the original discoverer but also heaped compliments on his listeners for becoming good and trustworthy citizens of "the Land of the Free," a reporter could describe their fervent response: "The great roar that rose from Nordic throats to Thor and Odin above the lowering gray clouds told that the pride of the race had been touched."[4]

In 1925 at the Minnesota State Fair descendants of Norwegian immigrants posed in front of a full-size replica of the small sloop Restauration, *built that year. The original brought the first boatload of Norwegian immigrants to America in 1825.*

The inveterate cultural pluralist Waldemar Ager viewed the festival as a major argument for a pluralistic society; he rejected the "melting-pot" concept—so clearly evoked in Coolidge's speech—as it would only lead to a "vulgarization" of American culture. As ethnic achievements and cultural idioms were paraded, the Norwegian American historical experience was—while not endorsing the idea of the melting pot—in an assimilative fashion placed within an American historical reality; the main message was nevertheless a defining positive ethnic identity and image. It was in reality a dual, or complementary, identity that the Norse-American Centennial projected in order to create acceptable ethnic credentials within the social reality of the decade's patriotic conformism, advancing consumer economy, and suburban expansion. For many Norwegian Americans in attendance, a home in the suburbs rather than an idyllic family farm might indeed have been the American Dream. The major components of a twofold Norwegian American identity were nevertheless a wholesome rural and religious heritage relating to pioneer days, brave and patriotic American citizenship, and ancient Viking roots, Leif Ericson serving as the quintessential hero and icon. These qualities established a usable past and continue in an ever-changing ethnic identity to be celebrated by Norwegian Americans as defining attributes.[5]

Local newspapers praised the festivities; the *Western Guard, Starbuck Times,* and *Swift County Monitor* all carried extensive reports. The *Western Guard* reprinted the entire centennial address given by President Coolidge for the benefit of those not among the many from Madison who had "the pleasure of hearing it"; they might instead read it and "preserve it for future reading" since "The address will bear reading over and over." The *Starbuck Times* listed the names of the many townspeople who attended; it noted the president's praise of the pioneers, the exhibits of tapestries and paintings in the women's building, and the pageant centering on Colonel Hans Christian Heg, commander of the Norwegian Fifteenth Wisconsin Regiment, "depicting the history of the Norsemen in America from the time they first landed to the present." The *Swift County Monitor* noted with pride that Benson was one of seven U.S. cities where "The special Norse-American two-cent and five cent stamps went on sale . . . May 17."[6]

A Place Called Home

Benson was the place called home for those who remained as well as for those who had left west-central Minnesota. For those who grew up there—just as memories of place in Norway had done for the immigrant generation—the town and its surroundings conveyed, to paraphrase James Duncan, a sense of themselves and of the landscape and places they inhabited and thought about. An example of the notions of community and place is provided by L. T. Christopherson, an earlier resident of Benson who in 1927 wrote nostalgically to the *Swift County Monitor* and confessed that he had "never been completely weaned from the place of [his] birth," even though a quarter century had passed since he last saw "the old home town." From Pomroy, Washington, he declared how he longed "to see the old meadows which were laden with the sweet odors of the wild flowers and vibrating with the song of the birds and the hum of bees, the placid stream of the Chippewa river, the old school house. . . . Yes the old times call across the span of years that separate me from my boyhood youth." Thus are such treasured, and perhaps idealized, memories poetically expressed.

Small-town life in the 1920s, as it was lived in Starbuck, Benson, Madison, and western Minnesota's other minor urban communities, might, however, have been more prosaic than romanticized recollections from childhood and youth would suggest. Yet the histories of the three towns were sufficiently long to allow for reflection and a sense of place for those who for one reason or another called them home. Norwegian-born author Martha Ostenso, in 1925 celebrated as "the youthful, fascinating queen of literary New York," claimed that her early life in Benson, a few years into her teens, "made that city know her best," and she embedded impressions from it and other western towns in her novels. Commenting on her 1925 novel *Wild Geese*—portraying farms and farmers of the Midwest—Ostenso mused, "A thousand stories are there still to be written."[7]

The place called home was greatly altered in the decades after World War I by a surge in popular culture, which frequently replaced ethnic festivities that otherwise might have taken place. Norwegian farm families were, however, attracted to town by the new entertainment. The Dreamland and Viking moving picture theatres in Benson entertained with such silent comedic productions as *A Desert Hero,* starring Fatty Arbuckle, *The Million Dollar Dollies,* with the Dolly Sisters, and other films featuring Charlie Chaplin but also, as announced in 1919, when the two theatres came under one management, "road shows, concerts, dances and for public hire." An ambitious "vaudeville," as it was advertised, at Dreamland featured bands and orchestra programs, including the Echoes of Norway Band, songs and dances, and moving pictures. The movies were competitors to the opera house—in Benson as elsewhere—and caused the decline of the formerly secure small-town institution.

Community entertainment was not totally absent in the new establishments: the twenty-five-piece Benson Community Orchestra under the direction of E. G. Nelson played at Dreamland Theatre, and even Bjørgvin Lodge might hire the theatre, as it did in December 1920, for a concert by the baritone soloist John Nyborg. Still, the movie theatres never attained the position of the opera house and, as Lewis Atherton deplores, precipitated a loss of "culturally inspired local citizens [who] stood ready to promote 'higher' artistic and intellectual standards"; earlier these enlightened citizens had, Atherton argues, kept the Main Street environment from becoming either barren or sterile for ordinary residents. In Benson, as in other midwestern towns and trading centers, the high school auditorium, well-attended high school athletic contests, and even the armory became competing venues—one may add the impact of the automobile and radio—further depriving the opera house of its role as a community center.[8]

Other troubling signs of waning ethnic life came to light. The segregated Norwegian American farming communities faced economic difficulties. It signaled the beginning of the end for strong ethnic rural enclaves; even so they persisted in some fashion well beyond the years of World War II. Business enterprise and commerce had from the earliest days been the central nexus of western urban growth. A farm depression affected western Minnesota, as it did the nation, after the agricultural prosperity of the war years; a general recession came in 1920, with recovery in the industrial sector two years later, while the economic difficulties for farmers endured. In Swift County, the number of farms operated by owners declined even though new land was put under the plow, and farms fell into the hands of absentee landlords. By 1930 nearly half of all farms were operated by tenants rather than by full owners, and the value of farms had dropped from its peak in 1920. These developments pointed toward a decline in the local agrarian society, one which would not only have an adverse economic effect but would cause social and community changes that undermined the maintenance of separate ethnic agricultural communities.

Benson relied on the buying power of its agricultural hinterland and, despite a large array of businesses, faced uncertain times alongside rural communities. Commercial activity was nevertheless lively throughout the twenties. In January 1920, the *Swift County Monitor* in a full-page advertisement carried New Year's greetings from fifty-six businesses in Benson. Listed were familiar farm-related businesses, such as Benson Cooperative Creamery, and other farming and marketing cooperatives and companies like the Benson Produce Company, the Benson Market

Company, the Farmers' Exchange, the Benson Livestock Shipping Association, and the Benson Mill & Elevator Company—"Manufacturers of Benson's Best." There were greetings from Benson Cooperative Mercantile Company—"The Profit-Sharing Store"—F. J. McCauley Farm Machinery, and J. A. Olson Automobiles and Farm Machinery, the latter expanding to join the many automobile dealers, including "The Famous Ford" sold at P. J. Falkenhagen & Son. There were two harness makers, three hardware stores, and as many banks: First National Bank, Security State Bank, and Swift County Bank—"The Bank That Backs the Farmer." There were the established general merchandise stores, Theodore Hansen, M. Hoban, and P. J. Larson, and Rekka Nermoe Millinary Shop, run by the only woman merchant. There were also places to congregate: the well-established Bakken's Bakery and Lunch Room, the more recent P. Berge & Sons Viking Restaurant, the Paris Café—"Home of the 50-Cent Plate Dinners"—and Leitte & Erenberg Billiards, Soft Drinks and Cigars, no legal liquor being available. This list of business enterprise speaks to continuity as well as to optimistic entrance into the new economic order and national business boom of the 1920s—the first mass-consumption society.

Dependence on agriculture created problems in the entire local economy. Second-generation Norwegian Herbert Monson, born in 1904 and working as a building contractor, describes Benson as "not good in the 1920s and 1930s." Because of business closings and bank holidays, "it was bad"; his father, John Monson, born in Hedmark, Norway, lost the large amount of $4,000 during a bank holiday. Nevertheless, the 1927 special issue of the *Swift County Monitor*, expressing chamber of commerce optimism, paints a picture of prosperity and growth, even claiming that "agriculture is making forward strides." Mayor Julius Thorson proudly assured his fellow citizens, "From a business point of view we have real grounds for optimism," pointing to Benson's reputation as an attractive town with highly rated schools, splendid churches, and "above all the high standard of her citizenship."[9]

NORWEGIAN FAMILY STABILITY

Norwegian American Thorson would most obviously view his fellow ethnics as being of a high standard. Economic uncertainties notwithstanding, Norwegians in Benson and their country cousins continued to exhibit great visibility. Throughout the 1920s and even later, there exists much evidence of a strong Norwegian presence. Leland Peterson relates that in some Benson stores business could be conducted in Norwegian in the interwar years and, in one or two businesses, until the late 1940s. Into the 1930s, as reported in the local press, there were "New Norse Books at Public Library . . . ready for circulation." Saturday, when the rural population paid a visit to town, Norwegian could be heard on the streets of Benson. In villages such as Starbuck and Sunburg, Norwegian persisted. Oral Lansverk relates, "Norwegian was still the major language in Sunburg into the 1950s." Starbuck did business in Norwegian into the same decade, and, according to Lavon Lund, patrons may still be heard speaking Norwegian in the local coffee shop. Norma Larson, born in 1929, recalls that when her parents went to Madison on Saturday night to buy groceries, "everyone on the street spoke Norwegian."[10]

Family stability reflected in a high rate of endogamy secured the persistence of a local Norwegian American community. Lowry Nelson in his 1943 article sees intermarriage as the final test of assimilation; his findings of a high endogamy rate in ethnic populations in rural Wright County, Minnesota, cause him to question the "melting-pot theory of amalgamation." He hypothesizes, "intermarriage appears to be influenced by numerical importance of the particular group in the population, residential propinquity, and religious differences." He further submits that "high rates of in-group marriages suggest the persistence of culturally deviant groups and a retardation of assimilation."[11]

Swift County's many compact and isolated ethnic enclaves, despite ominous precursors regarding their economic foundation, would encourage unions of individuals of a shared ethnicity and religious affiliation. Norwegian Lutherans often claim that when the time came, they were nearly obligated to look for a mate within the congregation's fold. Norwegian dominance in terms of numbers, neighborhood sociality, and Lutheran membership worked to the same end in the city of Benson. Investigation into selected Swift County townships and the city of Benson focused on the second generation, defined as a person having at least one Norwegian-born parent. The census figures, on which the findings are based, include only residents, leaving out those who had left the community and whose inclusion might conceivably have changed the results somewhat. The first- and second-generation rates of endogamy were not combined in order to avoid a distorted sense of Norwegian endogamous marriages, since many of the first generation were married prior to emigration or found a Norwegian spouse soon after arrival. Limiting the conclusions to those born in America—to those who may have been influenced by an ethnically pluralistic society, as reported in the 1920 federal census—will better test the cultural maintenance suggested by the union of people of the same ethnic origin.

A simple perusal of the weddings announced in the *Swift County Monitor* creates a strong impression of both bride and groom being Norwegian and of only a few marriages to non-Norwegians. A common entry might be: "Miss Ella Knutson, daughter of Mr. and Mrs. Knute Knutson of this city was married at seven o'clock Friday night, February 25, to George Torgerson of Grafton, N.D. at the Knutson home. Rev. O. J. Kvale of Our Savior's church performed the ceremony." A more grand one: "At an im-

TABLE 16

Intermarriage of Second-Generation Norwegians in 1920 in Swift County[a]

Spouse Ethnicity[b]	Benson City		Cashel Township		Six Mile Grove Township		Swenoda Township		Torning Township[c]	
	N	%	N	%	N	%	N	%	N	%
American	37	20.1	5	15.6	3	15.8	8	15.4	4	12.1
Canadian[d]	2	1.1	1	3.1	0	0	0	0	0	0
Danish	6	3.3	2	6.3	0	0	3	5.8	0	0
English	4	2.2	1	3.1	0	0	0	0	0	0
German	8	4.3	3	9.4	2	10.5	0	0	1	3.0
Irish	4	2.2	2	6.3	0	0	0	0	0	0
Norwegian	120	65.2	21	65.6	14	73.7	41	78.8	21	63.6
Swedish	22	12.0	4	12.5	1	5.3	4	7.7	7	21.2
Other or Unknown	4	2.2	0	0	1	5.3	0	0	1	3.0
Non-Duplicated Totals	184	100.0	32	100.0	19	100.0	52	100.0	33	100.0

Source: U.S. Census, 1920

a. Second-generation Norwegian determined by at least one parent born in Norway
b. Spouses include immigrants and second generation. Ethnicity determined by birthplace of spouse's father and/or mother
c. Torning Township, excluding Benson City
d. The majority of Canadians were French Canadian

pressive marriage ceremony Friday evening, September 24, at 8 o'clock at Our Savior's church, this city, Miss Hilda Halvorson, daughter of Ole Halvorson of Benson, became the bride of Julian Torgelson, son of Mrs. Anna Torgelson of Milan.... The bride ... was gowned in white bridal satin embroidered in white satin rope and pearls and set with rhinestones. Her court train, hung from the shoulders, was edged with Chantilly lace." And outside the city: "Miss Marie R. A. Hatlelid and Henry Erickson were married Saturday night, November 15, at seven o'clock at the home of the bride's mother, Mrs. H. Hatlelid, in Swenoda.... The bride wore a gown of white georgette crepe meteor.... Mr. And Mrs. Erickson ... will make their home on the groom's farm in Swenoda and their many friends wish for them every happiness."[12]

The rate of in-group marriage for second-generation Norwegians in Swenoda was nearly 80 percent, the highest of the townships under consideration. Outside the group they found mates among Swedish and Danish residents; only eight Norwegians, about 15 percent, married a non-Scandinavian, although in some cases those listed as "American" might actually be later-generation Scandinavians. The third-generation Norwegian American was visible but not identified by ethnicity in the

Wedding photograph of Henry B. Hanson and Julia Anderson in Six Mile Grove, November 15, 1913. The attendants are Henry Johnson and Tillie Hanson.

federal enumeration. By 1920 the balanced sex ratio among Norwegian Americans in Swift County was another basic factor that encouraged finding a Norwegian spouse, supplementing the congregational, cultural, and residential forces. The strikingly high endogamous rates in the city of Benson were perhaps the most unexpected finding. In more than 65 percent of all marriages among the second generation, both partners were Norwegian, an unusually high percentage that indicates ethnic cultural separateness. Anecdotal evidence suggests that social stratification among Norwegian residents played a part in spouse selection; children of the more prosperous south-side Norwegian Bensonites appeared to wed people who shared their social status. Swedish, Danish, and German Lutherans were the preferred marriage selections outside the group; though rare, in the small-town environment of Benson four unions were formed between a person of Irish descent and a second-generation Norwegian.[13]

"As long as the in-group marriage rate is at least 50 percent," Nelson states, "it is difficult to see how absorption or biological assimilation is going to take place." He further insists that even less than one-half marrying within the ethnic group would be sufficient to maintain what he terms a "hard core" of cultural identity. Even in the Norwegian colony in Chicago endogamy was high in the second generation, though understandably lower than in west-central Minnesota. With 46 percent of the second generation and 77 percent of the first in 1910 having wed another Norwegian, a pronounced ethnocentric environment was much in evidence. These statistics suggest the strength of Norwegian ethnocentricity regardless of locale. It is nevertheless striking that ten years later, as Table 16 documents, second-generation Norwegians in Cashel, Six Mile Grove, and Torning had rates of marriage to fellow Norwegians substantially above 50 percent. These locations obviously functioned as ethnic rural enclaves; they provide further evidence of the ethnic segregation possible on the western prairie.[14]

Marriage largely "within its own membership," as Nelson describes endogamy, "tends to perpetuate the native folkways, language, and cultural outlook." The family the union creates is more a cultural than a biological entity. Within the family structure, historical impulses and ethnic values and traditions are passed from one generation to the next, perhaps explaining why ethnic cuisine, as evidenced in personal interviews, remains a basic part of ethnic identity. The family generally operates as a conservative force, making family activities one of the most significant ways in which ethnic culture is expressed. The stability of family life indicated by the cultural unity of endogamy may be seen as the major counterforce to a relentless assimilative agitation throughout the interwar years.[15]

MAKING A LIVING

Livelihoods created social fellowship among people in similar socioeconomic circumstances; shared working experiences represented an additional uniting ethnic agency. Occupational life in Benson in the 1920s did not vary greatly from that of other villages and cities in western Minnesota. In the ten years after 1910, as recorded in the federal census, no major changes in the listed occupational categories occurred.

Considering the male population, the Norwegian ethnic stock, immigrants and their children, still displayed a lower percentage in professional occupations than either other immigrant groups or old-stock Americans; the percentage of Norwegian professional women, however, had grown to approximate that of the older American population. Many of these women, not only Norwegian but other immigrant and old-stock Americans as well, were employed as schoolteachers, nurses, librarians, and bookkeepers—in other words, in lower professional positions. Lois Munn Mitteness, of German background but married to Norwegian Donald Mitteness, tells of coming to Benson, where she worked as a bookkeeper at Swift County Bank. Other typical female professions existed. "Miss Esther Simenstad," the *Swift County Monitor* reported in 1926, "daughter of Mr. and Mrs. Anthon Simenstad of Swenoda, has announced that she will hold classes in music in Benson this winter." She had graduated from McPhail School of Music in Minneapolis after a three-year course.

Norwegian professional men were still most prominently exemplified in the Lutheran clergy, but they were also represented among Benson's pharmacists, physicians, veterinarians, and educators. There was, a respondent suggested, "the legendary Dr. [Silas W.] Giere"—American born of Norwegian heritage, who from 1921 and for some years practiced medicine in Benson—famed not only for his medical skills but

TABLE 17

Distribution Amongst Occupational Fields of Females and Working Males[a]
Aged 15 to 65 by Ethnic Origin in Benson City, 1920

Percentage of Ethnic Group Working in Occupational Field

	Males			Females		
	Norwegian	Other Immigrant	Old Stock[b]	Norwegian	Other Immigrant	Old Stock[b]
Professionals	5.5	9.8	11.9	7.4	5.0	7.9
Farmers	2.7	4.1	1.8	—	—	—
Managers, Officials, and Proprietors	16.9	19.6	20.2	0.6	0.4	—
Clerical Workers	6.4	3.6	4.6	6.5	3.8	9.4
Sales Workers	18.3	6.7	12.8	2.9	2.1	—
Craftsmen	17.8	20.6	17.4	—	—	—
Operatives	6.4	9.8	7.3	1.6	2.9	—
Service Workers	2.7	4.6	5.5	6.8	2.5	0.7
Laborers, including Farm Labor	23.3	21.1	18.3	—	—	—
At School, None, or Unspecified[c]				74.1	83.2	82.0
Total (*N*)	100 (219)	100 (194)	100 (109)	100 (309)	100 (238)	100 (139)

Source: U.S. Census, 1920

a. Persons with occupations listed as "at school" or "none" or not specified are excluded from tallies
b. "Old stock" defined as native born of native-born parents
c. Also includes "keeps house/housework/housewife"

also for his penchant for traveling the world to hunt and his interest in flying his own light plane. Immigrants joined the professions as well. Hans O. Sandbo, born in Gudbrandsdalen in 1866, came to America as a young man of sixteen, attended Willmar Seminary, taught school, and thereafter pursued a varied career, as Swift County register of deeds, in real estate and banking, and finally as deputy county treasurer, showing progress in occupational assimilation.

More Norwegian women—about 25 percent—in comparison both to other nationalities and to older American groups, worked outside the home, as they had done in 1880 and in 1900. Middle-class women like Kari O. Krogen Frovold, wife of Knud P. Frovold, born in 1849 in

Sigdal, Norway, Sophie Knudson Hoiland, wife of Andrew J. Hoiland, born in Molde, Norway, in 1859, and Dorothea Espelien Olson, wife of Adam Olson, born in Valdres, Norway, in 1864, are listed as housewives, as are wives of men in more ordinary social circumstances. The many who worked outside the home—as clerical and sales workers and in service occupations—suggest a level of economic need in Norwegian households.

The percentage of men occupied as managers, officials, and proprietors had declined relatively compared to 1880 and showed only a small increase since 1900. Benson's population in 1920, however, was more than 4.6 times larger than in 1880 and 1.4 times larger than in 1900. This particular category, while in 1920 encompassing many more individuals, would also cover a much broader variety of occupations, from hog dealer to newspaper publisher, grain buyer to city clerk, county treasurer to bank president, merchant to hotel keeper, building contractor to power plant superintendent. Norwegian men were found in these and similar occupational pursuits.

New employment opportunities and occupational choices increased as the city of Benson grew and developed greater economic diversity. Many Norwegian men were employed in sales or crafts. In addition to the traditional general merchandise and hardware stores, some were now automobile salesmen or agents for real estate and life insurance companies. Norwegian men were still well represented in carpentry and blacksmithing, and they practiced other crafts as well. A few examples will introduce the personal factor in these statistics—all listed in the 1920 federal census. Hans H. Strand, in the plumbing and heating business, had immigrated from Vanylven in Sunnmøre, Norway, at age twenty in 1888; Thore Knutson worked as a stonemason in Benson after arriving from Sjølset in Øksendal, Norway, in the early 1880s; Ole Syverson, from Valdres, Norway, who immigrated in 1886 at age twenty-four, might represent the 2.1 percent farmers listed in the census; he farmed until he moved to Benson in 1920. Laborers, including farm laborers, still constituted a substantial portion of Norwegian workers and in percentage of the total number employed was larger than the percentage for working males in the two other categories. In other words, the blue-collar category dominated. Haldor Anderson, who worked as a drainage contractor and plumber, had emigrated from

Måløy, Norway, at age twenty in 1884; he is a good representative of the successful blue-collar worker. Even though no strong class distinctions were drawn, in social life, church attendance, and festive gatherings the many Norwegian American common workers with their own social network and activities were likely the ones who represented a primary ethnicity—they simply were Norwegian—and thus a countercurrent that naturally preserved ethnic cultural expressions.[16]

POLITICS AND THE GREAT DEPRESSION

The Norwegian impulse from pioneer days continued in force in west-central Minnesota. More than 11 percent of Benson's citizens in 1920 were born in Norway and another 29 percent had Norwegian-born parents. In the region's relatively short history, decades of shared memories served as a bond among citizens of diverse ethnic and social backgrounds. In June 1930, at the start of the Great Depression, Benson celebrated the sixtieth anniversary of its founding with a grand three-day festival. The arrival of Hilda Christenson (Mrs. S. H. Bakken)—in 1867 the first white child born in Swift County—from her home in St. Paul reminded celebrants both of what in historical terms was a short distance in time from frontier conditions and the spectacular accomplishments since. She was the daughter of pioneer settlers Lars and Anna Christenson. The hard times beginning that decade might, however, have tempered a jubilant spirit; the years of depression remain a vivid part of the living memory of many western Minnesota residents.

The prosperity of the 1920s collapsed with the stock-market crash in October 1929, and the depression that followed touched every household in America, taking a great human toll. Unemployment grew alarmingly in Minnesota; farm prices dropped; foreclosures increased. In March 1934, as reported in the local press, 2,937 persons in Swift County, 20 percent of the population, were on federal or other relief rolls. Drought added to the misery. Homer Tjosaas, born in 1922 and growing up on his father's homestead in Six Mile Grove, recalls when the clouds of dust came and made it impossible to grow anything: "the worst years were 1933 and 1934." His neighbors were poor farmers. "We had our own beef," Tjosaas related, "and separated and churned butter, which we traded together with eggs for groceries. We didn't pay with money."[17]

Hilda Christenson (Mrs. S. H. Bakken), daughter of Lars and Anna Christenson, in 1867 was the first white child born in Swift County.

Nationality could still come to the aid of political conviction. The belief, seemingly supported by empirical evidence, is that in times of hardship ethnic groups unite. Where politics and ethnicity coincide the candidate's nationality clearly made a difference. In the 1930 gubernatorial race, Floyd B. Olson, born of Norwegian Swedish parentage in 1891 in North Minneapolis, won the election by a landslide to become the first Farmer-Labor governor. The outcome was clearly influenced by the hard times, but his Scandinavian background also attracted the Scandinavian vote. Olson handily beat both his Republican and Democratic opponents; the Democratic candidate, Edward Indrehus—an immigrant from Bergen, Norway, in 1890 as a young man of seventeen—had a particularly poor showing, indicating the Democratic Party's weakness in state elections rather than the issue of nationality. Indrehus received only 3.7 percent of the votes cast statewide. Swift County gave him 162 votes, or 3.3 percent, compared to 1,269 for the Republican contender and 3,662 for Olson. At its reunion in Starbuck in June 1931, Trønderlaget initiated the governor into the society, which represented the region of Norway from which his father, Paul Olson, had emigrated. His membership suggested both broad Norwegian support and regional pride among the Trønders, who claimed him as "one of us." Re-elected twice, Olson died in office in 1936.

Governor Olson was succeeded by Norwegian American Elmer A. Benson, born in 1895 in Appleton. Following in his parents' footsteps, Benson was a strong Farmer-Labor politician, a midwestern radical, and a crusader against the use of liquor. Among his political assets could be counted his orthodox progressive conviction, his Scandinavian background, and his service in the armed forces; in addition, his adult career as a cashier in a small independent Appleton bank gave Governor Benson the desirable rural flavor. He recognized the Nonpartisan League "as the springboard from which the Farmer Labor Party was organized in Minnesota." Benson and his supporters' liberal leadership of the Farmer-Labor Party was, however, at odds with the urban upper-middle-class leadership of the Democratic Party, hindering cooperation between the two political bodies.[18]

In a May 2002 interview, Ginter Rice related that he, as well as his father, Oscar Rice, were staunch Democrats; he emphasized that his reason for joining the Democrats was Franklin D. Roosevelt's establishment of the Works Progress Administration (wPA) in 1935 and the work and social relief it provided "when hardships were really bad." Howard W. Peterson, born on a farm near Benson in 1911 to parents of Swedish origin, tells how his father, Alfred Peterson, became an organizer of the Nonpartisan League in Torning and Benson townships after first having been attracted to the Populist and Socialist political causes; later he joined the Democratic Party because "all these far-left politics failed." Though Democrats and Farmer-Laborites nominated separate candidates for the governorship, on the national level Democratic tickets enjoyed the support of the Farmer-Labor Party and beginning in 1932 carried the state in five consecutive presidential elections. In 1932 Roosevelt was approved by Minnesota voters—the first time a Democrat had ever won the state for president. A fusion of the two parties was accomplished toward the end of World War II; the liberal faction, represented by the more radical Elmer Benson wing, was pushed out and replaced by new Democratic-Farmer-Labor (DFL) leaders. Their goal was to unite Democrats and Farmer-Laborites.[19]

Two local Norwegian American politicians stand out in the annals of the Democratic and Farmer-Labor parties. Congressman Paul J. Kvale, son of Ole J. Kvale, was elected to succeed his father, who died in office in 1929. Paul Kvale served as a Farmer-Labor representative of the large Seventh District until 1939; his informative letters from Washington, DC, were a regular feature of the *Swift County News*. Alfred Ingvald Johnson of Benson became an important local Democratic politician. Lawyer and prosecuting attorney Richard Hilleren, a close friend of Johnson's, described him as a brilliant man. Born to Norwegian immigrants Bryngel and Carrie Johnson in Six Mile Grove Township in 1898, he became a successful businessman in Benson. Politically he moved from the Non-partisan League to the Farmer-Labor Party and assisted in its fusion with the Democrats. Elected to the state House of Representatives in 1941, he was re-elected eight times. One may argue that political talent more easily comes to the fore in a small electorate, where family, business, and local political connections create a broad network of supporters. Further, Scandinavian name recognition may sway those less familiar with the candidate's platform and qualifications.[20]

WANING ETHNIC IDIOMS

Ethnicity expresses itself as a dynamic tale of accommodation and resistance. One may therefore well consider the special social, economic, and political environment in western Minnesota and its impact on ethnic cultural maintenance. A prevailing national discouragement of cultural diversity as a legacy of the "100 percent Americanism" of World War I remained during the interwar and World War II years and during the patriotic consensus-inspired decades that followed. There were, to be sure, forces that counteracted the agitation for a monocultural nation. In Swift County, Norwegian, Swedish, and German persisted as basic means of communication within families and in ethnic relations and were in religious services reminders of an immigrant heritage. On the other hand, an accent or foreign brogue might become a serious handicap. Thus parents, even when residing in an ethnic community, might decide to speak only English to their children. Verner Johnson recalls that his Swedish-born parents made a point "to speak English when the children were growing up."[21]

By 1940 regular Swedish and Norwegian Lutheran church services belonged mainly to the past; most were discontinued in the 1930s. Pastor Arthur W. Chell, who served Trinity Lutheran Church in Benson from 1930 to 1939, was the last pastor to offer services in both Swedish and English. A monolingual American-born clergy entered the ministry; they would emphasize the so-called English work. In 1925 statistics suggest that within the Norwegian Lutheran Church of America there were an equal number of services in the two languages, even though Norwegian services might gather only a few faithful adherents of the Norwegian work. One may follow Norwegian's declining use in religious services by perusing local newspapers, which regularly announced the language of the particular service, Norse or English. Madison's Ness Lutheran Church, the later First Lutheran Church, announced in 1925 that it would use English, rather than Norwegian, on alternate Sundays but that all "young people's meetings shall be conducted in English." The same year Madison Lutheran Church made English its "official language." Toward the end of World War II, less than seven percent of all services in American Lutheran churches were conducted in Norwegian. The adjective "Norwegian" was dropped from the name of the merged church body in 1946.[22]

The idea of "the flight of the second generation" may find some confirmation in the transition to English, first in Sunday school, then in confirmation classes, and gradually in church services. In Benson's Immanuel congregation, Pastor J. S. Strand, serving from 1912 to 1930, is credited with beginning the transition by establishing a class in English in the Sunday school the year he arrived. Occasional services in Norwegian continued during the tenure of Strand's successor, Reverend Herman E. Jorgensen, until 1939 and a few years beyond at the four congregations he served, either at the Immanuel edifice in Benson or at Lake Hazel, Six Mile Grove, or Swift Falls. Though a rare Norwegian service might occur at Our Savior's Church, for the most part by the 1930s it seemed to limit its Norwegian to a "Norse Bible Hour," reminding members—probably in concession to the older, Norwegian-speaking ones—to "Bring your Norse Bible." Still, Paul A. Mortenson, born in 1930, thought of Our Savior's as being "very Norwegian."

Loyalty to the old-country tongue in religious services might depend on the individual pastor's ability and propensity; Pastor Jorgensen, for example, left Immanuel to assume editorial responsibility for the church's Norwegian-language organ, *Lutheraneren* (The Lutheran); his interest in the Norwegian work was evident. It would, in spite of English's inroads, be a fallacy to dismiss ethnicity as having no role in congregants' lives. The overwhelming percentage of American-born Norwegians who found a spouse of their own nationality, in town as well as in the countryside, evidences a cogent ethnicity. The family units formed through marriage to a fellow Norwegian encouraged retention of ethnic identities, traditions, customs, and in many cases even the old-country language.[23]

The Depression in some conspicuous ways reinforced cultural and community loyalties. To clarify, consider the widely accepted maxim that in hard times ethnic groups pull together and assist each other. In a Norwegian urban colony like Chicago's, with social assistance provided by an array of mutual aid, burial, and sick benefit societies and by benevolent institutions, the parole has much credibility; in hard times theater and musical groups arranged benefit performances to help needy compatriots cope with the uncertainties of the urban environment. The situation in a small country town might obviously differ, but the special sense of coming to the aid of fellow Norwegians was much in evidence there as well. In the country town and in farming communities assistance was more commonly extended beyond the ethnic group, however. The pioneer Lutheran church in its rural setting exercised social outreach and came to the aid of parishioners and community members; "there was a community if you needed help," Paul Mortenson recalls. The moral and social challenges of the city made the congregation's social work in a harsh urban environment such as Chicago more direct and more confined to people of the same nationality.[24]

Lacking evidence in church records and organizational minutes to the contrary, the strong impression created in the public media is that the several ethnic populations in a city like Benson pooled resources to assist fellow Bensonites. The Benson Community Fund, organized in late 1931, had among its affiliate members both Lærken Lodge of the Daughters of Norway and Bjørgvin Lodge of the Sons of Norway. It staged charity balls at the armory, the proceeds of which were to "be used in relief locally."[25]

Concern for community welfare encouraged ethnic events and thus may, as in the Norwegian Chicago colony, have given renewed strength to the organizational aspect of ethnicity even when relief was not rendered exclusively to fellow Norwegians. Bjørgvin Lodge, for instance, regularly arranged dances in order to give communal support; the dances also became significant ethnic social occasions. Lærken, as another example, had social gatherings and cake sales, the latter to raise money for its charitable and organizational activities.

At a time of waning ethnic affirmation, religious institutions continued to mark Norwegian historical events. In 1930 was the 900th anniversary of the martyrdom of St. Olaf, Norway's eternal king, at the Battle of Stiklestad on July 29, 1030. His death and later sainthood established the

Christian church in Norway. Our Savior's Church, which in 1930 observed its own sixtieth anniversary, on May 17—Constitution Day—mindful both of its own history and of its Norwegian heritage, conducted a grand all-day dedication and musical festival the following year. Pastor Melvin O. Andrews, speaking in Norwegian, appealed "to all his listeners, Norse by descent but American by choice, to uphold the best traditions of Norway and America and thus assure the future of American civilization."

The message, whether expressed in a sacred or a profane context, might not differ much. The content given an ethnic identity served to honor an ancestral heritage that would ease entrance into American society. A remarkably accurate account of May 17, with quotes from the Norwegian constitution, appeared in the columns of the *Swift County News* in 1937. As was certainly the intent, these passages proved the compatibility of Norwegian immigrants to American democracy. One may here speak in terms of complementary identities, the one reinforcing the other, or even consider Werner Sollors's idea of a dual loyalty of *consent* and *descent* to distinguish between self-made and ancestral definitions of American identity. While *descent* defines loyalty to an ancestral heritage, *consent* defines loyalty to a new culture of individualism and political structures. Sollors sees the tension between these two as the central drama in American culture.[26]

Evidence of what Sollors defines as *descent* was throughout the interwar years visible. Touring groups of Norwegian American folk dancers and singers who performed in Benson reinforced ethnic loyalty, reminding citizens of a Norwegian American cultural world. In the countryside, as Orie Mills, who grew up south of Benson, relates, "there were a lot of Norwegian house parties. They cleared the living room and danced to accordion, violin, or guitar music."

In people's daily lives, however, ethnic cuisine continued as the most salient and persistent element of loyalty to an ancestral heritage. Religious institutions honored ethnic foods as well: Our Savior's Church regularly announced its annual lutefisk suppers. The Great Depression gave ethnic food a special status; the deprivations it caused made ethnic dishes—simple, affordable, nourishing—daily fare for many. Conrad Urke, a *klubb*-eating champion, grew up during the Depression: "we lived mainly on *klubb* and *graut* [potato and cream mush]." Ethnic dishes were not a later revival but a continuous tradition, for Urke personally but also within the larger Norwegian community.[27]

AMERICANISM AND THE ANCESTRAL HOMELAND

World War II was in ethnic terms an ambivalent force. Depending on the status of individual nationalities—friend or foe—the intense patriotism the conflict created did not automatically negate attachment to the homeland. In fact, German invasion of Norway on April 9, 1940, elevated Norway's position in the American public eye and, as Carl G. O. Hansen writes, had more than any other event a powerful effect "in creating solidarity among the Norwegian-American groups." The idea of assistance and gifts to the homeland had long traditions in all ethnic groups; specific emergencies produced an instantaneous response. No calamity created greater sympathy among the emigrant community than the five long years of Norway's occupation. On September 16, 1942, Roosevelt gave his treasured "Look to Norway" speech from his open car in Washington, DC, with Norwegian Crown Princess Märtha at his side. She and the royal children spent the war years in the United States. In June 1939 the crown princess had made a much-celebrated visit along with Crown Prince Olav to the Midwest; they received a rousing welcome from the Norwegian American community. The local Benson newspapers noted with pride that Katherine Jorgensen, daughter of the Reverend Herman Jorgensen, would, as a student at St. Olaf College, deliver the welcome speech when the royal couple visited the school. A positive image of the Norwegian homeland was promoted by these events, strengthening a sense of ethnicity as well as acceptance by American society.[28]

The code of the day was nevertheless Americanization. In September 1938 the senior social class of Benson High School presented "The Melting Pot." The program showed the arrival of immigrants who "went into the melting pot. . . . When they came out they were American." Appropriately, the high school band played "The Star-Spangled Banner" before the program and closed with "America." The immigrants came from Norway, France, Germany, England, and Ireland, and there was one lonely Jew.[29]

The following year American society gained added motivation to call for national unity. War broke out in Europe with the Nazi blitzkrieg against Poland on September 1, 1939, and the Anglo-French declaration of war two days later. Between April 9 and June 22, 1940, Nazi forces conquered Denmark, Norway, the Netherlands, Belgium, and France. The United States vigorously supported the Allies with direct aid and diplomatic actions in what may be described as "the undeclared war." Then the Japanese attack on Pearl Harbor on December 7, 1941, brought the United States directly into the global strife and committed the nation to intervene in world affairs. Following immediate declaration of war against Japan, Germany and Italy declared war on the United States and Congress in turn declared war on the Axis. These were, succinctly stated, the main events reported in local and national newspapers; as the war progressed it had profound repercussions on the nation and on its multitude of small communities.[30]

Front-page stories in the *Swift County Monitor*, published Fridays—or the *Swift County News*, published Tuesdays—relate both local patriotic fervor in support of the war effort and the fateful consequences of the clash of arms. War bond quotas and war loan campaigns, patriotic gatherings, collections of scrap iron, and rationing all received press attention and created strong patriotic emotions. The names and faces of inductees and volunteers became poignant reminders of the sacrifice and the disruption of individual lives the war exacted. The newspapers ran a series under the heading "Heroes on Parade," reporting on area men who served in the armed forces. Their numbers in Swift County increased greatly over the course of the war, from 167 National Guard and other servicemen in 1941 to 1,500 at the end of 1944, "with hundreds fighting on the German front, in Italy, and on the Pacific Islands." The human cost of war was brought home in reports of individual casualties. Sergeant Donald J. Juntilla of De Graff, the first Swift County inductee, was also the first to die. He was followed by many other servicemen: Seaman Omar J. Kolstad, Private First Class Wesley D. Tjosaas, Lieutenant Ira O. Bakken, among others. The deaths of two Benson teenage servicemen and boyhood friends from high school—Private First Class LuWayne Larson, age nineteen, in Germany, and Private First Class Kenneth B. Olson, age eighteen, in Iwo Jima—became an especially afflictive reminder of war's absurdity. Our Savior's Church in March 1944 held an "Honor Service Men" event for congregational members in the armed forces; there were seventy-eight names, five of which were women's, and the name of a serviceman "killed in action."[31]

During these momentous times the Norwegian American community felt compelled to launch a major relief effort for the old homeland. Setting the tone locally, the Immanuel congregation in 1942 conducted a May 17 service "in the Norwegian language"; a mixed chorus sang the two national anthems. It was not, as during World War I, considered inappropriate to celebrate, as Carl G. O. Hansen stated, "the national holiday of a country that so gallantly stood up in the fight." The Norwegian Lutheran Church of America, as the main, if not the only, national ethnic organization, assumed leadership in the relief efforts. Organization began only a few days after the April 9, 1940, attack on Norway. J. A. Aasgaard, church president, became president of American Relief for Norway, Inc., as well. This body, organized on April 27 and the result of early initiatives, promoted a large-scale nationwide relief effort among people of Norwegian birth and ancestry—from New York to San Francisco. The association's official resolution was written by Reverend Jorgensen; it expressed "heartfelt sympathy with Norway, the homeland of the pioneer fathers," realizing that "the basic principles of life in the Norway of yesterday are the foundation principles of American religious, civil, and personal liberty." These sentiments and identities were truly complementary. One may well ask—and the question was certainly taken seriously by those involved—could the United States ever receive better immigrants than those who had arrived from old Norway? Clothing, food, and money were collected and sent through neutral Sweden and occupied Denmark.[32]

Appeals were made to secular and religious Norwegian American audiences. Minnesota's Norwegians responded to the state committee's requests for donations, and there were many local efforts in the west-central part of the state. On May 17, 1940, Bjørgvin Lodge of the Sons of Norway in Benson sponsored "Syttende Mai Benefit Ball" at the armory, the proceeds going to American Relief for Norway. In 1943 it joined Lærken Lodge of the Daughters of Norway to sponsor the showing of the 1939 Norwegian film *Gjest Baardson*, about the nineteenth-century master thief, at the DeMarce Theatre in Benson for the benefit of Camp Little Norway. Located near Toronto in Canada, the camp was established to train Norwegian fliers for combat service. The Camp Little

Norway Association, formed in October 1941, eventually merged with American Relief for Norway.

Norway and its tragic straits became an engrossing engagement for much of the Norwegian American population, locally as well as nationally. As a part of "a nationwide fundraising program which reaches its climax on the Syttende Mai," Bjørgvin Lodge sponsored jointly with "the Lutheran congregations belonging to the N.L.C.A. synod in the Benson vicinity" a local celebration for "Norse Relief." The women in Our Savior's Church were in charge of the clothing drive, which continued after the end of hostilities. By the end of the war, greater pride and unity existed among Norwegian Americans. On May 8, 1945, by happy circumstance in celebration of V-E Day, DeMarce offered an "All-Norwegian Dialogue Film," *Trysil Knut*, smuggled out of occupied Norway. The tale was based on the legend of a champion skier in Trysil in Østerdalen, Norway's easternmost valley. On the same program was Sverre Kolterud; in 1932 he had represented Norway in Nordic combined skiing, cross-country and jumping, at the Olympic games in Lake Placid. In these and other activities, a Norwegian ethnic forte was made visible.[33]

THE CHANGING FACE OF THE POSTWAR YEARS

Economic and social change in the years following World War II saw the disparities between living in town and living on the farm swiftly lessening. The old dichotomy between rural and urban lost much of its relevance as country life to a large extent merged with that of the small town and city. The resumption of immigration was another social factor that influenced American society. For Norwegians, there had been a long break in the overseas movement to the United States. Norwegian immigration never became large after the war, although in the first years of peace delayed reunions hastened departures. The postwar movement, though gaining some momentum in the first few years following the end of hostilities, never attained great numerical significance; it reached its absolute maximum for any one year in 1952 with the emigration of 2,958 Norwegians. By 1980 some 50,000 Norwegians had moved to the United States. The newcomers settled mainly in large urban areas such as New York, Chicago, Minneapolis, Seattle, Los Angeles, and San Francisco; in these early centers of Norwegian settlement, they reinforced ethnic impulses. Few found a home in rural and small-town environments. Kirsten Vingerhagen Ricke, born in 1918 in Ringsaker, Norway, emigrated in 1947; she and her first husband, Christian Petersen, whom she met the day before she emigrated and got to know on the voyage, moved in 1948 to Benson, where she had an uncle. Aside from "British brides" who joined soldier husbands in Benson, she would be one of very few postwar immigrants in town.[34]

The Norwegian American community was, however, in a transitional phase, one that had begun before the war. It was losing its earlier structural qualities and sense of a national community. Ethnic boundaries were rapidly disappearing. Simply considering the decrease in the number of Norwegian-born Americans offers explanation. The 202,294 individuals of Norwegian birth in the United States in 1950—mainly people who had arrived before 1930—were reduced to 97,243 only two decades later, despite the arrival of new immigrants. Minnesota in 1970 had fewer than 10,000 Norwegian-born residents; in this older region of settlement, the recent influx of newcomers had been relatively modest. A postwar patriotism and a national search for unity rather than diversity further undermined ethnic maintenance.[35]

Benson and other small towns in western Minnesota were simultaneously experiencing economic difficulty and a loss of population. To quote from a recent article in *Minnesota Cities:* "Each decade the smaller towns and cities find it more and more difficult to keep up with the world around them." In a sensitive sociological study, *Small Town and the Nation* (1969), Don Martindale and R. Galen Hanson examine broadly "the conflict of local and translocal forces" as they have affected the city of Benson—its economy, power structures, and agencies of socialization. The current study, focusing as it does on ethnic and social circumstances, benefits most from the earlier study's findings about education. The great loss of the town's youth, revealed by looking at the plans and actions of graduating high school students, show, in the words of the text, "the cleavage between local and non local interests." Martindale and Hanson describe Benson's youth as the town's most valuable product but also as its most valuable export.[36]

St. Olaf, Luther, and Concordia colleges had from the early days of their existence recruited among young people in western Minnesota's Norwegian settlements; these institutions regularly brought their bands or choirs to Benson and other area towns. Theodore Jorgenson, professor of Norwegian at St. Olaf College, visited these same towns, both when campaigning as a DFL-endorsed candidate for the U.S. Senate in 1946 and more commonly at a variety of Norwegian American events. The message of higher education based on a Norwegian and Lutheran heritage was disseminated broadly; such schools gave young people a unique educational alternative. In the years following World War II, these private colleges still retained a strong cultural and religious attachment to their origin in a Norwegian immigrant past.[37]

Year after year, a majority of high school graduates left their small-town environment to seek employment or higher education elsewhere. Robert Mikkelson, a graduate of a large class of nearly 190 in 1968, estimated that only some fifteen "are still around the area." Mikkelson, born in 1950, returned to Benson as a special education teacher, choosing a career—teaching—that can be successfully pursued in a small town. He finds the advantages of small-town life far outweigh disadvantages: "There is no place in the world I would rather raise my children . . . how do you place a value on walking into almost any business in town and end up having a 'good talk' with the proprietor or another customer?" These and other treasured amenities bring townspeople back after their professional training.[38]

Most who continued their schooling did not attend a private school. By looking at the future plans of high school students as noted by the school counselor one may gain some insight into local occupational preferences among the many available possibilities. A survey of ninety-two graduating seniors the spring of 1999 showed a variety of "plans for the future." The largest group, twenty-three women and sixteen men, chose vocational-technical education, many at the two-year Ridgewater College in Willmar; they received training in business administration, accounting, the medical field, social work, and photography. Sixteen women and eight men selected public colleges and universities, and nine women and five men applied to private Lutheran colleges—Concordia College in Moorhead and Augustana College in Sioux Falls being the most popular; most of these students had not chosen a specific field of study. Six students chose work; two enrolled in the armed services; those remaining were undecided. As earlier surveys suggest, few would become permanent residents of Benson once they had completed their education. And to cite Martindale and Hanson in their analysis of a 1967 survey: "The more specialized one's college or university training, the less likely one is to find a niche in Benson."[39]

Personal Stories from Some Who Left

Extensive interviews were conducted with high school graduates who earned their diplomas in the late 1960s and pursued careers outside Benson. They all in one way or another relate to the small-town environment they left. Scott F. Anfinson, born in Benson in 1950, is today the Minnesota state archaeologist. Of five brothers, only Reed Anfinson remained in Benson, succeeding his father, Ronald Anfinson, as publisher of the *Swift County Monitor-News*. The other four established distinguished careers elsewhere. Scott Anfinson recalls:

> The one time of the year we really saw sort of our Norwegian heritage was at the smorgasbord at Our Redeemer's Church in the fall, and not much attention was given to being Norwegian or *Syttende mai*. . . . It did not hit me that I was something else than American, but Norwegian too, until I came into a big city and the University of Minnesota where there were lots of ethnic groups. . . .When I started taking anthropology courses I sort of became aware of ethnicity and what it meant, and . . . I started analyzing my own situation, and I went to my first Sons of Norway Lodge . . . on Lake Street [in Minneapolis].
>
> As children we noticed religious differences, and though we did not discriminate, the Catholics had their own school and lived in their own world. . . . Benson was all white, but we had Mexican migrant workers who came to town.

The presence of those laborers was the first time, Anfinson remembers, "where I was thinking of someone being from a different race or country." The one class distinction was "city people opposed to country people. . . . There was some tendency among some people to look down a bit on farmers," Anfinson believes. "They were farmers; we were townies."

Scott Anfinson reflects on his youth as being "a very idyllic time." There "were really no fences in Benson and really no crimes. . . . A typical summer day would be spent with us heading down to the swimming pool." Responding to the idea that place may define the deepest sense of identity, Anfinson reflected that even though he has lived many places, when asked where he is from, he invariably answers Benson. Perhaps sharing the dilemma of immigrants and their need for immutable memories of place, whether they left Norway or simply a place like Benson, Anfinson concedes, "what bothers me most . . . are the changes in the town, because I think I had such an idyllic childhood and that I think of that childhood very fondly." His disappointment does not deter Anfinson from describing Benson as a community that has "a will to be good . . . there is still that core of that small town, mainly Norwegian Lutherans, that is struggling against modern society in some ways to be the town it was in the 1950s. . . . The fact that it tries makes me want to go home."[40]

Rodney Paul Rice, born in Benson in 1955, in his interview described small towns as "a very good seedbed" but noted, "if you're going to succeed you have to go somewhere else, for the most part." Rice is now a professor of English at the South Dakota School of Mines in Rapid City; earlier he had served twenty-three years in the U.S. Air Force. As a child Rice was very much aware of his Norwegian background because "both [his] parents were proud of their ethnic heritage." He even sensed growing up "that those of us in Benson who were of Scandinavian or in particular Norwegian ancestry—because most of us were—felt, I think, . . . not arrogant but somehow that we're better than, say, somebody who might be Irish-Catholic or, you know, German-Catholic or German-Lutheran."

His doctoral work on the writings of Wright Morris, an author of the small town on the Great Plains, gives Rice a broad understanding of the country town:

I feel two different ways about Benson and sometimes I feel both at once. It's kind of a funny way to describe it. Part of me is repulsed by it: sort of the Sinclair Lewis narrow-minded, small-mindedness of it. The provincial aspect sort of nauseates me. But then another part of me is a little bit like Garrison Keillor's Lake

Wobegon: I'm very fond of it, I love it. So what I think I struggle with is this mixture of nostalgia and nausea both.

Rice elaborates further on his conflicting sentiments by concluding that "when I go there a big part of me is there and I owe a lot to that for helping me be who I am and establishing what I am, but another part of me is just repulsed by the same things that Sinclair Lewis was repulsed by." Rice quotes Morris: "Home is where you hang your childhood."[41]

The large Tennant Company, with corporate headquarters in Minneapolis, promotes itself as "creating a cleaner, safer world." Its chief executive officer and president is Janet Dolan, born in Benson in 1949. Dolan graduated from William Mitchell School of Law and worked as a trial lawyer for ten years before coming to Tennant. She grew up on a farm south of Danvers. Her father was third-generation Irish and her mother second-generation Norwegian; her mother converted to the Catholic faith. She remembers, "Anti-Catholicism was diluted by the time I grew up. I had Protestant cousins. In the interest of tolerance we did not talk about religion, or genuflect at funerals. My parents didn't wear religion on their sleeve, but they taught me about charity and commitment to other people." Dolan grew up more Irish American than Norwegian American—her father's family had a stronger tie to its roots: "I was the first in my family to go back to Ireland and Norway. It made me feel more ethnic and in tune with my heritage."

In discussing the nature of the small town, Dolan relates her own success to its supportive and confidence-building environment: "It is a wonderful place in which to grow up." For those who choose to enter public service, Dolan explains, "small towns are microcosms that help produce successful politicians. There is no gated community, and the town has a collective need and a collective will. Family and homogeneity help build networks." But, Dolan states, "Unless I make a lifestyle decision, the lack of career opportunity in a place like Benson would prevent me from moving back." There are also the negatives of gossip, an inability to keep a secret, the danger of becoming averse to taking risks or otherwise set in one's ways. The inherent provincialism of a country town can be overcome, however, Dolan insists, since "Your own ambition determines your cultural interests. As a child, my family went to the Guthrie Theater and the Walker Art Center in Minneapolis."[42]

ECONOMICS AND THE NORWEGIAN
AMERICAN COMMUNITY

Benson, the town those who have left continue to cherish as a place called home, experienced great changes in the final decades of the twentieth century. The repercussions from a drastic decline in the rural population had consequences not only for Swift County's agricultural communities but also for its trading centers. Local schools and churches that at an earlier date had formed the center of community life could no longer be maintained. In 1970 the last rural school district was dissolved; in 1950 there had been seventy-one country school districts, each supporting simple one-room schoolhouses. Those two decades saw the rapid loss of an educational institution that extended back to the pioneer settlers.

Changes in the average farm size tell their own story. Farms in active operation were in 1954 on average 256 acres, in 1978, 389 acres, and in 1997, 525 acres, many being much larger; corporate and other absentee ownership of land—apparent since the 1920s—increased. Larger farm operations took over the land as people moved out; the number of small farms decreased rapidly: during the decade before 1997 the number of farms dropped from 884 to 739. There were agricultural specializations, such as turkey operations, but grain farming predominated. Having grown up in Cashel Township, Richard Hilleren relates that small grain—oats and wheat—and corn were main crops, but his family also had livestock and hogs; other farmers might in addition have dairy cows, sheep, and poultry. On the family farm in Torning Township, Paul Mortenson diversified to turkeys. "Lots of small farms went out of business," he explained. Mortenson still lives on the farm, "but around me no one farms. It is just residential. The tight little community is lost." The new circumstances undermined the survival of rural ethnic enclaves and maintenance of the culture they embodied.[43]

The local Norwegian American community was itself weakened as members retained long-standing disjunctions in its sacred institutions. In Benson, early efforts in 1917 failed to merge the two Norwegian Lutheran congregations, Immanuel and Our Savior's, both at the time members of the newly formed Norwegian Lutheran Church of America. Despite the broader designation, there was apparently not sufficient common ground to form a single congregation. Immanuel had experienced bitter internal strife, blamed on divisions within the United Church, to which it belonged. Members took sides in the controversy; as a consequence, Immanuel withdrew from synodical membership until formation of the national Norwegian Lutheran church in 1917.

It took time to overcome differences. Not until June 6, 1949, did the two congregations vote to consolidate into one. There was still resistance, as reported in Our Savior's Church: "If three persons voting yes had cast negative ballots, the merger proposal would have been killed." The new congregation was incorporated December 4 and given the name Our Redeemer's Lutheran Church. An imposing edifice on the southeast section of Benson was dedicated in 1957. Our Redeemer's became the town's large Lutheran church. The misfortune that affected parishes in Norwegian agricultural communities, as financial realities deprived them of membership, came to aid the congregation in town. A majority of parishioners of rural churches, as these were dissolved, joined and augmented membership. Trinity of Swenoda was dissolved in 1961, Six Mile Grove Church in 1965, and Lake Hazel in 1967.

Separate congregational identities might hinder unity. As Jan Baukol describes it, distinctions existed among former parishioners of dissolved churches so that "if they were asked to put on a program, they would select people from their own group to serve on the committee." On the other hand, what "unites them is that they are all Norse." During research for this book, a uniting ethnic identity was much in evidence. At the morning service on Sunday, June 2, 2002, Reverend David Andert requested that those with "a smidgen of Norwegian blood rise." About 85 percent of the congregants present did so. In place of the annual lutefisk dinner, in 1954 the congregation introduced the enduring tradition, referred to by Scott Anfinson, of an annual "Norwegian Smorgasbord." Ethnic dishes common to the area were served: *rømmegrøt* (cream porridge), *søtsuppe* (sweet soup), *rullepølse* (collared lamb or beef pressed and sliced into cold cuts), blood *klubb*, potato *klubb*, flatbread, and *lefse.*[44]

Even with the infusion of new members from country parishes, an aging membership and the loss of many young people posed a serious threat to the welfare of town churches. Moreover, movement of people into town from outlying rural areas modulated the ethnic composition of Benson and other towns in the region. Trinity Lutheran, as Orie Mills, who grew up in Benson, recalls, was known as "the little Swedish church" and Redeemer was known as "the big Norwegian church." Trinity, like other congregations in town, suffered a decline in membership. "Twenty to thirty years ago," Mills observes, "75 percent of the congregation was losing hair or lost it. . . . Today the congregation is younger, whereas Redeemer is shrinking."

The new members altered the ethnic composition of the Trinity congregation. A survey taken at a Sunday service in September 2003 showed that of the 175 members present, more than half were born in Swift County and 35 percent were German, 30 percent Norwegian, 23 percent Swedish, and 11 percent of other ethnic backgrounds. Reverend Barbara Thompson explains that the large German contingent came from a Missouri Synod Church, Our Redeemer's in Danvers, when it closed in 1994. Norwegians joined, she felt, because they preferred the greater warmth of a small congregation. Pastor Thompson's Norwegian origin might give cause for ethnic humor; her gender, however, created serious concerns for some members. Quoting an older man, who complained, "it is hard to take communion from someone with red fingernails," Mills believes "Pastor Barbara has done a wonderful job of overcoming sexism against female pastors."[45]

The composition of Trinity's membership indicates the softening of ethnic differences and an increased ecumenical spirit. Nevertheless, denominational divisions persisted among some congregations. Whereas Pastor Thompson could exchange pulpits with the local Catholic priest, St. Mark's Lutheran Church of the Missouri Synod did not recognize her as a pastor. Father Steve Verhelst of St. Francis Xavier Catholic Church describes the increased ecumenical cooperation from the late 1960s and 1970s, following the Second Vatican Council in 1962–65: "Cooperation with mainline churches went smoothly, but due to their belief statements there are barriers with the local Pentecostals and the Missouri Synod." Openness offers no menace, Father Verhelst believes, but, echoing the fear of pioneer pastors and priests, "secularism and individualism is a greater threat to churches."[46]

The migration into Benson of people of German origin in 1940 brought about the founding of St. Mark's Lutheran Church. Demographically, if not in the common understanding, Benson was on its way to becoming a "German" rather than a "Norwegian" town. But the beginnings of St. Mark's history predated its formal organization. Services had been

A memorial on the site of the Six Mile Grove Lutheran Church. Similar memorials mark other churches that were torn down as the congregation was dissolved for lack of members.

conducted since 1926, when Danvers and Benson likely were one parish; from the early 1930s a Lutheran Mission held services for a small group of communicants in the public library basement. Membership increased when rural churches closed; new members, for instance, came from St. John's Lutheran Church of the Missouri Synod, located near the county border south of Benson. Many have roots in Fairfield Township and the village of Holloway in Moyer Township, Swift County's two main German townships. A poll in September 2003 identified 75 percent of the members as having German ancestry; about half were from Swift County.[47]

Benson faces a changing world, one that challenges its character, its ethnic identity, and its sense of social and political community. Residents might fear, to quote an article on town life in southwestern Minnesota, that "stores and downtown are closed, and people increasingly find their entertainment, goods and opportunities for a full life elsewhere." The city is, however, taking steps to adjust to and to counter the downward trend. New initiatives to create revenue and employment have been introduced with some success. These changes might eventually lead to an even greater demographic shift as people of non-European backgrounds move to Benson to work in the new industries.[48]

CHAMBER OF COMMERCE ETHNICITY

Regardless of new initiatives and their relative success, the general economic developments in Swift County affected agricultural communities and caused demographic changes in the county's trading centers. In a November 2003 editorial citing findings by the Center for Rural Affairs, located in Nebraska, the Minneapolis *Star Tribune* deplored how Minnesota's western counties shared in the economic downturn seen in the rural upper Great Plains. Jack Kjos, vice president of Benson's First Federal Savings Bank, maintains, however, that Benson "has thrived on itself, starting many new businesses, and is holding its own. . . . Holding its own is almost like expanding in this part of the country. . . . Younger people are returning because there are jobs." In fact, Benson's population grew from 3,235 to 3,376 during the final decade of the last century, reversing an earlier decline.

Economic hardship in western Minnesota and efforts to reverse the downward course, described in the editorial on rural poverty cited above, are not the focus of the present study. The changing economic situation simply forms a backdrop and causal explanation for the region's social and ethnic ecology. Joseph Amato and John Meyer's brief account *The Decline of Rural Minnesota* (1993) may serve as an incisive guide to shifting economic settings. The Center for Rural Affairs in particular faulted "federal agricultural policies for encouraging factory-scale operations, rather than assuring that family-sized farms remain viable." The deepening loss of family farms of course had an adverse impact on rural ethnic communities. A measure introduced in Congress in fall 2003 by Minnesota senator Norm Coleman—the Rural Renaissance Act, calling for federal involvement and funds "to revitalize rural America and rebuild main street"—might if enacted together with other federal and state measures help repopulate and reinvigorate the western counties.[49]

An ethnic renaissance or revival from the late 1960s and 1970s rejected the national consensus mode of the postwar era. During this national movement, America discovered itself as a culturally pluralistic society. In part a reaction against assimilation and the loss of cultural idioms that had occurred by then, the movement for many Americans became a search for roots. Family associations and reunions, enthusiasm for family history, and visits to the old country express an individualized and personal relationship to ethnic identity as well as historical continuity with the immigrant experience.[50]

In the 2000 census, 4,641,254 Americans nationwide subjectively claimed Norwegian ethnicity. This number nearly equaled the population of Minnesota (4,919,479) and actually surpassed the population of Norway (4,554,000) as estimated January 1, 2003. Since ethnicity has become a subjective choice for European ancestry groups, the large number identifying themselves as Norwegian is powerful evidence of a persistent and strong sense of ethnic identity in post-immigration generations. The subjective nature of ethnic identity justifies analysis of a postethnic America; it might be understood, to quote from *The Promise Fulfilled*, as "a cosmopolitan rejection of the narrowness of the involuntary dogma of cultural pluralism that *assigns* group identities." If one is European American one may, in a society where most people have

TABLE 18

Ancestry in Minnesota, Swift County, Benson City, Madison City, and Starbuck City, 2000

Ancestry[a]	Number and Percentage of Individuals									
	Minnesota		Swift County		Benson City		Madison City		Starbuck City	
	N	%	N	%	N	%	N	%	N	%
Danish	88,924	1.8	239	2.0	96	2.9	41	2.3	13	1.0
Dutch	99,944	2.0	291	2.4	51	1.5	35	2.0	13	1.0
English	309,802	6.3	552	4.6	206	6.1	75	4.3	67	5.0
French (except Basque)[b]	202,946	4.1	504	4.2	188	5.6	39	2.2	20	1.5
French Canadian[b]	59,719	1.2	65	0.5	17	0.5	4	0.2	6	0.5
German	1,806,650	36.7	5,011	41.9	1,533	45.6	706	40.2	412	31.0
Irish[b]	552,952	11.2	1,137	9.5	282	8.4	91	5.2	88	6.6
Norwegian	850,742	17.3	3,992	33.4	1,324	39.4	823	46.8	741	55.8
Polish	240,405	4.9	409	3.4	137	4.1	31	1.8	16	1.2
Swedish	486,507	9.9	1,062	8.9	271	8.1	151	8.6	137	10.3
Other Ancestries	1,483,151	30.1	2,173	18.2	405	12.0	124	7.1	135	10.2
Total Ancestries Reported	6,181,742	125.5	15,435	129.0	4,510	134.2	2,120	120.7	1,648	124.1
Total Population	4,919,479	100.0	11,956	100.0	3,364	100.0	1,757	100.0	1,329	100.0

Source: U.S. Bureau of the Census, Census 2000

a. Single or multiple

b. The data represent a combination of two ancestries shown separately in Summary File 3. French includes Alsatian. French Canadian includes Acadian/Cajun. Irish includes Celtic.

mixed national ancestries, choose ethnic identity and affiliation. The strength or importance of a specific ethnic identity for the individual is of course not denoted in the statistics.[51]

People of American Indian ancestry still suffer from the indiscriminate assignment of identifying symbols. Marie Lightning Koenigs, born in 1942 and good-humoredly declaring herself "Swift County's token Indian for many years," told how her mother wanted her "to forget old Indian ways and become white." Her older siblings spoke the Ojibwe language and had difficulty at school, so she as the youngest learned only to understand the language. Marie became more aware of her heritage when on a visit to Hawaii she encountered the multiracial society there. In 1969 she married Noel Koenigs, who is of German ancestry. Her goal upon moving to Benson was to educate people about Native American culture and to have her children be proud of their heritage. She fought to remove some biased mascots from Benson High School, such as the cheerleading squad "the Watipi Girls," who stereotyped Native Americans. Although she originally thought "Benson Braves," the name of the football team, might be a reminder of the area's indigenous people, she now feels that the time has come to remove this name as well. Native Americans should celebrate their own symbols, Koenigs explains, such as those made visible at powwows. Koenigs's experience in some significant respects resembles that of earlier immigrants; it also gives insight into the nature and insensitivities of American society.[52]

In Minnesota and according to self-identification, Norwegian Americans constitute the second-largest single ethnic group, second only to the German American population. Their acceptable symbols show both consistency and durability. Locally, the so-called new ethnicity manifested itself, as it did in other Norwegian centers, in many personal dimensions but also in public space as a community affair. On visits to Benson, Scott Anfinson from the 1970s noticed "more signs of Sons of Norway meetings reported in the paper, and all of a sudden we were taking Norwegian language classes." The sister benefit society, organized as the Daughters of Norway in Minneapolis in 1897, in 1950 merged with the Sons of Norway. In the postwar years, as the second-generation membership gained control, "the order moved from one with a working-class vision and identity to one of the middle-class." The American-born generations joined and took charge, and people other than those of Norwegian ancestry were admitted to membership. In social life the strictures against alcohol relaxed. English had replaced Norwegian as the order's official language in 1942. In time the "daughters" surpassed the "sons" in sheer numbers. An aging and diminishing membership surely warrants description of the order's lodge meetings as a "retirement culture."

May 17 festivities, much neglected in the postwar years, were revived. Indeed, a great increase in observances occurred coast-to-coast; May 17 in many places with a large Norwegian American presence evolved into a community celebration much like St. Patrick's Day. *Syttende mai* was becoming an ethnic festival as much as a marker of Norwegian ethnicity. Beginning in 1989, the Benson area chamber of commerce for some years sponsored observances of "May 17, Norwegian Independence Day," as reported in the *Swift County Monitor-News* in 1992, "with a full day of events that recognizes the strong Scandinavian influence that is a part of the area's heritage."[53]

Parading ethnicity at this juncture in Norwegian American history may, more so than previously, be substantially seen as a marketing strategy. Accepting such chamber of commerce motives does not negate the sense of heritage and multicultural appreciation that ethnic festivals encourage. Commercial initiatives are present, however, when the Wisconsin town of Mount Horeb advertises itself as the "Troll Capital of the World" and nearby New Glarus becomes "Little Switzerland." Colorful ethnic symbols, exhibits, and celebrations are intended to attract business and to revitalize communities.[54]

Madison in Lac qui Parle County evolved into "Lutefisk Capital USA." It had competition from Glenwood in Pope County, which also wished to capitalize on the image of this oft-maligned ethnic dish and is home to Mike's Fish & Seafood, a large lutefisk plant. How Madison won out shows the value of marketing ethnicity as well as distortions, ignorance, and frivolous interpretations of ethnic traditions. "Well, what's a little prairie town without a lake supposed to do to attract business?" full-blooded German American Scotty Kuehl queried in an interview. He and Norwegian American Richard "Dick" Jackson, owner of the local SuperValu store, had the idea of exploiting the lutefisk angle after his supplier, the Olson Fish Company in Minneapolis, commented: "You sure sell a lot of lutefisk down there."

The two men approached the Madison city council in December 1982, proposing to name the city the lutefisk capital of the United States. Armed with data that Madison consumes more lutefisk per capita than any other town, a marketing specialist, Robert Dunnom, invented the caricature, Mr. Lou T. Fisk, that adorns the water tower. A monument to the cod, declaring Madison the lutefisk capital of America, was erected in Jacobson Park. "Lou," as the fish originally was called, was paraded through the streets of Madison to Jacobson Park for the dedication ceremony on June 23, 1983, bringing great media attention, which of course was the purpose of the entire event. Lutefisk celebrations had, however, been introduced nearly ten years earlier. At the first celebration in 1974,

A monument to cod in Madison declaring the city the "Lutefisk Capital USA"

in mock beauty-queen style but with "hefty girl" requirements, Ivey Vonderharr was elected Lutefisk Queen by audience applause.

In 2003 the annual celebration—now "Norsefest," promoting Madison as a tourist area—was conducted November 6–8, with a potato *klubb* luncheon, a lutefisk and turkey supper, evening entertainment, outhouse races—competing teams pushing an occupied, wheeled outhouse—and for the media highlight a lutefisk eating contest, the latter two events injecting "American" competition into an ethnic festival. Third-generation Norwegian American Jerry Osteraas in 1988 became the first Lutefisk King by eating seven pounds of the smelly, gelatinous product in one hour; he has "only lost three times since." One may well ask how these fatuous public displays of ethnicity may affect a more serious attitude toward ancestral heritage, but Scotty Kuehl insists, "it makes us appreciate all ethnic groups more and enhances ethnicity."[55]

Starbuck on Lake Minnnewaska demonstrated culinary loyalty to the popular *lefse* in its ambitious move to direct attention to the "Land of Lefse, Lutherans, and Loons" advertised on its street banners. A majority of Starbuck's citizens claim Norwegian ancestry, and in Madison Norwegian Americans remain the largest group, but in both cities other ethnicities, in particular German, are increasing their presence. Still, the main ethnic symbols are Norwegian. Third-generation Norwegian American Arnold Pederson relates that the idea of baking the world's largest *lefse* was introduced as "a joking situation." Maurice Amundson suggested it at a planning session of the centennial committee for Starbuck's founding, organized by the chamber of commerce. Then the project became intertwined with restoring the Starbuck railroad depot, championed by the Starbuck Depot Society, formed in 1986. At the site of this important local landmark in 1983 the giant *lefse*—weighing 70 pounds and measuring 9 feet, 8 inches in diameter—was baked by eight members of the Starbuck Lions Club. "I oversaw about three practice sessions," Pederson commented. On May 16, 1987, with a clear connection to *Syttende mai,* the depot society sponsored the first *Lefse Dagen, Lefse* Day, to commemorate the world-class *lefse*'s anniversary. A *lefse*-shaped monument on the lawn west of the depot marks the spot, yet another symbol of strong Norwegian identity. "Even the dogs bark in Norwegian," Pederson jokes, "they say 'Woof-dah.'" The sixteenth annual Lefse Dagen, May 11, 2002, offered sausage rolled in *lefse,* a truly Norwegian American creation, alongside other fare on the "Scandinavian menu."[56]

The city of Benson in 1920 was 4.4 percent German, 11.2 percent Swedish, and 39.1 percent Norwegian. The 2000 federal decennial count shows that the German portion had expanded to 45.6 percent, the Swedish had reduced to 8.1 percent, and the Norwegian had remained nearly static at 39.4. Although these ethnic identities are subjective, they nevertheless address mobility and geographic assimilation. Yet an impression of Norwegian dominance remains. Jan Carr Luzum, an Irish Catholic who has lived in Benson since 1967, candidly stated that she still feels this dominance: "They always talk about their own things, show pictures of their visits to Norway, and have a cultural attitude that says Norwegian is better." Her comments relate to strong ethnocentric sentiments, which evidence suggests are persistent and strong among post-immigration Norwegian Americans.[57]

Ethnocentricity manifests itself in different venues. The 1990s en-

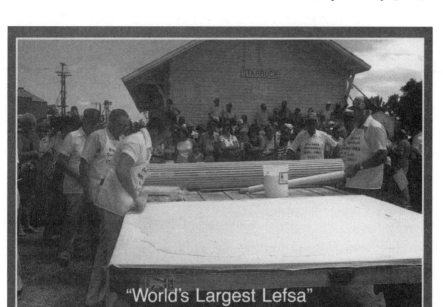

"World's Largest Lefsa"

The "World's Largest Lefse" was baked at Starbuck's centennial, July 1, 1983, on the Northern Pacific Depot grounds.

deavor to make Benson the "Klubb Capital of Minnesota" in connection with the May 17 observances may be seen in light of both business initiatives and ethnic enthusiasm. This culinary tradition was not dead but very much in play: four Benson restaurants at the time served *klubb* on a regular basis; two still offered this robust peasant fare during the research period for this study. Janet Lundebrek, born in 1946 and later president of the First Security Bank, took the lead. The May 17 competition occurred on the bank premises; Conrad Urke, a local law enforcement agent, won the first championship by eating more *klubb* than anyone else; he notes, "when we grew up that is mostly what we lived on." Explaining why celebrating Norwegian heritage was important to her, Lundebrek cheered the diversity of the United States: "The best we can do to understand all peoples is to understand the heritage, and my heritage was Norwegian, and even though we didn't live in Norway, a lot of our principles, I like to think, are a lot the same, because that's the way we grew up."[58]

NORWEGIANS AND THE COUNTRY TOWN

Tracing the Norwegian experience in west-central Minnesota from the 1860s to the present time documents a history—from first to last—of strong ethnic loyalties and a coextensive loyalty to American citizenship. The double allegiances indeed seem to function as complementary identities, the one reinforcing the other, as shared historical memories were created in a geographic environment vastly different from the scenery of the ancestral homeland.

Their sense of peoplehood, in Milton Gordon's term, in the special setting on the prairie remained in force well beyond the immigrant generation, though challenged by divisive Lutheran positions, localism, and political activism. Norwegians in the western counties constituted a larger percentage of the total population than anywhere else in Minnesota; consequently their visibility and influence continue in strength in that part of the state, though the Norwegian impulse in later generations is naturally weakened. In public, it expresses itself in a festival culture that involves the entire community. As central places, Starbuck, Benson, and Madison interacted with their rural hinterlands; a dominant blue-collar Norwegian workforce resided in town as other compatriots engaged in small business enterprise. A growing Norwegian professional class after 1900 indicated a maturing community; however, Yankee bankers and other professionally trained men played a significant role throughout most of these towns' histories.

The Norwegian small-town environment diverged both from Norwegian agricultural communities, whose greater segregation preserved ethnic idioms, and Norwegian colonies in large metropolitan areas, which operated as separate worlds in an environment of competing nationalities. In the small western town, ethnic groups could not separate to the same degree and instead frequently interacted as a community. Their new identity was thus tied to the town—the place called home—and was strengthened generation by generation.

Notes

Notes to Chapter 1

1. Ray A. Billington and Martin Ridge, *Westward Expansion: A History of the American Frontier,* 5th ed. (New York: MacMillan Publishing Co., Inc., 1982), 1–3, 6–8, quotes p.1, 6; Henry Bamford Parkes, *The United States of America: A History,* 3rd ed. (New York: Alfred A. Knopf, 1968), 163, 189–90, 422–23.

2. Ingrid Semmingsen, *Norway to America: A History of the Migration,* trans. Einar Haugen (Minneapolis: University of Minnesota Press, 1980), 121–23.

3. Billington and Ridge, *Westward Expansion,* 409–25, 629–43; Harvey Walker, *Village and Government in Minnesota,* Publication No. 6 (Minneapolis: University of Minnesota Press, 1927), 2–3; Odd S. Lovoll, "Norwegians on the Land: Address for the Society for the Study of Local and Regional History," in *Historical Essays on Rural Life* (Marshall, MN: Department of History, Southwest State University, 1992); Thomas White Harvey, "The Making of Railroad Towns in Minnesota's Red River Valley: A Thesis in Geography" (master's thesis, Pennsylvania State University, 1982), 2, n1; see also Oliver Knight, "Toward an Understanding of the Western Town," *The Western Historical Quarterly* 4 (1973): 27–28.

4. Odd S. Lovoll, *The Promise of America: A History of the Norwegian-American People* (Minneapolis: University of Minnesota Press, 1984; rev. ed., 1999), 126–28, 231; Lovoll, "Norwegians on the Land."

5. Lovoll, "Norwegians on the Land," 1.

6. Odd S. Lovoll, *The Promise Fulfilled: A Portrait of Norwegian Americans Today* (Minneapolis: University of Minnesota Press, 1998), 3–4, quote p.4; T. K. Derry, *A History of Modern Norway, 1814–1972* (Oxford: Clarendon Press, 1973), 93, 237–57; Milton M. Gordon, *Assimilation in American Life: The Role of Race, Religion, and National Origins* (New York: Oxford University Press, 1964), 30.

7. Thorstein Veblen, "The Country Town," *The Freeman* 12 (11 July 1923): 418.

8. Werner Sollors, *The Invention of Ethnicity* (New York: Oxford University Press, 1989), ix–xx; Marcus Lee Hansen, *The Immigrant in American History* (Cambridge, MA: Harvard University Press, 1940), 30, 93; see also David A. Hollinger, *Postethnic America: Beyond Multiculturalism* (New York: Basic Books, 1995); Mary C. Waters, *Ethnic Options: Choosing Identities in America* (Berkeley: University of California Press, 1990), 16–20, quote p.17.

9. Jon Gjerde, *The Minds of the West: Ethnocultural Evolution in the Rural Middle West, 1830–1917* (Chapel Hill: University of North Carolina Press, 1997).

10. Richard Lingeman, *Small Town America: A Narrative History 1620–The Present* (New York: G. P. Putnam's Sons, 1980), quote from front flap.

11. Nelson Klose, *A Concise Study Guide to the American Frontier* (Lincoln: University of Nebraska Press, 1964), 6, 50–61; Frederic L. Paxson, *History of the American Frontier 1763–1893* (Boston, MA: Houghton Mifflin Company, 1924), 289, 290–92. The frontier is also defined as an area containing not less than two nor more than six inhabitants per square mile. It may also be defined by stages: A. trappers and fur traders; B. cattlemen; C. miners; D. farmers; E. town dwellers. This study focuses mainly on the agricultural and village frontier.

12. Gary Clayton Anderson, *Little Crow: Spokesman for the Sioux* (St. Paul: Minnesota Historical Society [hereafter, MHS] Press, 1986), p.6 lists the seven tribes of the Sioux confederacy: Mdewakanton, Wahpeton, Wahpekute, Sisseton, Yankton, Yanktonai, and Teton. Mitchell E. Rubinstein and Alan R. Woolworth, "The Dakota and Ojibway," in ed. June Drenning Holmquist, *They Chose Minnesota: A Survey of the State's Ethnic Groups* (St. Paul: MHS Press, 1981), 18–20; Samuel W. Pond, *The Dakota or Sioux in Minnesota As They Were in 1834* (St. Paul: MHS Press, 1986), 26–31, quotes p.26, 27, 31.

13. Rubinstein and Woolworth, "Dakota and Ojibway," 17; William Watts Folwell, *History of Minnesota*, 4 vols. (St. Paul: MHS Press, 1921–26), 1:80–81, 146–47, 149.

14. Folwell, *History of Minnesota*, 1:132–33, 147; Theodore C. Blegen, *Minnesota: A History of the State* (Minneapolis: University of Minnesota Press, 1963), 85–86; Theodore C. Blegen, "The Pond Brothers," *Minnesota History* 15 (Sept. 1934): 273–81; W. M. Babcock, "Major Lawrence Taliaferro, Indian Agent," *Mississippi Valley Historical Review* 11 (Dec. 1924): 358–75; see also Grace Lee Nute, "Posts in the Minnesota Fur-Trading Area, 1660–1855," *Minnesota History* 11 (Dec. 1930): 353–85; Marcus Lee Hansen, *Old Fort Snelling, 1819–1858* (St. Paul: MHS Press, 1918; reprint, 1958).

15. Blegen, *Minnesota*, 159; Folwell, *History of Minnesota*, 1:225, 229–30; Paxson, *History of American Frontier*, 393–94.

16. Folwell, *History of Minnesota*, 1:241–46, 247–48; Blegen, *Minnesota*, 70, 163–64, 175–78, 243–48; Lovoll, *Promise of America*, 107. "Old-stock" is defined as native born of native-born parents.

17. Paxson, *History of American Frontier*, 424–25; Blegen, *Minnesota*, 129, 166–69; Folwell, *History of Minnesota*, 1:266–69, 353–54, 356; Rubinstein and Woolworth, "Dakota and Ojibway," 24.

18. Blegen, *Minnesota*, 175.

19. Blegen, *Minnesota*, 220–21.

20. Blegen, *Minnesota*, 228–29; Folwell, *History of Minnesota*, 2:1–3, 9–15.

21. Folwell, *History of Minnesota*, 2:14–16, quote p.14–15; Roy F. Nichols and

Eugene H. Berwanger, *The Stakes of Power, 1845–1877* (1961; rev. ed., New York: Hill & Wang, 1982), 47–48, 51–55.

22. Folwell, *History of Minnesota,* 2:2–3; Nichols and Berwanger, *Stakes of Power,* 59, 90–100; Jerry Rosholt, *Ole Goes to War: Men from Norway Who Fought in America's Civil War* (Decorah, IA: Vesterheim Norwegian-American Museum, 2003); Blegen, *Minnesota,* 233–34; Theodore C. Blegen, *Norwegian Migration to America: The American Transition* (Northfield, MN: Norwegian-American Historical Association [hereafter, NAHA], 1940), 389–91.

23. Blegen, *Minnesota,* 234, 262–64. The Homestead Act offered any citizen or intending citizen who was the head of a family and over twenty-one years of age 160 acres of surveyed public domain after five years of continuous residence and payment of a registration fee; under the act land could also be acquired after six months residence at $1.25 an acre.

24. Theodore Christianson, *Minnesota: A History of the State and Its People* (New York: The American Historical Society, Inc., 1935), 1:377–80.

25. Kenneth Carley, *The Dakota War of 1862: Minnesota's Other Civil War* (St. Paul: MHS Press, 1961; reprint, 1976), 1, 4, 7–9, 21, 72–75, 76–82; Folwell's number of white fatalities supports the lower figure; Paxson, *History of American Frontier,* 487; Rubinstein and Woolworth, "Dakota and Ojibway," 22. The authors explain that the 374 Dakota that remained in 1866 were mostly part-time residents allowed to return under permits. By 1870 most of them had also departed, leaving only 176 Dakota in the state. In 1909 the State of Minnesota erected a monument on the site of the Baker farm, where the Dakota War had begun.

26. Carley, *Dakota War,* 21, 23–24; Folwell, *History of Minnesota,* 2:392; Hjalmar Rued Holand, *De norske settlementers historie* (Ephraim, WI: privately published, 1909), 543–50; A. E. Strand, *A History of the Swedish-Americans of Minnesota* (Chicago: Lewis Publishing Company, 1910), 355–66; Victor E. Lawson, Martin E. Tew, and J. Emil Nelson, comps., *Illustrated History and Descriptive and Biographical Review of Kandiyohi County, Minnesota* (St. Paul, MN: The Compilers, 1905), 20–22.

27. Theodore C. Blegen, "Guri Endresen, Frontier Heroine," *Minnesota History* 10 (Dec. 1929): 425–30. In a letter to her mother dated 2 Dec. 1866, which Blegen presents in translation, Endresen relates that the two men were unhurt and helped her. In making her a heroine, Blegen relies on the accounts of the two she rescued, Solomon R. Foot and Oscar Erikson, printed in Lawson, Tew, and Nelson, *History of Kandiyohi County,* 106–10.

28. Theodore C. Blegen, ed., *Land of Their Choice: The Immigrants Write Home* (Minneapolis: University of Minnesota Press, 1955), 427, 428–30.

29. Blegen, *Land of Their Choice,* 428; Lovoll, *Promise of America,* 104–5.

30. Lovoll, *Promise of America,* 115; Fredrika Bremer, *Homes in the New World: Impressions of America,* trans. Mary Howitt, 2 vols. (New York: Putnam, 1853), 1:56.

31. The collective term "Scandinavian" was employed by the American press instead of the national appellations of Swedish, Norwegian, or Danish regardless of nationality. In the nineteenth century, and even later, the immigrants themselves might attach "Scandinavian" to the names of organizations, choruses, and congregations instead of a narrower designation. The historian has to determine the nationality of the memberships in order to establish a particular national identity. Bremer uses the term inclusively—Swedes, Norwegians, and Danes were Scandinavians—much like the term Nordic or the North of today, which has been extended to include the Finns. Adolph B. Benson and Naboth Hedin, *Americans from Sweden,* in The Peoples of America Series, Louis Adamic, ed. (New York: J. B. Lippincott Company, 1950), 161–62. In 1902 the spot of their settlement was marked by a tall, inscribed granite monument.

32. Carlton C. Qualey, *Norwegian Settlement in the United States* (Northfield, MN: NAHA, 1938), 111; Holand, *De norske settlementers historie,* 322–23, 325.

33. Lovoll, *Promise of America,* 8–10, 10–13, 13–16, 16–18; Odd S. Lovoll, "Norwegian Emigration to America: A Dramatic National Experience," *The Norseman* 4–5 (1999): 4–12.

34. Lovoll, *Promise of America,* 10–12; Arne Hassing, "Methodism from America to Norway," *Norwegian-American Studies* 28 (Northfield, MN: NAHA, 1979): 192–216.

35. Lovoll, *Promise of America,* 14. The name of the administrative unit was *amt* until 1918, when the designation was changed to *fylke.*

36. Qualey, *Norwegian Settlement,* 15–16; Lovoll, "Norwegians on the Land," 7, 8.

37. Odd S. Lovoll, *A Century of Urban Life: The Norwegians in Chicago before 1930* (Northfield, MN: NAHA, 1988); Odd S. Lovoll, "A Perspective on the Life of Norwegian America: Norwegian Enclaves in Chicago in the 1920s," *Migranten/ The Migrant* 1 (1988): 24–37; Lovoll, *Promise of America,* 47–51.

38. Lovoll, *Promise of America,* 46–47, 51–52.

39. Lovoll, *Promise of America,* 53–55, 70; Svein Nilsson, *A Chronicler of Immigrant Life,* ed. and trans. Clarence A. Clausen (Northfield, MN: NAHA, 1982), 132.

40. Lovoll, *Promise of America,* 55–58, quote p.58. Some scholars insist that the small, simple log church in West Koshkonong, built the fall of 1844 and dedicated 19 Dec., should be accorded the honor of being the first Norwegian Lutheran church in America. The Muskego Church, although not dedicated, was in use from early fall 1844, and thus preceded the West Koshkonong structure.

41. Lovoll, *Promise of America,* 55, 62–63; Qualey, *Norwegian Settlement,* 67, 69.

42. Holand, *De norske settlementers historie,* 320–22, 330; Lovoll, *Promise of America,* 116–17; Qualey, *Norwegian Settlement,* 78, 83–86, 91.

43. Holand, *De norske settlementers historie,* 320, 403–4, quote p.320, translated by the author.

44. Holand, *De norske settlementers historie,* 327, 484.

45. Lovoll, *Promise of America,* 118–21; Qualey, *Norwegian Settlement,* 97, 99.

46. Carlton C. Qualey, "A Typical Norwegian Settlement: Spring Grove, Minnesota," *Norwegian-American Studies and Records* 9 (Northfield, MN: NAHA, 1936): 54–55, quote p.55; see also Britt Unni Skjervold Geving, *An Evolving Heritage: The Norwegian Americans in Spring Grove, Minnesota, the 1850s to the 1990s* (master's thesis, Norwegian University of Science and Technology, Trondheim, 2001).

47. The Lake Park Region covers the counties of Becker, Otter Tail, Pope, Kandiyohi, Douglas, Swift, and Todd, western Stearns and Meeker counties, and eastern Grant and Stevens counties; Holand, *De norske settlementers historie,* 532, 538–43; Qualey, *Norwegian Settlement,* 124–25.

48. Folwell, *History of Minnesota,* 3:62.

49. Billington and Ridge, *Westward Expansion,* 6; Lingeman, *Small Town America,* 18, 107.

50. Lingeman, *Small Town America,* 259, 399, 443: Lingeman's excellent social history presents the variety of American small towns that came into being from colonial times; Lewis Eldon Atherton, *Main Street on the Middle Border* (Bloomington: Indiana University Press, 1954), 41.

51. Sinclair Lewis, *Main Street: The Story of Carol Kennicott,* intro. by Martin Bucco (1920; reprint, New York: Penguin Books, 1995), 240. The women served *römmegröd og lefse,* cream porridge and *lefse,* popular ethnic foods.

Notes to Chapter 2

1. Edward D. Neill, *History of the Minnesota Valley* (Minneapolis, MN: North Star Publishing Company, 1882), 165, 167.

2. Thomas Hughes, "History of Steamboating on the Minnesota River," *Collections of the Minnesota Historical Society* 10.1 (St. Paul: MHS, 1905): 138–57; Judson W. Bishop, "History of the St. Paul & Sioux City Railroad, 1864–1881," *Collections of the Minnesota Historical Society* 10.1 (St. Paul: MHS, 1905): 399–400, 401–2; Neill, *History of Minnesota Valley,* 913.

3. Blegen, *Minnesota,* 252, 296, 299–301; John H. Randall, "The Beginning of Railroad Building in Minnesota," *Collections of the Minnesota Historical Society* 15 (St. Paul: MHS, 1915): 215–20. After James J. Hill and associates became owners of the St. Paul and Pacific Railroad, they incorporated the property as St. Paul, Minneapolis and Manitoba Railroad Company in 1879; in 1885 it became a part of the Great Northern Railway.

4. Harvey, "Making of Railroad Towns," 3, 8; Stanley Holte Anonsen, *A History of Swift County* (master's thesis, University of Minnesota, 1929), 16–17; Blegen, *Minnesota,* 301, 304–5.

5. Lars Ljungmark, *For Sale—Minnesota: Organized Promotion of Scandinavian Immigration, 1866–1873* (Gothenburg, Sweden: Akademiförlaget, 1971),

78, 91–95, 267–68; Gordon S. Iseminger, "*Land and Emigration:* A Northern Pacific Railroad Company Newspaper," *North Dakota Quarterly* (Summer 1981): 70–89.

6. Ljungmark, *For Sale—Minnesota,* 59–60; see Sören Listoe, *Staten Minnesota i Nordamerika. Dens fordele for den skandinaviske indvandrer med særligt hensyn til jordbrugeren* (Minneapolis, MN: Published by S. Christensen for the State of Minnesota, 1869–70).

7. Ljungmark, *For Sale—Minnesota,* 57–64, 65–69; Odd S. Lovoll, "Paul Hjelm-Hansen: Norwegian 'Discoverer' of the Red River Valley of Minnesota and Settlement Promoter," in eds. Vidar Pedersen and Željka Švrljuga, *Performances in American Literature and Culture: Essays in Honor of Professor Orm Øverland on His 60th Birthday* (Bergen, Norway: University of Bergen, 1995), 165–68.

8. Odd S. Lovoll, "The Great Exodus," in ed. Erik J. Friis, *They Came from Norway* (New York: The Norwegian Immigration Sesquicentennial Commission, Inc., 1975), 10–15; Lovoll, *Promise of America,* 31–33, 33–37; Semmingsen, *Norway to America,* 112–13; Petter Jakob Bjerve, *Ekteskap, fødsler og vandringer i Norge, 1856–1960* (Oslo, Norway: Statistisk Sentralbyrå, 1965), 164.

9. Folwell, *History of Minnesota,* 3:58–59.

10. Qualey, *Norwegian Settlement,* 97–98, 112, 124–25, 232; Holand, *De norske settlementers historie,* 536.

11. Atherton, *Main Street,* 28–29; Warren Upham, "Minnesota Geographic Names: Their Origin and Historic Significance," *Collections of the Minnesota Historical Society* 17 (St. Paul: MHS, 1920): 190–95; Gary Richter, comp. and consl., *Starbuck 1883–1983* (Starbuck, MN: The Starbuck Centennial History Book Committee, 1983), 5–6.

12. Neill, *History of Minnesota Valley,* 950; Michael Fedo, comp., *The Pocket Guide to Minnesota Place Names* (St. Paul: MHS Press, 2002), 15, explains the name as follows: "Benson city and township (Swift County) are named for Ben H. Benson, an early area businessman."

13. Upham, "Minnesota Geographic Names," 540; *Benson Times,* 6 Oct. 1885; Department of the Interior, Census Office, *Statistics of Population of the United States at the Tenth Census, 1880* (New York: Norman Publishing, 1991).

14. Anonsen, *History of Swift County,* 355; Neill, *History of Minnesota Valley,* 955, gives 1867 as the date for Christenson's arrival; *Swift County Minnesota: A Collection of Historical Sketches and Family Histories* (Benson, MN: Swift County Historical Society), 11, maintains he arrived in 1866, as do other sources consulted; see his obituary in *Swift County Monitor,* 8 Dec. 1910.

15. Neill, *History of Minnesota Valley,* 356–57; Tom Schmiedeler, "Civic Geometry: Frontier Forms of Minnesota's County Seats," *Minnesota History* 57 (Fall 2001): 330–45, quote p.339. The city of Morris in Stevens County is named in honor of Charles Morris.

16. *Benson Times,* 23 Feb. and 11 Sept. 1876; *Swift County Review,* May 28, 1909; *Swift County Monitor,* 24 Apr. 1908, 19 May 1916, 1 July 1927; Neill, *His-*

tory of Minnesota Valley, 957; Anonsen, *History of Swift County,* 17–18; O. K. Smith, comp., *Review of the Progress of Benson Minnesota* (Benson, MN: Swift County Monitor Press, 1892), 15, 16; Ole Wenaus is listed in the 1875 Minnesota census as being born in Norway and immigrating in 1875, at thirty-one years of age; "Chippewa Landing" as Benson's earliest name is stated in a "Pilgrim Heritage Church, 1876–1975," pamphlet, 17 Oct. 1976, in author's possession.

17. *Swift County Monitor,* 24 June 1927; *Nordisk Folkeblad,* 8 July 1869; Odd S. Lovoll, "Paul Hjelm-Hansen: Norwegian Discoverer of the Red River Valley and Settlement Promoter," public lecture, Dawson, MN, 21 Feb. 1993; the quote about Hjelm-Hansen is from a bronze memorial tablet executed by Norwegian American artist Paul Fjelde and presented to the MHS in 1924 by the Norwegian-Danish Press Association of America.

18. Anonsen, *History of Swift County,* 18, 57; Benson Township, Swift County, *Minnesota State Census* (St. Paul, 1875); the General Law enacted in 1851 required a minimum resident population of three hundred in order to be incorporated as a village: see Walker, *Village and Government,* 42–43.

19. Folwell, *History of Minnesota,* 1:150–53; Blegen, "Pond Brothers"; Theodore C. Blegen, "Two Missionaries in the Sioux Country," *Minnesota History* 21 (Mar., June, Sept. 1940): 15–283; Pond, *Dakota in Minnesota; Swift County Monitor-News,* 10 June 1992, reports on the commemorative plaque placed in Ambush Park that year and the beginnings of the park in the 1960s.

20. Atherton, *Main Street,* 3; Anonsen, *History of Swift County,* 3–12; *Benson Times,* 4 July 1882, 16 Feb. 1877: in subsequent issues the newspaper prints the village ordinances.

21. Atherton, *Main Street,* 13; Anonsen, *History of Swift County,* 18–21, 26; *Swift County Minnesota,* 51; *Benson Times,* 21 Apr. 1877 and other issues announce various stagecoach departures.

22. Anonsen, *History of Swift County,* 20–21; *Swift County Monitor,* 4 Aug. 1921. Swift Falls never grew large, but in 1880 it got a general store, in 1893 a creamery, and in 1918 a bank, all founded and managed by J. M. Danelz.

23. Anonsen, *History of Swift County,* 18; *Swift County Monitor,* 21 July 1905; Neill, *History of Minnesota Valley,* 957–58; *Benson Times,* 24 July and 23 Dec. 1876.

24. Atherton, *Main Street,* discussed in chapter 1, 3–32, quote p.3; Atherton defines the "middle border" as consisting of Ohio, Indiana, Illinois, Missouri, Michigan, Minnesota, Wisconsin, and Iowa and the eastern fringe of Kansas, Nebraska, and the Dakotas.

25. Veblen, "Country Town," 417–20, quotes p.418; Lewis E. Atherton, "The Midwestern Country Town—Myth and Reality," *Agricultural History* 26 (July 1952): 73–80, reprinted in ed. Abraham Eisenstadt, *American History: Recent Interpretations,* Book 2 (New York: Thomas Y. Crowell Company, 1962), 137–48.

26. Atherton, "Midwestern Country Town," 139, 140; Billington and Ridge, *Westward Expansion,* 688; *Swift County Minnesota,* 874.

27. *Benson Times,* 31 Dec. 1876; Folwell, *History of Minnesota,* 3:66; Joseph A.

Amato, "Business First and Always," in eds. Richard O. Davies, Joseph A. Amato, and David R. Pichaske, *A Place Called Home: Writings on the Midwestern Small Town* (St. Paul: MHS Press, 2003), 416. Amato writes about Marshall, MN, but the reference applies equally well to Benson.

28. *Benson Times*, 16 Feb. and 10 Apr. 1876; Neill, *History of Minnesota Valley*, 955, 957–58.

29. Folwell, *History of Minnesota*, 3:93; Anonsen, *History of Swift County*, 22–23; *Benson Times*, 30 Dec. 1876; *Swift County Monitor*, 29 Dec. 1899, was published "In Honor of Settlers of Swift County" and carries a history of "Third of a Century."

30. The hopperdozer was a long pan with its bottom covered in tar to catch the locusts as it was drawn through the field; Anonsen, *History of Swift County*, 22–23, 24; *Benson Times*, 9 June and 21 July 1877, 12 Jan. 1878.

31. Neill, *History of Minnesota Valley*, 913–14, 955.

32. *Swift County Monitor-News*, 24 June 1927; Anonsen, *History of Swift County*, 12.

33. Anonsen, *History of Swift County*, 12.

34. Neill, *History of Minnesota Valley*, 955; *Swift County Monitor*, 29 Dec. 1899, 24 June 1927; Swift County Commissioner Records, 3 Jan. 1871, Swift County Courthouse, Benson; *Swift County Minnesota*, 175–76, 262.

35. Neill, *History of Minnesota Valley*, 955; Upham, "Minnesota Geographic Names," 542; *Swift County Minnesota*, 42, 642; Department of the Interior, *Tenth Census, 1880; Swift County Monitor*, 3 Oct. 1902; interview with Janet Lundebrek, 6 June 2002; Lundebrek, the great-great-granddaughter of Oley Thorson, provided additional material on Thorson and his family, including pages from *History of Swift Falls: Prepared for the Centennial Celebration, June 19, 20, 1976;* the 1870 federal census lists Thorson as Olie Thorson: the Norwegian name "Ole" was frequently altered to "Olie" or "Oley" in official records.

36. *Swift County Minnesota*, 132–34.

37. Department of the Interior, *Tenth Census, 1880; Swift County Minnesota*, 642, explains the name of Torning Township: "The name originally submitted to the commissioners was Tonning—after a town in Denmark, but in the Commissioners' records it was misspelled and became Torning"; the same source, p.384, explains the name of Hegbert Township as combining the first syllables of the original settlers, Ole E. Hegstad and Ernest Christianson Bertness, two young Norwegian immigrants who settled on the south shore of Long Lake in 1869.

38. Gjerde, *Minds of the West*, 81; Department of the Interior, *Tenth Census, 1880.*

39. Department of the Interior, *Tenth Census, 1880;* interview with Ernest E. Anderson, Benson, MN, 31 May and 24 July 2002; interview with Leonard Mitteness, Benson, MN, 30 May 2002; interview with Ginter Rice, Benson, MN, 30 May 2002.

40. James P. Shannon, *Catholic Colonization on the Western Frontier* (New Haven, CT: Yale University Press, 1957), 7, 46–51, 54, 57, 107–13, 260–61; *Swift County Advocate*, 3 May 1878; for an insightful portrait of early Graceville, see Bridget Connelly, *Forgetting Ireland* (St. Paul: MHS Press, 2003).

41. Shannon, *Catholic Colonization*, 55; Department of the Interior, *Tenth Census, 1880*.

42. Shannon, *Catholic Colonization*, 135–36.

43. Shannon, *Catholic Colonization*, 139–40; *Dedication of St. Francis Xavier School, a Memorial Pamphlet Issued by the Parish of St. Francis*, pamphlet, 28 Aug. 1953; interviews with William J. Luzum and Jan Carr Luzum, Benson, MN, 28 May 2002.

44. Hildegard Binder Johnson, "The Germans," in ed. Holmquist, *They Chose Minnesota*, 153, 154; Department of the Interior, *Tenth Census, 1880*; Gary G. Erickson, information on churches in western Swift County, 5 June 2003.

45. Frank Renkiewicz, "The Poles," in ed. Holmquist, *They Chose Minnesota*, 362, 363; Department of the Interior, *Tenth Census, 1880*; *Swift County Minnesota*, 315.

46. *Swift County Minnesota*, 599–600; Department of the Interior, *Tenth Census, 1880*.

47. Interview with Susan M. Pirsig, executive director, Swift County Grow, 4 June 2002; Pirsig related how Benson citizens, many in prominent positions, in 1993–94 opposed plans to recruit a substantial number of Hmong immigrants to alleviate the shortage of workers in a manufacturing company in Benson. She cited well-educated younger persons who complained, "If they can't speak American, why do they want to be in the United States?" Many schoolteachers and civic leaders talked against the proposal; representatives for the Hmong realized they would not be welcome and decided to abandon the plan. "It's our loss," Pirsig concluded. In its racial attitude Benson is of course not unique.

48. See Einar Haugen, *The Norwegian Language in America: A Study in Bilingual Behavior*, 2 vols. (Bloomington: Indiana University Press, 1969).

49. Odd S. Lovoll, *A Folk Epic: The Bygdelag in America* (Boston, MA: Twayne Publishers, 1975), 3–6, 40–43; Arthur C. Paulson quoted in Lowell J. Soike, *Norwegian Americans and the Politics of Dissent, 1880–1924* (Northfield, MN: NAHA, 1891), 11; Rasmus B. Anderson, *Bygdejævning. Artikler af repræsentanter fra de forskjellige bygder i Norge om, hvad deres sambygdinger har udrettet i Vesterheimen* (Madison, WI: Amerika's Forlag, 1903), 338, 342; Rudolph J. Vecoli, "The Italian Americans," in eds. Leonard Dinnerstein and Frederic Cole Jaher, *Uncertain Americans: Readings in Ethnic History* (New York: Oxford University Press, 1977), 202–3. In America's great cities, Italians formed stable "Little Italys" where they might, Vecoli explains, group "themselves along certain blocks according to provinces or even villages of origin." In these closed neighborhoods the Italian peasants—*contadini*—re-created much of the rural folk life they were familiar with from the old country.

50. *Swift County Monitor-News*, 6 July 1967; *Swift County Minnesota*, 132–34; O. M. Norlie, *Norsk lutherske menigheter i Amerika 1843–1916* (Minneapolis, MN: Augsburg Publishing House, 1918), 647; "Lake Hazel Lutheran Church Centennial, 1871–1971," pamphlet, n.d.; Leland G. Pederson, letter to the author, 16 Jan. 2003; Verna Gomer, letter to the author, 11 Jan. 2003; interview with Verna Gomer, 23 July 2002; Gjerde, *Minds of the West*, 8; the church structure and cemetery are cared for by the Lake Hazel Lutheran Church Memorial Association.

51. J. D. Korstad, "Swift Falls, Benson, Swift County, Minn.," in ed. L. M. Gimmestad, *Nordfjordingernes historie i Amerika* (Minneapolis, MN: Lutheran Free Church Publishing Company, 1940), 231–32; Norlie, *Norsk lutherske menigheter i Amerika*, 649.

52. *Swift County Minnesota*, 405; J. S. Johnson, *Minnesota: En kortfattet historie av nordmændenes bebyggelse av staten, deres gjøremaal, foreninger og livsvilkaar* (Minneapolis: Minnesota-Norway 1914 Centennial Exposition Association, 1914), 66–67; *Hope Lutheran Church, Sunburg, Minnesota Centennial 1875–1975*, pamphlet, 1975; *Official County Plat Book and Farmers' Directory of Swift County Minnesota* (ca. 1940), 31, Swift County Historical Society, Benson, MN; *Atlas of Swift County Minnesota* (Fergus Falls, MN: Thomas O. Nelson Co., 1961), 11.

53. *Benson Times*, 17 Apr. 1876, 14 July 1877, 7 Jan. 1881; Gjerde, *Minds of the West*, 8; the hospital for the insane in St. Peter, MN, was opened in 1866.

54. *Compendium of History and Biography of Central and Northern Minnesota* (Chicago: George A. Ogle & Co., 1904), 330–31; Odd S. Lovoll, "The Norwegian Press in North Dakota," *Norwegian-American Studies* 24 (Northfield, MN: NAHA, 1970): 78–101, quote p.79.

55. *Compendium of History and Biography*, 330–31, 412; the quote is from an interview with Meredith Sherman Ulstad, Northfield, MN, 22 Nov. 2002, in regard to Hantho Township, Lac qui Parle County, but has wide application in many parts of west-central Minnesota.

56. "The Six Mile Grove Town Records," held in the town hall, were kindly made available to us by Charles McGee, board supervisor, 11 June 2003; Walker, *Village and Government*, 83; Bernt A. Nissen, *Det nye Norge grunnlegges. Vårt folks historie*, vol. 6 (Oslo, Norway: Aschehoug & Co. [W. Nygaard], 1964): 288–95.

57. George M. Stephenson, "The Mind of the Scandinavian Immigrant," *Norwegian-American Studies and Records* 4 (Northfield, MN: NAHA, 1929): 71.

NOTES TO CHAPTER 3

1. Atherton, *Main Street*, 207; *Minnesota Tidende*, 7 Apr. 1899; Yvonne Hanson Dewar, comp., "The Hansons of Six Mile Grove" (Crookston, MN: privately printed, 1988); Gjerde, *Minds of the West*, 203–21.

2. Hanson Dewar, "Hansons of Six Mile Grove," 1, 9–10, 29–30, 39–41; Gjerde, *Minds of the West*, 8; Norlie, *Norsk lutherske menigheter i Amerika*, 647.

3. Merle Curti, *The Making of an American Community: A Case Study of Democracy in a Frontier County* (Stanford, CA: Stanford University Press, 1959), 222–23, 448; Parkes, *United States of America*, 200–202; Patricia Nelson Limerick, *The Legacy of Conquest: The Unbroken Past of the American West* (New York: W. W. Norton & Company, 1988), 20–23, quote p.20; Paul S. Boyer, et al., *The Enduring Vision: A History of the American People* (New York: Houghton Mifflin Company, 4th ed., 2002), 349.

4. Hanson Dewar, "Hansons of Six Mile Grove," 40; interview with Homer Tjosaas, Benson, MN, 13 Nov. 2001; Ana and Erich Hanson were the great grandparents of Homer Tjosaas.

5. Walter D. Kamphoefner, *The Westfalians: From Germany to Missouri* (Princeton, NJ: Princeton University Press, 1987), 83–84.

6. Department of the Interior, *Tenth Census, 1880*; Lovoll, *Promise of America*, 139; *Benson Times*, 7 Aug. 1883.

7. *Benson Times*, 11 July 1882, 10 July 1883, 10 June 1884.

8. Walker, *Village and Government*, 33–38.

9. *Benson Times*, 3, 10, 17, 24, and 31 Mar. and 23 June 1877, 3 May 1878; *Swift County Monitor*, 29 Dec. 1899, 14 Jan. 1926, 22 July 1927.

10. *Benson Times*, 15 July 1881, 31 Mar. 1877; Department of the Interior, *Tenth Census, 1880*.

11. *Swift County Monitor*, 27 May 1892; U.S. Bureau of the Census, *Fourteenth Census of the United States, 1920* (Washington, DC: GPO, 1923).

12. U.S. Bureau of the Census, *Fourteenth Census, 1920*; *Trinity Lutheran Church 125 Years, Benson, Minnesota 1874–1999* (Benson, MN: privately printed, 1999), 5–9; *He Lives: St. Francis Xavier Catholic Church, 1882 Benson, Minnesota, 1982* (Benson, MN: privately printed, 1982); *Benson Times*, 10 July 1890.

13. See the insightful discussion of class and ethnicity by John Higham, "From Process to Structure," in eds. Peter Kivisto and Dag Blanck, *American Immigrants and Their Generations: Studies and Commentaries on the Hansen Thesis after Fifty Years* (Chicago: University of Illinois Press, 1990), 11–41, quote p.18; Lovoll, *Century of Urban Life*, 165–72, 268–72.

14. *Benson Times*, 28 Mar. 1879; *Swift County Review*, 19 Mar. 1909; *Swift County Monitor*, 6 Jan. 1928; Atherton, *Main Street*, 75, 166.

15. Curti, *Making of an American Community*, 253–58; Hanson Dewar, "Hansons of Six Mile Grove," 220–21.

16. Department of the Interior, *Tenth Census, 1880*; Curti, *Making of an American Community*, 250.

17. Atherton, *Main Street*, 161, 174; *Swift County Minnesota*, 29–30; *Benson Times*, 15 July 1887; the Merchants' Hotel was built and operated by Ole Thorson in the mid-1870s.

18. *Benson Times*, 24 May 1880, 14 Oct. 1902, 21 Jan. 1908; *Swift County Monitor*, 29 Dec. 1899, 27 Nov. 1925, 24 June 1927; *Swift County Review*, 10 Apr.

1917; *Review of Progress of Benson*, 24–25; Neill, *History of Minnesota Valley*, 958; Atherton, *Main Street*, 148–49.

19. Neill, *History of Minnesota Valley*, 958; Department of the Interior, *Tenth Census, 1880*.

20. *Swift County Monitor*, 24 Apr. 1908, 28 May 1909, 24 June 1927; *Review of Progress of Benson*, 15; Neill, *History of Minnesota Valley*, 957.

21. *Swift County Monitor*, 24 June 1927; *Swift County Review*, 19 Nov. 1910.

22. Tage G. Mandt from Telemark, Norway, learned the blacksmith trade in his father's smithy on their farm in Dane County, Wisconsin. He constructed the Stoughton wagon, much used in the Midwest in the decades after the Civil War. *Swift County Monitor*, 4 Nov. 1898, 19 Jan. 1900, 22 July 1927; *Benson Times*, 24 Apr. 1876, 13 Feb. 1880, 11 July 1882; *Benson Posten*, 19 July 1878, printed as a section of *Benson Times*; Neill, *History of Minnesota Valley*, 960; Department of the Interior, *Tenth Census, 1880*.

23. *Swift County Monitor*, 15 Jan. 1920, 24 June 1927.

24. *Swift County Monitor*, 25 May 1919, 24 June 1927.

25. *Swift County Monitor*, 24 June 1927; *Swift County Review*, 24 Aug. 1906, 28 June 1912.

26. *Swift County Monitor*, 28 May 1909, 24 June 1927; *Benson Times*, 6 Aug. 1880, 8 July 1881; Anonsen, *History of Swift County*, 38. Madison in Lac qui Parle County, for instance, suffered several fires in the 1890s and early 1900s that took most of Main Street; brick buildings gradually replaced the wooden structures destroyed by fire.

27. *Benson Times*, 7 July 1877, 9 Feb. 1882; *Swift County News*, 7 Apr. 1921; Department of the Interior, *Tenth Census, 1880;* Isaac L. Preus was a member of a prominent Norwegian American family active in the Lutheran church.

28. *He Lives: St. Francis Xavier; Swift County Monitor*, 1 Nov. 1918.

29. *Benson Posten*, 22 May 1876, 28 June 1878; *Benson Times*, 18 Nov. 1876; *Budstikken*, 18 Apr. 1877; Lovoll, *Promise of America*, 180–81; Johs. B. Wist, ed., *Norsk-amerikanernes festskrift 1914* (Decorah, IA: The Symra Company, 1914), 167; *Fakkelen* (The Torch) was published in Glenwood from 1885 to 1886.

30. *Benson Times*, 23 Feb. and 24 Nov. 1877; *Swift County Monitor*, 24 June 1927; *Swift County Minnesota*, 879–80; additional information on Ole Thorson provided by Terje Mikael Hasle Joranger, e-mail correspondence, 30 June 2003.

31. Gjerde, *Minds of the West*, 68, 72; Billington and Ridge, *Westward Expansion*, 688; Lovoll, *Promise of America*, 143.

32. *Benson Times*, 21 Aug., 21 Oct., and 9 and 16 Dec. 1876, 26 Jan. 1877, 31 Oct. 1879; "Pilgrim Heritage Church, 1976–1975"; Church Records of Christ Church, National Register of Historic Places—nomination form, newspaper data relating to Christ Church, all in Swift County Historical Museum, Benson, MN; Lovoll, *Century of Urban Life*, 58–60, 61–62, 235–36; Neill, *History of Minnesota Valley*, 958; see Arlow W. Andersen, *The Salt of the Earth: A History of*

Norwegian-Danish Methodism in America (Nashville, TN: Norwegian-Danish Methodist Society, 1962), 152; Neil A. Markus, "Areal Patterns of Religious Denominationalism in Minnesota, 1950" (master's thesis, University of Minnesota, 1961), 142–44; L. R. Moyer and O. G. Dale, *History of Chippewa and Lac qui Parle Counties* (Indianapolis, IN: B. F. Bowen & Company, Inc., 1916), 1:286.

33. See for an interpretation of anti-Catholicism among Norwegian Americans Soike, *Norwegian Americans; Benson Times,* 8 May 1876; *He Lives: St. Francis Xavier.*

34. *Trinity Lutheran Church 125 Years,* 5–9; Sture Lindmark, *Swedish America, 1914–1932* (Uppsala, Sweden: Läromedelsförlagen, 1971), 248–53; Allan Kastrup, *The Swedish Heritage in America* (Minneapolis, MN: Swedish Council of America, 1975), 201–2. The Norwegians left the Scandinavian Augustana in 1870 and formed a Norwegian Augustana. Later the same year a majority of congregations left and formed a more nationalistic church known as the Conference. The Swedish church never used the national designation in its name.

35. Laurence M. Larson, "The Collection and Preservation of Sources," *Norwegian-American Studies and Records* 9 (Northfield, MN: NAHA, 1936): 98–99; Eugene L. Fevold, "The Norwegian Immigrant and His Church," *Norwegian-American Studies* 23 (Northfield, MN: NAHA, 1967): 3–16, quote p.7.

36. Norlie, *Norsk lutherske menigheter i Amerika,* 646; "Christ Our Hope, Our Redeemer's Lutheran Church, Benson, Minnesota, 1870–1970," pamphlet, 1970; "The Sixtieth Anniversary of Our Savior's and Trinity Lutheran Churches," pamphlet, 1930, 4–5; C. S. Pederson, *Rev. Chr. Pederson 1852–1930* (Benson, MN: privately printed, n.d.), 5–7, 12–13, 14; East and West Zion History Book Committee, *East and West Zion Lutheran Celebrating 125 Years, 1871–1996* (n.p.: privately printed, 1996), 4–6.

37. "Our Savior's Lutheran Church, Benson, Minnesota, Diamond Anniversary 1870–1945," pamphlet, 1945, 6.

38. Norlie, *Norsk lutherske menigheter i Amerika,* 646; *Swift County Monitor,* 21 May 1937; "The Seventy-Fifth Anniversary of Immanuel Lutheran Church, Benson, Minnesota," pamphlet, 1972; some sources suggest that Immanuel and Six Mile Grove did not separate completely until 1879.

39. *Benson Times,* 8 and 15 May 1876; Norlie, *Norsk lutherske prester i Amerika,* 137, 151; Lovoll, *Promise of America,* 114–15, 143–45.

40. "Christ Our Hope"; congregational minutes of Trinity Lutheran Church, 1870–1886, translated from the Norwegian by Oliver Skare, Our Redeemer's Lutheran Church, Benson, MN.

41. Marion John Nelson, "A Pioneer Artist and His Masterpiece, *Norwegian-American Studies* 22 (Northfield, MN: NAHA, 1965): 3–17, quotes p.14, 18; see also Lena R. Christenson's biography of her father, "Sketch about Lars Christenson of Benson, Minnesota, and the Altar He Carved during His Spare Time," in the Vesterheim Museum, Decorah, IA.

42. Congregational minutes of Trinity Lutheran; Fevold, "The Norwegian Immigrant and His Church," 10.

43. Hansen, *Immigrant in American History,* 120; Blegen, *Norwegian Migration,* 222.

44. Blegen, *Norwegian Migration,* 222; Fevold, "The Norwegian Immigrant and His Church," 10; Lovoll, *Promise of America,* 78–80, 149–50; Norlie, *Norsk lutherske menigheter i Amerika,* 645–50.

45. *Benson Times,* 11 and 18 Apr. 1879, 2 Jan. and 30 Apr. 1880, 24 June 1885; congregational minutes of Trinity Lutheran.

46. *Benson Times,* 1 Mar. 1878. The Order of the Blue Ribbon was founded by F. Murphy in Pittsburgh, PA, in 1877; members wore a blue ribbon in accordance with the book of Numbers, 15:38–39.

47. Curti, *Making of an American Community,* 100.

48. Fevold, "The Norwegian Immigrant and His Church," 12–13; Ewa Morawska, *For Bread with Butter: Life-Worlds of East Central Europeans in Johnstown, Pennsylvania, 1890–1940* (Cambridge, England: Cambridge University Press, 1985), 10.

49. Odd S. Lovoll, "The Changing Role of May 17 as a Norwegian-American Key Symbol," in eds. Brit Marie Hovland and Olaf Aagedal, *Nasjonaldagsfeiring i flerkulturelle demokrati* (Copenhagen, Denmark: Nordisk Ministerråd, 2001), 65–78, quote p.70; Lovoll, *Century of Urban Life,* 245.

50. *Budstikken,* 9 and 23 May 1876; *Benson Times,* 8 and 22 May 1876; Blegen, *Norwegian Migration,* 214–15.

51. *Benson Times,* 30 Dec. 1876, 20 Jan. and 18 May 1877, 17 and 24 May 1878, 23 May 1879, 21 May 1880, 20 May, 10 June, and 1 July 1881; *Benson Posten,* 12 and 19 Apr. and 24 May 1878.

52. *Benson Times,* 13 Nov. 1883, 10 Feb. 1885.

53. *Benson Times,* 19 Dec. 1882, 7 Oct. 1884.

54. *Benson Times,* 31 Mar. 1877, 3 Apr. 1883, 18 and 26 Feb. and 1 Apr. 1884; the Benson Dramatic Company or Association announces simple productions in the *Benson Times* from early 1877.

55. *Benson Times,* 8 Dec. 1877, 17 and 24 Apr. and 22 May 1883.

56. Todd W. Nichol, tr. and intro., *Vivacious Daughter: Seven Lectures on the Religious Situation Among Norwegians in America, by H. A. Preus* (Northfield, MN: NAHA, 1990).

57. Per Nordahl, "Lost and Found—A Place to Be: The Organization of Provincial Societies in Chicago from the 1890s to 1933," in ed. Daniel Lindmark, *Swedishness Reconsidered: Three Centuries of Swedish-American Identities* (Umeå, Sweden: Kulturgräns Norr, 1999), 65–89, discusses the concept of place and landscape as identifying factors; see also David Duncan and Davi Ley, eds., *Place/Culture/Representation* (New York: Routledge, 1993): "the authors explore the ways in which a more fluid and sensitive geographer's art can help us make sense of ourselves and the landscapes and places we inhabit and think about."

NOTES TO CHAPTER 4

1. *The Centennial History of Kandiyohi County, Minnesota, 1870–1970* (Willmar, MN: Kandiyohi County Historical Society, 1970), 37.

2. *Centennial History of Kandiyohi County,* 32, 33, 37–38, 199; Johnson, *Minnesota,* 63–66; U.S. Bureau of the Census, *Twelfth Census of the United States, 1900* (New York: Norman Ross Publishing, 1997); J. W. Arctander later moved his law office to Minneapolis.

3. Neill, *History of Minnesota Valley,* 964; *Benson Times,* 19 Mar. 1891; "Charter, City of Glenwood, Pope County, Minnesota. Adopted at a Special Election, July 29, 1912" (Glenwood, MN: Glenwood Gopher-Press Print, 1912), 3; U.S. Bureau of the Census, *Twelfth Census, 1900.*

4. U.S. Bureau of the Census, *Twelfth Census, 1900.*

5. Billington and Ridge, *Western Expansion,* 6–7.

6. "Ft. Lake Johanna & Iverson Cabin," plaque erected in Fort Lake Johanna Park in 1999 by Fort Lake Johanna Historical Park Association; Hannah A. Sanders, *Historical Sketches from "The Cradle of Pope County"* (n.p.: privately printed, 1992); Richter, *Starbuck 1883–1983,* 6.

7. Stockholm, the story goes, was named in honor of a local Swedish bootlegger known as "Whiskey Swede"; more likely it got its name from the Scandinavian settlers in the area. The meeting to usher Pope County into existence on 4 Sept. 1866 was held in the log home of Ole Peterson, an extensive landholder from Valdres, Norway, and the county's first sheriff and later treasurer. The log cabin was moved to the Pope County Historical Museum.

8. Sanders, *Historical Sketches;* Jeanne David and Alice Tripp, eds., *Remembering Lake Scandi* (n.p.: privately printed, 1990), 12–13, 21–22; U.S. Bureau of the Census, *Twelfth Census, 1900.*

9. East and West Zion History Book Committee, *East and West Zion Lutheran Celebrating 125 Years 1871–1996,* 5; Arnold P. Pederson, "Aslaksons in Pope County Minnesota from 1871," typescript (Mar. 1989), in author's possession.

10. Calvin E. Pederson, "Norske Bygder—Represented in Pope County," map showing regional origin in Norway; Terje Mikael Hasle Joranger of Oslo, Norway, provided me with a copy, for which I thank him most sincerely.

11. Richter, *Starbuck 1883–1983,* 3, 10–11; additional information on the Wollan family from Jostein Molde in Trondheim, Norway.

12. Richter, *Starbuck 1883–1983,* 3, 10–11; U.S. Bureau of the Census, *Twelfth Census, 1900;* effective 1 July 1975 by statute all Minnesota villages became cities: see Minnesota Secretary of State, *The Minnesota Legislative Manual* (St. Paul: State of Minnesota, 1975–1976); Kathleen Neils Conzen, "Mainstream and Side Channels: The Localization of Immigrant Cultures," *Journal of American Ethnic History* (Fall 1991): 5–20.

13. Richter, *Starbuck 1883–1983,* 3; U.S. Bureau of the Census, *Twelfth Census, 1900.*

14. Richter, *Starbuck 1883–1983*, 3; U.S. Bureau of the Census, *Twelfth Census, 1900;* David LaVigne, analysis of collected data (July 2002).

15. Richter, *Starbuck 1883–1983*, 12–13, 14–15, 22; "The Fremad Store," typescript (n.d.), Pope County Historical Society, Glenwood, MN.

16. Richter, *Starbuck 1883–1983*, 92; Norlie, *Norsk lutherske menigheter i Amerika*, 557. Norlie gives 1869 as the year of founding; distance in 1872 caused a split because of "too long way to church." Indherred, now Innherad, denotes the districts around the inner part of the Trondheimsfjord in the county of North Trøndelag.

17. Richter, *Starbuck 1883–1983*, 92–93, 98–99; Norlie, *Norsk lutherske menigheter i Amerika*, 553, 554, 557, 558, 559, 560, 561; *Minnewaska Lutheran Church 90th Anniversary, 1973* (Starbuck, MN: Minnewaska Congregation, 1973); Rasmus Malmin, O. M. Norlie, and O. A. Tingelstad, trans. and rev., *Who's Who Among Pastors in all the Norwegian Synods of America 1843–1927* (Minneapolis, MN: Augsburg Publishing House, 1928), 642.

18. Richter, *Starbuck 1883–1983*, 95–97; Norlie, *Norsk lutherske menigheter i Amerika*, 556; Malmin, Norlie, Tingelstad, *Who's Who Among Pastors,* 314; M. Casper Johnshoy, comp., *A Brief History of Fron Evangelical Lutheran Congregation, 1880–1942* (Starbuck, MN: Fron Congregation, 1942); between 1857 and 1876, until the Norwegian Synod could establish its own theological training school, its ministers were trained at the Missouri Synod's Concordia Seminary in St. Louis.

19. Norlie, *Norsk lutherske menigheter i Amerika*, 556, 557, 558, 561; *Illustrated Album of Biography of Pope and Stevens Counties, Minnesota* (Chicago: Alden, Ogle & Company, 1888), 176–77; Timothy L. Smith, "Religion and Ethnicity in America," *American Historical Review* 83 (Dec. 1978): 1155–81; John Bodnar, *The Transplanted: A History of Immigrants in Urban America* (Bloomington: Indiana University Press, 1985), 145; Peter A. Munch, "Segregation and Assimilation of Norwegian Settlements in Wisconsin," *Norwegian-American Studies and Records* 18 (Northfield, MN: NAHA, 1954): 136; Bjørg Seland, on the faculty of Agder University College, Kristiansand, Norway, provided information on low-churchly societies.

20. U.S. Bureau of the Census, *Twelfth Census, 1900;* a monument in the joint cemetery of the two Swedish Lutheran churches gives the following years for their existence: Bethany, 1877–1996, Bethesda, 1879–1966; Richter, *Starbuck 1883–1983*, 99, gives 1896 as the year the Bethesda Church was organized; see same page for Congregational Church; P. E. Christenson, "A Biography of Dr. C. R. Christenson," typescript (1955), Pope County Historical Society, Glenwood, MN; *Starbuck Times*, 8 June 1877.

21. In many interviews individuals dwelled on the socially conservative and stable practices at home, on the farm, and in the village, the criticism of those who broke social convention, and the frugality born of the need that circumscribed their lives; this theme remained consistent as individuals related their

family histories and the experience of early settlers in western Minnesota. See C. F. Midelfort and H. C. Midelfort, "Norwegian Families," in eds. Monica McGoldrick, John K. Pearce, and Joseph Giordano, *Ethnicity and Family Therapy* (New York: Guilford Press, 1956), 438–56; Lovoll, *Promise Fulfilled*, 186–92; Conzen, "Mainstream and Side Channels," quote p.13.

22. U.S. Bureau of the Census, *Twelfth Census, 1900.*

23. U.S. Bureau of the Census, *Twelfth Census, 1900; Prairie Chronicle: A History of Lac qui Parle County* (n.p.: Curtis Media, Inc., 1995), 176, 194, 388–90, 433–34; Anne Maguire, ed., *Madison Historical Album* (Madison, MN: Lac qui Parle County Historical Society, n.d.), 11–12; Moyer and Dale, *History of Chippewa and Lac qui Parle*, 1:411–13, 1:566–72; Martin Ulvestad, *Nordmændene i Amerika, deres historie og rekord* (Minneapolis, MN: History Book Company's Forlag, 1907), 102–3; William Anderson, *City Charter Making in Minnesota* (Minneapolis: University of Minnesota, 1922), 11, 38; file on medical doctors, Lac qui Parle History Center, Madison, MN; Madison opted for a city charter under the general city incorporation law of 1870, codified as revised in 1894, rather than under home-rule provisions.

24. Minnesota Secretary of State, *Legislative Manual of the State of Minnesota* (St. Paul, MN: The State, 1907); plat book of Lac qui Parle County (1907), Lac qui Parle Historical Society, Madison, MN; Moyer and Dale, *History of Chippewa and Lac qui Parle*, 1:421–22, 1:427–28; Jon Leirfall, *Liv og lagnad i Stjørdalsbygdene* 1.2 (Trondheim, Norway: Stjørdal og Meråker Kommuner, 1968), 72–73, 74; Maguire, *Madison Historical Album*, 16; U.S. Bureau of the Census, *Twelfth Census, 1900.*

25. Moyer and Dale, *History of Chippewa and Lac qui Parle*, 1:445–56, quotes p.448, 449, 454, 455, *Independent Press* quote p.454; Ulvestad, *Nordmændene i Amerika*, 381; *St. Paul Dispatch*, 30 Oct. 1926.

26. See Thomas Harvey, "Small-Town Minnesota," in ed. Clifford E. Clark, Jr., *Minnesota in a Century of Change: The State and Its People Since 1900* (St. Paul: MHS Press, 1989), 99–127; Maguire, *Madison Historical Album*, 24–25, quote p.30; Moyer and Dale, *History of Chippewa and Lac qui Parle*, 1:112–14, 1:177–78; Einar Hoidale papers, NAHA, Northfield, MN; the courthouse moved from Lac qui Parle Village was at that time placed on Seventh Avenue, where it was divided into two: one half was remodeled into a dwelling that still stands today.

27. U.S. Bureau of the Census, *Twelfth Census, 1900.*

28. G. T. Lee, *Lidt om det kirkelige Arbeide i Pope County, Minnesota, 1865–1909* (Glenwood, MN: Herald Printing Co.'s Forlag, 1909), 27–30; Wist, *Norsk-amerikanernes festskrift*, 260–61, 263; Lovoll, *Promise of America*, 163.

29. Wist, *Norsk-amerikanernes festskrift*, 232–40, 253; Lovoll, *Promise of America*, 152.

30. Rev. H. O. Hendrikson, ed., *In Retrospect: A History of the Lutheran Normal School, 1892–1932* (Lake Mills, IA: Graphic Publishing Company, 1958),

4, 9–10, 29, 103, 107–11; "Den Lutherske Normalskole, Madison, Minn.," in supplement to *Minnesota Tidende*, 18 Nov. 1897; *Western Guard*, 24 July and 25 Sept. 1895; the controversy in the Norwegian Synod which in 1887 caused a split dealt with the doctrine on predestination.

31. Supplement to *Western Guard*, 30 June 1960; interview with Inez Gualtieri, Madison, MN, 14 Apr. 2003.

32. The Socialist and labor leader Marcus Thrane (1817–90) organized labor societies in Norway; his activities led to arrest and imprisonment; after his discharge he immigrated to America in 1863. He resided in Chicago and later in Eau Claire, WI, where his son Arthur Thrane, father of the younger Marcus Thrane, was a medical doctor. In Dec. 1881 the older Marcus Thrane went on a lecture tour to western Minnesota, speaking in Benson to an audience that was not very large, "owing to the fact of his lecture not being known, but his address was very well spoken of," *Benson Times*, 29 Dec. 1881. On the older Marcus Thrane, see Terje I. Leiren, *Marcus Thrane: A Norwegian Radical in America* (Northfield, MN: NAHA, 1987); *Madison Tidende*, 18 Apr. 1895, 27 May 1897; file on medical doctors, Lac qui Parle History Center, Madison, MN; Gualtieri interview.

33. *Madison Tidende*, 18 Apr. 1895, 25 June 1896; *Minnesota Tidende*, 12 Aug. 1897; Wist, *Norsk-Amerikanernes festskrift*, 170–71; *A Souvenir . . . Madison, Minnesota* (Minneapolis, MN: Wall & Haines, 1900).

34. Wist, *Norsk-amerikanernes festskrift*, 171; *Western Guard*, 5 Jan. and 28 Oct. 1891.

35. Einar Hoidale papers, NAHA, Northfield, MN; supplement to *Western Guard*, 30 June 1960; in ten chapters, beginning in its 22 June 1898 issue and concluding 26 Aug. 1898, the *Western Guard* exposed "The Rise of the Ring."

36. Jon Willand, conversations and e-mail exchanges, 2002–03: interview with Fr. Eugene Hackert, New Ulm, MN, 13 Apr. 2003; supplement to *Western Guard*, 30 June 1960; *Western Guard*, 22 June 1898; *Independent Press*, 30 Nov. 1929; Norlie, *Norsk lutherske menigheter i Amerika*, 589–98; *75th Anniversary First Lutheran Church, 1879–1954* (Madison, MN: privately printed, 1954); Joseph Tetlie, *Madison Lutheran Church, Fiftieth Anniversary Festival, 1885–1935* (Madison, MN: privately printed, 1935); *Centennial History and Reminiscence Book, Garfield Lutheran Church, 1892–1992* (Madison, MN: privately printed, 1992); Moyer and Dale, *History of Chippewa and Lac qui Parle*, 1:411; Malmin, Norlie, and Tingelstad, *Who's Who Among Pastors*, 441, 583.

37. Connelly, *Forgetting Ireland*, 199–204, relates how Fr. Peter Rosen was suspended for writing a tract criticizing Archbishop John Ireland and accusing him of dishonesty in his colonization promotion.

38. *Independent Press*, 3 Jan. 1896; supplement to *Western Guard*, 30 June 1960; Norlie, *Norsk lutherske menigheter i Amerika*, 593–94, 596–97; Soike, *Norwegian Americans*, 192; U.S. Bureau of the Census, *Twelfth Census, 1900*.

39. See discussion in Soike, *Norwegian Americans*, 191–92; interviews with

Fr. Eugene Hackert, New Ulm, MN, 7 June 2003, Ann Maguire, Madison, MN, 10 June 2003, and Fr. Steve Verhelst, Benson, MN, 12 June 2003; Ray Allen Billington, *The Protestant Crusade, 1800–1860: A Study of the Origins of American Nativism* (New York: Rinehart & Company, Inc., 1938), 1–31, quote p.1; interview with Robert Joseph Dineen, Benson, MN, 29 May 2002; several Catholics in Madison declined to be interviewed because they did not wish to revive painful memories of anti-Catholic discrimination.

40. *Swift County Monitor*, 24 June 1927; *Agralite Cooperative, Benson, Minnesota, 1940–1965. A Special Report on a Quarter Century of Service* (Benson, MN: privately printed, 1965), 7–15; Richter, *Starbuck 1883–1983*, 30; Paul Kittelson, information on Benson power plant, correspondence, 21 Oct. 2002; Moyer and Dale, *History of Chippewa and Lac qui Parle*, 1:572–77; Mollie Hoben, *NANA . . . The Benson Years* (St. Paul, MN: privately printed, 1979). The Agralite Cooperative was consolidated 4 May 1939, though the rural electrification movement in Stevens, Big Stone, Swift, and southern Pope counties dates from 1935. The first rural electric meter of the Agralite Cooperative was set on 4 Mar. 1940 near Starbuck.

41. Atherton, *Main Street*, 285; Hoben, *NANA*; J. B. A. Benoit, a resident of Benson, is credited with making the first automobile in Benson, in 1902: see account in *Swift County Monitor*, 27 June 1927, 12 Apr. 1940.

42. Rosanne E. Gjencke, "Record-Setting Judge Norwegian Emigrant," *Kandi Express* (Willmar, MN: Kandiyohi Historical Society, May 1981); Søren B. Laache, *Norsk medicin i hundrede aar* (Oslo, Norway: Steen'ske bogtrykkeri, 1911), 253, cited also in Øivind Larsen, Ole Berg, and Fritz Hodne, *Legene og samfunnet* (Oslo, Norway: Den norske lægeforening, 1986), 49; *The West Central Minnesota Daily Tribune*, 1 Feb. 1951; Anonsen, *History of Swift County*, 48–49; *Swift County News*, 31 Oct. 1939, 4 July 1950; *Benson Times*, 11 May and 8 June 1909.

43. *Swift County Monitor*, 4 Feb. 1898, 24 June and 28 Oct. 1927, 28 Apr. 1950; *Swift County Review*, 9 Sept. 1904; *Benson Times*, 6 Feb. and 12 June 1906, 11 Feb. 1908, 12 Oct. 1909; *Budstikken*, 16 May 1876; *Swift County, Minnesota: A Collection of Historical Sketches and Family Histories* (Benson, MN: Swift County Historical Society, 1979), 854; U.S. Bureau of the Census, *Twelfth Census, 1900*; Rolf Klevstrand, *From Apothek to Drugstore: Norwegian Immigrant Pharmacists in the United States of America* (Oslo, Norway: Cygnus forlag AS, 2003); David LaVigne, notes (20 July 2002); W. R. Smith purchased Lion Drug Store in 1908.

44. Department of the Interior, *Tenth Census, 1880*; U.S. Bureau of the Census, *Twelfth Census, 1900*.

45. Atherton, *Main Street*, 285, 290–95; *Benson Times*, 9 July 1880.

46. Atherton, *Main Street*, 287–88, 292.

47. *Madison Historical Album*, 178; *Benson Times*, 21 Aug., 4 Sept., and 18 Nov. 1876, 14 Oct. 1902; *Swift County News*, 7 Apr. 1921; Catherine McNicol

Stock, "Compromise and Its Limits," in eds. Davies, Amato, and Pichaske, *Place Called Home*, 232.

48. Lovoll, *Promise of America*, 289–92.

49. Carl G. O. Hansen, *History of Sons of Norway* (Minneapolis, MN: Sons of Norway Supreme Lodge, 1944), 31, 50, 138–39.

50. Interview with Bernice Oellien, Madison, MN, 9 June 2003; *Sons of Norway Bjørgvin Lodge 10, Benson, Minnesota, 100 Years, 1902–2002* (Benson, MN: privately printed, 2002); Richter, *Starbuck 1883–1983*, 167, 170; *Starbuck Times*, 15 May 1903, 15 May 1908.

51. *Western Guard*, 18 May 1898.

52. *Benson Times*, 10 June 1884, 6 July 1892; *Western Guard*, 18 May 1898.

NOTES TO CHAPTER 5

1. Anderson, *City Charter Making*, 40–41, 61–62; *Swift County News*, 21 Jan. 1926; *Benson Times*, 25 Feb., 3 Mar., and 14 Apr. 1908; a copy of the "City Charter of the City of Benson" (25 Feb. 1908) was provided by Mayor Paul Kittelson.

2. Atherton, *Main Street*, quotes p.72, 75, see discussion 72–76; "City Charter of Benson"; *Benson Times*, 12 May 1903, 14 Apr. 1908, 12 Apr. 1909, 12 Apr. 1910; exhibit text at Swift County Historical Museum, Benson, MN; in April 1909 S. H. Hudson was elected mayor.

3. *Swift County Monitor*, 10 Jan. 1919, 24 June 1927; *Swift County Monitor-News*, 27 June 1990; information from Swift County Historical Society, Benson, MN.

4. *Swift County News*, 30 Dec. 1947; *Swift County Monitor*, 24 June 1927; *Decorah-Posten*, 1 Jan. 1948; *The Lutheran*, 7 Jan. 1948.

5. List of Benson school board members assembled by Marlys Gallagher, Swift County Historical Society, Benson, MN; *Swift County News*, 21 Apr. 1936.

6. *Swift County Monitor*, 16 June 1899, 19 Jan. 1900, 24 June 1927; school records, Swift County Historical Society, Benson, MN; by 1870 all rural schools in Swift County had been consolidated; Robert Bly, "Being a Lutheran God-boy in Minnesota," in ed. Chester G. Anderson, *Growing Up in Minnesota: Ten Writers Remember Their Childhoods* (Minneapolis: University of Minnesota Press, 1976), 207.

7. *Benson Times*, 5 Feb. 1884; congregational minutes of Trinity Lutheran Church; congregational minutes of Six Mile Grove Congregation, 1879–1931, Our Redeemer's Lutheran Church, Benson, MN.

8. *Swift County Review*, 23 Apr. 1909; Hoben, *NANA*; Minnesota Independent School District #777 (Benson) Records, 1901–76, and Benson High School Record Book, 1906–13, MHS, St. Paul, MN; *Swift County Monitor* makes reference to Norse classes and teachers in the following issues: 6 Feb. 1914, 21 May 1915, 26 May and 1 Sept. 1916, 31 Aug. 1917, 30 Aug. 1918.

9. Hoben, *NANA*; *Benson Times*, 19 Sept. 1905.

10. Lovoll, *Promise of America,* 29.

11. E. John B. Allen, *From Skisport to Skiing: One Hundred Years of an American Sport, 1840–1940* (Amherst: University of Massachusetts, 1993), 5.

12. Richter, *Starbuck 1883–1983,* 174; *Swift County Review,* 26 Feb. 1909; *Benson Times,* 23 Feb. 1909.

13. Atherton, *Main Street,* 135–36; *Images of America: Swift County Minnesota* (Benson, MN: Swift County Historical Society, 2000), 92; *Benson Times,* 8 Dec. 1903, 15 and 22 Nov. 1904; Seland's humorous stories are published in such collections as *Nye skjemtesoger* (Banter Stories), 1920, and *Morostubbar* (Amusing Tales), 1942.

14. *Benson Times,* 13 and 20 June 1905; *Decorah-Posten,* 9 June 1905; see also Lovoll, "Changing Role of May 17," 65–78; the idea of "key symbols" was developed by anthropologist Sherry Ortner in her article "On Key Symbols," *American Anthropologist* 75:5 (Oct. 1973): 1339–47.

15. *Benson Times,* 10 Apr. 1906, 29 Nov. 1910; *Swift County Monitor,* 29 May 1914; Lovoll, *Folk Epic,* 119–20; a number of histories of Norway can be consulted, including John Midgaard, *A Brief History of Norway* (1963; rev. ed., Oslo, Norway: Tano, 1986). Erling Bjørnson (1868–1959), Bjørnstjerne Bjørnson's youngest son, having grown up in both Germany and Norway had deep roots in both cultures; in Norway, he served in the Storting as an elected member of the agricultural party. Dagfinn Worren, University of Oslo, Oslo, Norway, provided additional information on Seland and Bjørnson.

16. *Benson Times,* 22 May 1906, 29 Nov. 1910; Lovoll, *Folk Epic,* 99–100, 117–18.

17. Lovoll, *Folk Epic,* 119; Odd S. Lovoll, "The Norwegian-American Old-Home Societies Viewed as a Mediating Culture Between 'Consent' and 'Descent,'" in eds. Lars Olsson and Sune Åckerman, *Hembygden och världen. Festskrift till Ulf Beijbom* (Gothenburg, Sweden: Svenska Emigrantinstitutet, 2002), 117–33, quote p.119; Nordahl, "Lost and Found," 65–89.

18. Lovoll, *Folk Epic,* 65; *Swift County Monitor,* 18 June and 2 July 1915, 1 Jan. 1920; *Benson Times,* 24 Oct. 1905, 29 Dec. 1908; "Raport Bog for Kvindeforeningens Sekretær af Vor Frelsers Menighed, Benson, Minnesota, 1914–1924," Ladies Aid minutes, Our Redeemer's Lutheran Church, Benson, MN.

19. *Swift County Monitor,* 26 June 1914, 7 June and 12 July 1918; Lovoll, *Folk Epic,* 249.

20. *Swift County Monitor,* 17 Jan. 1936; *Swift County News,* 14 Jan. 1936; Lovoll, *Folk Epic,* 118.

21. *Benson Times,* 24 May 1904, 26 May 1906, 14 and 24 May 1907, 26 May 1908, 23 May 1911; Lovoll, "Changing Role of May 17," 66.

22. Waters, *Ethnic Options,* 134; Gjerde, *Minds of the West,* 236–37, quote p.237, where Conzen is also quoted; see Conzen, "Mainstream and Side Channels," 5–20; Leonard Mitteness interview.

23. The painstaking and time-consuming work of determining Norwegian

landholdings in Swift County, as well as preparing a table, map, and chart, was conducted entirely by Gary G. Erickson of Willmar, MN, on a voluntary basis. I am greatly indebted to him and grateful for his enthusiastic and competent assistance.

24. Interview with Ellsworth Smogard, Philip Nygard, and Philip Greseth, Madison, MN, 14 Apr. 2003.

25. Anderson interviews; Gjerde, *Minds of the West*, 8; Walter Kamphoefner, *Westfalians*, 129–34, quote p.134.

26. Interview with Ginter Rice, Benson, MN, 24 July 2002; Ginter Rice, "The Life and History of Ginter Rice" and "The Life and Family of Ginter Rice," typescripts (2002), in author's possession; Mons Sotendahl and N. J. Njus, *Festskrift. En fremstilling af det kirkelige arbeide i Norway Lake fra 1862–1916* (n.p.: n.d.), 73–76.

27. Interviews with Verna Gomer, Benson, MN, 13 Mar. and 23 July 2002.

28. Lee Benson, *The Concept of Jacksonian Democracy: New York as a Test Case* (Princeton, NJ: Princeton University Press, 1961), 165; Soike, *Norwegian Americans*, 3–9.

29. Blegen, *Norwegian Migration*, 555; see discussion in Lovoll, *Promise of America*, 189–202.

30. Soike, *Norwegian Americans*, 189–90.

31. Soike, *Norwegian Americans*, 7, 185–97; Paul Kleppner, *The Cross of Culture: A Social Analysis of Midwestern Politics, 1850–1900* (New York: Free Press, 1970), 84–88, 103, quotes p.87; Sten Carlsson, *Skandinaviska politiker i Minnesota 1882–1900: En studie rörande den etniske faktorns roll vid politiska val i en immigrantstat* (Uppsala, Sweden: University of Uppsala, 1970), 57–58; see also Richard J. Jensen, *The Winning of the Midwest: Social and Political Conflict, 1888–96* (Chicago: University of Chicago Press, 1971); on the final point, see Bodnar, *The Transplanted*, 205.

32. Soike, *Norwegian Americans*, 45–46, 66, 191–92; J. L. Nydahl, *Afholdssagens historie* (Minneapolis, MN: Forfatterens Forlag, 1896), 304, 314; Jennifer A. Delton, *Making Minnesota Liberal: Civil Rights and the Transformation of the Democratic Party* (Minneapolis: University of Minnesota Press, 2002), 2.

33. *Benson Times*, 18 Nov. 1876, 2 and 18 Nov. 1877, 14 June 1878, 7 Nov. 1884, 28 Aug. 1888; *Swift County Advocate*, 19 Oct. and 2 Nov. 1877; *Swift County Press*, 24 Oct. 1883; Ole Lien was a frequent contributor to *Budstikken:* see its reports on the 1876 and 1877 elections, 24 and 31 Oct. and 8 and 14 Nov. 1876, 31 Oct. and 7 and 14 Nov. 1877; Anonsen, *History of Swift County*, 67; Martin Ridge, "Ignatius Donnelly: Minnesota Congressman, 1863–69," *Minnesota History* 36:5 (Mar. 1959): 183; Martin Ridge, *Ignatius Donnelly: The Portrait of a Politician* (1962; reprint, St. Paul: MHS Press, 1991), 160–61; *Swift County, Minnesota: A Collection*, 725; Sons of Norway information on the founders of Bjørgvin Lodge, Benson, MN.

34. Soike, *Norwegian Americans,* 50–51; Anonsen, *History of Swift County,* 55–56, 67–68; David LaVigne, "County, State, and National Politics in Benson City and Swift County, 1876–1926: Basic Developments and Reflections," typescript (8 Aug. 2002), in author's possession; Kendric Charles Babcock, *The Scandinavian Element in the United States* (Urbana: University of Illinois Press, 1914), 140–41.

35. Anonsen, *History of Swift County,* 55; *Benson Times,* 14 Nov. 1879; *Swift County Review,* 10 Apr. 1917; Bruce M. White et al., *Minnesota Votes: Election Returns by County for President, Senators, Congressmen, and Governors, 1857–1977* (St. Paul: MHS, 1977), 156–57; Delton, *Making Minnesota Liberal,* 2; *Budstikken,* 17 Oct. 1883; Babcock, *Scandinavian Element,* 140–41.

36. Anonsen, *History of Swift County,* 68–69; *Swift County Review,* 12 Oct. 1906, 28 May 1909; *Swift County Monitor,* 26 Oct. 1894, 28 Oct. 1904, 10 Sept. 1909, 1 Nov. 1912, 22 Jan. 1920, 22 July 1927, 9 Mar. 1928, 29 June 1934, 9 June 1944; the first county officers in 1871 were appointed, not elected.

37. Blegen, *Norwegian Migration,* 556; Jensen, *Winning of the Midwest,* 84.

38. *Benson Times,* 9 Nov. 1886; LaVigne, "County, State, and National Politics"; White, *Minnesota Votes,* 163–64; Blegen, *Minnesota,* 386.

39. *Swift County Monitor,* 7 Nov. 1890; *Western Guard,* 30 June 1960; Blegen, *Minnesota,* 388; White, *Minnesota Votes,* 165–66.

40. For a major treatise on Knute Nelson and his career, see Millard L. Gieske and Steven J. Keillor, *Norwegian Yankee: Knute Nelson and the Failure of American Politics, 1860–1923* (Northfield, MN: NAHA, 1995); *Benson Times,* 8 Nov. 1904.

41. LaVigne, "County, State, and National Politics"; White, *Minnesota Votes,* 82–84, 168; *Swift County Monitor,* 9 Nov. 1894; James M. Youngdale, *Third Party Footprint: An Anthology from Writings and Speeches of Midwest Radicals* (Minneapolis, MN: Ross & Haines, Inc., 1966), 62–85.

42. John D. Hicks, "The Persistence of Populism," in eds. Rhoda R. Gilman and June Drenning Holmquist, *Selections from Minnesota History: A Fiftieth Anniversary Anthology* (St. Paul: MHS, 1965), 272–85; Blegen, *Minnesota,* 433; White, *Minnesota Votes,* 169–71; LaVigne, "County, State, and National Politics"; *Benson Times,* 15 Nov. 1910; Youngdale, *Third Party Footprint,* 31.

43. *Swift County Monitor,* 13 Nov. 1908; *Benson Times,* 3 Nov. 1908, 8 Nov. 1912; White, *Minnesota Votes,* 18, 177–78; Carl H. Chrislock, *The Progressive Era in Minnesota, 1899–1918* (St. Paul: MHS Press, 1971), 34.

44. Carl H. Chrislock, *Ethnicity Challenged: The Upper Midwest Norwegian-American Experience in World War I* (Northfield, MN: NAHA, 1981), 4, 8, 68–76, Grevstad quote p.70; John Higham, *Strangers in the Land: Patterns of American Nativism 1860–1925* (New York: Atheneum, 1977), 195; Blegen, *Minnesota,* 478.

45. Youngdale, *Third Party Footprint,* 49–53; Robert L. Morlan, *Political*

Prairie Fire: The Nonpartisan League, 1915–1922 (Minneapolis: University of Minnesota Press, 1955), 110–12, 279–80, quote p.110; White, *Minnesota Votes,* 185; Blegen, *Minnesota,* 477; *Swift County Monitor,* 4 Nov. 1920.

46. Youngdale, *Third Party Footprint,* 110–11; Chrislock, *Ethnicity Challenged,* 30–31, 33; admiration for "German civilization" was expressed by John O. Evjen, professor of church history at Augsburg Seminary, Minneapolis, MN.

47. *Swift County Monitor,* 6 Apr., 22 and 29 June, 6 July, and 7 Sept., 1917, 15 Mar., 9, 12, and 19 Apr., 14 June, 21 Sept., 15 Nov., and 20 Dec. 1918; Richter, *Starbuck 1883–1983,* 203; Blegen, *Minnesota,* 473; Chrislock, *Ethnicity Challenged,* 98–100.

48. *Swift County Monitor,* 28 Oct. and 4 Nov. 1920; *Willmar Tribune,* 15 Sept. 1926; Youngdale, *Third Party Footprint,* 110–11.

49. *Swift County Monitor,* 16 Nov. 1922, 6 Nov. 1924, 24 June 1927; *Swift County News,* 9 Nov. 1922; Youngdale, *Third Party Footprint,* 210–17, 218–30; White, *Minnesota Votes,* 20, 37, 104–7, 186–88; Delton, *Making Minnesota Liberal,* 5–6.

50. Moyer and Dale, *History of Chippewa and Lac qui Parle,* 2:224–25; *Swift County Monitor,* 16 Nov. 1922, 6 Nov. 1924; *Glenwood Herald,* 13 Nov. 1924; *Western Guard,* 14 Nov. 1924, 4 Nov. 1926; LaVigne, "County, State, and National Politics."

51. Nydahl, *Afholdssagens historie,* 224, 231, 249, 267, translation by the author; interview with Ginter Rice, Benson, MN, 3 June 2002; Jon Willand, "Making Sin Pay," 2, chapter 17 in a larger study of Madison and Lac qui Parle County, which Professor Willand kindly shared with me; *Starbuck Times,* 1 Oct. 1997.

52. Philip Nygard, letter to the author, 21 Nov. 2003; Hoben, *NANA.*

53. Willand, "Making Sin Pay," 4; *Swift County Monitor,* 10 Apr. 1914, 14 May 1915; P. J. Youngdahl, *A Birthright Restored; or, County Option, What It Is and How It Will Work* (n.p.: Minnesota Anti-Saloon League, 1910), 4; Ernest H. Cherrington, comp. and ed., *The Anti-Saloon League Year Book 1919* (Westerville, OH: Anti-Saloon League of America, 1919), 125–26; Starbuck remained dry until 1976.

54. *Swift County Monitor,* 8 Nov. 1910, 22 Jan. 1915, 6 Oct. 1916; *Benson Times,* 4 Oct. 1910; *Swift County Review,* 7 Oct. 1910.

55. *Swift County Monitor,* 6 Oct. 1916; Cherrington, *Anti-Saloon League Year Book,* 125; Waldemar Ager, *Afholdsfolkets festskrift 1914* (Eau Claire, WI: Reform Publishing Company, 1914), 12, 17; Lovoll, *Century of Urban Life,* 123.

56. *Swift County Monitor,* 17 June, 30 Sept., and 4 and 18 Nov. 1920; White, *Minnesota Votes,* 89, 226; Youngdale, *Third Party Footprint,* 218–19; Chrislock, *Ethnicity Challenged,* Nelson quote p.116.

57. Blegen, *Minnesota,* 481; *Swift County Monitor,* 2 Dec. 1920, 16 June 1921, 13 Sept. 1923; Willand, "Making Sin Pay," 68, 70, *Dawson Sentinel* quote p.70; a respondent in Benson provided me with a list of known Norwegian bootleggers

but subsequently withdrew his permission to use the information; Deborah Miller, research librarian at the MHS in St. Paul, assisted in locating information on the temperance issue: I am most grateful to her for her assistance.

58. *Swift County Monitor,* 13 Oct. 1921, 15 Sept. 1933, 7 Oct. 1938, 17 and 24 Oct. 1947, 7 Jan. 1949; *Starbuck Times,* 3 and 17 Nov. and 15 Dec. 1976; city of Starbuck, council minutes, located by city clerk Marilyn Mortenson at the request of Arnold Pederson; State of Minnesota, Office of Liquor Control Commissioner, records, MHS, St. Paul; Pope and Lac qui Parle remained among Minnesota's nine "dry" counties following the 1961 referendum, as reported in the *St. Paul Dispatch,* 3 Oct. 1961; U.S. Bureau of the Census, *Thirteenth Census of the United States, 1910* (Washington, DC: GPO, 1912–14); Lovoll, *Promise of America,* 231–32, 274–75.

NOTES TO CHAPTER 6

1. Lovoll, *Promise of America,* 300–303; Lovoll, *Folk Epic,* 140–41.

2. *Swift County Monitor,* 20 May 1920, 12 and 19 May 1921; Kirsti Alette Blomvik, "Heritage, Sisterhood, and Self-reliance: The Evolution and Significance of the Daughters of Norway, 1897–1950" (master's thesis, Norwegian University of Science and Technology, Trondheim, 2002), 58–62, 103. The Daughters of Norway (*Døtre af Norge*) was organized in Minneapolis on 31 Mar. 1897; by 1914 there were forty-five lodges and about 3,100 members. Larken, the name of the society in 1876, might have influenced the selection of Lærken as a name; the modern Norwegian form is *lerken,* meaning the songbird the lark.

3. Lovoll, *Folk Epic,* 164–71; Carl H. Chrislock, "The First Two Centennials, 1914 and 1925," in *Norwegian Sesquicentennial, 1825–1975* (Minneapolis, MN: Norwegian American 1975 Sesquicentennial Association, 1975), 34–37.

4. See April R. Schultz, *Ethnicity on Parade: Inventing the Norwegian-American through Celebration* (Amherst: University of Massachusetts Press, 1994); Lovoll, *Folk Epic,* 167; Odd S. Lovoll, "Leiv Eriksson som symbol i det norske Amerika," in eds. Jan Ragnar Hagland and Steinar Supphellen, *Leiv Eriksson og Vinland. Kjelder og tradisjonar* (Trondheim, Norway: Det kongelig norske videnskabers selskab, 2001), 119–33.

5. Lovoll, *Folk Epic,* 169; John R. Jenswold, "Becoming American, Becoming Suburban: Norwegians in the 1920s," *Norwegian-American Studies* 33 (Northfield, MN: NAHA, 1992): 3–26.

6. *Western Guard,* 5 and 12 June 1925; *Starbuck Times,* 3 Apr. and 12 June 1925; *Swift County Monitor,* 23 Apr., 7 and 21 May, and 4 and 11 June 1925. The cities chosen for the opening sale were Benson, Northfield, St. Paul, and Minneapolis, MN; Decorah, IA; Chicago, IL; and Washington, DC; Benson was selected because it was the home of congressman Ole J. Kvale, author of the bill providing for the printing of special stamps.

7. *Swift County Monitor,* 22 Oct. 1924, 20 Nov. 1925, 28 Nov. 1927; Martha Ostenso, *Wild Geese* (New York: Dodd, Mead and Company, 1925); Duncan and Ley, eds., *Place/Culture/Representation,* i.

8. Atherton, *Main Street,* 141–42; *Swift County Monitor,* 11 and 25 July, 29 Aug., and 30 Oct., 1919, 8 Apr., 26 Nov., and 2 Dec. 1920, 14 Jan. 1926, 7 Jan. and 24 June 1927.

9. *Swift County Monitor,* 1 Jan. 1920; Blegen, *Minnesota,* 480–81; U.S. Census Reports, agricultural statistics, 1880–1930; for a treatment of 1920s economic life, see Ellis W. Hawley, *The Great War and the Search for Modern Order* (New York: St. Martin's Press, 1979); interview with Herbert Monson, Scofield Place, Benson, MN, 31 May 2002.

10. Interview with Leland and Michael Pederson, Benson, MN, 7 June 2002; interview with Norma Larson, Madison, MN, 14 Apr. 2003; interview with Janet K. Lundebrek, Benson, MN, 6 June 2002; interview with Oral Landsverk, Benson, MN, 3 June 2002; interview with Lavon and Vera (Brandt) Lund, Benson, MN, 2 June 2002; *Swift County News,* 26 Apr. 1932; interview with Joel Lee, conducted by Gary G. Erickson, Benson, MN, 13 June 2002: Mr. Lee stated, "It was all Norwegian. You went to town here on Saturday night, they sat and talked Norwegian."

11. Lowry Nelson, "Intermarriage Among Nationality Groups in a Rural Area of Minnesota," *American Journal of Sociology* 48:5 (Mar. 1943): 585–92, see Table 8 for rates of marriage.

12. *Swift County Monitor,* 20 Nov. 1919, 3 Mar. 1921, 30 Sept. 1926.

13. For additional studies of intermarriage, see Donna L. Pagnini and S. Philip Morgan, "Intermarriage and Social Distance Among U.S. Immigrants at the Turn of the Century," *American Journal of Sociology* 96:2 (Sept. 1990): 405–32, and Albert Ernest Jenks, "Ethnic Census in Minneapolis," *American Journal of Sociology* 17:6 (May 1912): 776–82.

14. Nelson, "Intermarriage," 591; Lovoll, *Century of Urban Life,* 230–31.

15. Nelson, "Intermarriage," 591; Lovoll, *Promise Fulfilled,* 186–90.

16. U.S. Bureau of the Census, *Twelfth Census, 1900; Swift County Monitor,* 17 Nov. 1917, 26 Aug. and 2 Dec. 1926, 12 and 19 Apr. 1929, 29 Apr. 1949; *Swift County News,* 23 June 1931; *Swift County Review,* 24 Sept. 1910; interview with Donald and Lois (Munn) Mitteness, Benson, MN, 29 May 2002; *Swift County Minnesota,* 744; interview with Richard H. Hilleren, Benson, MN, 31 May 2002; see discussion of class and ethnicity in Gordon, *Assimilation in American Life,* 44–49.

17. Tjosaas interview; Blegen, *Minnesota,* 524–25; *Swift County Minnesota,* 577; *Swift County News,* 10 June 1930, 10 Apr. 1934.

18. Blegen, *Minnesota,* 523; White, *Minnesota Votes,* 191–96; Youngdale, *Third Party Footprint,* 314–15, 321; George H. Mayer, *The Political Career of Floyd B. Olson* (St. Paul: MHS Press, 1987), 56, 116, 250, 282–83, 293, 299; *Swift*

County News, 16 June 1931; information on Edward Indrehus was provided by Deborah Miller, MHS, St. Paul.

19. Ginter Rice interview, 30 May 2002; Thomas C. Cochran, *The Great Depression and World War II, 1929–1945* (Glenview, IL: Scott, Foreman, and Company, 1968), 56, 77, 81–82, 105, 148; Blegen, *Minnesota,* 576–78; interview with Howard W. Peterson, Benson Nursing Home, Benson, MN, 5 June 2002.

20. Hilleren interview; interview with Marilyn Johnson LaMourea, Starbuck, MN, 26 May 2002; *Swift County Minnesota,* 777–78; *Montevideo News,* 11 Oct. 1929; *Skandinaven,* 15 Dec. 1936; *Swift County News,* 15 Mar. and 21 June 1938.

21. Lois Munn Mitteness, born in 1932 in Stevens County, related that she grew up speaking German; Lavon Lund, born in 1932 in Starbuck, told that his family spoke Norwegian when they visited neighbors; Oral Landsverk, born in 1924 in Kerkhoven Township, described how natural it was in the neighborhood to speak Norwegian: she "never thought about it"; interview with Alfrida Hilda (Hegland) and Verner Johnson, Benson, MN, 3 June 2002.

22. *Trinity Lutheran Church 125 Years,* 23; Verner Johnson interview; Lovoll, *Promise of America,* 326–28; *Western Guard,* 30 Jan. and 13 Feb. 1925.

23. "'A Historical View of Our Pastoral Founders': Our Redeemer's Lutheran Church, Benson, Minnesota, 1870–1995," Our Redeemer's Lutheran Church, Benson, MN; *Swift County News,* 28 Nov. 1933, 9 Jan. 1934, 14 June 1938, 30 May 1939; interview with Paul A. Mortenson, Benson, MN, 4 June 2002.

24. Lovoll, *Century of Urban Life,* 120–30, 205–21; Mortenson interview.

25. *Swift County News,* 1 Dec. 1931, 6 Dec. 1932.

26. *Swift County News,* 20 and 27 Jan. and 19 May 1931, 16 May 1933, 18 May and 21 Sept. 1937, 22 Feb. 1938; Werner Sollors, *Beyond Ethnicity: Consent and Descent in American Culture* (New York: Oxford University Press, 1986), 5–6.

27. *Swift County News,* 18 Apr. 1933, 18 Nov. 1937, 22 Feb. 1938; Norrøna Leikaring and Thorstein Skarning and his Norwegian Hillbillies, both from Minneapolis, performed in Benson; interview with Orie Mills, Benson, MN, 13 Mar. 2002; interview with Conrad Urke, Benson, MN, 7 June 2002.

28. *Swift County News,* 11 Apr. 1939; Carl G. O. Hansen, *My Minneapolis: A Chronicle of What Has Been Observed About the Norwegians in Minneapolis Through One Hundred Years* (Minneapolis, MN: privately published, 1956), 335–45; Harry T. Cleven, Norse Federation, Oslo, Norway, provided information on the "Look to Norway" speech.

29. *The Gopher's Whistle,* 20 Sept. 1938.

30. Cochran, *Great Depression and World War II,* 146–58.

31. *Swift County News,* 21 and 28 Apr. 1942, 16 and 23 Feb. and 14 Sept. 1943, 14 Mar., 4 Apr., 14 Aug., and 3 and 31 Oct. 1944, 19 June 1945; *Swift County Monitor,* 30 Mar. 1945, 15 Mar. 1946; *Swift County Monitor,* published on Friday,

became *Swift County News* on Tuesday; the same editor handled both DFL organs.

32. *Swift County News*, 12 May 1942; A. N. Rygg, *American Relief for Norway: A Survey of American Relief Work for Norway During and After the Second World War* (Chicago: American Relief for Norway, Inc., 1947), 9–21, quote p.14; Hansen, *My Minneapolis*, 270, 346.

33. *Swift County News*, 13 July 1943, 17 Apr., 8 May, and 25 Dec. 1945; *Swift County Monitor*, 17 May 1940, 16 May 1941; Hansen, *My Minneapolis*, 346–48.

34. Odd S. Lovoll, "From Norway to America: A Tradition of Immigration Fades," in ed. Dennis Laurence Cuddy, *Contemporary American Immigration: Interpretive Essays* (Boston, MA: Twayne Publishers, 1982), 90, 93; interview with Kirsten Vingerhagen Ricke, Benson, MN, 2 June 2002; Kirsten Vingerhagen Ricke, letter to the author, 9 Mar. 2004; *Swift County Monitor*, 10 May 1946; see discussion of social change in Blegen, *Minnesota*, 574–76.

35. Lovoll, "From Norway to America," 99, 100.

36. Joseph Amato with John Meyer, "More of the Same, More with Less: Toward the Year 2000 in Minnesota," *Minnesota Cities* (July 1991): 12–16; Don Martindale and R. Galen Hanson, *Small Town and the Nation: The Conflict of Local and Translocal Forces* (Westport, CT: Greenwood Publishing Corporation, 1969), 112–24, quotes and paraphrasing p.123, 124.

37. *Swift County Monitor*, 7 June 1946.

38. Interview with Robert J. Mikkelson, Benson, MN, 11 Mar. 2002; Robert J. Mikkelson, e-mail correspondence, 19 and 24 Feb. and 9 Mar. 2004.

39. Surveys for the years 1999–2003 were provided by Jessica Ebling, counselor at Benson High School; Martindale and Hanson, *Small Town and Nation*, 124.

40. Interview with Scott F. Anfinson, Northfield, MN, 13 Feb. and 6 Aug. 2002; interview with Reed Anfinson, Benson, MN, 21 June 2001; interview with Patricia Ann and Ronald Anfinson, Benson, MN, 12 Mar. 2002.

41. Interview with Rodney Paul Rice, Northfield, MN, 30 July 2002; Rodney is the son of Marion and Ginter Rice.

42. Interview with Janet Dolan, Golden Valley, MN, 3 Dec. 2003; Janet's parents are Robert and Helen Dolan.

43. Information on public schools from Swift County Historical Museum, Benson, MN; information on agriculture from Edward Pederson, Swift County assessor, 17 Feb. 2004; "Census of Agriculture for Swift County" provided by Douglas Hartwig, Minnesota Agricultural Statistics Service, St. Paul, MN; Hilleren interview; Mortenson interview; Mikkelson interview.

44. Interview with Jan Baukol, Benson, MN, 4 June 2002; documents stored in Our Redeemer's Lutheran Church archives, Benson, MN, including "Fælles-Komiternes Rapport," 13 and 27 Aug. 1917; historical records prepared by Alice Skarsten; minutes, 20 Mar. 1917 to 8 Jan. 1924; historical background of Our

Redeemer's Lutheran Church; Our Redeemer's 41st Annual Norwegian Smorgasbord; and undated newspaper clippings from *Swift County Monitor-News*.

45. Interviews with Orie Mills, Benson, MN, 13 Mar. and 31 May 2002; interview with Rev. Barbara Thompson, Benson, MN, 29 May 2002; the survey was conducted by Mr. Mills and Pastor Thompson; John Thompson determined that Our Redeemer's has suffered a great loss of members, reflecting the congregation's age composition: in 1966 there were 2,370 baptized members, in 1990, 1,644, in 2003, 1,415.

46. Thompson interview; Mills interviews; Verhelst interview.

47. *50th Anniversary, 1940–1990, St. Mark's Lutheran Church, Benson, Minnesota* (Benson, Minnesota: privately printed, 1990); Rev. Dennis J. McManus conducted the survey and graciously answered questions as well as provided a copy of the history when I visited the church in Mar. 2002; see announcements in *Swift County Monitor,* 30 May 1939.

48. Amato with Meyer, "More of the Same," paraphrasing and quote p.14.

49. Interview with Jack Kjos, Benson, MN, 3 June 2002; (Minneapolis) *Star Tribune*, 11 Nov. 2003; Joseph A. Amato and John W. Meyer, *The Decline of Rural Minnesota* (Marshall, MN: Crossings Press, 1993); "Rural Renaissance Act," Senate Bill 1796, Thomas Legislative Information, http://thomas.loc.gov.

50. Lovoll, *Promise Fulfilled,* 42–47, 262.

51. Lovoll, *Promise Fulfilled,* 34; U.S. Bureau of the Census, *Census 2000,* http://govpubs.lib.umn.edu/census/profile.phtml; Solveig Hofossbråten, ed., *Minifakta om Norge 2003* (Oslo, Norway: Kongelige norske utenriksdepartement, 2003); see Hollinger, *Postethnic America.*

52. Interview with Marie Lightning Koenigs, Benson, MN, 4 June 2002; interview with Marie Lightning Koenigs, by telephone, 25 Apr. 2004.

53. Scott Anfinson interview, 6 August 2002; Lovoll, *Promise Fulfilled,* 197–203, quote p.202; newspaper clippings, 1990–94, undated, from *Swift County Monitor-News,* provided by Janet K. Lundebrek, president, First Security Bank, who was active in May 17 arrangements. Despite heated debate the official name of the Sons of Norway never changed after the merger; the name is actually the opening line of the first Norwegian national anthem (words by Henrik Anker Bjerregaard, music by C. Blom): "Sønner af Norge, det ældgamle Rige" (Sons of Norway, that ancient kingdom); "Sons of Norway" may thus be taken to mean all Norwegians, sons and daughters. In 1820 the song was awarded a prize and designated "the enthroned Norwegian national anthem"; see Hansen, *History of Sons of Norway,* 11–12.

54. Lovoll, *Promise of America,* 65–66.

55. Lovoll, *Promise of America,* 91–93; interview with Scotty Kuehl, Madison, MN, 16 Oct. 2002; interview with Ivey Vonderharr, Madison, MN, 16 Oct. 2002; interview with Jerry Osteraa, Madison, MN, 14 Apr. 2003; *Visitor's Guide to Madison, Minnesota, 2003 (Western Guard);* Ethel Shelstad at the *Western*

Guard was most helpful in providing information about the history of Madison; second-generation Norwegian American Gerda Hofseth Dolman, earlier curator of the Lac qui Parle County History Center and interviewed with Kuehl, agreed that Norsefest enhanced appreciation of ethnicity.

56. Interview with Arnold Pederson, Starbuck, MN, 16 Apr. 2003; *Starbuck Times,* 8 May 2002; "Sixteenth Annual Lefse Dagen," program (2002); *Starbuck Railroad Times,* 16 May 1992; Schibsted Book of Records in Norway recognizes the *lefse* as the world's largest ever baked; in Norway sausage is rolled in *lumpe,* a small potato cake, which might have been the idea behind wrapping sausage in *lefse.*

57. Jan Carr Luzum interview; Lovoll, *Promise Fulfilled,* demonstrates a continuous Norwegian American ethnocentric strength.

58. Interview with Janet K. Lundebrek, Benson, MN, 25 July 2002; Urke interview; Conrad Urke telephone interview, 13 Mar. 2004.

Index

Note: *Italic* page numbers indicate illustrations (maps, tables, and photographs)

Illustration Credits

page 5
Map from Ingrid Semmingsen,
*Norway to America: A History of
the Migration,* Einar Haugen, trans.
(Minneapolis: University of Min-
nesota Press, 1978)

page 9
Norske folkemuseum (Oslo)

page 18
CartoGraphics, Inc.

page 23
Hjalmar Rued Holand, *De norske
settlementers historie* (Chicago,
1912)

pages 27, 131
Norwegian Emigrant Museum,
Norway

page 32
Map drawn by Tone Anda. In Einar
Haugen, *The Norwegians in Amer-
ica: A Students' Guide to Localized
History* (New York: Teachers Col-
lege Press, 1967), viii

pages 47, 49, 74, 85, 98, 108, 109, 189,
198, 237, 243
Swift County Historical Society

pages 58, 230
Minnesota Historical Society

pages 60, 133, 149, 194
Maps by Gary G. Erickson

page 67
Courtesy Harvey Rodahl

page 70
Courtesy Eleanor Anderson
Pederson

page 112
Our Redeemer's Lutheran Church,
Benson, MN

page 115
Vesterheim Norwegian-American
Museum, Decorah, IA

pages 135, 221
Pope County Historical Society

pages 151, 156, 180
Lac qui Parle County Historical
Society

page 183
Courtesy Stephen P. Hippe

page 193
Chart by Gary G. Erickson

page 261
Photo by Odd S. Lovoll

page 267
Photograph by Charles Smith from
C. Edwards Studio; reprinted by
permission of the Madison Area
Chamber of Commerce

page 269
Starbuck Depot Society

Norwegians on the Prairie was designed and set in type by Wendy Holdman at Prism Publishing Center in Minneapolis. The text typeface is Warnock Pro, a new Adobe Originals Open Type font designed by Robert Slimbach and named after John Warnock, the co-founder of Adobe Systems. This book was printed by Maple Press, York, Pennsylvania.